FRANK N. MEYER

Plant Hunter in Asia

The greatest service which can be rendered any country is to add a useful plant to its culture.

— THOMAS JEFFERSON

FRANK N. MEYER

Plant Hunter in Asia

B Y *Isabel Shipley Cunningham*

The Iowa State University Press

A M E S

© 1984 The Iowa State University Press. All Rights Reserved
Composed and printed by The Iowa State University Press, Ames, Iowa 50010.

First edition, 1984

Library of Congress Cataloging in Publication Data

Cunningham, Isabel Shipley, 1919–
 Frank N. Meyer, plant hunter in Asia.

 Bibliography: p.
 1. Meyer, Frank Nicholas. 2. Plant collectors — United States — Biography. 3. Plant intro-
duction — United States — History. 4. Botany, Economic — Asia — History. 5. United States.
Dept. of Agriculture — Officials and employees — Biography. I. Title.
SB63.M55C86   1984   631.5′2′0924 [B]   83–12920
ISBN 0–8138–1148–1

To my mother and father
CLAUDINE WELSH SHIPLEY AND MARVIN R. SHIPLEY
and to my husband's mother
EDNA MOEHRING CUNNINGHAM
ardent gardeners all

In the Shipley garden I first saw recent plant introductions.
In the Cunningham library I met the plant hunters
and glimpsed Frank Nicholas Meyer.

CONTENTS

ix

THE SECOND EXPEDITION

THE THIRD EXPEDITION

THE FOURTH EXPEDITION

JOURNEY'S END

M A P S

PREFACE

L E A D E R S in many fields of human endeavor have been forgotten in the course of the continuing development of the work that they pioneered; Frank Meyer fits that familiar pattern. British authors have said that his name should be a household word in America and that American farmers should celebrate an annual Meyer festival in grateful remembrance of his work in Asia. Yet few Americans are aware of their debt to the man who expanded the horizons of American agriculture during the early years of the twentieth century. Meyer's colleagues at the United States Department of Agriculture believed that some record of his work and personal activities should be written for publication; nevertheless, for sixty years Meyer's pioneering work in Asia has remained a neglected segment of America's heritage. People have forgotten that his drought-resistant shade trees, hardy yellow rose, blight-resistant chestnuts, and improved fruits, grains, and vegetables have enriched waste lands and have helped to feed millions. At a time when many Americans are expressing concern about feeding a growing population and about the loss of crop genetic resources, Meyer's search for better foods and for hardy and drought-resistant plants has become relevant.

This account of Frank Meyer's endeavors is based primarily on his letters to members of the staff of the Foreign Seed and Plant Introduction Section of the United States Department of Agriculture and to his family and friends in Holland. My task has been to weave together the strands of information that he recorded in more than 2,500 pages of letters about the places he visited, the plants he collected, the people he met, and the historical events of the early years of this century. But Frank Meyer's letters tell more than this; as he revealed his hopes and fears, his limitations and accomplishments, and his struggles with external forces and with himself, a whole portrait of the man emerges. When all the pieces of the puzzle are in place, apparent contradictions disappear.

Though British plant hunters also traveled to remote regions in Asia during the early years of the nineteenth century, they generally collected ornamentals for individual subscribers or private institutions; Meyer alone represented a government and searched primarily for economically useful rather than ornamental plants. Entering China near the dawn of the era when explorers could travel freely there, he concentrated on fruits, nuts, grains, and fodder crops. Not many years after his death, the borders of China and of the USSR were closed. No one before him traveled for ten years across the mountains and deserts and through the farms, orchards, and forests of Asia in search of food crops; no one has done so since.

At the time of his death, devoted friends on three continents mourned the loss of a man whose personal qualities were as unique as his contributions. Frank Meyer loved his adopted country and gave his life in the course of fulfilling its needs. I hope that his fellow countrymen will enjoy this account of his experiences and appreciate his efforts to make America a better place to live.

In quoting from Meyer's letters, I have not used ellipses to indicate omitted words, phrases, or sentences; however, these omissions do not distort the meaning or alter the spirit of his original text. All unidentified quotations are from Meyer's letters.

Many changes have occurred in Asia during this century. Areas that Meyer would have recognized as parts of Mongolia and Tibet are no longer within those boundaries. Manchuria, the scene of conflict between Japan and Russia when Meyer explored there, is now a part of the People's Republic of China. I have referred to the geographic boundaries and the political status of these regions as he knew them between 1905 and 1918.

Since Meyer's lifetime, the names of many towns, cities, and provinces have changed, particularly as a result of the adoption of the Pinyin system of romanization in 1978. I have followed Meyer's usage, usually adding the current equivalent in parentheses unless the name is unchanged. For the Pinyin spelling, I have used the *Gazetteer of the People's Republic of China,* prepared by the Defense Mapping Agency, Washington, D.C., July, 1979, and the National Geographic Society map of the People's Republic of China.

The appendix contains the U.S. Department of Agriculture's Plant Introduction (PI) numbers for some of Meyer's introductions. These numbers are essential tools for tracing plants through the USDA records. When botanical names have changed, both forms are given initially and in Appendix A and B; former and current names are cross-referenced in the index.

ACKNOWLEDGMENTS

I T is a pleasure to acknowledge my indebtedness to Dr. John L. Creech, last chief of the New Crops Research Branch of the Agricultural Research Service, retired director of the U.S. National Arboretum, and an internationally acclaimed plant collector, for suggesting the subject of this study, commenting on the manuscript, and imparting his broad knowledge of plant exploration. I also want to express my gratitude to Dr. Vivian Wiser, historian, USDA, for sharing her professional expertise throughout the long process of research, composition, and revision. I am especially grateful to Dr. Frederick G. Meyer, supervisory botanist at the National Arboretum and an experienced plant collector, whose kindness and guidance encouraged and enlightened me as I struggled with unfamiliar nomenclature. Dr. Meyer checked the botanical names throughout the text; if errors occur, they are mine alone. He also helped to obtain photographs from the National Arboretum collection and answered innumerable questions patiently.

In addition, Harold F. Winters, retired chief of the Germplasm Resources Laboratory, USDA Agricultural Research Center, Beltsville, Maryland, and a veteran of plant hunting expeditions to New Guinea and elsewhere, gave meticulous attention to the text, offered helpful suggestions, and pointed out obscure reference material. I owe special thanks to Dr. Theodore R. Dudley, research botanist at the National Arboretum and a member of the 1980 Sino-American Botanical Expedition, for reviewing the manuscript and providing precise information and perceptive comments. I also appreciate the advice and support of two friends, Oretha D. Swartz, author of *Service Etiquette,* and Esther T. Travis, a skilled editor who has read successive drafts of the manuscript and contributed many constructive suggestions.

Those who have generously imparted their specialized knowledge of the current value of Frank Meyer's collections include William L. Ackerman, Roland M. Jefferson, and Sylvester March of the National Arboretum, as well as John L. Creech, Frederick G. Meyer, and Harold F. Winters. I am particularly indebted to Dr. Ackerman, research horticulturist, for sharing the results of years of work with Meyer's introductions at the Chico, California, and the Glenn Dale, Maryland, plant introduction stations. I also wish to thank Dr. George A. White, plant introduction officer, and Dr. Howard Brooks, Dr. Harold W. Fogle, Dr. Wayne Porter, Dr. David C. Smith, Jr., and Dr. Ramon Webb, specialists working with fruits, grains, and vegetables at the USDA Agricultural Research Center at Beltsville, Maryland, for their important contributions. I am especially grateful to Gregory Williams, Director, Appalachian Region, International Tree Crops Institute, U.S.A., whose keen interest in agroforestry enabled him to respond to many inquiries with accuracy and enthusiasm.

Dr. John Popenoe, director of the Fairchild Tropical Garden in Miami, provided material from his files; the Honorable Marjorie S. Holt, Congresswoman from Maryland, furnished photocopies from the Library of Congress; and Mrs. George C. Gerber of McLean, Virginia, permitted me to quote from letters written by her father, Nelson T. Johnson, first American ambassador to China. I also appreciate the assistance given by Deborah Strauss, managing editor of *Diversity,* Barbara Carr of the secretarial staff of the National Arboretum, and Barbara Kuhn of the American Genetic Association.

Faculty members at various state universities have furnished invaluable data. I owe special thanks to Dr. Melvin N. Westwood, professor of horticulture and curator of the plant germplasm repository at Oregon State University, Corvallis, and to Dr. Paul Lyrene, Fruit Crops Department, University of Florida, Gainesville, for their helpful replies to numerous questions. Others who have contributed information include Dr. William Beres, Dr. Claron O. Hesse, Dr. Dale Kester, Dr. Dan E. Parfitt, Dr. Calvin O. Qualset, and Dr. Kay Ryugo of the University of California at Davis; Dr. Sidney D. Thibodeaux of Nicholls State University, Thibodaux, Louisiana, and Dr. Gisela J. Lozata, Louisiana State University, Baton Rouge; Dr. James B. Shanks of the University of Maryland, College Park; Dr. Robert L. Anderson, Michigan State University, Lansing; Professor Charles Burnham (retired) of the University of Minnesota, St. Paul; Dr. Dale E. Herman of the North Dakota State University, Fargo; Dr. Catherine H. Bailey (retired) of Rutgers, the State University of New Jersey, New Brunswick; and Dr. David L. Chapman, Dr. Henry Dethloff, Dr. R. S. Dewers, Dr. Fred Miller, Dr. Keith F. Schertz, and Dr. Oliver E. Smith of Texas A & M University, College Station.

For information about Meyer germplasm currently held by the USDA, I am indebted to Dr. Louis N. Bass, USDA National Seed Storage Laboratory, Colorado State University, Fort Collins, and to the coordinators of the four regional plant introduction stations: Dr. S. M. Dietz of Washington State University, Pullman; Dr. Desmond D. Dolan of Geneva, New York;

Dr. Gilbert R. Lovell of Experiment, Georgia; and Dr. Willis H. Skrdla of Iowa State University, Ames.

Other USDA professionals who have assisted in the search for surviving Meyer introductions are Stephen K. Salvo and William H. Fry of the National Plant Materials Center, Beltsville, Maryland; James Henry of the Plant Materials Center, Elsberry, Missouri; and Dr. Douglas Helms, historian, all of the Soil Conservation Service; Dr. Mason Miller, Cooperative State Research Service, Washington, D.C.; Dr. William Preston and Gerald A. Seaton, formerly of the Glenn Dale Plant Introduction Station, Glenn Dale, Maryland; Elizabeth L. Ley of the National Arboretum; Dr. Richard A. Jaynes, Connecticut Agricultural Experiment Station, New Haven; Dr. William D. Horton and Dr. W. R. Okie of the Fruit and Tree Nut Laboratory, Byron, Georgia; Dr. J. C. Hearn, USDA Horticultural Laboratory, Orlando, Florida; Dr. Knud E. Clausen, North Central Forest. Experiment Station, Carbondale, Illinois; E. W. Johnson, formerly superintendent of the Plant Materials Center, Woodward, Oklahoma; Marilyn J. Samuel, High Plains Grasslands Research Station, Cheyenne, Wyoming; Dr. Richard A. Cunningham, Northern Great Plains Research Laboratory, Mandan, North Dakota; and Lloyd E. Joley, formerly superintendent, Chico Plant Introduction Garden, Chico, California. I also appreciate the cooperation of representatives of the USDA Forest Service: Robert Fewin of Lubbock, Texas; Frank Gottbrath of Buena Vista, Virginia; and Dr. William B. Critchfield of the Institute of Forest Genetics, Placerville, California.

Those outside the USDA who have helped to locate Meyer germplasm include Gary L. Koller, supervisor of the Living Collections at the Arnold Arboretum, Jamaica Plain, Massachusetts; James Bauml and Clair Martin of the Huntington Botanical Gardens at San Marino, California; and Richard Haubrich, Quail Botanical Gardens, Encinitas, California. I am also indebted to Lynn M. Collicut of the Canadian Agricultural Research Station, Morden, Manitoba, and W. J. Cody of the Vascular Plant Herbarium, Canadian Department of Agriculture, Ottawa; J. Roy Quinby, Pioneer Hi-Bred International, Plainview, Texas; William E. Rinne, USDI Bureau of Reclamation, Boulder City, Nevada; Daniel Barth of Gridley, California; Paul H. Thomson, founder, and Pat Sawyer, president, California Rare Fruit Growers, Fullerton, California; Dr. Irvin May of Houston, Texas, formerly National Park Service archivist; Dr. David Herold of White Bear Lake, Minnesota; Edward M. Simmons, McIlhenny Enterprises, Avery Island, Louisiana; George L. Taber, Jr., Glen Saint Mary Nurseries Company, Glen Saint Mary, Florida; David C. Andrews, Oxon Hill, Maryland; and Mrs. Barbara J. Todd of the Litchfield Historical Society, Litchfield, Connecticut.

Members of the staffs of the National Agricultural Library at Beltsville,

Maryland, the library of the National Arboretum in Washington, the Annapolis and Anne Arundel County Public Library, and the Koninklijke Bibliotheek in The Hague, Holland, have helped me locate research materials that are not readily accessible. In addition, Helen Ulibarri and Dr. Douglas Helms of the Natural Resources Branch of the National Archives, made archival records available to me. Without the records filed at the National Archives, a comprehensive study of Frank Meyer would be impossible. I also owe special thanks to Jayne T. MacLean and Shirley Gaventa of the National Agricultural Library and to Diny Winthagen, librarian at the Hugo de Vries Laboratory at the University of Amsterdam, for their assistance.

I am grateful to a native of The Hague, the late Jeannette Bouter Bernaerts of Amberly, Annapolis, Maryland, who translated Dutch sources with skill and enthusiasm. Dr. F. A. Stafleu of the International Association for Plant Taxonomy at Utrecht and Diny Winthagen of the University of Amsterdam assisted me in attempts to locate Frank Meyer's relatives now living in Ermelo, Holland.

This book would not have been possible without the patience and support of my late husband, Chipman Woodward Cunningham, who shared my time with Frank Meyer for three years. Finally, the implicit faith that my children, Deborah Chipman Cunningham and David Woodward Cunningham, have expressed in my ability to complete this project has made it impossible for me to falter.

Setting the Stage

Photograph of Frank N. Meyer as a young man in Amsterdam, taken in 1898, when he was 23. Reproduced from *De Aarde en Haar Volken*.

David Fairchild and Meyer in Fairchild's office in the old USDA building at 14th and B Streets in 1908. (The desk shown is now in the office of the director of the National Arboretum in Washington.)

Scientific staff of the Bureau of Plant Industry, January 14, 1912. Front (left to right): David Fairchild, P. H. Dorsett, Beverly T. Galloway, Erwin F. Smith; Back (left to right): W. T. Swingle, Merton B. Waite, Mark A. Carleton, Albert F. Woods.

The Past Is Prologue

WE were all to be actors in a gigantic drama.
Its importance has meant little to the press...
but I believe that history will evaluate our work
more highly.
DAVID FAIRCHILD, *The World Was My Garden*

FOR ten years Frank Meyer traveled across the continent of Asia looking for useful plants and fulfilling his promise to "skim the earth in search of things good for man." No hardship or danger deterred him if facing that obstacle might lead to the discovery of a promising fruit, grain, or tree. He walked thousands of miles over lofty mountains and parched deserts, through snowstorms and dust storms, and into primeval forests never before seen by a white man. Wading across swift and icy rivers, balancing a donkey on a fragile bamboo bridge over a chasm, or following a narrow crumbling footpath along a steep precipice, he had a single goal: "I will do all I can to enrich the United States of America with things good for her people."[1] He faced bands of brigands in China, crossed the shifting glacier that formed the Mussart Pass over the Tien Shan in Chinese Turkestan, endured Siberian winters with temperatures −40°F, and visited Kalmuck and Kirghiz settlements where only a generation earlier men had been offered as human sacrifices. He fought off an attack by three murderous ruffians in Khabarovsk and barely escaped being shot by soldiers in the Kansu (Gansu) Province of China. Deserted by his interpreter near the border of Tibet and by his assistant and interpreter in Samarkand, he went doggedly on with a map and a compass as guides.

As a result of his dedication to his work, his vast knowledge of plants, and his devotion to his adopted country, he sent the Department of Agriculture hundreds of shipments of live cuttings and thousands of sacks filled with seeds. His 2,500 plant introductions have changed the landscape and improved the economy of the United States. Today Americans eat the foods and enjoy the shrubs that he found in Asia; from the Dakotas to Texas his elms serve as windbreaks on formerly treeless prairies; and, perhaps most important of all, plant breeders are still using the genes that his introductions added to America's crop germplasm in order to produce better grains, fruits, vegetables, and ornamentals.

But, since his death in China in 1918, Meyer has been forgotten by most of his countrymen. Few people know the intriguing story of his life; fewer still appreciate the character of this magnetic and complex man who revealed his thoughts and hopes in more than 2,500 pages of letters to his family, friends, and associates. Frank Meyer served as an agricultural explorer for the Foreign Seed and Plant Introduction Section of the United States Department of Agriculture; his expeditions are a part of the larger drama of the early years of that organization.

By the end of the nineteenth century, American farmers had won their long struggle against ranchers. Settlers filling the northern prairies and the arid Southwest were appealing to the Department of Agriculture for help in finding grains that could ripen in the coldest states or crops that might adapt to dry or alkaline soil. In 1897 James Wilson, the secretary of agriculture, had sent Niels E. Hansen to Russia to search for hardy fruits and grains. But the vast unexplored resources of China, where agriculture had been developing for more than four thousand years, offered a greater opportunity and challenge.

Ever since Marco Polo's return from fabled Cathay, Westerners had longed for the horticultural treasures of China, where earth's richest flora had survived untouched by the Third Ice Age that had covered much of Europe and North America. The Chinese government, however, had limited foreigners for centuries to the open ports of Canton and Macao. After the Opium Wars of the 1840s resulted in greater privileges for Westerners, Robert Fortune, a Scottish plant hunter, spent nineteen years near the treaty ports, occasionally managing to travel two hundred miles into the interior disguised as a Chinese beggar with shaved head and pigtail. Later, amateurs like the French missionary-botanist Father Armand David and the Irish consular official Dr. Augustine Henry collected dried herbarium specimens of many new plants, revealing the richness and variety of China's flora.[2]

At the turn of the century, the Boxer Rebellion gave European powers a chance to extend their influence; at last plant hunters could travel with a fair degree of safety into western China. In 1899 Veitch and Sons, a famous English nursery firm, sent a young collector named Ernest H. Wilson to find the ornamentals described by Father David. Wilson collected seeds of three hundred species, nine hundred pressed specimens, and thirty-five Wardian cases of living plants before he returned to England in 1902. Realizing that agricultural exploration would yield equally great rewards, David Fairchild, head of the infant Foreign Seed and Plant Introduction Section of the USDA, eagerly anticipated sending an explorer to China. But first he needed to find the right man to search vast areas, identify useful plants, and transport them to America.

In 1889 Beverly T. Galloway, head of the Division of Plant Pathology of the USDA, had brought nineteen-year-old David Fairchild to Washington to join five plant pathologists who were working in attic rooms of the old red brick department building. Galloway's Wisconsin classmate, P. Howard Dorsett, soon joined the group. A little later, Fairchild's Kansas State classmate, shy and scholarly Walter T. Swingle, arrived with his growing library of agricultural references in five or six languages. Seeking an opportunity to learn about the flora of foreign countries, Fairchild accepted a Smithsonian fellowship to study in Europe. Aboard ship he met Barbour Lathrop, a well-to-do gentleman who later took him on an extended tour of the Pacific and showed him fruits, grains, and ornamental plants that could be valuable in America. Returning to Washington in 1897, David Fairchild knew exactly what he wanted to do with his life.[3]

With the help of W. T. Swingle, he conceived a plan to divert twenty thousand dollars of the funds appropriated for the wasteful Congressional Seed Distribution Service in order to finance a section for the specific purpose of introducing new and useful crops into the United States. He enthusiastically presented this idea to the secretary of agriculture, James Wilson, who approved the plan and asked him to organize the new section. Housed on the fifth floor under the eaves of the old Department of Agriculture building and staffed by one teenage secretary, the Foreign Seed and Plant Introduction Section became a reality when Congress passed the revised appropriation bill in July, 1898. With these funds Fairchild sent Seaman A. Knapp to Japan to look for new varieties of upland rice, Mark Carleton to Russia to find desperately needed winter wheats, and W. T. Swingle to Algeria and Asia Minor to investigate figs and dates as possible crops for the Southwest. Their success won public support of government sponsored plant introduction.[4]

Though Fairchild traveled for the next several years as special agent of the Foreign Seed and Plant Introduction Section, he never forgot his hope of sending a long-term plant explorer to China. In England he visited Augustine Henry to try to persuade that distinguished amateur botanist to return to Asia as a collector for the Department of Agriculture. Though Dr. Henry declined Fairchild's offer, his enthusiastic account of the unexplored fertile plains and useful plants of the western Chinese provinces made a deep impression on David Fairchild.

He returned to Washington in 1903, determined to initiate agricultural exploration in the Orient. By this time the Foreign Seed and Plant Introduction Section had become a part of the Bureau of Plant Industry directed by Beverly T. Galloway. Galloway agreed that the collector Fairchild sought must be a good botanist who could recognize those plants that were both new and useful; a practical gardener who could gather and transport live material — scions and cuttings as well as seeds; and a man of great endurance who could tolerate all sorts of physical discomforts and walk thousands of miles where no roads existed. Choosing a plant hunter who combined these qualifications became Fairchild's chief concern.

In June of 1904 he began a series of visits to experiment stations and individual correspondents who were testing plants being introduced by the Department of Agriculture. Among the people most interested in plant exploration, he hoped to find a qualified man to collect for the department in China. In Boston he called on Charles Sprague Sargent, the director of Harvard's world-famous Arnold Arboretum. Though these two men devoted their lives to related goals, their personalities offered a sharp contrast. Sargent, a Bostonian of ample means, assured social position, and established reputation, was strong-willed and often sarcastic, while the younger man from the Kansas prairies attracted friends everywhere because of his diplomacy and enthusiasm. Sargent mentioned that he was negotiating for the services of E. H. Wilson, who was making his second journey to the Orient for Veitch and Sons. Because of the rivalry that was developing between these two leaders in American plant exploration, this information spurred Fairchild's desire to send a collector to China.

From Boston he gradually worked his way across the country until he reached the new USDA plant introduction garden at Chico, California. There P. Howard Dorsett, with a small and dedicated staff working from dawn until sunset in temperatures as high as 117°F, had built greenhouses and installed a pumping plant for irrigation. Returning from California by a southern route, Fairchild reached Washington in October; he had spent four months talking to plant enthusiasts throughout the country, but still he had not found the agricultural explorer he needed.

For some time Adrian J. Pieters, who had directed the Foreign Seed and Plant Introduction office during the last months of Fairchild's travels abroad, had been thinking of recommending an untested plant collector for this challenging assignment. Eventually he suggested that Frank Meyer, a gardener who had worked for the department during Fairchild's long absence, might be the man Fairchild sought. Meyer, who shared Pieters's own Dutch heritage, liked to travel to distant places and to walk hundreds of miles. He had come to America with a letter of recommendation from Hugo de Vries to Erwin F. Smith, one of the five plant pathologists who were working with Galloway when Fairchild first arrived in Washington in 1889. Fairchild eagerly questioned Smith about Frank Meyer, and he liked what he heard.[5]

Meyer had been interested in growing plants since boyhood. At the age of fourteen he began to work at the Amsterdam Botanical Garden. After several years he became supervisor of the experimental garden of the exacting botanist and geneticist, Hugo de Vries. Resigning as head gardener, he had walked across Europe, observing the flora everywhere he went. Erwin Smith enjoyed telling Fairchild the story of Meyer's journey to see orange groves and vineyards. Setting out with maps and a compass, he had ignored roads and walked across the Alps, where he nearly lost his life in a blizzard. Descending into the foothills in Italy, he had startled a farmer who asked where he had come from. "Across the mountains," replied Meyer. "Impossible," the farmer objected. "There are no roads."[6] After seeing much of Europe, Meyer had worked in commercial nurseries in England. In October of 1901 he emigrated to America.

Pieters added his favorite account of Meyer's activities after Dr. Smith had found him a modest job as a gardener in the USDA greenhouses on the Mall. During one of his first outings, Meyer had hiked along the Potomac to Mount Vernon. On the return trip he had spent the night in a barn and had heard noises that he thought might have been made by Indians. He reported with some disappointment that he had not seen a single Indian in Virginia. His previous impressions of rural America had been based on the novels of James Fenimore Cooper. After almost a year in Washington, where Pieters and Dorsett became his friends, he decided to see more of America. In September, 1902, he moved to southern California. Later he wandered across Mexico studying plant life and then found work at the Missouri Botanical Garden in Saint Louis.

An exciting picture was emerging, one that must have reminded David Fairchild of many great plant hunters of the past. Thoughts of finding a twentieth-century David Douglas or John Gibson, outstanding plant collectors of the Golden Age (1768–1836), must have raised his hopes. He was especially impressed by Meyer's willingness to walk great distances and by his journey to study the flora of Mexico at his own expense. Pieters warned that Meyer was unwilling to stay in one place, but Fairchild needed a man who would search the continent of Asia for plants that might be useful in America. To the recommendations of Pieters, Smith, and Galloway, George Oliver, Meyer's supervisor in the greenhouses, added his endorsement. In March Fairchild asked Pieters to wire Frank Meyer to ask whether he would be interested in going to China as an agricultural explorer. At last Fairchild had made his decision; time would test the wisdom of his choice.

In the Beginning

Let the fields and the gliding streams in the
valleys delight me. Inglorious, let me court the
rivers and the forests.

VIRGIL, *Georgics* 2

O N November 29, 1875, Frans Meyer was born into a family that
had recently suffered tragedy. When Jan Franciscus Meyer became
ill, his wife and children faced hardships. Jan Meyer survived the
illness that invaded his home, but two of his four children died, leaving only
two daughters. Thereafter Frans Nicholas and Jan Martinus Meyer were
born. (In the Netherlands their surname was spelled Meijer; Frans Meijer
became Frank Meyer when he came to America.) The two boys and their
older sisters grew up in a small house at 11 Lodewyck Trip Street in Houthaven, near the harbor in Amsterdam. Jan Franciscus Meyer, who had been
a sailor in his youth, supported his family as a harbor policeman who
guided ships into the Amsterdam harbor in all kinds of weather. His wife,
Maria Catherina Haasters Meyer, had worked as a young girl in the home of
a doctor. When she married, her employer attended her wedding and promised to give her lifelong medical care in appreciation of her loyal service to
his household. Frans was devoted to his mother and to his older sisters,
Alida Wilhelmina Adriana and Maria Francisco Dorothea.[1] Throughout his
life, he called Alida and Maria "Da" and "Mie," the names he had used in
his childhood.

A quiet boy who loved plants and animals, Frans earned praise as a
good student. After school, instead of rolling his hoop with the other boys,
he often took long walks, read travel stories, and worked in his family's
garden. When he finished the sixth grade, his parents asked him what sort
of work he planned to do; he replied that he wanted to be a world traveler
who studied plants. His father explained that they could not afford the
scientific education that would be necessary for such a career. Instead of

evening, but Mr. and Mrs. Janssen became his lifelong friends and corresponded with him wherever he went thereafter.

Frans Meyer explored Europe happily for several months. He walked through Belgium, Germany, France, Switzerland, and Italy, using a map and a compass as guides. He returned to Holland after he had seen the orange groves and the vineyards he had yearned to visit. Before he could fulfill his dream of going to America, he needed to earn money for his passage. Since he had not seen England, he decided to spend the next year working there. On the day that he left Amsterdam, his whole family went with him to the harbor to say good-bye, realizing that this parting would last a long time.

For more than a year he worked in commercial nurseries near London, growing fruits and vegetables in greenhouses and espaliering fruit trees. On October 12 he left Southampton on the S.S. *Philadelphia*.[2] The day before he sailed he wrote to the Janssens to thank them for their sympathetic letters. "I am pessimistic by nature," he admitted, "and have not found a road which leads to relaxation. I withdraw from humanity and try to find relaxation with plants. I live now in expectation of what will come."

When the *Philadelphia* reached New York on October 19, immigration authorities at Ellis Island searched his luggage, interrogated him, and then directed him to the railroad station to wait for a train to Washington. He marveled at American trains that traveled "at racing speed," twice as fast as those in Holland. Though he feared that they might explode, they were more comfortable than European trains. Everyone sat on soft cushions "behind each other, not staring in other people's faces." Each coach had drinking water in a cooler, and the lavatories were equipped with soap and towels. Most wonderful of all, everyone traveled in accommodations of the same class.

At 7:30 A.M. on October 20, 1901, he reached Washington. Carrying his letters of introduction from de Vries and van Eden, he sought an acquaintance of de Vries, Dr. Erwin F. Smith, who had won international recognition as a pioneer in bacteriology. Meeting this distinguished scientist, who was known for his kindness and interest in young people, was Meyer's good fortune when he came to Washington as a stranger.[3] With Smith's help, he found work in the USDA greenhouses on the Mall near the present location of the National Art Gallery.

Three days later he wrote his parents that he had a fine job; "Is het niet kolossaal wonderbaar?" He had worked for two days for good wages — six hundred dollars a year, and he had found a "safe harbor," a boardinghouse where his landlady served two hot meals daily. He had already climbed the nine hundred steps in the Washington Monument, seen the Capitol, and ridden on "electric trams that flew at high speeds." More wonderful still, the trees had turned scarlet during Indian summer. Outside the city, along the banks of the Potomac, the scenery was so beautiful that "I have trouble to believe my eyes." The water reflected the different colors of the foliage of trees and shrubs, reminding him of valleys he had seen in Switzerland. Being in America seemed like a dream, and he felt that he would be happy there for a long time.

After he had lived in Washington for a month, he wrote his parents that people lived in their own homes in America as comfortably as hotel guests. All houses had bathrooms and he could take a bath in hot or cold water as often as he pleased. Even the middle class enjoyed steam heat, simply turning a little knob to be warmer. In a large department store he had ridden in elevators with mirrors and electric lights and had watched a vacuum tube carry his money to a distant cashier and return with his change. People dressed so neatly that one could not tell an employer from an employee. Only the poor Negroes were an exception, but they dressed "very fine" when they could afford to do so. He was finding courage and strength to live according to his own ideas and was beginning to make friends.

When winter came, he enjoyed the frost and snow and gradually began to see "the sunny side" of life. Since the other men at his boardinghouse were quiet bachelors, he missed stimulating conversation in the evenings. As a diversion he went out to dinner at restaurants and tried new foods. He liked Chinese dishes and preferred Chinese tea to American tea; however, he soon realized that everything that he bought in America was expensive and his salary was not as generous as he had thought at first.

As the months passed, he began to build friendships that lasted his entire life. Erwin Smith continued to take an interest in him and invited Meyer and A. J. Pieters to his home. They spent long hours talking about the nature of the universe and man's place in it. Meyer, an articulate conversationalist, expressed the ideas he had absorbed in discussions at Our House in Amsterdam. Smith remembered long afterward his interest in Buddhist concepts and in the philosophy of Schopenhauer. Howard Dorsett also befriended the young man. At the Dorsett's home Meyer enjoyed being with a family again, for the Dorsetts had two sons and two daughters. In addition to Smith, Pieters, and Dorsett, Meyer admired his supervisor, George W. Oliver, director of plant testing and propagation at the USDA greenhouses.

When April came and willows were in leaf, he thought of spring in Holland and asked his parents whether his azalea was blooming in the little garden at Houthaven; by May he found the heat in Washington almost unbearable. Every evening he swam in the Potomac, for the humidity made him feel lazy and miserable. In addition, a letter forwarded from Holland informed him that a routine check of males born in 1875 had revealed that he was not free of military service. Unless he completed a second year in the Dutch army, he could be classified as a deserter. This information surprised and disturbed him, but he found refuge in the growing plants around him.

During the summer the heat continued to trouble him; however, he attended the theater and lectures, took long walks, and gradually began "to feel like an American." He decided that people could tolerate the humid weather in Washington because every household had an icebox and there was ice in all the water pitchers. Americans also ate quantities of ice cream and drank "ice cream in soda water," but the treat he enjoyed most was cold watermelon.

By the end of the summer, he had decided to see more of America. In a letter to the Janssens he tried to analyze his difficulty in finding contentment: "My life is without purpose. . . . I say to myself, 'Don't worry,' but unfortunately pessimistic thoughts come. Sometimes I care too much about something. And, when I worry too much, I need the uttermost thought to get relaxed again. How strange is this life—to exist and not to know why—to suffer and not to know why. I deceive myself often and say, 'Once it will be clear. I must wait.' And I wait and wait." Work was his remedy for melancholy; he found that it cured him as surely as medicine helped people who were ill.

In September of 1902 he traveled across the United States by train. "America is so big one can scarcely believe it," he wrote his parents. Even a fast train took twenty-six hours to go from Washington to Chicago, twenty-six from Chicago to Denver, and another twenty-six from Denver to Salt Lake City. He stopped there to see the Great Salt Lake and to attend a service at the Mormon Tabernacle, where the beauty of the organ music and the choir of six hundred voices impressed him deeply. The journey from Salt Lake City to San Francisco lasted thirty-two hours; from San Francisco he traveled south for nineteen more hours to Santa Ana near Los Angeles. There he soon found work at the short-lived USDA plant improvement garden and a home in a pleasant boardinghouse.

The beauty of nature and the variety of new plants that grew in southern California immediately absorbed his attention. Though the rainfall was sparse, the land was fertile. He saw palms, oranges, and lemons growing everywhere. "Here a boy can eat as many walnuts, peaches, figs, or watermelons as he wants. The fruit rots on the trees, so plentiful is the supply," he wrote A. J. Pieters. He took long walks, observed plants in a different environment, and felt content in his new location,

As fall changed to winter, he missed the snow and cold winds. With no thunderstorms and almost no rain to break the monotony, he began to feel bored by the perpetually sunny skies. He expressed his restlessness to his friend Pieters, who reminded him that he would succeed in his work only if he would "stick to it." Meyer replied, "I'll try. But it seems to me that the more a man travels, the less he feels himself attached to a certain place. A man is constantly wishing and longing for farther off and unseen places. Why do we have that desire?"

Perhaps Pieters was not surprised the following April when Meyer wrote that he was resigning. "This is a great country and I have still much to see and learn before I settle down," he explained. But this was not the main reason for his leaving Santa Ana after only seven months. In Washington he had enjoyed the friendship of educated men, but at Santa Ana he had been treated "just like a very common laborer," given no desk or even soap and towels or "a decent toilet room. These are but little personal things. Another more weighty matter is the garden itself. Treatment of plants is by far not satisfying. Plants received from the Seed and Plant Introduction Section died from lack of proper care. I do not say these things in anger but simply for justifying myself."

With the money he had saved, he wandered north for several weeks. Southern California, with its sparse population that included many descendants of Spaniards and Indians, seemed to him a very young country. "It is odd I have to wander so much," he wrote the Janssens. "I must have lived very strange in my former life. Could I only lift that veil!" His wandering ended at Montecito in a valley where the beauty of the mountains and the sea impressed him so deeply that he did not want to leave.

At Montecito he became head gardener in a commercial nursery that specialized in carnations and other cut flowers. In 1903 Montecito was only a village with the post office located in the combined grocery and general store. Raising greenhouse plants in the open was a new experience for Meyer and keeping them watered, a never-ending task. He did not plan to remain there more than a year, even though he enjoyed looking at the mountains at sunrise and sunset, swimming in the Pacific in the moonlight, and listening to the waves at night. He wanted to see the tropics next and then to go to the World's Fair at Saint Louis in 1904. As the new year began, he admitted to Dorsett that he felt depressed and he tried to analyze the reason: "I long for a bit more change in the weather. This is a splendid climate for old and sick people, but not for a normal, healthy person. I think sometimes with pleasure how a snowstorm would do me good or a heavy, warm rain, as we have them in the old country and in the East. You have seen yourself, Mr. Dorsett, how miserable I began to feel in Santa Ana."

His family could not understand why he continued to move about without mentioning returning home. Alida suggested that he start a little nursery in Holland, but he reminded her how depressed he had become just before he had traveled to Italy and Switzerland. Seeing new plants and new places had satisfied him then, and the same remedy could cure him again. "Happiness I don't find, but who finds that? No one I have met. The wonder is that stupid and silly people are the happiest."

A month later he had found the cure he sought. "By mutual agreement I am going to leave a few months earlier than our first intentions were, and so by March first I am a free man again," he wrote Dorsett. "The song of liberty is so sweet. Now in these last days the sun shines brighter, the birds sing more gaily, and everything seems more laughing now that my prison walls are crumbling away under the steady hammer strokes of Father Time." His letter concluded as usual with "kind rememberings" to Pieters, Smith, and Oliver, as well as to Mrs. Dorsett and the children.

When March finally brought the freedom that Meyer longed for, he left Armstrong's nursery and traveled to San Francisco. In cooler weather he enjoyed walking around the city observing plum and cherry trees in bloom. He also investigated the possibility of employment with Luther Burbank at Santa Rosa, but he learned that Burbank was doing much of his work alone and did not need a gardener. He wandered through the narrow streets of Chinatown, noticing the men, who wore long queues, and their pretty wives and children. But he could not see the "opium basements," for no white man was admitted. As he explored San Francisco, he felt free and content. After he had learned all that he could there, he took a steamer to San Blas, hoping to discover strange and rare plants in Mexico.

Rendezvous with Destiny

Our destiny exercises its influence over us even
when we have not learned its nature: it is our
future that lays down the law of our today.
                                        NIETZSCHE

A FTER a calm voyage over water as still as a mirror, Meyer
reached San Blas and began a 260-mile hike to Guadalajara. Along
the way he slept outdoors or in the huts of the natives. Near San
Blas he had to climb a slender tree to reach the bamboo flooring on which
he slept. During the night he heard insects crawling on the palm leaves
above him and "didn't sleep exactly quietly" for fear that a spider or a
scorpion might descend on him. By day he walked, stopping for meals with
the Mexicans and eating whatever was available, including stewed dog
meat. Though he enjoyed the beautiful scenery, he found the heat oppressive and sometimes had difficulty getting enough food in rural areas, where
everything edible was consumed by the impoverished Mexicans.

Fourteen days later he reached Guadalajara. He had discovered fruits
and flowers that were new to him, but he was disappointed to learn that the
inhabitants took little interest in plants and few nurseries existed in Mexico.
Because the roads were dusty during the dry season and the temperature was
high at midday, he traveled by train from Guadalajara to Mexico City.

After three weeks spent near Mexico City, he walked sixty miles to
Cuernavaca in two days. "For scenery this is wonderful country," he told
Dorsett. "Where I am now, I hardly think I ever saw a finer spot — a lovely
valley with range after range of mountains around. One peak in the distance
is an extinct volcano covered perpetually with snow. Its name is Popocate-
petl." Though he missed no opportunity to enjoy the beauty of Mexico, he
continued to look for a job where he could learn more about native trees
and plants. Since plenty of cheap labor was available, no one would employ
a skilled gardener. As he investigated the flora, he wrote Dorsett that "there
hardly passes a day that I do not discover some unknown fruits or flowers.

A few days ago I found the genuine wild potato growing at elevations between nine and ten thousand feet. Awful small they are, and I am really surprised that the modern 'Murphies' are their descendants. I felt just as glad as if I had found a nugget, for a botanist can have his 'strikes' too, as the miners term it."

Between Córdoba and Jalapa he saw begonias, sensitive plants, dahlias, and other familiar cultivated plants growing like weeds along the road. "I have learned more about the true nature of plants during this two-month trip in the wilderness than all the books or hothouses could have brought me in ten years," he told Dorsett. He also mailed eight varieties of seeds for trial at the new Chico Plant Introduction Garden, with a careful description of each type. These seeds, the first of hundreds of shipments that he sent to the USDA, included an apricot, an ash, an ornamental cherry, a small lupine, and a yellow chili pepper. His journey across Mexico ended abruptly at Vera Cruz, where a yellow fever epidemic forced him to leave immediately for Cuba.

When he tried to enter Cuba, American officials placed him in quarantine because he could have been exposed to yellow fever at Vera Cruz. Since this disease had caused such tragic loss of life during the recent Spanish-American War, the new American administration strictly enforced laws to prevent the entrance of anyone who might be infected. He did not find the food or the company pleasant during five days in quarantine. Confinement, high temperatures, and humidity made his two weeks in Cuba less enjoyable than the remainder of his journey; however, he enjoyed seeing the beautiful parks in Havana and the pineapples and other tropical fruits in the markets. At the house where he lodged he met another Dutchman, the son of the governor of a West Indian island. Conversing in Dutch and sipping tall Cuban drinks mixed with fruit and ice helped Meyer to forget the intense heat. Hearing Dutch spoken again also made him long for news of his family, for he had not received mail from home in the three months since he had left Montecito.

From Havana he went to New Orleans. His long trip across Mexico had cost four hundred dollars and had exhausted all his savings. Looking for employment as he traveled, he moved on to Birmingham, Alabama. After working for a few weeks in the enervating climate there, in late July he had enough money to go to Saint Louis where he found an opening at the Missouri Botanical Garden. "It is a good thing I got this place, for financially I am in pretty bad shape," he admitted to the Dorsetts. Answering their invitation to visit them at their new home in Chico, he wrote, "California occupies still a very large place in my heart. Notwithstanding the troubles I had there, I do love the Golden State. I have spent there most of the time since I lived in the United States, which I come to regard already as my native land."

At the Missouri Botanical Garden, Dr. William Trelease employed

Meyer as a propagator of herbaceous material and assigned him the task of raising about ten thousand plants from seeds. In addition, Meyer initiated preparation of a list of seeds available for exchange with botanical gardens in foreign countries. He found a pleasant boarding house with an Irish landlady near the botanical garden. In his leisure he walked in the country-side where he discovered grapes, persimmons, pawpaws, and nuts. Often he swam in a lake or in the Mississippi. When fall came, he experienced "a wonderful strange feeling of pleasure and sorrow mingled" as the green leaves turned to flame colors.

Since the World's Fair had attracted him to Saint Louis, he spent many hours exploring all the buildings. He described to his parents the wonders that he had seen: an electric sewing machine that operated when one pushed a button, pianos that played automatically, statues and scenes carved from butter, Turkish wheat, African diamonds, and "big automobiles" that could carry forty people. Two Dutch generals who had recently served in the Boer War were in charge of the South African exhibit. Meyer spoke to General Cronje in Dutch and "had a few glasses of beer with him." He also was one of twenty thousand people who saw President Theodore Roosevelt when he attended the fair with his wife and daughter.

But the American agricultural exhibits attracted him more than inventions or foreign displays. He drank freshly squeezed "apple wine," ate pancakes made of banana flour, and examined many varieties of grapes, apples, and peaches. "In agriculture there is a wonderful fine display," he told Dorsett. "I spent a couple of hours alone to look at the exhibit of the Bureau of Plant Industry, the new fruits and plants they are importing and so many more things." He enjoyed the opportunity to talk to both Beverly T. Galloway, head of the Bureau of Plant Industry, and Adrian J. Pieters, who came to Saint Louis in connection with the USDA exhibit.

Promoters of the Exposition held an International Congress of Art and Science on the fairgrounds in September. They invited as guests one hundred speakers from Europe and one hundred from the United States. Hugo de Vries, who had recently published *The Theory of Mutation*, was one of the distinguished guests. Trelease entertained de Vries in his home and guided him through the Missouri Botanical Garden. De Vries did not know that his former protégé was employed in Saint Louis, and Trelease did not guess that Meyer had worked for de Vries. When Trelease attempted to introduce his skilled gardener to de Vries, Meyer enjoyed the amazement on their faces as de Vries warmly greeted his former pupil.

Early in November Pieters sent Meyer a telegram asking him to be a member of the Forestry Jury at the fair. Meyer hesitated because he knew that the panel members were expected to dress formally. He had never worn a high hat or evening dress and he did not plan to begin now. When he explained that he could not afford to buy formal clothes, he learned that a business suit would be sufficient if he bought a white vest, "a fine shirt and tie," and gloves. Judging presented no problems for him, but he felt less at home at affairs in the evening. Most of the guests were elegantly dressed, "at least, the gentlemen; the ladies wore low-cut dresses with naked arms, more undressed than dressed." Walking in the country gave him more pleasure than formal events.

Winter brought gray skies, icy winds, and a feeling of restlessness. After two years among palm and lemon trees, he missed the flowers and warm weather and complained about the smoke and fog in Saint Louis. Writing to the Janssens in Holland, he admitted that "traveling and wandering are the only things that interest me. I get tired in regular surroundings. I think of countries I have not seen that might give me rest. If I were wealthy, I would go around the world and after I had seen it all, buy a little piece of land where I liked best." He was hoping to leave Saint Louis in the fall and go to South America to explore the Andes. Life had become dull again, he wrote Dorsett. "Still we have to live it through whether we like it or not." The pattern had become familiar: enthusiasm in a new setting, then boredom, frustration, and the need to cast off fetters and move on.

Suddenly the miracle happened; the dream of his youth came true. On March 10, 1905, a telegram from Adrian J. Pieters opened new horizons for Frank Meyer. His boredom changed to enthusiastic acceptance of the challenge of exploring China for the United States Department of Agriculture. The wire that he sent Pieters reflected his ebullient reaction: "Great thanks for your offer. Accept it. Will be ready any time but would like to stay here a few weeks yet." On the evening that he received the telegram he wrote to his "dear mother" to congratulate her on her birthday. "I have big news," he told her, explaining that he had been asked to accompany Professor Sargent to China to collect new plants for the American government. Arrangements were not definite, but "the offer is a beautiful one even if it does not go through."

After expressing his surprise and gratitude to Pieters, he asked about the nature of his work. "China is quite a wild country as I understand it, and one is most of the time pretty far away from civilization. Well, that's all right." He also inquired whether he would need to take photographs. "If I have to do it, I will start directly and learn that art." Though Eastman had produced the roll-film camera a decade earlier, dependable film had not been developed. Plant explorers had to carry a large camera, a tripod, heavy glass plates, and a black cloth for draping camera and photographer.

Pieters followed the telegram with a request that Meyer suggest the salary he would require. Meyer answered, "About the compensation, I leave that better to you. I haven't any idea how big my expenses will be in that country. Does the government supply us with suits, arms, horses, or any other things we may need?" After Pieters insisted that Meyer make a suggestion, he hesitantly proposed a salary of $50 a month, adding that expenses abroad are always larger than one may think. When the department eventually offered $1,000 a year plus an allowance for expenses, this problem was solved.

Three months passed before Meyer left Saint Louis. Spring brought thaws that left the streets near his boardinghouse deep in mud, but finally the grass turned green and flowers began to bloom. Even with several men to help him at the botanical garden, he could scarcely tend the thousands of young plants that were his responsibility. Though the garden was closed on Sundays and the gardeners had that day off, Meyer was busier than ever. "I can't leave those little plants uncared for on the Sabbath," he wrote his parents. Reluctant to lose such a dedicated and competent gardener, Trelease sometimes hoped that the expedition to China would not materialize. Meyer knew that Sargent had canceled his proposed trip to the Orient and that Fairchild was hoping to be able to accompany him instead. Since he believed that he would eventually reach China, he accepted a series of revised plans and enjoyed the coming of spring in Saint Louis. "In a way I am not sorry I am not going yet," he told Pieters, "for the magnolia trees in this garden are in full bloom and it is a soul-inspiring sight."

After several postponements, in late June Fairchild asked Frank Meyer to come to Washington. For the first of hundreds of times Meyer wrote directly to Fairchild, thanking him and also "the other gentlemen who have given you such nice statements about me that you offer me such an important position without ever having seen me. It is certainly a very fine opportunity to do some noble work for this, my adopted country, and I surely hope to prove that I realize the grandness of this exploration of a practically new field. Just now I am almost burning to have a talk with you about how many we will be, the language, the transportation of collected material from the railroadless interior to the harbor towns, and many more things."

More than thirty years later David Fairchild recalled vividly his first meeting with Meyer on a hot and humid July day. For Meyer this interview was the culmination of four months of waiting. Fairchild too had been looking forward to forming his own estimate of his agriculture explorer. He met a man of medium height, broad-shouldered and strong, with regular features, blue eyes, brown hair, and beard. Sitting eagerly on the edge of his chair, Meyer was completely unconscious that his striped shirt had become soaked with perspiration and the colors had run together. But Fairchild was more interested in observing his quick intelligence and his love of plants. "From the first time I set eyes upon him, I believed in him," he told Pieters months afterwards. When Meyer described his distress because the bamboo that Fairchild had sent to Santa Ana had died after the director had refused to allow Meyer to mulch the plants, Fairchild looked beyond Meyer's unconventional clothes and muscular body and glimpsed his sensitive soul.

Years later Fairchild wrote, "From that moment Meyer and I were friends, and for thirteen years I traveled with him, in spirit if not in body, through the farms, gardens, forests, and deserts of Asia."[1]

A few months earlier Fairchild had married the younger daughter of Alexander Graham Bell. After his return from his travels abroad, he had been invited to one of Mr. Bell's Wednesday Evenings, occasions when twenty-five or thirty scientists gathered for discussion and refreshments in the paneled library at 1331 Connecticut Avenue in Washington. Fairchild developed a lifelong admiration for Bell, a man of great vigor, charm, and kindness; soon he found in Marian Bell a rival to his interest in plant introduction. Though he wanted to introduce Meyer to his wife's distinguished family, he had to "spruce him up a bit" before he could take his unconventional plant hunter to the Bells for dinner. As he had guessed, the family was fascinated by Meyer, especially by his keen interest in everything and his eagerness to learn. An interesting conversationalist as well as a good listener, Meyer talked enthusiastically about places that he had visited, justifying Fairchild's pride in his protégé.[2]

From Washington Meyer wrote his parents the exciting news that his trip to China had been confirmed. "It is a beautiful prospect. People here have been good to me. I have been invited to dinners and parties, but I get tired of that. Last Saturday I visited the home of a millionaire. He has only fifteen millions! Everyone asked about my trip to Mexico. That trip did me a lot of good. . . . I can hardly believe I got such a beautiful job." He would be allowed thousands of guilders to travel, hire helpers and horses, and buy plants. Only one problem remained—the difficulty of the Chinese language. "There are more than three thousand letters in that alphabet. I am afraid I cannot master that whole language. Well, I shall try with all my powers, and I think I will succeed."

July of 1905 proved to be busy and exciting enough to compensate for four months of waiting. He met the secretary of agriculture, received his letter of authorization and his appropriation, and emerged from a conference at the Treasury Department bonded. Because Meyer needed to become familiar with plants that had already been collected in China, Fairchild arranged a ten-day trip to the New York Botanical Garden, Henry L. Hicks's Nursery at Westbury, Long Island, and Harvard University's Arnold Arboretum at Jamaica Plain near Boston. Completed in 1900, the "Crystal Palace" in the Bronx contained nearly nine thousand living specimens and the dome of the palatial palm house rose ninety feet above eleven connecting greenhouses, but Meyer focused his attention on herbarium specimens collected by Augustine Henry and on books about the flora of China. It was not the splendor of the New York Botanical Garden that impressed him but the Arnold Arboretum, the two-hundred acre home of one of the world's outstanding plant collections. Meeting the director, Charles Sprague

Sargent, and seeing such a tremendous variety of trees and shrubs during the four days he spent there increased his determination to succeed in his new assignment.

Two days after returning to Washington, Frank Meyer began his long journey. At the Chico Plant Introduction Garden in California he saw P. H. Dorsett. On the second of August, he left San Francisco aboard the *Coptic*. Neither Sargent nor Fairchild could arrange to introduce him to the work of a plant hunter in China; therefore, Meyer traveled alone to a strange continent. Though the confinement of an ocean voyage made him impatient, he felt "very happy at the thought of giving people many new plants and fruits from China." Aboard ship he had time to remember the advice that Sargent had given him at the Arnold Arbóretum, to review his notes about people whom Fairchild wanted him to meet, and to think of the chance that he would soon have to prove his ability as an agricultural explorer. During the year ahead he would be tested, but he felt ready to meet the challenge.

The First Expedition

THE
United States of America

DEPARTMENT OF AGRICULTURE

To all who shall see these presents greeting:

Be it known that **Mr. Frank N. Meyer,**

an Agricultural Explorer in the United States Department of Agriculture.

a Citizen of the State of Missouri and of the United States of America, whose signature appears on the margin hereof, will, in the immediate future, visit Manchuria and other parts of China for the purpose of Aiding in Agricultural Development, especially along the line of Pomology.

He is hereby introduced and cordially commended to all persons interested in Agricultural Development, especially along Pomological lines, and to all Friends and Official Representatives of the Government of the United States of America in China and such other countries as he may visit.

Frank N. Meyer

In witness whereof, I have hereunto subscribed my name and caused the seal of the Department of Agriculture to be affixed. Done at the City of Washington, District of Columbia this Twenty-ninth day of August, A.D. 1905, and of the Independence of the United States of America the One Hundred and Thirtieth.

James Wilson
Secretary of Agriculture

Official document authorizing Frank N. Meyer to go as an agricultural explorer to *"Manchuria and other parts of China"* as a representative of the USDA, August 29, 1905. Courtesy Dr. George A. White, Plant Introduction Officer, Agricultural Research Center, Beltsville, Maryland.

Meyer's *"little caravan halting for a rest in a beautiful ravine, where the ax of the woodsman has not done much damage as yet."* Southern Manchuria, June 26, 1906.

Meyer's carts *"crossing a rickety shakey bridge without falling through,"* northern Korea, August 1, 1906.

The barren Wu Tai Shan, *"our caravan creeping its way through the now dry bed of a river,"* April 14, 1907. President Theodore Roosevelt used this photograph in his conservation message to Congress in 1908.

Meyer (top) with four professors from Shansi University on a 700-year-old *Thuja orientalis* in the courtyard of an old temple at Tsintse, May 5, 1907, during a rare relaxed moment with Westerners.

"A piece of rugged mountain scenery at an elevation of between 8000 and 10,000 ft.," Wu Tai Shan.

"These plants and seeds, weighing altogether between fifteen and twenty tons, and which the explorer accompanied for four weary weeks on the tank oil steamer 'Ashtabula,' are at last landed on American soil, waiting to be inspected and fumigated," San Francisco, June 13, 1908.

FIRST EXPEDITION, 1905–1909

CHAPTER 4

Stranger in China

Near Peking
SEPTEMBER TO DECEMBER, 1905

MEYER enjoyed his voyage across the Pacific. The captain of the *Coptic* knew Amsterdam well and invited Meyer to sit at his table, where Chinese mess boys wearing long queues served everyone. During a brief stop in Hawaii, Meyer visited the small USDA Experiment Station and the larger Territorial Station. After they left the islands, a fierce three-day storm pounded the ship, but the remainder of the trip was pleasant. Discovering that at sea he made friends easily, Meyer relaxed among his congenial fellow passengers until he disembarked at Yokohama.

As soon as he landed, Meyer visited H. Suzuki at the Yokohama Nursery and sent Fairchild copious notes about plants that could be tested at a proposed USDA plant introduction garden in Hawaii. He also bought a bale of sphagnum moss to put aboard the steamer, for he remembered Sargent's warning that he would not find that essential item in China. In Tokyo he admired beautiful temples and gardens and noticed strange sights—parasols made of bamboo and silk, straw shoes with wooden soles, and people traveling in jinrikishas pulled by men who traveled as fast as horses. "Japan is a very clean country, but it somewhat makes upon me the impression of being a doll country," he wrote Charles Monroe Mansfield, a friend at the plant introduction office in Washington. "Everything is so little—men, horses, trees, gardens, cups, everything." Aboard ship again and steaming slowly through the inland sea, every view seemed like a dream. At Nagasaki he called on the brother and sister of A. J. Pieters; then, leaving his new acquaintances on the *Coptic* with regret, he transferred to a ship bound for Shanghai.

The steamer weathered a typhoon in the South China Sea, and gale winds were blowing when it docked at Shanghai. After the storm struck, the swollen river left water several feet deep in the streets, uprooting hundreds of trees and flooding the hotel basement where Meyer had stored his big box of official stationery, inventory notebooks, vouchers, and the precious bale of sphagnum moss. His dismay about the damage to the department's supplies dissipated when he realized that other hotel guests had lost thousands of dollars worth of fine silks and art, while the losses of merchants who had sugar, cotton, and tobacco stored in warehouses amounted to millions.

After calling on the American consul general, he visited nurseries and consulted people about forwarding his future shipments to the United States. He soon made a lifelong friend of the superintendent of parks and open spaces, D. MacGregor, who promised to care for any plants that he might ship to Shanghai.[1] His official duties completed, Meyer explored streets covered with a foot of mud. He noticed ladies riding in low carriages pulled by men or small horses, and a man pushing five or six others who sat in a sort of wheelbarrow. That the Chinese police force had authority only over the natives surprised him; English and Irish policemen protected Caucasians. He related these observations to his father, who had seen Far Eastern ports as a sailor in his youth.

En route by sea to Tientsin, at Chefoo (Yantai) Meyer called on Dr. Yamei Kin and Mrs. John L. Nevius, the widow of a medical missionary who had introduced Western fruit trees there. These ladies, friends of David Fairchild, shared their considerable knowledge of the flora of northern China and showed Meyer several fine gardens. They also invited him "to take many a cup of tea" and to eat a typical Chinese dinner. Afterward, loaded with gifts of fruit and mooncakes, he rode to the steamship in a jinrikisha. "And it was more luck than wisdom that I wasn't thrown out on the road, for there are a few things in this country which are simply fierce," he told Pieters, "and these things are the state of the roads and the filth. It is sometimes staggering to see that utter disregard for the most rudimentary ideas of sanitation."

He reached Tientsin (Tianjin) in mid-September and made calls on the American consul, shipping agencies, and nurserymen. In the markets he saw "a strange persimmon, perfectly seedless," he reported to Fairchild. "Then there are very strange quinces here. They look like fine yellow pears and one kind looks like a small yellow apple, but they are quinces and they are melting in one's mouth. The big trouble is now, where do they come from? Most say, 'Tientsin have no got.' " Soon he discovered that wholesale dealers bought from transporters who traveled by boat for many miles up or down the numerous canals or rivers to buy from the growers. "The wholesalers sell again to the middlemen and these to the retailers, so it is no wonder nobody knows where things come from." Though he took a twenty-mile walk beyond the city and saw vineyards with fine grapes, he failed to find the fruits that he sought.

Arriving in Peking (Beijing) at last, he explored that colossal city of 700,000 inhabitants. The foreign quarter, a walled village within the city, housed the various embassies. Outside the foreign quarter, crowds filled the streets. Meyer met sailors of all nationalities, talked to Dutch marines, and ate black bread and cold soup with Russian sailors. China's problems, he thought, resulted from corrupt government and a language so difficult that even educated Chinese could not agree on the meaning of a contract.

He described to Charles Mansfield some of the less pleasant aspects of life in China: "You people in America haven't any idea of the filth here. In one place people are eating their dinner, while next to them ragpickers are emptying their bags. Opposite these parties is an open sewer into which refuse is dumped, and some men are sitting on the edge obeying the call of nature!" Along some city streets residents had dug drainage trenches. "The water that used to run into their houses now accumulates in these holes. Vegetable sellers sprinkle their vegetables with it, children bathe in it, mosquitoes multiply in it, and on dark nights many a poor soul falls into it."[2] Lack of sanitation and the appalling poverty of the masses distressed him.

As soon as he settled in Peking, he planned a ten-day plant-hunting trip to the mountains sixty miles northeast of the city. His first journey set a pattern that he would follow on expeditions ranging over many hundreds of miles. He had heard that large peaches, pearlike quinces, fine apples, and almonds grew in the mountains. He therefore hired a guide from that region, as well as a coolie, a cart, a driver, and donkeys. After packing food, cooking utensils, bedding, candles, inventory notebooks, sphagnum moss, copper labels, oiled paper, twine, seed bags, and a roll of burlap, he began his journey.

When his party stopped at a small village in the mountains and everyone came to look at the foreigner, he patiently allowed the curious natives to examine him. After feeling his boots and pants and making remarks about the color of his blue eyes, the villagers became interested in his flashlight. "Time after time they requested me to blow the candle out," he told Fairchild. "One man wanted to know what I had in a small bottle. Well, it was pepper, and, not knowing the Chinese word, I made the movement of taking a little to my nose and sneezing. To my amazement the whole crowd wanted some of it and sniffed it up through their nostrils. They cried and wept and coughed and shouted, and I couldn't keep myself straight from laughing." Later, when Meyer added pepper to his soup, they understood that it was a seasoning. "All of those who hadn't partaken roared at those who had been so silly. Then I found they had supposed the stuff to be a foreign snuff." After this encounter, he spent several days searching for desirable nuts and fruits. Returning to Peking, he rode a donkey down steep, rocky slopes for twelve hours. Having started the day at a high altitude where the cold wind and rarified atmosphere made him shiver, he finally reached the hot, dusty plain north of Peking and then crossed the city to his hotel.

In his report to Fairchild, he withheld until last the news of his first important discovery: "Almonds did not exist at all there, neither those big late peaches, neither quince-pears or that special kind of apple, but there were little orchards of apricots, early peaches, medium pears, and walnuts, and last but not least, very large seedless persimmons (*Diospyros kaki*). Some of these were four inches in diameter. As soon as the leaves are off, I'll go back to these trees and will try to send you a thousand scions." These sweet Chinese persimmons, unlike the American persimmon, remained firm even when ripe and therefore could be transported and marketed.

Though he devoted most of his time to finding useful crops, Meyer also eagerly complied with the USDA policy of collecting ornamentals "when encountered." Early in October, accompanied by Mr. and Mrs. E. T. Williams of the American Legation, he traveled for sixteen days in the Wei-tsan or Western Mountains about fifty miles from Peking. There he discovered that the original vegetation had survived centuries of cultivation only around the temples and monasteries. At one temple he found a hundred-foot-tall *Catalpa bungei*, still very rare in the States; at another he saw graceful bamboo forty or fifty feet high. Other unusual ornamentals that he thought Americans might appreciate included the spreading Chinese horse chestnut (*Aesculus chinensis*) and "those curious white-bark pines (*Pinus bungeana*) which for all the world look like being whitewashed."

Meyer's next journey took him two hundred miles northeast of Peking into an agricultural section of Mongolia that no white man had visited before. Rumors of a paper-shell walnut led him to Changli and then to the village of Gopo. There he found orchards with a few paper-shells scattered among the hard-shell walnuts; however, there were no nuts on the trees, and the farmers, frightened by the appearance of a "foreign devil," were unwilling to point out the rare paper-shells. Meyer later sent Dorsett a single nut with the warning, "Be good to that paper-shell, for it is the only large one I was able to lay hands on and the owner wouldn't show me the tree." On one farm he made cuttings of a beautiful table grape similar to a Muscatel. He took pictures of the grapes, but the villagers, though fascinated by his camera, were afraid to be photographed. The farmers admired his pruning shears and "howled with delight when I chopped a heavy branch clean through." In addition to the grapes, he saw a "fine white, long-headed cabbage, more like a giant long-headed lettuce," beautiful red turnips like large, round radishes, and purplish carrots which were as red as beets when scraped. Gathering seeds of these vegetables proved to be a major problem because each farmer saved only enough for his own use, eating or selling all his surplus.

In addition to vegetables, he collected the wild persimmon (*Diospyros lotus*) because he had observed that the Chinese used it successfully as a rootstock for the cultivated persimmon. The trees in their orchards sometimes lived to be centuries old; yet they remained productive. Furthermore, the drought-resistant wild Chinese persimmon promised to be admirably suited to the semiarid Southwestern states. Untested as a rootstock before Meyer introduced it for that purpose, in twenty years it superseded all other stocks in use in California, producing thrifty, rapid-growing, uniform stands of nursery trees with excellent root systems.[3] In the mountains near Shan Haikwan (Shanhaiguan), he discovered a columnar juniper which Fairchild later named *Juniperus chinensis* 'Columnaris'. This evergreen now forms handsome hedges at the Glenn Dale Plant Introduction Station in Maryland and at the National Arboretum in Washington.

On this trip he stayed overnight at rural inns and became accustomed to brick beds, holes in the walls for ventilation, and the lack of tables, chairs, or lamps. The filthy inns swarmed with lice, bedbugs, and centipedes. His guide killed a large scorpion, explaining that "one is only sick for three days when they bite one." He described to Pieters his first bath in a Chinese bathhouse where everyone undressed in a big room with broad benches along the side walls. Ten or twenty people washed together in a small closed room in a three-foot pool of very hot water. Each bather received a basin of cold water to rinse himself. By that time the room had filled with spectators, gathered to see the foreigner. "I had to dry and dress in great show just to let them see how we do. Happily no buttons came off, so I hope I left a good impression. I often wish you could be with me here. We could laugh many a time."

By the end of October, Meyer had traveled west of Peking to Hsuanhwa (Xuanhua), a region with sterile soil, no trees, and ice already thick on ponds. Following a mountain trail with rocks above and a river five hundred feet below, he and his small party were caught in a gravel and sand storm while an icy wind nearly blew them down the precipice. Finally they came to an inn where Meyer saw on the wall in French an "amusing and disgusting inscription: 'Hotel of 1000 Bedbugs.' " To avoid being bitten, he improvised a bed by putting three small tables together in the middle of the room. He later confessed that his "spirits ran low" for a while because he had to choose between sleeping in bitter cold without a fire or building a fire that filled the room with smoke and caused the bugs to become active. In many rural inns, everyone slept in one room. If a private room was available, partitions usually did not reach the ceiling and a curtain often served as a door. Furthermore, he wrote Dorsett, "When I tell you that chamberpots and water closets are unknown, you may imagine the rest."

After returning to Peking through another dust storm, he packed his harvest and mailed bundles to the Chico Plant Introduction Garden, to Washington, and to Sargent at the Arnold Arboretum. To Dorsett he sent grape, apricot, poplar, and catalpa cuttings and elm, pear, and persimmon scions and to Fairchild an assortment of seeds including those of the maidenhair tree (*Ginkgo biloba*) and the silvery white-barked pine, "beautiful and serene enough to worship." He had seen on the grave of the second Ming Emperor a specimen that measured 10 feet in circumference and stood more than 120 feet high. Though several of these pines were already growing in the United States, including a small one at the Arnold Arboretum, he wanted America to have many more. After one century it "makes a nice impression," he commented, "but after two or three centuries it really becomes imposing." In the beautiful Ming Tombs Valley he had gathered acorns from a large-leafed oak which had turned a gorgeous crimson and seeds of maples that had become beautiful masses of scarlet, orange, and yellow. "To see the sunlight play on these colors is like listening to the most inspiring music. I felt good and was at peace with the whole creation sitting under such a tree." In mid-December he dispatched twenty-three more packages, warning Fairchild to give seeds of the fine white cabbage and red turnips only to experts for testing.

Mailing packages to America often proved a frustrating task. Meyer did not trust anyone else to pack his collection or to sew burlap covers over each large bundle to protect the poplar and willow cuttings, walnut scions, or hawthorn budwood. If the plant material dried completely it would die; excess moisture also could be fatal. He therefore would wring water out of the sphagnum moss that he used for packing until he thought that it contained just the necessary amount of dampness. In rural areas he had difficulty finding a post office that would accept parcels addressed to the consul general in Shanghai or to Washington. After packing, writing detailed descriptions in duplicate, and labeling, he often had to spend hours waiting for a qualified person to arrive at the post office or express company, only to find that they did not have the necessary forms for international shipments. After clerks had assured him that the weight limit for mail to the United States was eleven pounds, he bought tins and packed valuable seeds. Later he learned that eleven pounds was acceptable for mail going to England, but the limit to the United States was only four and a half pounds. "Things go very slow here," he told Fairchild, "and one who is in a hurry wears himself out and accomplishes nothing."

Finding and keeping Chinese employees presented a continuing problem. The Chinese disliked being away from their friends and relatives and wanted to go home soon after starting a journey. They did not like to walk, preferring to ride in a cart unless the track was too rough or too steep. Because Meyer walked great distances without resting, his guide thought that he must have iron legs. Though he complained about their faults, Meyer assured Dorsett that "China is going to come to the front, for the people are a solid kind of men and they possess many sterling virtues. In agriculture, they are experts." To Pieters he wrote, "China needs an intelligent government to make this country one of the finest countries on the face of the globe." But he treasured pictures of American scenes "to keep in my own thoughts green the memory of the best country on earth."

Difficulties with mailing packages, keeping employees, and adjusting to the declining rate of exchange upset him far less than news of the death of Mrs. Dorsett. The Dorsetts had been especially kind to him when he first came to America, and he remembered their hospitality gratefully. Though Mrs. Dorsett had been ill at the time that he had visited Chico in July, word of her death in August did not reach him until December. Then he wrote his friend, "How it grieves me to hear of the death of Mrs. Dorsett. Why? Why? In my last two letters I had already the feeling that she did not live any more on this earth. It aches me too that I was not able to see her when I was with you at Chico. I can't give you consolation — but be brave!" Meyer did not know that both of Dorsett's daughters also were ill with a malaria-like fever and both would soon die.

In December a wave of antiforeign feeling swept China. Five years after the Boxer Rebellion, many Chinese bitterly resented the presence of foreigners. The American Legation staff did not expect another general uprising, but they did predict local disturbances. Meyer remembered that while he was in Shan Haikwan collecting dry-land rice, a Westerner, believing that he had been insulted, beat a Chinese man with his cane. A mob formed, tore the foreigner's clothes, and took his possessions. Meyer had dressed the foreigner's wounds and continued his journey. In Changli, Chinese soldiers at first refused to allow him to enter an inn. Later, while he was eating dinner, they had stared at him until he offered them food "of which they made liberal use"; however, he had experienced no serious trouble.

When his mother wrote that she feared for his safety among so many foreigners, Meyer answered that he always treated the Chinese well and took care not to offend them. His guide and carters told the villagers that their employer was an unusually strong man who could crack a nut in one hand, break a rope with his two hands, and walk many miles without tiring. The Chinese sometimes asked to see his arm and leg muscles and his mysterious canned food. Whenever he realized that they feared the foreign demon, he would sit down among them, eat a piece of fruit, and let them see that he was not as strange as they had thought. "I stay healthy and strong," he assured his family. "Sometimes I am surprised at myself because I get so easily through so many difficulties." He explained that he did not mind traveling in a cart without springs and sleeping on a hard brick bed. A fire of leaves, grass, or dried dung under the bed kept it warm, though the heat also activated insects. His first journeys had yielded new fruit trees, vegetables, and ornamentals that had brought praise from his employers; "I will prove that I am worth their choice."

Though physical discomforts and dangers did not trouble him, he did admit to feeling lonely and missing friends with whom he could share his joys and sorrows. Letters from Fairchild arrived regularly, but a few days before Christmas Meyer asked him to "put a little less officialness in your letters and a little more warmth, for I am all alone here and am not much in conversation with my fellowmen so one needs a little sympathy in his letters." Almost three months later Meyer received Fairchild's reply saying that he could appreciate Meyer's feelings because he too had enjoyed encouraging letters when he was in the field. Meyer then admitted that his request had been "somewhat childish." Yet he enjoyed receiving letters "of a far less brief character" and hearing that his work was appreciated in Washington.

Despite loneliness, the feeling that he was doing a good job usually kept him cheerful. He wrote confidently to Charles Mansfield, recalling pleasant fishing trips along the beautiful banks of the Potomac and a February night when they "almost froze to death" at Great Falls. To him Meyer confided that Fairchild " 'trusts' that I'll be able to keep up. Do you think that when I want to make a success of a thing, I wouldn't be able to do so? Ha! Hear me laugh! I'll show them that the selection of Frank Meyer was a good one." After a night spent on a brick bed in a smoky room with fragments of torn paper at the windows flapping noisily, he sometimes felt discouraged, "but when the sun comes out and I see the beautiful bluish mountains in the distance, I feel again that it isn't so bad after all." His determination to succeed and his desire to find useful crops, shrubs, and trees for his adopted country kept his spirits high as his first harvest season in China ended.

The First Winter

Near Peking and Shanghai
JANUARY TO APRIL, 1906

A S the temperature dropped to zero and ice froze a foot thick on the canals in late December, Meyer continued to collect near Peking. Three days after spending Christmas with Mr. and Mrs. E. T. Williams of the American Legation, he sent the department bundles including grape cuttings, peach budsticks, a yellow rose (*Rosa xanthina*) to be shared with Sargent, and a new grass that, according to the gardener at the German Legation in Peking, stayed short and green. If it should prove successful in the United States, he commented, it might "revolutionize the lawn mower business."

On December 29 he set out toward the Western Mountains in fine snow. In the temple yard that he had visited in the fall, he took cuttings of the male Chinese pistachio (*Pistacia chinensis*), the Chinese horse chestnut (*Aesculus chinensis*), the *Catalpa bungei*, and a willow suitable to very dry regions (*Salix matsudana* 'Umbraculifera'). These trees were not new to botanists, but they never had been introduced into general cultivation in America. Meyer admired the Chinese pistachio especially because the delicate new foliage emerged wine red in the spring, it offered dense shade in the summer, and the leaves turned flaming scarlet in the autumn. This tree is now a popular ornamental in California. During the next two days he followed the trail of the famous Pai li or Peking pear (*Pyrus pyrifolia* var. *culta*) for which he had been looking ever since he had arrived in China. On New Year's Day he found it; "then my joy was great to begin 1906 in such a nice way."

After this promising start he went on to the mountains, riding a donkey until the trail became too steep. At one point he fell and his donkey fell on him, "but having a heavy coat on, none of my ribs broke." In crevices between rocks he found peach trees (*Prunus davidiana*) and took cuttings for propagators to use in breeding hardier fruit trees and ornamentals. While he was collecting persimmons and bush cherries, eight men and boys followed him for ten or twelve miles to see what the "foreign devil" was doing. Meyer complained that he felt like a monkey in the zoo.

Searching for fruit trees in a bleak region after having had only a small breakfast, he became hungry about eleven o'clock and asked villagers where he could find an inn. They assured him that he would reach a good place one mile farther along his route. Later, a second group said that he would need to travel another mile and a half. This misdirection continued until 3:00 P.M. when he finally found a place "to stretch my cold weary limbs on a brick bedstead with a nice fire underneath. I closed my door rather hard, for I was mad with all those lying rascals, but after a pretty substantial meal, I began to feel better and to think that they probably did it that way not to discourage us by telling us that we had to go from eleven to three before we could get anything to eat." Though he understood their reasoning, he often became irritated with the Chinese because they told him whatever they thought he wanted to hear instead of telling the truth.

During this journey a visit to a Chinese hothouse offered vivid sensory impressions. Made of sorghum stems heavily plastered with mud and heated by flues, the hothouse had paper windows on the south side only. Large open vessels filled with water maintained humidity while other open vessels contained liquid night soil, the traditional fertilizer of China. Despite the unpleasant odor permeating the hothouse, Meyer found much to admire: beautiful forced peonies that sold for fifty cents a bloom, small orange trees full of fruit, and fine cucumbers, luxuries for the wealthy at fifty cents each. "If a young cucumber shows a tendency of going to be crooked, the Chinese simply hang a piece of stone tied to a string on it and force it to be straight," he told Fairchild. "Could we only do this thing to crooked people too!" Eight half-naked coolies kept a furnace burning to maintain a temperature of 90°F and the heat, in addition to the odor of the onions and "the vessels with certain liquids referred to," did not make the hothouse an inviting place to have lunch. He nevertheless accepted an invitation to join the staff for tea, onion sprouts, and forced young leaves of the Tree of Heaven (*Ailanthus altissima*). The heat, the odors, and the novel food made him feel far from well until he went outdoors where the temperature registered 20°F.

Eleven days of travel in bitter cold yielded a good harvest. His collection included a Chinese maple (*Acer truncatum*) that later showed promise at the Chico Plant Introduction Garden because of its graceful foliage and beautiful autumn leaf colors.[1] Within a few hours after collecting scions and cuttings, Meyer wrapped them in dampened sphagnum moss, which soon froze in unheated rural inns. When he returned to Peking, he packed twenty-seven bundles with infinite care and sent them to America. He included diseased pear twigs for Merton Waite, a USDA plant pathologist who had been one of five men working with Galloway when Fairchild first came to Washington in 1889. Meyer incorrectly identified the disease as pear blight; when Waite corrected his error he apologized, "for it isn't quite honorable that I should have made a mistake."

At his hotel he found instructions requiring that he record all expenditures in Chinese currency. Since China had no stable currency, numerous brass, copper, and silver coins were in use, but their value changed every five miles. "How I am going to square the job is a puzzle to me," he wrote Dorsett. "If I am going to translate that money into official money, then I want a bookkeeper and an accountant all the time with me. I am a botanist and not a banker." He explained to Fairchild that the official Chinese coin, the tael, existed only on paper, for it simply represented a measure of a lump of silver; the measure varied with purity as well as weight from town to town. Furthermore, people used Mexican, Hong Kong, and Chinese dollars, each with a different value. To convert his accounts to taels seemed impossible.

Despite this problem, he had begun to plan an extended expedition into previously unexplored regions. Since he had come to China especially to find hardy crops for the northern states, he asked the American Legation to try to obtain permission for him to collect in Manchuria. Japan was occupying both southern Manchuria and northern Korea; therefore, the consul general had to cable his request to Tokyo. At the end of January the Japanese government wired the American Legation that they had approved Meyer's application.

On January 27 he received authorization from Beverly T. Galloway, head of the Bureau of Plant Industry, to proceed to Shanghai whenever the weather became too cold to continue to work in northern China. After his first year in the field, Meyer never considered going south or resting during the winter as most explorers did. In 1906, however, as heavy snow fell and icy dust storms gripped Peking, he decided to take the newly completed railroad to Hankow (Hangou), a seven-hundred-mile journey. From Hankow he would travel down the Yangtze to Shanghai. On February first he left Peking on an unheated train without sleeping or dining accommodations. Each passenger carried his own bedding and food, but the bitter cold made sleeping difficult. On the third day of the trip, temperatures became milder and the train (apparently exhausted by its exertions, Meyer said) stopped at 3:00 P.M. at a town that boasted an inn with a "foreign bed." The proprietor proudly showed Meyer a dirty mattress on an iron bedstead; "blankets, sheets, and pillows had gone long since." The next morning the journey continued before sunrise. The temperature rose hourly as the train passed bamboo groves, rice fields, and wheat several inches high. That evening Meyer reached Hankow and saw for the first time "the royal Yangtze River (Chang Jiang), a splendid body of water."

After dinner Meyer explored the native section of town. As he walked, the dark streets became narrower and he realized that "some rowdies" were following him. When he turned back toward his hotel after half an hour, "they jumped me with their fists in the back, a few put their hands in my coat pockets, and they put up a terrible howl." People gathered and merchants came out of their shops, but they "apparently liked this way of doing, for they all joined in the howling and sneering. I knew if I became angry, they would have robbed me of everything and probably beaten me too, if not worse, so I just did as if I took this howling for an ovation, and took my hat off and bowed in all directions and smiled like a president on his inauguration trip. At the same time, though, I took the greatest haste in marching on and didn't stop until I was safely in the foreign quarter."

When he called at the American Consulate the next morning, the consul warned him that foreigners were not safe in the native section of the city at night. Meyer accepted his experience philosophically, remarking that "these little incidents add zest to travel." He visited gardens and nurseries for three days but found nothing of agricultural interest in Hankow; he did collect seeds of *Euonymus japonica*, an attractive semiprostrate shrub with beautiful foliage.

On February 7 he boarded the steamer *Tien-shan* for the three-day trip to Shanghai. In contrast to the train, where he was the only white passenger, the ship's officers were Englishmen, Scots, and Australians, with whom he enjoyed talking. They shared "a good table with wine and beer" and told stories of their adventures. Though the officers had traveled widely, they envied Meyer because he had seen a little of the interior of China. So soon after the Boxer Rebellion, few white men shared that experience. The days on the steamer passed too quickly, and Meyer reluctantly left his new acquaintances when they reached Shanghai.

The formalities observed at the Astor Hotel did not appeal to him. The menu offered twenty-five or thirty choices, but he enjoyed this luxury only a few days; then he longed for "the little pan of food" that he used to take from home to the Amsterdam Botanical Garden. Beyond the foreign quarter, he discovered muddy canals and families living in poverty, some spending their entire lives on crowded houseboats. When he saw people buying sticks of sugar cane from a man who had just washed them in a mud puddle beside the road, he wondered how the Chinese survived such unsanitary practices.

After making the obligatory call on the consul general, he collected cuttings of peaches and scions of persimmons and apricots. He noticed that the Chinese ate lotus rhizomes raw, boiled, pickled, and preserved in sugar; they also enjoyed bamboo and alfalfa shoots and water chestnuts. Hesitat-

ing to send home unfamiliar foods that Americans might consider "rubbish," he sought Fairchild's advice about these vegetables.

Scrupulously honest and exceedingly thrifty, he felt troubled when the
government auditor questioned his expenditures. He had listed a disburse-
ment of $1.40 to boys hired at $0.20 each to gather seeds, for example, but
the auditor disallowed the item because the illiterate boys had not signed
subvouchers. Gradually Meyer became more stoical about audits of his
accounts. "From the financial quarter I expect many a storm yet to come,"
he told Fairchild. "At least, I will get weathered and then they won't disturb
my sleep anymore."

His efforts to arrange a trip 150 miles southwest of Shanghai were
complicated by the usual problem of finding a guide to accompany him.
Rumors of a general massacre of foreigners to take place on February 25
caused consular officials to warn him to stay in Shanghai where foreign
troops were stationed. As soon as February 25 passed uneventfully, he hired
a junk and sailed south. For two days he shared the cabin with seven
Chinese, eating with them although everyone put his chopsticks into his
mouth and then into the common bowl. Heavy rain had left some roads
under two feet of water, and at higher altitudes snow covered the ground.
Nevertheless, with the help of Alexander Kennedy of the Grace Mission at
Tangsi (Dongsi), he found an early-flowering cherry that grew along the
canal between Suchow (Suzhou) and Hangchow (Hangzhou). At the Chico
Garden, this cherry (distributed as *Prunus pseudocerasus*) flowered ten
days before any other and proved to be a different species from any Western
cherry. While working near Hangchow, he stayed at the home of the American consul, F. D. Cloud, who advised strongly against a journey farther into
the interior because the natives in that area resented foreigners. During
Meyer's visit, Cloud received a letter warning that all foreigners in the
region were to be murdered.

Reporting to his family, Meyer minimized the risks of travel and emphasized encouraging news. His friends in America had sent him newspaper
articles mentioning his work, and his employers had decided to publish his
descriptions of Chinese plants. "I will become famous," he promised. "Just
wait a century or two."

Though tension grew in Shanghai, Meyer was more concerned with
shipping his collection to the United States in good condition than with the
possibility of an uprising against foreigners. Dorsett had written that a
package of cuttings had arrived damp and moldy; later another had come
with buds dead, apparently the result of being kept too near the boilers on
the four-week ocean voyage. Meyer experimented with various packing
methods to overcome the wide variations in temperature. He sent some
scions in wet, and others in slightly damp, sphagnum moss and some seeds
in charcoal and others coated with paraffin. He learned that cuttings and

scions traveled best in damp peat moss or damp cypress sawdust, wrapped well in oiled or paraffin paper. Insects presented a problem, for he had no facilities for fumigating the plant material that he was collecting as he moved about. Most of the trees in China were infested by scale insects, and he repeatedly reminded Dorsett and Fairchild that his cuttings and scions must be thoroughly fumigated in case eggs were hidden in crevices in the bark.

Since Fairchild had urged him to find hemp to replant the recently abandoned rice fields in South Carolina, he investigated the matting rushes that grew up the Yangtze near Nanking (Nanjing).[2] Bad food and poor accommodations made this cold and rainy nine-day trip unpleasant, but he returned to Shanghai with the hemp plants and pages of notes on planting, harvesting, and curing the rushes and weaving the mats. Because the weight of the rushes exceeded the postal limit, the consul general arranged to send them by diplomatic pouch, though he feared that the State Department might disapprove. On later expeditions to more remote areas, the Agriculture Department secured permission for Meyer to use this method of sending valuable plant material to Washington.

Meyer rejoiced when he received a telegram from the secretary of agriculture authorizing his trip to Manchuria. "There are big robber bands there," he wrote Fairchild, "and I talked with fellows who showed me scars of wounds they had received in combat with these chaps, so I have some interesting trips ahead of me." He had learned that he must appear before the commander in chief of the Japanese army when he reached Manchuria in order to get the necessary permit to travel there. Since Russia occupied northern Manchuria, he must also secure a Russian permit.

In March Fairchild wrote that he and his wife had bought forty acres in the Maryland countryside near Chevy Chase. Though it was ten miles from the Capitol and accessible only by an unimproved lane, Rock Creek flowed through the property and old trees made a fine setting for their new home which they called "In the Woods." They had ordered from Suzuki's nursery in Yokohama 125 flowering cherry trees.[3] Meyer responded with enthusiasm: "If you plant cherries as a spring delight, do not fail to plant Japanese maples for fall effects. . . . Have you a brook? If so, plant *Iris kaempferi*. There are dreams of beauty among them." Perhaps he sensed that In the Woods would become a beloved retreat for him as well as for the Fairchilds. In any case, he offered advice generously: "Do you love weeping trees? The Weeping Pagoda Tree is delightful. Plant also a few clumps of the Chinese tree peony and have some big Chinese porcelain vessels in which you can plant lotus. Have also a few clumps of magnolias. They are so noble in the early spring. Have some white-barked birches, the most elegant of all northern trees. If you can get a specimen of the *Davidia involucrata* sent to England by Wilson, do try it." For a little while, his thoughts wandered far from troublesome permits, bands of outlaws, and financial accounting.

Meyer and MacGregor, the superintendent of parks in Shanghai, became good friends. MacGregor told Meyer that E. H. Wilson had spent about twenty thousand dollars each year when he was collecting in China for Veitch and Sons. MacGregor also described Wilson's preparation at the Royal Botanic Gardens at Kew, training at the Arnold Arboretum, conferences with Augustine Henry, and opportunity to study at the Hong Kong Botanical Garden. The contrast with his own frugal budget and his few days at the New York Botanical Garden and the Arnold Arboretum became painfully apparent to Meyer. Including his railroad and steamship tickets to Shanghai from Washington, his own expenses would total about $2,500 for the year plus his annual salary of $1,000, leaving the department a balance of $1,500 from his appropriation.

Though eighteen men-of-war, including five American battleships, remained in the harbor, he wrote A. J. Pieters that foreigners in Shanghai were not living in hourly expectation of death, "as some of the correspondents of different papers have tried to make out. We all feel that the Chinese won't try to murder wholesale. They know that the white men are prepared to sell their hides pretty dear. I personally bother myself very little about these matters. I found out that the facing of a danger is most times a perfect solution of it."

Loneliness, not danger, troubled Meyer most. He observed that many white men who had come to the coastal cities of China just to make money "lead fast lives and go to the dogs." He did not care for their company. "Loneliness hangs always around the man who leaves his own race and moves among an alien population," he acknowledged, but he found consolation in Ibsen's statement that the strongest man is he who stands alone. Even more comforting was his firm belief in the importance of his work. Because he felt that he was making a contribution to mankind, he was willing to tolerate loneliness and to decline offers of more remunerative employment as landscape gardener for a Chinese millionaire, superintendent of a European nursery, or horticultural instructor for the Chinese government at a salary of $4,000.

As he prepared to leave Shanghai in April, he was troubled by a new rule requiring that all expenditures be filed within twenty days of the time they were incurred. He argued that it would be impossible to comply in unsettled parts of Manchuria or Siberia and asked, "Have these gentlemen who drew up all these regulations ever been out in a foreign country like China?" Yet he remained enthusiastic about agricultural exploration, admitting to Fairchild, "I love the work so well that I would hate to give it up."

Before going north, he bought a revolver and a hundred cartridges in order to be ready for "the goodly lot of outlaws" in Manchuria. On April 11 he left Shanghai.

After an ocean voyage to Tientsin, he spent six days in Peking securing letters of introduction from W. W. Rockhill, the American minister, and from the Russian minister, in addition to his Japanese permit. Just before his departure he heard the shocking news of the San Francisco earthquake and saw newspaper photographs of the effect of the fire. Appalled by the destruction, he thought first of Dorsett and the USDA testing garden at Chico and then of Luther Burbank and his propagation garden. Seven weeks passed before he learned that both men and their work were safe.

Meyer's former guide refused to leave his family for six or eight months and to face the dangers reported in Manchuria, but in Tientsin he was able to engage another man. On April 23 he wrote Fairchild that, if no one succeeded in frightening his guide that night, he planned to start for Manchuria in the morning. Apparenly no problems developed. Six days later he reached Newchwang (Yingkou), Manchuria, completing the first step in a long journey through regions never before seen by a white man.

CHAPTER 6

Journey to the North

Manchuria and Korea
MAY TO SEPTEMBER, 1906

T H O U G H Meyer wanted to travel across Manchuria, the consul general at Newchwang warned him that the Japanese occupied the south, the Russians controlled the north, and the military administration had closed central Manchuria to travelers. In addition, powerful bands of Chinese outlaws, "who levy blackmail on all who pass," held the western section. Only the officials at Japanese army headquarters at Port Arthur could grant his request to proceed.

While he waited for permission to go to Port Arthur (Lüshun), he journeyed a hundred miles north of Newchwang. In that region farmers had destroyed the original vegetation, leaving only the stumps of large old trees. Missionaries there told him that robbers recently had besieged a whole town. Meyer carried his loaded revolver constantly. He wrote Dorsett that he was about to enter wild country where he might meet robber bands, leopards, tigers, bears, and wolves. He did not fear wild animals or the danger of being murdered, "but the robbing part of it is unpleasant, for without supplies and money one may starve."

At Newchwang he heard from Fairchild that the plant introduction office had not yet received an appropriation to extend his appointment for a second year. He had already submitted his plan to travel overland along the Yalu and Tumen rivers to Vladivostok and then by cart back to Newchwang by way of Harbin and Mukden, a journey of about six months. Since he was eager to remain in the field for the autumn harvest, he answered, "If the government doesn't see fit any more to pay my expenses, couldn't we write to some millionaire or to some wealthy nurseryman to defray the costs until winter? If I am called back, it is not necessary for me to come back, is it — if I settle the financial matters all right?" He concluded with the comforting thought that he would soon be out of touch with post offices.

After three weeks of waiting, he received permission to travel to Port Arthur to secure a pass from the Japanese authorities. Unfortunately, no one told him that he should carry blankets and food on the train. After a cold and uncomfortable trip, he reported to the Japanese commander in chief, Major General Ochiai. General Ochiai refused to allow him to travel in central Manchuria, where bands of robbers roamed. Meyer then asked to cross northern Korea instead. Ochiai agreed to this proposal, provided that he submit his route for approval.

During the two-day wait for his pass, he climbed the famous 203 Meter Hill, recently captured by the Japanese at the cost of ten thousand lives, and found it littered with shells, cartridges, clothing, and bones. "So much innocent blood was spilled. Awful, isn't it?," he wrote David Fairchild. "And yet the skies were blue and hills were purple in the distance and Siberian Edelwies was in snowy garb and here and there a Sempervivum was peeping through pieces of rock." The Japanese had already planted a million pine trees to reforest this barren region, but he noticed that the trees appeared unsuited to such a dry area and many were dying.

At nearby Dalny (Lüda, formerly Dairen), where the Japanese had taken over a Russian experiment garden, paved streets and stone and brick homes with shade trees reminded him of the white men who had lived there. Now he saw at the windows the faces of the Japanese conquerors. Mistaking him for a Russian, they sneered and laughed as he passed to express their contempt for the white man.

Soon after returning to Newchwang, he stored his trunk at the consulate and mailed the USDA a number of varieties of dry-land rice and beans. Two of the latter were soybeans (*Glycine max,* formerly *G. hispida*) that yielded superior oil; the variety called 'Virginia' is now held at the National Seed Storage Laboratory at Fort Collins, Colorado. Late in May he told his parents about the journey he was beginning: "The trip ahead is difficult, but I'm sure I'll make it. In a month I will be in Siberia. It will be fun." Thinking of spring at home, he asked about the begonias and clivias that he had planted in the little garden at Houthaven.

He and his guide arrived in Mukden (Shenyang) in a howling dust storm that lasted three days. Though his eyes ached and his throat felt parched, Meyer called on the local missionaries to learn where he might find useful plants. About ten miles outside of Mukden he visited North Tombs, a park situated in a forested area with trees and shrubs that revealed what a beautiful region this part of Manchuria had been before the Chinese destroyed the vegetation. Not far away an early Manchu Emperor rested at East Tombs among large pines, oaks, and lindens.

After six days near Mukden, Meyer left by cart for Liaoyang. In the mountains he found mistletoe with red berries and an alfalfa that he expected to withstand any drought, for the area had little rainfall. As usual on rural journeys, he was plagued by filthy inns and bitten by "not less than six kinds of vermin"; yet he enjoyed traveling through the Chien Shan or Thousand Peaks, which looked like a gigantic saw from the distance. In this densely wooded countryside, he identified pines, oaks, lindens, walnuts, elms, pears, apricots, honey locusts, catalpas, poplars, and two new willows. Each ravine offered its own characteristic vegetation. In some he found beautiful white tree peonies blooming among scrub growth "as if some artist had painted them there." He believed that this region should be preserved as a national park, for so many other lovely places had already been "exterminated" by the Chinese.

At Liaoyang he ate supper with missionaries and often stayed rather late, but his guide and coolie feared to venture far alone. They told the servant of one of the missionaries that tigers had chased Meyer in the mountains; he insisted that they had heard only the growling of wolves.[1] Stories of five men shot by eleven armed brigands east of Liaoyang and of a Chinese man roasted alive by a robber band alarmed the servants, though Meyer pointed out that Chinese troops had caught and decapitated the outlaws. While he was spending the night with Dr. Westwater, a missionary, his men disappeared "with wages in advance," probably having found a Chinese junk headed for Tientsin.

After returning to Newchwang to find a guide who was not "paralyzed by fear when he thinks of going away from home," Meyer complained that Chinese men would rather remain in their mud shacks than "see something of the world and get new experiences." Eager to continue his journey, he failed to understand that they wanted to avoid experiences like being roasted alive. Finally, on June 22 at 6:00 A.M., he began his challenging trip with two strong carts drawn by five mules, two drivers, an intelligent and honest guide, and a coolie "of doubtful character."

For ten days, as they followed the course of streams over mountains, down steep precipices, and through valleys, Meyer enjoyed the beautiful wild countryside and the brooks lined with willows and alders. Sometimes he and his men waded across the same cold stream ten times in a day. Near the trail he saw lilies, clematis, and roses. He frequently paused to make herbarium specimens of new trees and shrubs as he traveled "amidst the rolling of thunder and flashing of lightning through gorgeous mountain valleys." On several occasions his drivers refused to follow trails because they had heard of robbers there. Meyer usually walked ahead, acting as guard and scout because he was carrying several hundred dollars in silver. When the carts passed through low valleys, he climbed the slopes to scan the horizon and cautiously advanced through narrow mountain passes ahead of his companions.

One day, in the majestic wild mountain range called Fong Whan Shan, a band of outlaws deliberately misdirected his party into a nearly impenetrable region. When night came, the little caravan was hopelessly lost in a pathless wilderness. In the dusk Meyer saw an overhanging rock that would provide some shelter from the falling rain. Knowing that a bear or wolf may have sought the same refuge earlier, he shot his revolver at a point below the rock and heard an animal run away. After spending the night in dripping wet clothes under the sheltering boulder, they found their way back to a trail, avoiding the outlaw band.

Often they did not pass another cart all day, but occasionally they spent the night at a small village where everyone gathered to see the "foreign beast." Arriving wet, tired, and hungry, Meyer did not enjoy washing, eating, undressing, and sleeping before an audience. He asked his guide to announce that he charged ten cents for the privilege of looking at him, but the villagers only laughed and continued to stare. In Manchurian inns everyone slept on one long brick bedstead built along the wall in the same room where food was cooked. Dogs, pigs, and chickens "had free admission" during the day and countless fleas bit the sleepers at night; Meyer said that the natives "seemed very glad that they bite a foreigner so well."

Japanese soldiers occasionally examined Meyer's baggage. Never having seen rubber, they scrutinized his sponge and the bulb of his camera with amazement. At one village the soldiers mistook him for a Russian spy. "One shook me up out of a sleep" while another kicked his guide. One night a knocking on the inn door and shouts outside awakened him. He heard two shots and ran outside looking for the troublemakers. Since all was quiet, he concluded that the innkeeper had fired at the intruders and frightened them away.

In this region he noticed a number of unfamiliar plants. For the first time in Asia, at elevations close to four thousand feet, he saw spruce trees. He also discovered beautiful ferns, a white climbing rose, red bush roses, and orange, pink, and white lilies. Since he had no equipment for pressing plant material, daily rain prevented successful drying of a large number of herbarium specimens he had gathered. At Liaoyang in June and again near Antung in July, he collected seeds of a large-leafed spinach (*Spinacia oleracea*) that grew all winter in sheltered places. When blight and wilt first threatened the spinach industry in America, J. B. Norton of the USDA furnished the Virginia Truck Experiment Station with seeds of Meyer's Manchurian spinach. Plant breeders there used this strain to incorporate disease resistance into the variety called 'Virginia Savoy' that saved the spinach canning industry.[2] The value of that single introduction, according to Fairchild, more than paid all the expenses of Meyer's expedition.

After a strenuous ten-day trip, Meyer found the town of Antung (Dandong) flooded and none of the expected mail waiting for him. As far as he knew, the appropriation for his work might end as he left Manchuria. On July 11 he nevertheless hired a sampan, crossed the Yalu River to the Korean side, and arranged to hire pack animals. Carts would be of no use, for wagon trails did not exist and footpaths were sometimes under two feet of water during the rainy season. Unable to engage a Korean guide who could speak English, he settled for one who spoke Chinese and communicated with him through his Chinese guide. "This coming trip along the Yalu and Tumen rivers and through grand wild mountains will be full of interesting adventures," he wrote Fairchild. Until he reached Vladivostok, he would be traveling through virtually unexplored country. Once in Siberia he hoped to find hardy plants for the northern tier of states. "If you do not hear from me by October 15," he warned Fairchild, "I may have met with an accident."

For almost a month Meyer and his party crossed a mass of mountains intersected by narrow valleys and twisting rivers. Rickety bridges sometimes spanned smaller streams; they waded through wider rivers. One day his small caravan climbed three mountain ranges and crossed a river twenty-five times. Another day the current swept the Korean guide off his feet as they waded across a swift river. Narrow mountain trails, never more than three feet wide, often skirted the edge of a precipice. Near Pyah-tong (Pyoktong) about two hundred feet above the Yalu, one horse slipped his traces and rolled down the mountainside. Though the horse regained his footing near the river bank, a large box of provisions fell into the water. Meyer followed it promptly. He grabbed the box before the strong current caught it and swam with it to the shore. The horse escaped injury, but the other box that he had carried was crushed and the contents were scattered over the mountainside. Since no replacements were available, everyone searched for several hours until they found all the cooking utensils and supplies. Korean horses were small, but they compensated for their size by having vicious tempers and biting fiercely. When a horse bit one driver severely, Meyer dressed the wound and regretted being unable to stitch it properly.

Because the trail was washed out from Pyah-tong to Chosan, Meyer decided to detour by junk. The trip took much longer than he had expected and the unsanitary conditions and nearly inedible food caused him to develop a high fever. "That is the last time they catch me in a junk on the Yalu," he wrote Fairchild indignantly. Near the Yalu he made one of the first collections of zoysia grass (*Zoysia japonica*) to reach the USDA. Because zoysia required little rainfall and infrequent mowing, he knew that it would be valuable for lawns and golf courses. After leaving the river for high mountain valleys, he felt well again and admired the scarlet lilies, bluebells, and huge apricot trees. As they traveled he collected herbarium material, grass seed, and red berries growing on blackberry bushes. William A. Taylor, a USDA specialist in pomology, later expressed great interest in this "red blackberry" (*Rubus* sp.).

At first it did not surprise Meyer that the Japanese had conquered the

Koreans, who appeared weak and stupid. After further observation, however, he decided that the Koreans were "well-behaved and gentle and impotent," possibly because they lacked wholesome food, especially fresh fruit and vegetables. Their diet distressed him, for he noticed that their brass bowls and cups contained little except a poor red rice, crushed beans, cucumber soup, and fresh cucumbers. They grew only tobacco, sorghum, millet, rice, soybeans, buckwheat, and hemp (*Cannabis sativa*), which supplied fibers for weaving all their clothing, even their sandals.

As Meyer and his men continued north from Kang-ko, they passed through primeval forests, sometimes camping at night in hunters' cabins among splendid larches, spruce, pines, lindens, birches, poplars, and gigantic willows. The dense undergrowth, tangled vines, fallen trees, and peat bogs prevented exploring beyond the edge of the trail. In the forest solitude, as they built their campfires, cooked their food, and warmed themselves, he felt as he imagined his primitive forefathers must have felt many thousands of years before. "Vague memories came back of some kind of life long, long ago," he wrote A. J. Pieters. "My men didn't feel so comfortable in these primeval wilds, but to me it was like a delightful dream, lasting too short." He rarely saw animals, birds, or men, and the silence and semidarkness eventually began to be oppressive.

Since they did not carry canned food because it was heavy and occupied too much space, they had little to eat except boiled oats for almost two weeks. Nevertheless, living on the Spartan fare that was available in the countryside, they continued to cover at least twenty miles each day. One day they walked thirty-five miles over mountains. Along the way Meyer collected a pyramidal wild cherry with bright green foliage. The Arnold Arboretum later considered it a desirable ornamental and named it *Prunus meyeri*.[3] As early as August 23 Meyer recorded a killing frost. He could bathe in the frigid mountain streams only a few minutes, "although I am a lover of cold water." The strenuous trip took much longer than he had expected because of the difficult terrain, but he found little comfort when at last they reached a mud-plastered inn at Hoi-ryong (Hoeryong). From a camp bed surrounded by hundreds of flies, he wrote his report while a "multitude" of Japanese and Koreans watched with interest. On September 7, he crossed the Tumen River and reached Pos'yet in Siberia. There he and his men boarded a steamer for the short trip to Vladivostok.

CHAPTER 7

The Journey Continued

Eastern Siberia and Manchuria
SEPTEMBER, 1906, TO JANUARY, 1907

A T Vladivostok a telegram from the secretary of agriculture informed Meyer briefly, "Authorization renewed." This meant that he would not need to pay the considerable expenses of the last two months, a risk he had accepted. But the long and arduous trip had taken a toll that could not be measured in dollars. The strain of the journey had caused his men to feel dull and to lose weight. The Korean guide had smoked opium so habitually that Meyer finally paid him and sent him back to Antung. "I myself became somewhat stupid," he admitted to Dorsett, "and feel like taking a long rest." Adequate food and housing restored his physical strength, but he felt "mentally weary" because he had missed books and congenial companions.

The high cost of lodging, food, and clothing in Vladivostok presented an immediate problem. Meyer had worn out several suits and three pairs of boots in three months. To buy winter outfits and boots in Russia would have been so expensive that he sent his trustworthy Chinese guide to Tientsin by steamer to retrieve some of the clothes he had stored at the consulate and to purchase the new clothing they both needed. Though his tall guide was "a faithful good fellow," he failed to secure all the necessary receipts for his expenditures, causing Meyer to lament that "this money part of exploring work will make me old before age."

While he waited for a pass to enable him to travel farther into Siberia, he learned as much as possible about Vladivostok. The military commander warned him not to go near fortifications because he might be arrested or shot. He saw as many soldiers as civilians. Though he enjoyed dining with some Russian officers, he sympathized with the poorly paid soldiers who could not afford even an occasional glass of beer. Russians comprised a minority of the population; there were many Germans and also Chinese, Japanese, and Koreans. The poor lived in little huts, while the rich resided in palaces, but he observed that both had to stay indoors at night to avoid robbers.

He found the Russians "a little rough and uncouth"; yet, he wrote Dorsett, "one feels intuitively that there is a very great future for this race, and the strange thing is that I like them. To look in the face of an open-hearted, simple-minded Russian farmer makes one feel a better man." Some day "when we Anglo-Saxons begin to decline," he told Pieters, "the Slav race will probably ascend," but first they must have enlightened government.

Many outlaws, both Russian and Chinese, were active in Vladivostok. A party of Caucasians held up a bank in daylight and escaped with thirty-five thousand rubles. Later a group of Chinese boarded a steamer "under the disguise of ordinary passengers" and took seven thousand rubles from other travelers. When Meyer heard an American comment that Vladivostok "is almost like Chicago," he remembered that "at home also everything is not always pie-nice."

Since there was no parcel post agreement between the United States and Russia, he sent twenty-two packages to the American Consulate in Shanghai to be forwarded to America. This shipment, largely from Korea, included 220 kinds of seeds of lawn grasses, leguminous plants, wild peonies, lilies, vegetables, and cuttings of ornamental trees and plants, as well as herbarium material. Sargent had written Fairchild, "I am glad to hear that Meyer is doing so well, but I hope that you will insist on his making herbarium specimens, for without these his work cannot have any solid scientific basis and must prove unsatisfactory." Fairchild commented to Meyer that the Department of Agriculture "did not place that much importance on herbarium specimens"; later Meyer bitterly regretted his failure to collect additional herbarium material of the unknown flora of northern Korea.[1]

After engaging a Russian interpreter with whom he could converse in German, on October 14 he started a three-week journey north to Nikolsk (Ussuriysk, formerly Voroshilov) and Khabarovsk. Though he had been warned that he might meet both Russian and Chinese outlaws, he concentrated on collecting hardy grains, trusting his letters of introduction and his revolver and bowie knife for protection. "I count on my own courage," he told Pieters, "and also on the best wishes of you all, so these things together will assure me a good journey." At Nikolsk the government forester gave him seven packages of seeds in exchange for his promise of seeds of hardy apples from the USDA. From Nikolsk he mailed his accounts for the quarter, despite the lack of an American consul to validate them. In addition to innkeepers unable to sign vouchers, he had to deal with Chinese, Mexican,

Japanese, and Russian currencies, as well as Manchurian and Korean war notes issued by Japan.

Leaving Nikolsk, he continued his trip north by cart and on foot, noticing oats, barley, wheat, and buckwheat under cultivation. Along the way he collected seeds of a bushy maple tree (*Acer ginnala*) bearing an abundance of rosy red fruits. Somewhere between Nikolsk and Iman he had silently celebrated an anniversary long anticipated. "On the twenty-second of October, 1906, it will be five years since I took out that paper, so I will declare myself an American citizen on that date," he wrote Fairchild. "In my heart I am it since long ago." At Iman (Dal'nerechensk) on November 1 he swam in the Amur River. That evening a snowstorm began "nicely and beautifully, so I danced from pure joy in the first snow of the year." By the next day the gentle snow had turned into an icy blizzard. Within twenty-four hours the Siberian winter had begun. He left Iman by train because travel by boat was impossible with the Amur full of ice.

He had heard that scores of people had been murdered that year between Vladivostok and Khabarovsk and that tigers, panthers, and wild boars roamed that area; however, he had no misadventures. The cold journey produced little that was new, though he collected nuts, pears, plums, wheat, and barley, as well as the beautiful Amur lilac. He also found grasses for C. V. Piper, head of Forage Crop Investigation, to test for pasture or hay. He liked the Russian peasants he met. "Such children they are," he told David Fairchild. "A firearm or compass is regarded with awe and big rough soldiers beg me a page out of an American magazine as a souvenir from a country where they intend to go as soon as they see the chance. My heart leaped up to them from sympathy."

Fifteen letters from the staff of the plant introduction office reached him at Khabarovsk. Though he felt gratified because the USDA had sent many of his introductions to experiment gardens and to nurserymen, he replied that the plant explorer's contribution formed only a small part of the total picture. "My work is only preliminary. The establishing is the thing." Nevertheless, he was glad to learn that horticulturists expected to breed hardier apples and pears as a result of his efforts. A letter from A. J. Pieters told of his resignation from the department. Meyer regretted his departure because Pieters had first suggested employing him as a plant hunter and had continued to feel "sort of personally responsible" for his performance.

As his thirty-first birthday approached, Meyer considered his present life and future plans. After a hard journey, he admitted to Fairchild that he would say to himself, "It is enough now." But, as soon as he had rested a few weeks and enjoyed some good food, "I cannot be held down any more. When happily married, I suppose even the strongest wanderer must feel tied to his home with such pleasant ties. Between you and me though, let me roam around as yet; the whole world is mine. I am too young to settle. First

I will skim the earth in search of things good for man. Asia is so big that one can explore for a whole lifetime and not visit it all."

Despite dangers and hardships he remained healthy and content, though he felt lonely at times. He wrote the Janssens that he longed to see his parents again and to tell them about his experiences. "But, if they ask, 'Young one, did you find what you were looking for?' I would have to say, 'No, I am as far as when I started'; therefore, when you ask how it is on the inside, I can tell you only that room is closed and I have thrown away the key."

At Khabarovsk the head forester of the Imperial Russian Domains gave him seeds of twenty-two varieties of trees and shrubs, and the Russian government agronomist added fifteen kinds of seeds of economic plants. In return Meyer promised nuts, apples, and pears, as well as vegetable and flower seeds that would germinate in North Dakota. Despite bitterly cold temperatures that sometimes reached $-40°F$, he liked to go at dusk to the town park by the river, where "it is a joy to see the sun set across the ice fields of the Amur and the beautiful silhouettes of the white birches against the dying purple of the West."

One evening, as he was returning to his inn after dinner, Meyer noticed that he was being followed along a quiet street by three men. Suddenly "a piece of cloth was drawn around my throat and they got me down on the ground." While the third man kept watch for anyone approaching, the first two struck his head several heavy blows. As he returned their assault, he drew the bowie knife he was wearing and plunged it into the stomach of the leader. When they realized that they were meeting armed resistance, all three men ran away with Meyer in pursuit until he remembered that he was helpless without his revolver. The next morning the police found the frozen body of a well-dressed man, possibly a victim of the same gang, near the place where the three men had attacked Meyer. Only a few days earlier, policemen told him, they had come upon the bodies of four murder victims under a bridge.[2]

This experience did not deter Meyer from collecting useful plants, packing them carefully, and then spending half a day at the post office getting them off to America. Three large packages of cereals and grains for cold climates included a promising strain of black oats. Four others held apples and wild grape scions, conifer seeds, Manchurian walnuts, hazelnuts, a hardy rush, and a pamphlet from the agricultural station for Mark Carleton, who could read Russian.

Writing from Khabarovsk to de Vries, Meyer acknowledged receiving a copy of his speech on experimental evolution and described finding pines, ginkgo, mistletoe, and other plants in a state of mutation. He enclosed varied clover leaves that he had gathered in an old cemetery in Newchwang. "You are right," he wrote. "My life is strange. It seems predestined that way.

You remember how I always wanted to travel and how long I suppressed that desire because I always liked to work with you. . . . It is strange for a man born in a low flat country like Holland to like mountains more and more. To climb mountains becomes more pleasant every day."

After visiting outlying regions in Siberia at a season when other plant hunters sought comfortable winter quarters, Meyer at last headed south by train, leaving Khabarovsk on November 26 and arriving two days later at Hailin, Manchuria. There he hired carts and proceeded to Ninguta in search of fine white pears; however, the pears proved to be only a rumor. At this point he faced the no man's land between the Russian- and the Japanese-occupied sections of Manchuria. He had planned to return to Harbin by sledge along the Sungari River (Songhua Jiang), a branch of the Amur, but civil and military authorities at Ninguta argued that such a trip would be foolhardy. The police warned that "it was pretty certain that I would never return anymore because of robber bands who plunder travelers." He decided to take heed, "for it doesn't pay to be murdered." On December 1 he returned to Hailin by cart and boarded a train for Harbin, even agreeing to have a convoy of four soldiers escort him to the station because a merchant had been attacked by outlaws on the same road the evening before. Military posts at each station and soldiers on board the train to guard the passengers convinced him of the danger to travelers.

After working and traveling in snowstorms with the temperature at zero, Meyer had a severe cold at Harbin and took an enforced rest for ten days. During this time he noticed that streets were in disrepair, even though Harbin had been the Russian headquarters during the recent Russo-Japanese War. Frequent robberies on the unlighted streets forced people to stay in their homes at night. As he considered the results of his trip north, he felt satisfied because he believed that his collection would eventually extend the growing area of grains and fruit trees in America several hundred miles northward. This work can scarcely be compared with empire building, he told Fairchild, and yet it is "a kind of empire building too."

A few days before Christmas he left Harbin by rail, going south to Kwan Tsientse (Changchun) where he spent the holiday at the home of Dr. F. J. Gordon of the Irish Presbyterian Mission. The homes of the missionaries seemed "like little oases." Though appreciative of their hospitality, he noted that "they leave the religious side out; otherwise there would be a coolness." Dr. Gordon promised to collect rice and crab apple seeds for the department in return for vegetable and flower seeds. Gradually Meyer established a large network of exchanges with missionaries in many parts of Asia. David Fairchild cooperated by putting a high priority on filling Meyer's requests promptly, because he recognized the value of missionary-collectors in remote areas.

From Kwan Tientse Meyer continued his journey southward by cart.

He celebrated the coming of 1907 in Kirin (Jilin) at the home of a medical missionary whose guests included Russian officers and other Westerners. Though the group spoke several different languages, Meyer enjoyed being able to talk to Europeans again. At Kirin Chinese officials demanded his passport eleven times in several days, but he kept on the trail of a rumored peach tree that had survived in that cold climate. After an exhausting search, he found the tree in the garden of a Buddhist temple and paid the priest who nurtured it two dollars for cuttings. He hoped that this peach would help in developing frost-resistant varieties for cold parts of the United States.

Though the weather moderated as he continued south, he experienced bitter cold as he rode in a springless cart between 4:00 and 8:00 A.M., when the temperature read $-25°F$. He wrote his sister that it was hard to laugh while the cold wind pierced his clothes. Even when he wore two pairs of pants, an undercoat and a sheepskin-lined coat, sheepskin stockings, a bearskin hat, a scarf, earmuffs, and a piece of sheepskin over his nose, he almost froze if he sat still as long as half an hour. As he set out each day just before dawn, he felt compensated for the bitter cold by the wonderful scenery. In the hours before daybreak, stars shone in the sky and the moon hung low on the horizon; then a pink glow slowly suffused the sky and a strange light spread over the landscape; finally the rising sun colored the mountaintops rosy red. The cold air often froze his beard and mustache to his scarf and he had to thaw them over a fire. Nevertheless, he was content because he had found new millets, beans, wheat, and dry-land rice growing at the forty-fourth parallel of latitude, giving hope of success with these crops as far north as Dakota.

Closer to Mukden he passed hundreds of carts loaded with grain, pork, venison, wild boar, and fish. Near the war zone he noticed again that the inhabitants sneered and laughed at him because the white race had lost the war. While he was looking for an inn, thirty or forty villagers crowded about him closely and some "used nasty words. I got angry and took hold of a ten-foot pole standing close at hand and went at them." This behavior proved effective, for the group of men scattered in all directions.

Meyer reached Mukden on January 21, prepared to finish collecting in Manchuria before going to the rich Shantung Province of China. He had to change his plans, however, when he found a telegram from the secretary of agriculture awaiting him: "Wilson leaves San Francisco January 3 for Upper Yangtze bringing you instructions. Meet him in Shanghai before February 10. Telegraph him in care of Hong Kong–Shanghai Bank." Regardless of his personal feelings, Meyer immediately wired E. H. Wilson, who was collecting for the Arnold Arboretum, "Will meet you in Shanghai. Wait for me." Before going to Tientsin in order to allow his guide to have a promised visit with his relatives, he shipped twenty large sacks of cereals and beans from Mukden to the United States. A week later a hurried trip took him through Liaoyang to Newchwang. There he wrote Fairchild that he was shipping "quite a few nice things," including five kinds of pears and alfalfa seeds. He felt frustrated because he was forced to rush across a region where he had spotted plants that he wanted to collect, but he withheld comment until he could learn the purpose of his unexpected journey to Shanghai.

Assignment to the Wu Tai Shan

Shanghai, Shansi, and Peking
FEBRUARY TO JUNE, 1907

A F T E R stopping briefly in Peking, Meyer arrived in Shanghai two days before the deadline specified in the telegram that had changed his plans. Fairchild had sent him nine issues of the *Gardeners' Chronicle* containing articles about E. H. Wilson's considerable success as a plant hunter in China. Meyer read all of them before meeting Wilson on February 8 for the first of a series of conferences. He soon learned that Fairchild had agreed to a trade with the Arnold Arboretum. In return for Wilson's promise to send the USDA economically useful plants from the upper Yangtze, Meyer was to collect botanical specimens for the arboretum in the Wu Tai Shan (Wu Tai Mountains) in Shansi Province.

Believing that the department undervalued the work he had planned to accomplish in Manchuria and that the trip to the Wu Tai Shan would be unproductive, he made no effort to appear content with Fairchild's bargain. Letters from both Meyer and Wilson reflect their failure to achieve rapport. Meyer told Fairchild that Wilson "likes to pay his respect to the Hundred and One officials. I, on the other hand, come as little as possible in contact with the officials. Most of them are frightfully ignorant of the products of the country." Wilson wrote Sargent that Meyer lacked a sense of humor and had very little understanding of Chinese manners and customs.[1] In an effort to overcome Meyer's misgivings, Wilson rashly said that he would be as willing to go to the Wu Tai Shan as to the upper Yangtze. Meyer promptly suggested trading assignments, but Wilson "had no ears for that." He specified that Meyer must prepare herbarium specimens, keep field notes, and take photographs at the Wu Tai Shan. Meyer agreed, but he made it clear that thereafter "they have no claim any more upon me and I will be free again to collect plants of greater economic importance."

As soon as Wilson left Shanghai, Meyer expressed his indignation to Fairchild, maintaining that the arrangements with Wilson could have been made by letter without interrupting his expedition. Frustrated because he must do "this rather empty botanical work," he added, "I hope the department receives its money's worth from the trade you made. Mr. Wilson is very hopeful about the prospects of the Wu Tai Shan, but he never was in North China. My hopes are not as great, but let us see."

Neither the interruption of his plans to work in Manchuria nor the assignment to the Wu Tai Shan was the primary cause of Meyer's discontent; he felt deeply hurt because Fairchild appeared willing to disrupt the work of his own untested collector when he had an opportunity to engage the services of a plant explorer of established reputation. Meyer pointed out that Wilson had enjoyed "special costly training" and had worked in an area known to be rich in new plants; for three years he had stayed in one region where he could train men to collect, pack, and ship; furthermore, his botanical work was easier than finding plants of economic value. "Wilson doesn't have to look into crevices to find a green shrub," he wrote. "Of course my work will not be appreciated until many years after."

The arrangement with Sargent included Meyer's return to the Wu Tai Shan to collect seeds in the winter, forcing the department to make a hasty decision to keep him in China a third year. He accepted this extension without complaining, but he did suggest that the department consider increasing his salary. Many more remunerative positions had been offered to him. At Mukden the governor general had offered him more than five times his current earnings if he would serve as agricultural advisor in Manchuria. Fairchild did recommend his promotion thereafter, noting that Meyer was "too valuable a man to go over to the Chinese service."

Because he had not been consulted about changes affecting his immediate future, Meyer protected his long-range plans by listing his goals. He wanted to visit experiment stations in various regions of the United States in order to learn their needs; to go to Holland in the fall of 1909 to see his elderly parents; to study collections of Asian material in European botanical gardens; to work at the Saint Petersburg Botanical Garden long enough to learn to speak Russian; and to collect in Central Asia—the Caucasus, Turkestan, and Mongolia. For more than five years he had been far away from his parents who were in their seventies and eager to see him. "I myself am longing to see them again," he wrote Fairchild. Accounts of excellent grapes, apricots, melons, and other products of Central Asia had convinced him that he must visit that region next. After he had explored there, he would return to China because he had "only skimmed a little edge of this part of the world."

While Meyer was still unhappy about abandoning his own work in order to cooperate with the Arnold Arboretum, Fairchild wrote that

Sargent felt "keenly disappointed that we have not encouraged your collecting more botanical specimens of the species of which you have sent us seeds." Meyer answered that "this criticism is really somewhat comical. It would be just as if the department people were disappointed when Professor Sargent didn't collect plants of economic interest on his journeys." From Vladivostok he had shipped two boxes of herbarium material collected on his trip north, but the ship carrying the boxes had been caught in a typhoon and the cargo badly damaged. Since he felt this loss keenly, criticism only compounded his disappointment.

Unaware that Meyer would see the trade with the Arnold Arboretum as expressing lack of confidence in him, Fairchild chose this time to convey Swingle's recommendation that Meyer have an interpreter write in Chinese characters the names of all the plants that he was sending to the USDA. Often Swingle had difficulty in recognizing the particular variety of fruit, grain, or vegetable that Meyer had sent. The department needed to identify the products of Chinese agriculture that they were introducing, as well as those still uncollected. Though Meyer understood the reason for Swingle's request, he also realized that persuading a well-educated Chinese interpreter to travel to isolated regions would be difficult, if not impossible.

Despite his reaction to his new assignment, Meyer remained enthusiastic about his current work and his future plans. He had sent Dorsett fourteen parcels containing scions, cuttings, and plants for the Chico Garden and mailed to Washington seeds of dwarf cherries, a valuable alfalfa, black barley, and six bags of beans. Upon completion of his expedition to the Wu Tai Shan, he hoped to go to Shantung Province to collect new fruits and vegetables. "There goes nothing above fresh air, a blue sky above one's head, and if some mountains or lakes can be added, then life is worth living," he told Fairchild. "I love exploring better than anything else."

His letters to Holland did not mention his problems. Instead he described the Chinese New Year festivities—the altars with candles, the delicacies, and the colorfully dressed children. Because of the celebration, he had been unable to hire anyone to help him pack his collection; as a result, he had sprained his wrist handling heavy bundles alone. A few of the wealthy Chinese owned automobiles, he told his parents. The Chinese "will live like the white race some day," he predicted, "and then maybe they will chase white people out of the country."[2]

Instead of nearing the end of a two-year tour of duty, he realized that he had completed only about half of a three-year assignment. "I feel like a much older man as when I left," he told Dorsett. "I don't mean physically. I mean mentally. I have increased my wisdom and widened my views. But I long to be back among you folks." He revealed his longing in his plans to go to Chico to see his plant introductions, to visit friends in Los Angeles and Saint Louis, and to return to Washington. When he learned that Dorsett would no longer be at the Chico Plant Introduction Garden to care for his shipments, he was troubled; however, he could only hope that the new superintendent would nurture his plants faithfully. In the meantime, he spent a few weeks collecting near Shanghai, while his friend Dr. S. P. Barchet of the American Embassy provided the Chinese names for the fruit trees he had found in Manchuria.

Early in April he returned to Peking to prepare for his journey to the Wu Tai Shan. William Woodville Rockhill, the American minister at Peking, told him that he would find those mountains barren. He nevertheless secured the necessary Chinese permit, completed his quarterly accounts in seven currencies, and engaged an intelligent interpreter who knew the Chinese names for plants. New voucher forms that the auditor had sent were too large to fit his pocket and so imposing that rural Chinese refused to sign them. Though they might be "beautiful to use in an experiment station," he told Fairchild, "for a traveler they are not fit."

On April 11 Meyer, his guide, and his interpreter went by train to the countryside and then continued their journey by cart in heavy rain. As they traveled into the interior, trails became so rough that they had to use mules instead of carts. Far from coastal cities, silver valued by weight replaced the familiar Mexican and Hong Kong dollars as the medium of exchange. In fact, Meyer found that banks charged a premium of 30 percent for silver coins but gave him lumps of silver at par. When he converted some of his silver to copper cash, he had to hire another mule to carry the heavy coins.

On April 20 he arrived at the Wu Tai Shan in a snowstorm that lasted three days and made him grateful for his fur clothes and the brisk fire under his brick bed. He found the vegetation sparse where splendid forests had once grown. Only the Buddhist and Taoist priests at monasteries and temples had preserved some trees and shrubs. Meyer took photographs of the almost completely barren landscape, mailing the pictures to Fairchild with the hope that he would send them to Sargent. Instead of waiting until mid-June as E. H. Wilson had suggested, early in May he left the Wu Tai Shan. "Caesar of old went to the Senate and said, 'Veni, Vidi, Vici,' " he wrote Fairchild, "and I went to the Wu Tai Shan and saw and went away, for it is as barren as the plains of Nebraska." When Sargent complained that he should have waited there until more vegetation appeared, Meyer answered that he could not have done so "unless I was of a barnacle nature, which God help me I never hope to become."

Sargent later insisted that Meyer had failed to appreciate the rarity of the material that he collected that spring and the following February. "To show you how badly he grasped the situation," Sargent wrote, "I will tell you that among the conifers from Wu t'ai of which he sent herbarium specimens . . . were certainly three new species of *Picea*, perhaps four, a new *Larix*, and a very remarkable pine. . . . The field, you see, was a very rich one, although he thought it not worth his attention."[3] Two years later William Purdom searched the Wu Tai Shan for Sargent. Purdom reported that there was scarcely a blade of grass on the mountains and nothing further to collect. From the viewpoint of a dendrologist who wanted to record new species, it could be called a rich field, but to an agricultural explorer, it represented only a pitiful example of the terrible results of deforestation. Perhaps Meyer was correct in guessing that the department would not benefit from the trade with Sargent, for E. H. Wilson took no interest in economic species and committed the nearly unpardonable crime of sending the USDA some naked barley marked *wheat*.[4]

As Meyer searched for new plants south of the Wu Tai Shan, he encountered curious natives and cheerless inns. When he entered a village after having walked twenty-five or thirty miles, children cried and dogs barked. Nevertheless, the villagers generally decided that he was not dangerous and crowded around to question his guide. If there was no fire burning at the inn, he wore two coats while he ate a cold supper. At such times he occasionally wondered whether his life was worthwhile; however, he usually felt content despite hardships because he was finding "good things" to send to America. Among them were a fine rice that flourished at three thousand feet and thousands of yellow roses previously known to botanists only through Chinese drawings. This semidouble rose, which he had collected in small quantities north of Peking, became extremely important in propagation because it bloomed early and freely and withstood long periods of drought. *Rosa xanthina* eventually helped to produce hardy yellow roses for New England and the northern prairies.[5]

At Taiyuan, the capital of Shansi Province, crowds of hundreds of noisy villagers tore the paper windows off his room to get a better view of the "foreign animal." He found tossing buckets of water at them "the most satisfactory remedy." In contrast, English missionaries, an American businessman, and four English-speaking professors on the faculty of Shansi University invited him to lunch and dinner. He appreciated the company of other Caucasians more than ever because he missed stimulating conversation; libraries, and botanical gardens. At Taiyuan he mourned for the rare plants that the Chinese had destroyed and observed the heartbreaking results of deforestation — floods in the rainy season and dry river beds where big ships had once navigated.

Since he planned to travel across Honan to Shantung Province, on May 11 he sent four bundles to the Chico garden. After hiring carts for the trip, his preparations ended in frustration when his employees refused to accompany him. While he had explored, his educated interpreter had stayed indoors because he feared the wolves. Even the guide had seen too much of the interior. Both men were unwilling to contend with poor food, hard journeys, tigers and wolves, country dialects, and natives who deliberately misdirected them, misnamed plants, and tried to cheat them. Meyer could not find suitable assistants in Shansi. He therefore returned to Peking, doubtful of the future of China as a great power because Chinese men hesitated to face new adventures.

At Peking he found Fairchild's tactful reply to his indignant reaction to the trade with Sargent. Now aware that Meyer thought that his own work had been slighted, Fairchild tried to reassure him: "You have the ideal spirit of an explorer. You have your heart set on the main issues and are willing to forgive us if we are in error at times in our directions to you. . . . I do not believe that any explorer has ever been as successful as you have been in landing in living condition in this country such a large number of introductions and valuable scions and plants."

Despite the disappointing journey that he had recently completed, Meyer responded with enthusiasm: "Our short life will never be long enough to find out all about this mighty land. When I think about all these unexplored areas, I get fairly dazzled; one will never be able to cover them all. I will have to roam around in my next life." His recipe for happiness still included "blue sky, some mountains in the distance, and a rippling brook or foaming sea close by."

Fairchild suggested that he study Chinese instead of Russian, but Meyer explained that learning to read and speak Mandarin, as well as a score of local dialects, was an almost impossible task. Though he could communicate in Chinese words and phrases, it was not possible to learn to speak Mandarin from books; acquiring just a basic vocabulary required two years of conscientious study. He wished that he could speak Mandarin so that he could talk to educated people who might offer him not only information but companionship as well. Natives spoke scores of different dialects in various parts of China. Missionaries who had lived there for thirty years often could not understand the dialect used twenty miles away from their homes. These discouraging facts had ended his original hope of becoming fluent in the Chinese language.

During the spring of 1907 Fairchild assigned Meyer a new task—to identify the insect pests that he was finding, as well as their natural enemies. Meyer had often warned Fairchild and Dorsett that many of the fruit trees that he collected were infested with scale insects; in Manchuria he had found so many beetles and caterpillars that he had repeatedly reminded the department that all shipments must be fumigated to prevent accidental introduction of destructive pests. "There always lurks that great danger of introducing insects and diseases," he admitted. Though he promised to send samples of insects and to make notes of their natural enemies, he reminded Fairchild that he had much to learn about entomology. "If I had had the luck of being born in the United States, I would have studied more thoroughly and might even be a M.S. by now, but in Holland higher education is only for the privileged ones, and so I became a specialist in the plant line only. Will I ever have time to qualify myself in other lines relating to this work? I hope so." Regardless of inadequate academic qualifications, thereafter he regularly sent entomological specimens to the USDA.

Because the department had been urging him to collect bamboo, especially the large timber-producing varieties, Meyer decided to go south in the summer of 1907. Before he left Peking, he bought three hundred bamboo plants native to northern China and ten rare blue spruce to take to America the following spring. He wanted to buy white-barked pines in Peking as well, but small trees were "scandalously dear" at sixteen Mexican dollars. In late June he boarded a steamer for Shanghai, taking with him the three hundred bamboo plants and ten blue spruce.

The Riches of Shantung (Shandong)

JUNE TO NOVEMBER, 1907

MEYER had several problems to solve before he could leave Shanghai. First of all, he needed to find a place to store the three hundred northern bamboo, where they could adapt to a warmer climate before traveling to America. He also had to arrange to establish in a cooler area the bamboo varieties that he planned to collect in hot and humid Chekiang (Zhejiang) Province. Fortunately MacGregor, superintendent of parks in Shanghai, agreed to care for both the northern and southern bamboo for almost a year. Meyer then sought a way to avoid transplanting the whole collection the following spring, risking damage to the root systems just before a long sea voyage. Despite the inconvenience and expense of moving many heavy cases, planting hundreds of bamboo in large boxes of soil seemed to be the only solution.

These matters settled, on June 20 he left Shanghai by launch. At Tangsi (Dongsi) he contracted for sixty boxes of bamboo, ten boxes of each of the three main timber varieties (*Phyllostachys pubescens*, largest and most common), and thirty boxes containing the ornamental and edible types. Arranging the contracts became complex because the natives of Chekiang Province spoke six different dialects and his guide knew only northern Chinese. Meyer later also purchased ten boxes of each of the most promising varieties of bamboo in the province. This time he had to supervise the transplanting personally, a trying task in the hot and sultry valleys. Today one bamboo from this collection is known as *Phyllostachys meyeri*.

Near the quiet old city of Ningpo (Ningbo), the ruined towns and fields full of weeds testified mutely to the destruction caused by the Taiping Rebellion. He could not dry the herbarium specimens that he collected there; in fact, the high humidity made his shoes turn green with mold overnight. Though he felt miserable in the "fierce moist heat" and battled hordes of

67

mosquitoes, he clung to the hope that the bamboo he was collecting would prove useful in the United States. Observing the red clay hillsides of Chekiang Province, he thought that bamboo might thrive in Georgia, especially if it could first be conditioned in a warmer location such as Puerto Rico.

The combination of heat, humidity, insects, and "some harmful bacteria" made him ill before he returned to Shanghai in mid-July. He nevertheless was able to pack and mail to the USDA three parcels including entomological specimens and thirty-two pounds of stones of the wild peach (*Prunus davidiana*) that Chinese farmers used as a stock for all stone fruits. Because it was remarkably drought-resistant, he believed that settlers in the arid Southwest would be able to graft fruit trees to this rootstock.

His continuing illness, which was similar to cholera, did not temper his indignant protest when he received a letter informing him that his charges for baggage in excess of the fifty-cent allowance had been disallowed. He explained that he had to carry provisions, bedding, a stove, packing materials, seeds, plants, and a hundred pounds of silver and copper; for all this, fifty cents per transfer seemed grossly inadequate. His protests evidently failed to convince the auditor, for Fairchild advanced $14.99 on Meyer's behalf to cover the charges for excess baggage. Meyer also objected to the new voucher form which required him to swear that his expenses were incurred "under urgent and unforeseen public necessity." He stated firmly, "My work is absolutely not unforeseen."

Before returning to Peking he intended to collect the honey jujubes, fine peaches, rare pears, and other products of the rich province of Shantung (Shandong). At the end of July he traveled by steamer from Shanghai to Tsingtao (Qingdao). In the cooler climate of Shantung he completely recovered from his illness and, early in August, began his journey through the mountains called the Lau Shan. While he was staying for six nights in an old temple, he discovered to his surprise that German interests were operating extensive nurseries and reforesting the Lau Shan at the expense of German taxpayers. As he journeyed across rocky mountains and valleys, the sea appeared "either in the distance like a mirror" or close below the steep overhanging cliffs. Along the way he collected a rare dwarf sorghum (*Sorghum bicolor*, formerly *S. vulgare*) and noticed not only the white-flowered *Catalpa bungei* but also a yellow-flowered catalpa that seemed to be a new discovery. He observed that the natives roasted the cocoon of a caterpillar that attacked pine trees and ate the chrysalis. Since he always sampled new foods in his travels, he tried this unusual item and found it similar in flavor to shrimp.

He paused on his journey near the seashore at a temple surrounded by a wealth of shrubs and trees. Making his headquarters there for five days, he collected many ornamentals and enjoyed seeing one-hundred-year-old crepe myrtle, boxwood, camellias, and a gigantic spreading ginkgo with a trunk sixteen feet in circumference. At Chingchou (Yidu) he found the flat sweet jujube, a great rarity like the Chinese saucer peach, and the Shantung plum-cot, a cross between a plum and an apricot. By the time that he reached Tsinan (Jinan) on August 25, Shantung had proved as rich in fruits as he had hoped. Watermelon varieties included melons with white, yellow, pink, and red meat, the yellow being especially sweet, though the color was not appealing. He collected not only the double yellow rose but also a single yellow (*Rosa xanthina* f. *spontanea*) that bloomed profusely, even in dry, rocky soil. From Tsinan he mailed Fairchild a box of live epiphytic orchids with small greenish-red flowers, suggesting that they might interest botanists at the Royal Botanic Gardens at Kew. Fairchild considered these orchids of great interest and did forward them to England.

Despite his love for his work, Meyer's third year in China was beginning to exact a toll. "Too long in China kills one's brain," he wrote Fairchild, citing as examples missionaries who had lost interest in events in the outside world. Since his interpreter and guide were not "of the brightest," he felt lonesome. He also had trouble sleeping at inns infested with vermin, flies, and mosquitoes. No mail had reached him for three months, making him feel doubly isolated. He nevertheless enthusiastically planned the next phase of his expedition.

With his guide and interpreter, he traveled southwest through a hilly region in search of the finest peaches in China. As he stood guard while his companions slept, three armed soldiers rode quickly toward his little caravan to warn him that many bands of robbers were active in that area. Later, while he was having lunch at a rural inn, a soldier brought in the body of a well-dressed Chinese gentleman with "fearful gashes" on his head. Suddenly Meyer lost his appetite. Chinese soldiers offered to escort his party but, having heard of their arrogance, he preferred to arm his men with large knives and to rely on his ten-shot automatic pistol.[1] The following day they met a group of "apparent outlaws." Meyer held his pistol "glistening in their eyes" and saw the leader signal his men not to attack. To his surprise he felt almost disappointed, for "the Samurai or Bushido spirit takes hold of one, and one actually wishes for a while that something might happen."

The famous pound peach (*Prunus persica*) that grew near the town of Feicheng made the risks of the journey worthwhile. Meyer wrote that these peaches were marvels — sweet, juicy, an excellent shipper, and quite large, some weighing over a pound. For generations farmers in the region had grown this clingstone with white flesh and downy light yellow skin with "a wee bit of blush," though it did not exist anywhere else in China. In 1907 the orchards could supply only one-fifth of an imperial order for 800,000 of the finest of these peaches. Hoping that the Fei peach would become popular in America, Meyer arranged to ship a large number of scions to the United States during the winter.

Traveling southward for two days, he visited hospitable German Catholic missionaries near Chiningchow (Jiningzhou). They offered him beer and cognac, rare treats in the interior, and warned him against traveling to Chontcho before the sorghum was cut. In this area where the Boxers had been especially active, brigands concealed themselves in the tall sorghum. Meyer therefore decided to go directly to Chufu to see the ancient trees around the tomb of Confucius.

At Chufu he found the streets a series of mudholes and the inns so infested with vermin that he slept in his clothes and boots for protection from scorpions. Despite these wretched conditions, he marveled at "trees that count their age by centuries." He admired a two- or three-hundred-year-old male *Pistacia chinensis, Juniperus chinensis* that could be a thousand years old, and a *Pinus bungeana* sixteen feet in circumference and at least fifteen hundred years old. *Thuja orientalis* (now called *Platycladus orientalis*), "a wonderful branch variation of the ordinary arborvitae which the Chinese call the rising phoenix tree," also made his trip memorable.

Proceeding toward Taian, he noticed cabbages (*Brassica pekinensis*) weighing up to forty pounds growing in heavily manured and irrigated fields. He was surprised to see that farmers had stored corn on rooftops and in trees for protection from rats and thieves. After he reached the interesting old city of Taian, the Reverend A. G. Moule of the Church of England Mission showed him fine gardens. Then they climbed the steep Tai Shan or Sacred Mountain. All the original vegetation had disappeared from the top of the mountain, leaving it bare except for ancient monuments and inscriptions. When the climbers became lost in a maze of small ravines, Mrs. Moule sent other missionaries to find them. At lower altitudes Meyer felt awed by venerable arborvitae, wisteria that appeared to be several centuries old, and fifteen-hundred- to two-thousand-year-old junipers. He looked at them with reverence because they may have existed before Christ was born. "Our California trees beat all these," he told Fairchild, "but these trees here have a different charm. Ours are wild; these are all reared under human supervision."

On September 14 he left Taian for Poshan (Boshan) in search of a promising grape. Along the way he passed orchards of hawthorns (*Crataegus pinnatifida*) bred to produce fruit which made delicious jelly and preserves. The orchards were a product of the patience of Chinese farmers, who had propagated these unpromising trees for generations. Meyer could not use carts to cross the trackless mountains; therefore, though he disliked "using fellow-men as draft animals," he was forced to resort to wheelbarrows pushed by coolies. Working far ahead of his men, he reached an empty watchhouse at sunset and went to sleep there. After an hour he was awakened by two men armed with a drawn sword and a club. Thinking that they were robbers, Meyer drew his revolver and they fled. Soon a large group of villagers armed with various tools and implements aroused him. Assured by Meyer of his good intentions, one of the men offered his pipe as a peaceful gesture and Meyer smoked a few puffs. Groups of villagers returned again and again to see the foreigner. When his interpreter and guide arrived at 10:00 P.M., Meyer and his party went to the village inn for food and rest on a brick bedstead. During the next two days a cold rainstorm flooded the trails and soaked the men's clothing. Meyer felt guilty when the coolies had to push and pull wheelbarrows through the mud. At the end of each day, hot tea and stewed beef "tasted like a banquet." After supper they slept on beds made of dried mud, which stuck to their wet clothes.

Plant material at Poshan justified all the discomfort, for Meyer discovered not only the sweet opalescent grapes, one bunch weighing five pounds, but he also collected seeds of the silk tree, a rare yellow-fruited hawthorn, and a dogwood loaded with dark green berries used as a source of oil for lamps. The next day he returned to Tsinan on a freight train that traveled on a spur to a coal mine near Poshan.

After five days spent near Tsinan collecting large pears, the flat jujube, and fine peaches, he and his men turned north. On September 27 they crossed the Yellow River (Huang He) on a barge, despite the torrent of water that formed a strong current. Three days of traveling through monotonous level country brought them to the village of Laoling. There Meyer found the famous seedless jujube without a stone or a pit. Because of its rarity, the court at Peking bought the entire harvest. In response to Fairchild's request, Meyer made extensive notes on jujube culture. He learned that the trees would thrive where little else would grow, continuing to bear for fifty years. The choice honey jujubes were first dried in the sun and boiled; then dried, split, boiled, and dried again; and finally boiled with sugar and dried. Though the Chinese considered them a great delicacy, Meyer admitted that they were not as good as Persian dates and "will not be luxuries with us." Fairchild, who needed crops for barren areas, believed that the adaptable jujube would surely become an important crop in the Southwest because it fruited abundantly, even in the Imperial Valley in California where temperatures reached 120°F. An orchard of Meyer's jujubes eventually bore fruit at Chico, but they never challenged Swingle's introduction, the Persian date.

From Laoling, four days travel across alkaline land with donkeys and carts brought Meyer to Tientsin on October 4. Along the way he had noticed not only the wild peach but also the northern wild pear (*Pyrus ussuriensis*) being used as a stock in alkaline soil. He collected seeds for use in developing stock for propagation of fruit trees in arid sections of the United States. Because the pear bore an abundance of small fruit, he believed that it might become an ornamental tree as well.

After having spent four months collecting seeds and cuttings of hundreds of varieties of plants and trees, Meyer reached Peking where he found many letters from Fairchild and fifty more from relatives and friends. Fairchild's letters brought the good news of Meyer's promotion with an increase in salary of four hundred dollars annually. They also conveyed official approval of his plan to visit nurseries and botanical gardens in Europe and to work in Central Asia after he had studied the needs of the northern states. "What a prospect! I am most thankful to you all there in Washington," he exulted. "I hope to do my very best to enrich the United States of America with things good for her people and their households. Please extend thanks to Dr. Galloway and the Honorable Secretary of Agriculture."

Despite this good news, Meyer felt "tired mentally" and he adjusted to sedentary work with difficulty after his long journey. He had to describe and pack the fruits, vegetables, and ornamentals that he had collected in Shantung, although he "would rather chop wood three days than do desk work half a day." After wandering in the countryside, he yearned for "the burning sun and the smell of the mountains." He disliked sitting in a room where he could not hear the wind, see the mountains, or inhale fresh air. In cooler weather two weeks later he wrote Fairchild that "my head feels less tired" and "the old energy returns"; yet he still experienced "a strange kind of tiredness at times." Though this feeling of lethargy dissipated as soon as he started another journey, to Fairchild's inquiry about spending a fourth year in China he answered firmly, "I need a change."

When he told his parents about his successful journey and his promotion, he added that one pays a price for everything. He had paid in lonely evenings at uncomfortable inns where he often thought of his family and friends. Missionaries in the interior had always received him kindly, and the wife of a Scottish missionary had baked delicious loaves of white bread for him to take with him. Opportunities to talk with other Westerners helped to overcome his loneliness. When he found himself among educated people, however, sometimes he regretted his own lack of higher education. To continue academic work would require both time and money, but he would like to do that if he could find the necessary time.

One of the men whose company he enjoyed in Peking was Nelson T. Johnson, who later became the first American ambassador to China. When Meyer had dinner at the embassy mess, they would frequently talk and drink beer together until two or three o'clock in the morning. Sometimes Meyer would speak of his adventures. Johnson never forgot how he "made our hair stand on end" by telling that he awakened one night in Mongolia to find one of his men standing over him with a drawn knife.[2] At other times Meyer would show Johnson common plants that could be used for their fiber or as fodder. Thirty years later Johnson recalled "the thrill I had one day when he turned back the leaves of some weed by the roadside and showed me some little aphids herding their honey-bearing ant cows."[3]

Meyer firmly believed that "any ordinary botanist" could collect new shrubs and trees; the agricultural explorer's effort to identify unknown plants that might be of great economic importance seemed to him much more challenging. "The world at large looks rather down upon the purely economic part of our work," he told Fairchild; however, he considered recognizing useful grains, fruits, and vegetables that would benefit mankind truly rewarding. When he heard that many of his introductions were thriving at Chico, he rejoiced, but he pointed out that "exploring and collecting is only a side issue. The growing of the things in America is the important thing. After all, what would it amount to if they didn't succeed at home?" But much remained to be done in China. "This is a tremendous country with hosts of important unintroduced things as yet and several explorers will have all they can do for this next ten or twenty years, if not longer, and I am willing to do my share."

After newspapers had reported the attack on him at Khabarovsk, American journalists had been seeking more stories about him. He believed that publicity should be focused on plants of economic value to American farmers and not on his adventures. When his family wrote that newspapers in Holland had mentioned his work, he felt pleased; however, he resented inaccurate accounts that emphasized sensational aspects of his journeys. "Our line of work," he insisted, "is interesting enough to be described as it is." He found "quite a few" mistakes in an article that a friend had sent him from the *Los Angeles Times*, and he called another clipping "absurd." The *Kansas City Star* had published his picture identified as David Fairchild, an error that embarrassed Fairchild and amused Meyer, who wrote, "When looking at my picture where I look like a robber headman, I am not quite sorry my chief's name has been put underneath." To Fairchild's suggestion that he publish the story of his journeys in book form, he responded with interest. He also completed an application for *Who's Who in America*, "though I don't see why they should ask me. I am only beginning to do some work." But he confided in his parents, "I believe I start to be famous."

Early in November he posted nineteen kinds of seeds to Washington and four heavy cases to Chico, urging the new director to fumigate the shipment. It included a rare zelkova, one sack of wetland rice for irrigated valleys in Utah or California, mountain buckwheat and oats, the wild peach to be used as a stock for all stone fruits, and a rare dwarf sorghum. With his collection he sent labels listing the names of all plants in both Chinese characters and roman letters, evidence that he must have employed Chow-hai Ting, the interpreter who accompanied him during all his later expeditions. After sending the department a draft for the unexpended balance of his appropriation for the past fiscal year, he was ready to begin his next journey. "Out in the wilderness again," he assured Fairchild, "I will be very soon the same as I was last winter."

A Harvest for America

Jehol, Peking, Shansi, and Chekiang
NOVEMBER, 1907, TO JUNE, 1908

W I T H   only six months left to complete his work in China, Meyer planned a month-long journey to Jehol; thereafter he was obligated to return to the Wu Tai Shan, to collect in the region around Peking, and to go south to Tangsi for bamboo. If he could complete these projects, he felt that he would be able to "give this tour a fitting end."

In preparation for his journey to Jehol, an isolated province located between Mongolia and Manchuria, he applied to the ruler, Prince Chiang, for permission to visit the Imperial Palace grounds. In Jehol he might see tigers, panthers, wolves, wild boars, mountain sheep, and "most marvelous of all, it is probably the only place in the world so far north where monkeys live." Doubtful that any zoological collection in America had these northern monkeys, he suggested to Fairchild that he try to obtain a few.

With his interpreter, guide, two carts, mules, and drivers, in mid-November he headed north in a heavy snowstorm. When the weather cleared in the afternoon, the snowy landscape "appeared like a wonderland." This illusion was shattered when he met thousands of Chinese soldiers with modern rifles and artillery. Meyer wondered what the future might bring because he had observed "the military spirit making gigantic strides of late." He did not foresee that the revolution establishing the first Chinese Republic was just three years away. Neither the snow nor the soldiers prevented his collecting acorns of oaks that looked like chestnut trees (*Quercus variabilis*) and several hundred scions of a tree bearing persimmons that weighed a pound and a half.

In the mountains called the Pang Shan, he replaced the mules with donkeys that carried seven sacks of currency in addition to their other burdens. He had prepared for any contingency by taking Mexican, Hong Kong, and Hupeh dollars, as well as lump silver, silver coins, and copper cash. The value of a thousand copper cash might be 140 pieces in one village, 480 at a second, and 990 at a third; however, at some villages up to half of the coins proved to be counterfeit.

For six days he stayed in an old temple once occupied briefly by a Chinese emperor. "More interesting yet," a very old priest told him that "Russian doctors" had lodged there while collecting plants many years before. Meyer believed that the "Russian doctors" must have been Dr. Bunge and Dr. Bretschneider, German botanists in the service of Russia; the latter mentioned having collected in this area in his *History of European Botanical Discoveries in China*, a volume that Meyer carried with him and consulted often. Though a fire kindled from pine needles and dry oak leaves burned beneath his brick bedstead, he needed the protection of his sheepskin clothing while a snowstorm raged outside. A bitter wind penetrated the cracks in the walls of the temple, freezing his teapot to the table and turning the water in his washbasin to solid ice. Walnut, chestnut, oak, apricot, and peach trees as well as ornamental shrubs grew near the temple, but the fierce storm forced him to spend two days writing and resting instead of collecting.

Meyer's interpreter returned to Peking because of the cold, but he and his two guides, four drivers, and six donkeys continued northward through a forested region where dense undergrowth shredded their baggage covers. Splendid stands of pines, oaks, lindens, elms, wild pears, crab apples, maples, and poplars reminded him of the forests of northern Korea. He discovered "glorious bunches" of mistletoe with red and yellow berries, but he regretted the damage that it did to trees that "died an untimely death through its ravages." When they came to frozen rivers or frail bridges, he and his men had to carry the baggage and help the skittish donkeys to keep their footing. In the forests they often noticed tracks of wolves. Several entered the courtyard of their inn one night and killed three pigs. The biting wind chilled even the interior of rural inns, and hard brick bedsteads offered little comfort. Though the northern monkeys kept out of sight in the forests, Meyer observed two in captivity and decided that they appeared to be quite intelligent.

In the city of Jehol (Chengde), capital of the province of Jehol, he marveled at "scenes that speak of past splendor," though he felt concern for the future of the region. He admired the beautifully laid out Imperial Park and the temple groves with their picturesque herd of tame deer, but he despaired when he heard that farmers were cutting trees as fast as the government opened new areas to settlement. Already floods had occurred in cleared areas. Meyer feared that this once fertile region would soon become an extension of the Mongolian desert.

He returned to Peking through biting dust storms, passing valleys already devastated by floods. "I see with sad eyes the last vestiges of a once grand vegetation," he told Fairchild. The Chinese had been guilty of "enormous crimes in destroying the balance of nature. Every wild tree or shrub is mercilessly cut down; every edible bird is trapped and eaten. Their mountains are barren wastes which let the rains rush off with great velocity, bearing with them arable soil and covering valleys with stony and sandy matter. Their climate gets drier year after year and famines result. Their birds are being exterminated; caterpillars of all descriptions destroy whole plantations of pine trees and catalpas and fruit orchards." In contrast to his distress at the destruction of vegetation, his twenty-six photographs of undefiled country acted as "food to one's craving for beautiful things."

As a result of his month-long trip, he sent forty-five parcels to Washington and twenty-eight to the Chico Plant Introduction Garden. They contained "some novelties in the line of insects," the rare red- and yellow-berried mistletoe, many varieties of pears, packages of chestnuts, large seedless persimmons, and hardy ornamental shrubs. Two weeks later he posted thirty-eight bundles of seeds, entomological specimens, algae, lichens, rare fungi, lespedezas, and grasses.

In response to inquiries about his collection, he promised Fairchild that he would bring blue spruce and white-barked pines to America with him and would try to obtain roots of the "exquisitely beautiful" white peony. "As a forced winter flower it makes a most artistic effect in a tastefully furnished room, especially when put in an antique Chinaware vessel." He had collected more varieties of soybeans than either the Japanese or the American government already had; however, he explained that countless strains must exist because the rural Chinese did not have seed stores and each farmer saved his own seeds. Since freight charges on his heavy boxes of bamboo plants promised to be almost prohibitive, he offered to pay part of the freight from his own funds, if necessary. Longing to see his introductions actually growing in the United States, he inquired eagerly, "How are my persimmons, pears, apricots, and grasses doing? Do the rushes grow in the Carolinas? And my dry-land rice?"

Two of the letters that Meyer found waiting at Peking annoyed him. In response to criticism about his covering too much territory (which he correctly identified as "probably suggested by Professor Sargent"), Meyer replied that he had to cover enormous areas in order to find useful plants. It would be simpler to stay in one place for several months and collect botanical specimens, but "I feel that I have a better mission: the obtaining of products that will prove to be of use in making our nation wealthier and better." Packages of new vouchers with instructions relating to "accounts current, abstracts, and Heaven knows what more" also disturbed him. Fairchild wrote that these matters "are the necessary framework upon which successful exploration is built." Meyer agreed, but he added, "When a framework gets too heavy the whole structure comes right down." As he predicted, Chinese merchants regarded the large blue and white vouchers with suspicion and refused to sign them.

During warmer weather he had located a number of plants that he wanted to collect in the mountains north and west of Peking, but he could not take cuttings and scions until winter. After engaging an interpreter and guide to accompany him, on January 15 he hired donkeys and set out. That night a heavy snowfall began and continued for two days. Meyer and his guide nevertheless worked in the deep snow, making cuttings of fruit trees and gathering a sackful of soaptree pods to be analyzed chemically. Though his feet nearly froze when wet snow penetrated his leather boots, Meyer thought that the snow-covered landscape formed "a sublime scene," especially when the full moon cast an "almost weird" silver light at night. Surrounded by "mysterious ghost-like silence, one could not help feeling exalted."

As he continued his journey, donkeys and men fell on the steep and slippery mountain passes, but an ancient horse chestnut tree, as well as a white-barked pine and a ginkgo, each twenty-one feet in circumference, made the risks worthwhile. Traveling through deep snow, he collected scions and seeds of the white-barked pine; however, he was unable to dig roots of the white peony from the firmly frozen soil. Of the pines he wrote, "The more one sees of them, the more one loves them—in rain, bright sunshine, soft moonlight, or snow laden, their exquisite appearance cannot fail to exert an uplifting influence on one's mind." Two days later more snow fell. Before Meyer found shelter at an icy temple, even the donkeys had difficulty climbing the narrow trail. Despite the cold weather, he succeeded in collecting cuttings of persimmons, apricots, yellow plums, the drought-resistant globular willow with an umbrella-shaped top, and a rare small-leaved, pyramidal white poplar (*Populus tomentosa*). On January 30 at a Presbyterian mission, he discovered a free-flowering pale pink rose (*Rosa odorata*) that later became an important grafting stock for greenhouse roses.[1] The next day at 4:00 A.M. he and his helpers loaded the pack mules and set out "under the small disc of the waning moon." When they reached the railroad at 3:00 P.M., they ate their first full meal that day and then boarded the train for Peking.

Returning from a journey meant listing, labeling, and packing the harvest. Thirty large bundles barely held all the cuttings and scions of various fruit trees, the rare Chinese horse chestnut, and other ornamental trees. Meyer identified each with names in both roman letters and Chinese characters, evidence that Chow-hai Ting was his interpreter. Five days later he mailed more parcels including the yellow rose, preserved jujubes for W. T. Swingle, and pods of a small spiny locust (*Gleditsia heterophylla*) that might be developed as a hedge plant. Since "nearly every tree produces pods which differ from those from other trees," Meyer concluded that it was in a state of mutation and asked that sets of pods be sent to Hugo de Vries and to Sargent.

Though he did not expect to find anything to justify the time and trouble, he prepared to leave for the Wu Tai Shan as soon as the Chinese New Year's festivities ended. He had noticed that the Chinese forgot their usual virtues of sobriety and thrift during the celebration. When "eating houses" and post offices reopened and "trains run also again," he was ready to start.

After leaving Peking, he passed through "nice rocky mountainous scenery" until he found a fairly clean inn that evening. On February 19, accompanied by his interpreter, guide, drivers, and six mules, he set off along roads that had become one-hundred-foot-deep gullies after centuries of use by mules and carts. During the rainy season these roads flooded; on one occasion a cloudburst destroyed forty carts with men and mules. Instead of rain, however, Meyer traveled through clouds of dust. He reported that his men "got into a bit of a scrap" with other mule drivers on the fourth day of the trip. "We were the biggest and heaviest loaded party so we had right of way, but the other party thought different and in no time there was a fight in which whips and fists were freely used, and they pulled each other's queues to such an extent that I expected them to come off. When I came between, they soon stopped." No one was hurt, "except for a few hairs pulled out," and everyone enjoyed the break in the monotony of the journey.

Arriving chilled and tired at the Wu Tai Shan, Meyer spent a miserable night in a cold, smoky inn. The following day he moved to a temple that was clean but so bitingly cold that ink froze on his pen. Priests told him that ancient ruins adjacent to the temple were four thousand years old. For five days, "during which we had only three snowstorms," he studied the conifers carefully. As a result of his two trips, he collected several spruce, a pine, and a larch that had not been recorded previously. In addition, he found two willows, a lilac, a rose, rhubarb, naked oats, and an extremely rare hull-less barley.

After six days Meyer left the Wu Tai Shan in an icy, cutting wind and passed through an isolated area where frightened natives ran when he approached them. In one village the inhabitants were so curious about him that he had to ask the local police to move crowds out of the inn yard. As he sat on a brick bed with a single candle for illumination, he wrote de Vries that he was burdened not only with bedding, food, clothes, and cooking equipment, but also with a large quantity of copper coins and lump silver. He believed that China needed a universal currency as desperately as a universal language.

On March 4 he reached the famous pear district of Tongchangdi. Pack animals of all kinds, even camels, came there and carried the fragrant pears to distant places. Because Meyer was the first white man to visit that region, people climbed onto rooftops to see him. He realized that even the headman of the village feared him. While the curious natives watched from a safe distance, he collected scions of the pears.

On his homeward journey he visited English missionaries and later had the unpleasant experience of losing his balance as he reached for seeds and tumbling down a precipice. Remembering not to resist the downward movement as he fell, he arrived at the bottom "only a little scratched and shaky." After collecting seeds and cuttings of the hardy yellow rose, four varieties of jujubes, six kinds of peaches, and entomological specimens, he returned to Peking.

As soon as the journey ended, the less congenial task of packing began. He then dispatched twenty-eight bundles of cuttings, scions, herbaceous material, and entomological specimens to Washington. In addition to the evergreens and grains from the Wu Tai Shan, this important shipment included jujubes, haws, six species of elms, a rhododendron, and the yellow rose. Handling numerous bundles, which often measured four or five feet in length and several feet in width, required considerable exertion. He also made duplicate inventory cards and attached labels to each item, giving the names in Chinese characters and in English with the assistance of Chow-hai Ting.

"Many interesting things remain to be introduced," Meyer wrote Fairchild in his final letter from Peking. "The whole Yellow River district has not been touched yet, and Shantung, Honan, Shansi, and Shensi are just calling me to search them." But he felt that one is always an exile in China. "I am longing to enjoy a good rest among more congenial surroundings," he admitted. "One always has to turn in to himself for advice or consolation here and that is not good."

Only a few details remained to be settled. He expected to take the department a large quantity of scions of the dry-land elm (*Ulmus pumila*) and of a rare weeping elm that he had recently collected from a tree on a grave at Fengtai. There he also had discovered a dwarf lemon tree (*Citrus* × *meyeri*) that the Chinese used as a house plant. They valued it both as a decorative and as a source of excellent fruit. Testing in the United States later confirmed Meyer's belief that it could be useful in private homes in America and could be grown commercially as well. In addition, he planned to buy evergreens at nurseries in Peking and to take them with him to America. One of this group was a silver-blue juniper of dense habit that the Chinese called the Fish-tail Juniper. The H. L. Hicks Nursery on Long Island grew it for many years as "Meyer's Juniper"; it still thrives at the Arnold Arboretum where it is called *Juniperus squamata* 'Meyeri'. Another valuable plant that he purchased at a nursery was a lilac that the Chinese used for pot culture because it flowered when it was only a few inches high. The lustrous dark green leaves and violet flowers that fade to lavender make this lilac (*Syringa meyeri*) a desirable shrub. Well-branched and symmetrical, it reaches a height of five feet outdoors. In 1965 Donald Hoag of the North Dakota Agricultural Experiment Station at Fargo reported that *Syringa meyeri* withstood severe winters without injury and promised to become the most valuable lilac on the northern plains.² Today it grows as far north as Morden, Manitoba.

Before he left Peking, Meyer also had to inspect two monkeys and decide whether they would accompany him to America. Fairchild had sent him an enthusiastic response from Dr. Frank Baker, Director of the National Zoological Park, along with instructions for caring for monkeys of the rare type that he had seen in Jehol. Dr. Baker wrote that they must be either *Macacus lasiotis* or *Macacus tcheliensis.*"Both are heavily furred and handsome animals, but very few specimens have been brought out alive, and I doubt whether any have come to the United States."³

After completing his tasks in Peking, Meyer packed all his possessions and embarked on the *Hsin-feng* for Shanghai. A restful sea voyage offered ample time for correspondence but limited opportunity for conversation because he was the only white man aboard. At the American Consulate at Shanghai, Dr. S. P. Barchet enjoyed his beautiful photographs and urged him to publish his pictures of views rarely seen by Westerners. Letters waiting for Meyer at the consulate included Fairchild's comment that he was using some of these photographs as lantern slides to illustrate his lectures on foreign plant introduction.

Less pleasant mail concerned his accounts. Though he had submitted his bills and receipts for the quarter and had reported a surplus of one thousand dollars for the year, he nevertheless received what he considered a severe reprimand from the auditor: "It is mandatory upon all agents of this department to use the forms prescribed by the Treasury Department if it is their wish to continue handling public funds." Though this was simply a reminder of a rule that he found difficult to follow in rural China, Meyer regarded it as a serious personal criticism. He considered offering his resignation, for he thought that would be the honorable response if the auditors disapproved of his handling of public funds. For a while he felt tempted to return to America "a free man" by way of India or Australia. Then he remembered his obligation to the department and thought of his plants "with nobody to care for them." No acceptable alternative existed. "I have decided to stick to the thing," he wrote Fairchild. "It was bad though on my head, and I was obliged to lay for three nights and two days on the bricks of a Chinese bedstead, not being able to do a thing. I was physically tired also. Many islands and dreamy countries call me where I don't have to bother about all this money business. I will not go out any more under the present financial regulations." His brief period of depression ended as soon as he reached a decision. He then made his final trip south to Tangsi and Hangchow for bamboo and other plants.

Three weeks later he returned to Shanghai to supervise the packing of his tremendous collection. His inventory listed seventy-seven different species and varieties, including one hundred boxes of thirty kinds of bamboo.

Among the ornamental trees were twenty-two white-barked pines, twelve blue spruce, five blue junipers, two zelkovas, a weeping juniper, a Chinese holly, and one hundred drought-resistant elms. He also had collected five ornamental lemons, ten white-fruited loquats, four dwarf plums, and two dwarf quinces. Seeds of plants of economic interest included seven kinds of asparagus, clover, oats, hemp, and cotton, as well as eighteen varieties of soybeans with descriptions of the characteristics and uses of each. He had not neglected shrubs and flowers, for he had assembled eighteen lilacs, a rhododendron, four viburnums, two spireas, a daphne, ten yellow roses, four lilies, and three epiphytic orchids. To all of this he added two live monkeys!

After negotiating with four steamship companies, he had chosen a Standard Oil steamer, the *Ashtabula*, because it offered the best conditions for his plants. As time grew short, temperatures rose and rain fell constantly; yet he not only supervised but also helped to assemble, pack, and store twenty tons of material. "It was only with the utmost hurry that I got at last my plants on the boat and Jupiter Pluvius reigned in full glory during those last days. Water rushed out of my shoes and clothes when, a few hours before leaving, we had the plants at last on the boat." Meyer, the only passenger aboard the *Ashtabula,* kept busy during the four-week voyage. He not only had to expose the plants to sun and air as often as possible, but he also cared for the monkeys. "They cause me as much trouble as babies," he wrote, adding that a plant explorer is "some kind of mother to his charges in any case." When the ship docked in San Francisco on June 12, he was glad to exchange the "rolling boat" for a hotel.

His first day in the United States began with visits from immigration and customs officials as well as horticulture inspectors, for California alone had strict quarantine laws in 1908. "The amount of time and paper we wasted in connection with these Customs matters was something fierce," he complained. Much more upsetting, the horticulture inspectors noticed some small scales on the bamboo and fumigated the one hundred boxes thoroughly. Most varieties eventually died as a result of treatment that he considered excessive. Fairchild later wrote that this loss "nearly broke Meyer's heart." Reporters soon descended on him, taking special interest in the monkeys and "writing all kinds of nonsense about them." Before leaving San Francisco, he supervised packing the tons of plants and seeds, barely managing to cram everything into a Southern Pacific freight car.

Moving on to Chico, he waited impatiently for his collection for five days; however, he enjoyed his first mail in two months, "like dew on the desert, received gratefully." He also had leisure to inspect the plant introduction garden and to regret Dorsett's departure. Conditions at Chico had deteriorated and many of the scions and cuttings that he had gathered with such great effort had died. Propagation facilities seemed "vastly insufficient" and management incompetent. When his carload of plants finally arrived, he repacked part of the collection and sent it to Washington. Though the temperature at Chico even in June reached the nineties, the bamboo had to be planted in the open. After supervising that task, Meyer visited friends near Los Angeles. "I long to see you all there after the long absence," he wrote Fairchild. "This country is too big and travel too slow!" On June 26 he left California to inspect the new plant introduction garden at Ames, Iowa.

CHAPTER 11

A Plant Explorer at Home

The United States
JULY, 1908, TO JULY, 1909

BEFORE beginning his next expedition, Meyer intended to develop a list of "desiderata" to guide him in his search for useful plants. Fairchild, knowing how much Meyer would dislike being confined to an office, agreed that he should visit plant introduction gardens, agricultural colleges, and experiment stations to learn the specific needs of various regions of the United States. Meyer began this project at Iowa State College (now Iowa State University). Accompanied by Professor S. A. Beach, he inspected the plant introduction garden at Ames, spoke to a student seminar about his work in China, and questioned the group to learn the needs of settlers in the upper Mississippi Valley. From Ames he went to see friends in Saint Louis before continuing his journey to the capital.

Though he had lived in southern California and in Saint Louis, coming home meant returning to Washington. Friends at the department invited him to dinners and parties, as many as four in one week. At their Maryland home, In the Woods, the Fairchilds celebrated his return with a barbecue for the entire staff of the Foreign Seed and Plant Introduction Section. On a moonlit evening everyone gathered around a campfire. When some of the younger staff members spiked the Fairchilds' cider, the party became festive. Several speakers complimented Meyer on the successful completion of his expedition. He responded by relating some of his experiences and singing Dutch songs beside the glowing embers of the dying bonfire.

But he did not spend much time relaxing; he was soon assigned a desk in the plant introduction office. In the area reserved for receiving shipments, he unpacked his baggage and removed the dinner jacket Fairchild had given him to wear in diplomatic circles in China. It had never been unfolded and was green with mold, but Fairchild understood Meyer's appreciation of the gift when he carefully repacked it. Meyer's first assignment was to study the inventory cards for the seeds, scions, and cuttings that he had shipped from China and to analyze the reasons for some failures. Of his introductions, 1,397 of the 1,664 numbered varieties had survived. Over 50 percent of the 479 varieties sent as scions or plants were growing in America, a remarkable record in the days of slow transit and exposure to extremes of temperature.[1] Meyer's report criticized the practice of storing plants near the boiler room on shipboard, overzealous fumigation, neglect of valuable plant material at Chico, and inadequate propagation facilities in Washington. He also classified his negatives and photographs, requesting permission to use them if he should write a book about his travels. Answering inquiries about his introductions gave him pleasure; requests were already coming from Texas and Arizona for his wild peach and from Nevada for fruit trees and the dry-land elm.

On June 26 he applied for citizenship papers. A month later he filed his petition, renouncing his allegiance to Wilhelmina, queen of the Netherlands. He then had to wait three months before appearing in person at the Supreme Court of the District of Columbia, accompanied by two people who had known him for five years.

In the meantime he visited agricultural colleges and experiment stations in the northern states. Less than four weeks after his arrival in America, he attended a conference of professors of agriculture at Cornell, where he spoke to forty people about dry-land farming in China. Professors representing colleges from Alabama to Nebraska were glad to describe their research projects to an agricultural explorer who would seek plants for use in their work. Meyer kept adding to his list of desiderata as he conferred with specialists including Liberty Hyde Bailey, author of many standard reference books about botany and horticulture.

Meyer left Ithaca the following day for a two-week tour of the northern states, guided by William A. Taylor of the Pomology Section of the USDA. At the New York State Agricultural Experiment Station at Geneva, Meyer noted U. P. Hedrick's need for hardy fungus-resistant plums, large mildew-resistant currants, and blight-resistant pears. Taylor then guided Meyer by steamer from Rochester to Montreal and by train to Ottawa. Since Canadian agriculturists shared many problems with farmers in the States, Fairchild had worked out a reciprocal arrangement with William Saunders, head of the Canadian Department of Agriculture. Working at the Ottawa Experiment Farm with early-maturing wheats from Russia and from the Himalayas, he and his son, Charles Saunders, were developing Marquis wheat, which ripened in the short season so far north. When an acute wheat shortage threatened the Allied powers during World War I, the Marquis wheat of Canada tipped the balance for the Allies by providing a tremendous yield.[2] Finding two thriving willows that he had sent from Siberia pleased Meyer, and he gladly recorded Saunders's request for ornamentals and fruit trees that could survive Canadian winters.

After three hours at Niagara Falls, he and W. A. Taylor continued their journey that night by train to Madison, Wisconsin. Meyer observed with admiration that Taylor managed to spend almost every daylight hour working for the department at widely scattered locations. In Madison Meyer spoke to the University Club and promised specialists at the Wisconsin Agricultural Experiment Station to seek hardier strains of apples, apricots, plums, and peaches.

The following morning Meyer and Taylor waited five hours for someone to drive them from the railroad station to the North Dakota Agriculture College at Fargo where they found conditions "pretty raw yet." Another sleeping car took them to Brookings, South Dakota, "without a bath or a sleep in a regular bed for a week." On the train they met Harry Benjamin Derr, a barley expert from the department's Office of Grain Investigation. Derr hoped to develop grains that would enable settlers in the northern Rocky Mountains to grow their own "bread foods." He asked Meyer to find an early, hull-less, large-grained barley suitable for high altitudes. Months later in Central Asia Meyer sent hardy grains to the department for Derr.

Arriving at Brookings at 5:00 A.M., the men napped in chairs on the porch of a hotel until breakfast time. Meyer found the South Dakota Agriculture Experiment Station tastelessly planned and the director, Niels E. Hansen, away on a plant exploration trip. Noticing plants overgrown with weeds, Meyer concluded that Hansen was trying to do too much to be able to maintain the experiment garden properly. The next issue of the Coleman newspaper quoted Meyer as having said that the South Dakota experiment station was "abreast of any in the country as far as original research and experimentation is concerned, while the work of Professor Hansen is approached only by that of Burbank." Meyer's indignation at this fabrication is reflected in his note attached to a clipping of the article: "I did *not* say anything they mentioned here. *Pure invention.* F. N. M."[3]

The next night Meyer and Taylor traveled to the Minnesota Agricultural Experiment Station in Minneapolis where Professor LeRoy Cady pointed out the work of plant propagators who were breeding hardier apples, apricots, peaches, and plums. After a good night's rest in a bed for the first time in about ten days and visits to Como Park in Saint Paul and the Excelsior Fruit Farm near beautiful Lake Minnetonka, Meyer decided that to be born in this part of Minnesota would be good fortune indeed.

On the evening of August 12, W. A. Taylor departed on still another sleeper, leaving Meyer to proceed to Chicago. His fourteen-story hotel filled him with admiration, for skyscrapers were still new to him. After studying exhibits of botanical material at the Field Museum, he inspected city parks where he noticed smoke damage to ornamentals and the need for "shade trees to live with factories." Following an absence of two weeks, he returned to Washington.

This trip yielded unexpected dividends. Not only had he added to his list of desiderata, but he also felt amply rewarded for all his efforts in China because so many plant breeders had expressed their appreciation of his work. An insight of greater importance resulted from his tour. For the first time he fully comprehended the possibilities hidden in plants. "In the future we will create unheard-of strains of fruits and trees and shrubs and flowering plants. All we need now is to build up collections so as to have the material at hand," he told Fairchild. "If I did not go to Asia again, I certainly would take some of these hybridization problems." Before World War I, the Department of Agriculture emphasized finding and introducing plants for direct cultivation. In the 1920s emphasis shifted to hybridization and selection, and collectors looked for new genes that might be valuable in breeding better plants.[4] Meyer never heard the terms gene pool or germplasm, but in 1908 he grasped the concept that now motivates international efforts to store earth's plant resources before they are lost forever. This understanding led him to risk his life in barren and sparsely populated regions along the borders of Turkestan, Mongolia, and Siberia.

When Meyer returned to Washington in late August, Fairchild suggested another project, which Meyer undertook reluctantly. President Theodore Roosevelt was preparing a message to Congress about the importance of conservation. Henry L. Hicks, the Long Island nurseryman Meyer had visited in 1905, wanted Meyer to show the president photographs of the Wu Tai Shan and to tell him about the terrible results of deforestation in China. Though Meyer hesitated, he could scarcely refuse when Fairchild urged him to cooperate for the benefit of the department. But he almost missed the opportunity when he returned to his room at the St. James Hotel in Washington and found a wire from Hicks saying that the president would see them at Oyster Bay at 10:30 the next morning. After managing to reserve a berth on a night train, he reached Long Island at 9:00 A.M. Hicks met him in an automobile, a rarity in 1908, and they "puffed off" to Oyster Bay.

Driving up Sagamore Hill, they saw Roosevelt "strenuously engaged in a game of tennis, his highly colored cheeks and bronzed neck looking all the healthier in contrast with his white woolen sweater, while his broad shoulders and strong calves, together with his massive head, gave one at once the impression of an all-around strong man." In a large reception hall, Meyer observed buffalo and moose heads mounted on the wall, big grizzly and black bearskins on the floor, and "nice small metal bears," one with diamond eyes, in an antique display case. Soon the president arrived. Seated in a leather armchair, he chatted about conditions in China, tigers in Siberia, his hunting trip in Africa, and Meyer's proposed expedition to Central

Asia. By the time the president praised the work of the Agriculture Department and asked to see the photographs, Meyer felt at ease. Roosevelt quickly decided that he could use Meyer's pictures and observations in his message to Congress. He asked Meyer to draw up a concise illustrated report showing the disastrous effects of deforestation in China. After the president called their visit "a delight," Meyer and Hicks "whirled" along the roads to Westbury. Some of the "whirling" must have been in Meyer's thoughts, for his photographs were to become the first visual aids used by a president in a message to Congress.

During the next five days Hicks guided Meyer on a tour of New York and New Jersey gardens. First they visited the New York Botanical Garden and the Carnegie Institute Experiment Station at Cold Spring. Carrying letters of introduction from Fairchild, Hicks and Meyer then traveled from Long Island by auto, train, ferry, subway, and several streetcar lines to see two distinguished hybridizers in New Jersey. After a tiring trip, they met Dr. Walter Van Fleet and Fairchild's uncle, Dr. Byron Halstead. At Rutgers University, where Galloway had recruited young David Fairchild nineteen years earlier, Halstead showed them the crosses that he was making in his effort to develop a tomato with fewer seeds and more meat. On Labor Day Meyer left Long Island on a coach filled with holiday crowds.

Before vacationing on Cape Cod in Massachusetts, he wanted to study the extensive collection of arboreal material at the Arnold Arboretum. In Sargent's absence Jackson Dawson, the superintendent of plantings at the arboretum, showed Meyer the Chinese collection. Meyer inspected the seed flats with great interest, especially the material Wilson was sending. Though he refrained from commenting, he wrote Fairchild that E. H. Wilson had sent ten tons of live plants in sand or clay instead of sphagnum moss and all had arrived dead. Wilson never attempted to take cuttings or scions, and both Wilson and Sargent were incredulous when Fairchild told them that many of Meyer's most successful introductions had been received as living budwood or cuttings.[5]

At last the time had come for Meyer to rest from his travels. He began his vacation at Dexter House at Sandwich on September 10. Perhaps Fairchild had suggested that Meyer could relax and work on his manuscript there, but resting and writing did not appeal to him. Though he enjoyed the climate and scenery, he felt like "the last bird of summer." By late September he was the only guest at Dexter House. After so many months of activity, he was lonesome. He nevertheless shared some good news with Fairchild. The auditor had finally settled his accounts and had concluded that he was entitled to a reimbursement of sixty-three cents, "an unexpected windfall. I will use it as the foundation of a still to be built fortune."

When Meyer left Dexter House on October 1, he spent three days conferring with Sargent and studying herbarium material at the Arnold

Arboretum and at the Gray Herbarium in Cambridge. Sargent used this opportunity to reprimand Meyer for his failure to make an extensive collection of herbarium specimens in China. Meyer responded that the department had sent him to collect economic material; privately he wrote Fairchild that he now agreed with Sargent about the critical importance of having authentic material in herbariums. When Sargent asked for specimens of all the arborescent plants that he might find in the future, Meyer recommended that the department authorize him to fulfill this request.

In preparation for his expedition to Central Asia, he journeyed to New Haven to confer with Ellsworth Huntington, a veteran of travels in Mongolia and Turkestan. Huntington gave him valuable information about the products and the customs of isolated parts of Central Asia, but he warned that visitors must have special Russian permits to travel to those places. He suggested that Meyer and Fairchild pay calls on the British, Russian, and Chinese legations in Washington to explain Meyer's mission and request their cooperation. He also advised Meyer to take presents for the numerous officials that he would meet. They talked until midnight, and Meyer left feeling so excited about exploring Central Asia that he wished he could go immediately.

During the following week he studied the agricultural needs of the tobacco growers in the Connecticut Valley and then departed for New York. There he called on people to whom Fairchild had provided letters of introduction and inspected camping equipment at Abercrombie and Fitch. "All that going about by underground, by elevated, and by various other railways" grew tiresome. On October 13 he gladly returned to "quiet Washington."

The three-month interval of waiting for approval of his petition to become an American citizen had ended at last. On November 2, seven years after his original application for naturalization, Meyer appeared at the District Supreme Court with his attorney and character witnesses. After he answered many questions and "swore with my right hand on the Bible," he finally attained citizenship.

Several tasks were waiting for him at the plant introduction office. He enjoyed preparing notes and lantern slides for a lecture that he gave at the annual meeting of the Society of American Foresters. In addition, he had to find a permanent home for the bamboo plants that he had transported from China. The department granted him an appropriation of three hundred dollars to be used for surveying possible sites. Since the Foreign Seed and Plant Introduction Section had no funds for purchasing land, his task included persuading owners of suitable acreage to allow the USDA to use the land without buying it.

Early in November he journeyed to Charleston to meet F. W. Clarke, an employee of the USDA who knew the South as W. A. Taylor knew the northern states. Because temperatures ranged too low to grow bamboo near Charleston, Meyer and Clarke moved on to Augusta and Savannah; however, Meyer believed that bamboo would not thrive in the light soil or stand the occasional periods of cold there. Near Jacksonville and Saint Augustine the sandy soil could not support the tall timber bamboo. At the USDA garden in Miami water rose too near the surface of the soil for the root system of the plants. The search led next to Gainesville, Florida. Still the region appeared unsuitable for bamboo culture.

Traveling by buggy across rolling hills to Brooksville, Florida, Meyer grew hopeful as he observed big timber and tropical fruits growing on clay soil. He explained to officials at Brooksville that the USDA wanted land in that area to grow bamboo, but the government lacked funds to buy the property. At a hastily called meeting of the Board of Trade, he secured a deed of trust to suitable acreage. On Christmas Eve he and Clarke journeyed to Tampa to investigate facilities for shipping bamboo products.

Christmas day forced him to rest briefly before completing his survey, but he and Clarke boarded a sleeping car that evening. The next day they eliminated the Tallahassee area and visited Hume's nursery at Glen Saint Mary, where Meyer enjoyed seeing small trees growing from persimmon seeds that he had sent from China. Since funds were running low, he offered to pay any expenses in excess of their joint appropriation. Eliminating Abbeville, Louisiana, he and Clarke boarded a train for Houston, arriving at midnight. After determining that the soil was too poorly drained for bamboo culture, they went to Pierce, Texas, where Meyer enjoyed visiting Clarke's family and seeing the livestock at A. P. Borden's ranch. "I am in love with the beautiful, good-natured Indian cattle, remarkably gentle fellows they are, loving petting as much as a lady's horse," he wrote Fairchild. "I would be only too glad if I could see them coming around my house asking to be petted."

Meyer missed his congenial companion when he went on to Victoria. He was shocked to find farmers growing citrus fruits where the mercury had dropped to −4°F in the 1894 freeze. After arriving at Brownsville at the southernmost tip of Texas at midnight, he spent the next morning studying the department's South Texas Garden with Professor Green. Insufficient rainfall and extremes of temperature ranging from −12°F to over 100°F made people long for shade trees that would survive in that climate. Meyer remembered their need when he collected the Kashgar elm in Turkestan.

The following evening he spoke to the Commercial Club of the Lower Rio Grande Valley, "a wonderful audience, typical of border country." The men wore big Texas hats and top boots and some even loosened their shirt collars. Meyer recommended planting sorghum and alfalfa and advised against planting figs, bananas, or oranges, precipitating a noisy argument between farmers and an aggressive group of land agents. One farmer vehemently denounced land sharks, the agents described the ability of orange trees to replace damaged growth after it had frozen, an intoxicated schoolmaster recited a poem, and Meyer heartily enjoyed the lively evening.[6]

From Brownsville he turned homeward, moving on to San Antonio and then to Opelousas and New Iberia in Louisiana. In pouring rain he inspected possible sites for bamboo until his buggy mired in deep mud. After stopping briefly in New Orleans and at Huntsville, Alabama, he returned to Washington, ending more than six weeks on the road. Despite a conscientious search, he had found no place better suited to bamboo culture than Brooksville. The department therefore confirmed that choice.

President Theodore Roosevelt had delivered his conservation message to Congress in Meyer's absence and had mentioned his name twice. Newspapers had devoted two full columns to his report on deforestation in China. The president had also used some of Meyer's photographs, as well as several taken in 1904 by Bailey Wills.

Except for occasional lecture tours, Meyer spent most of the next six months in Washington waiting for the appropriation for his expedition to Central Asia to become available. The Foreign Seed and Plant Introduction Section was then housed in what Fairchild later called "a series of leaky private houses, basements, and storerooms." In an office in a "shaky building" on B Street, Meyer worked on his bulletin about the fruits and nuts of northern China and also contributed to several other publications. He felt like a caged bird when he had to live in the city and sit at a desk. He disliked the narrow social conventions of the capital and confided to Erwin Smith that in Washington "the sky is too near."

Various groups invited him to lecture about his work. He traveled to Cheyenne in February to address the Dry Land Agricultural Congress and to Denver and Chicago to speak to the chambers of commerce. A few years earlier, he told his parents, he would not have had the courage to give lectures before important people; now he simply pretended that they were his friends. In Washington he showed lantern slides to fifty heads of departments. Even James Wilson, the secretary of agriculture, attended. People in Holland were hearing of his work, and de Vries wrote to say that he felt proud of his former protégé.

During the winter Meyer longed to see his family. Nowhere else in the world had he tasted vegetable soup like his mother's, he told his sister, and the fine pastries he had enjoyed at home were unknown in America. But one roadblock stood in the way of his return to Amsterdam. When he asked the Dutch ambassador whether or not Dutch authorities "still have a hold on me," the ambassador inquired at the Department of Defense in Holland. The department indicated that he might be held accountable because he had been allowed to emigrate without completing his military service. "If so, I won't see that little country," he wrote; however, he did plan a reunion with his relatives in any event.

As winter changed to spring, the Fairchilds' home offered him sanctuary from the city. Often he and David Fairchild labored on some outdoor project while young Alexander Graham Fairchild toddled after them; at other times Meyer talked about his early life in Holland and his experiences in China. In contrast to pleasant weekends at In the Woods, being "cooped up in that little office in hot and humid Washington" was a miserable experience. "I hope I will never again be subjected to such a compulsory sit-down-at-your-desk treatment," he wrote Fairchild afterward. Knowing that eventually he would be able to see his elderly parents, visit European botanical gardens, and explore Central Asia, he managed to complete his important bulletin, *Agricultural Exploration in the Fruit and Nut Orchards of China*.

When he finally received his appropriation and letter of authorization on August 4, he decided that his unfinished manuscript on Chinese dry-land agriculture "would be better in a drawer somewhere" and prepared to leave Washington.[7] After spending four hours at the Treasury Department, he emerged bonded and "had the sensation of having a check for six thousand dollars in my hand." The following day he and Beverly T. Galloway conferred with the secretary of agriculture, James Wilson. Because the Fairchilds had left for England, Meyer spent that night at their home, inspecting the garden and grounds before his departure. He assured Fairchild that everything was in fine condition, the Chinese cabbage "wonderfully good," and added, "Today I have sworn again to defend the Constitution. Now the great packing in." On August 14 he left New York on the *Carmania* of the Cunard Line.

The Second Expedition

Meyer with a *"variety of native wild Caucasian quince* (Cydonia vulgaris) *producing a bank of pinkish white flowers which resemble strikingly our American dogwood,"* Tiflis, April 25, 1910.

Meyer's route through the rugged mountains of the northern Caucasus en route to Vladikavkas, May 1, 1910. *"The mountains now had become wild and rugged, vegetation was scarce and utterly at rest and snow was all around us, making the winds at times chilly and piercing."*

Meyer in a *"veritable jungle of* Tamarix *bushes,"* Chinese Turkestan, February 18, 1911.

Meyer's party in the Tien Shan at 9000 feet. *"The faithful dog 'Shamrah' walked with us all the way from Aksu to Kuldja. He won't sit still, however."* Left to right: the guard, the Russo-Turki interpreter, the man in charge of horses, and the handyman. March 7, 1911.

"On dreaded Mussart or Ice Pass," Tien Shan, Chinese Turkestan. *"Our caravan climbing over a very rough part of the glacier. Yawning crevices on all sides and stones rolling down at intervals. Altitude 10,500 feet."* March 8, 1911.

"Kirghiz encampment where we stayed...the night a wolf came prowling around and our rest was far from being undisturbed." Near Kuldja, Chinese Turkestan, April 20, 1911.

Meyer and laden carts under a tall larch tree near Markakul, the Altai, southwestern Siberia, June 1911.

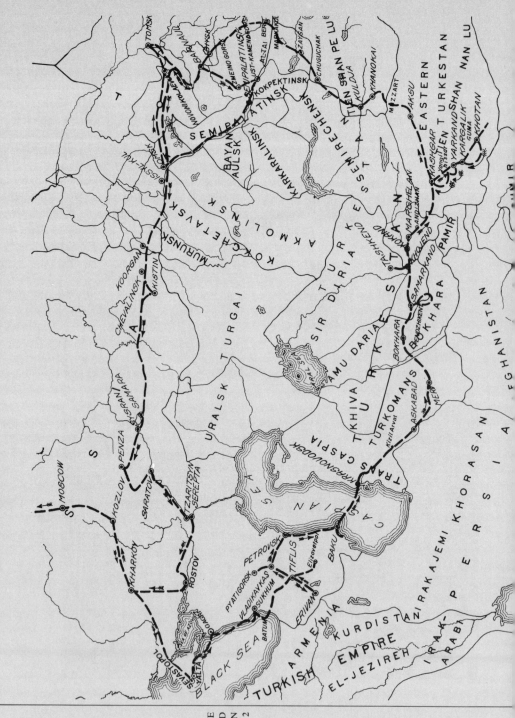

THE
SECOND
EXPEDITION
1909–1912

CHAPTER 12

Europe Revisited

England, Belgium, France, Germany, and Russia
AUGUST, 1909, TO JANUARY, 1910

ABOARD the luxurious *Carmania*, attended by numerous stewards and waiters, Meyer grew impatient to start work. He found the sea "a real nuisance and would not mind a bit if we could overbridge it. Not that I get seasick," he wrote Dorsett, "but I consider it such a waste of time to stay aboard a ship." Journeys by land, on the other hand, offered constant change. A concert and a minstrel show helped to while away the hours until the *Carmania* docked at Liverpool.

Meyer shipped most of his baggage directly to Saint Petersburg (Leningrad) before going to the capital. Hoping that Fairchild might still be in London, he looked for him at the Royal Horticultural Society flower show. His search was unsuccessful, but he did discover an exhibit of nearly two hundred fine photographs that E. H. Wilson had taken in China. Soon afterward he received a letter from Fairchild suggesting that he try to confer with George Forrest, a Scottish plant explorer who had returned recently from his first expedition to the Orient. Meyer met all the other British collectors of the Grand Age of plant exploration in China; unfortunately, he lacked time to go to Cheshire to talk to Forrest.

He spent most of his few days in England at the Royal Botanic Gardens at Kew and at the famous Veitch nursery in Surrey. At Kew E. H. Wilson pointed out the plants that he had sent from China. The following day Wilson met Meyer at Veitch and Sons and again showed him his numerous introductions. Not only the richness and variety of this plant material impressed Meyer, but also its tremendous latent possibilities for hybridization. During the remainder of the week he studied the "wonderfully rich" Kew herbarium. "If I had known that Kew after all is rather poor in northern Chinese material and that this material is of *immense assistance* to an explorer, I most certainly would have collected more," he wrote Fairchild. "It really hurts me now to find out how much more useful I could have been to mankind." Though he was eager to begin field work, he knew that he needed first "to pass through European centers of accumulated knowledge to find out what the world knows." He had received a tempting invitation to go to Edinburgh to visit MacGregor, his friend from Shanghai, but he could not linger in Britain. His itinerary required many stops in Western Europe before reaching Saint Petersburg ahead of frost that would kill vegetation there.

Nevertheless, he reserved four days for a reunion with his relatives who were "all too eager to see the exile who has been away for eight long years." Because he was not sure of his status with the Dutch military authorities, he did not go to Amsterdam. Instead he chose to give his entire family a vacation in Antwerp. "All my near relatives are here," he wrote Fairchild, "and we are a crowd of eight people. I am, of course, the most popular member and they want me to talk for hours and hours about all my experiences." The group included his father and mother, his brother Jan, his sister Alida, his sister Maria Hoogland, Jan N. Hoogland, and their young daughter Maria. At the age of thirty-three Frans Meyer was returning to his family after extensive travels and considerable success as an agricultural explorer. Yet he could say sincerely, "We all find that we haven't changed very much after all." Four days did not compensate for such a long absence. When Monday morning came and Meyer had to go to the botanical garden in Brussels, he took his entire family with him, extending their vacation three more days.

Afterward he journeyed to Paris, where the crowds of people made him impatient to move on. After studying in the herbarium at the Jardin des Plantes and visiting museums, he tired of the "so-called civilized life" and longed to be "already in the wilderness." The several days that he spent inspecting the fine collection of Asian plants at the Vilmorin arboretum and nurseries suited him much better. The Vilmorin family in France, like Veitch in England, had been established for generations, and their gardens at Les Barres and Verriers included a large number of trees and shrubs collected by missionaries in China and Tibet. When Meyer saw new plants that could prove useful in the United States, he suggested trading his yellow rose and Chinese pistachio for them.

Visiting Maurice and Philippe Vilmorin convinced him that the USDA must develop a seed exchange list to offer to people in foreign countries. He began such a list at once and arranged exchanges as he traveled across Europe. Today, as he envisioned, the USDA's National Arboretum conducts an exchange of seeds and plants with three hundred individuals and institutions in other countries, the most extensive plant distribution program in the world.[1]

Meyer then traveled to the quiet and charming old town of Angers to investigate the problem of crown gall in apple trees that nurseries exported to America. Though he conferred with thirteen nurserymen, they refused to admit that the disease was a problem, fearing that their export trade would suffer. Continuing his study in Orléans, Meyer again met nurserymen who denied that crown gall infested their apple trees. In order to elicit the information that he needed, Meyer held a conference and deliberately described varieties that appeared resistant as especially subject to crown gall. His ruse worked. The nurserymen quickly corrected him, thereby admitting the existence of the disease and giving him an opportunity to glean the facts he sought.

That assignment completed, Meyer left for Berlin. The Berlin Botanical Garden and the celebrated Spaeth Nurseries offered him a variety of plant material to study. Spaeth readily agreed to exchange with the USDA, since he wanted the Chinese globular-headed willow and pyramidal poplar. Meyer considered the geographic arrangement of material at the Berlin Botanical Garden ineffective, but he reserved his most severe criticism for the "despotic" director of the new Dahlem Botanical Garden. Not only was the garden divided geographically, but the director allowed no one to take photographs and permitted no children under the age of ten to enter. "This last direction is semi-barbaric," Meyer commented after he saw a couple with a child excluded. Worst of all, the garden was closed on Sundays and holidays. Most men had to work six days a week and could not afford to take a day off. "I hope the Berlin public will raise a howling protest against these outrageous rules," he wrote indignantly.

Though the Russian government delayed replying to his request for permission to explore in Central Asia, Meyer did receive letters from his former interpreters in Russian Poland and in Turkestan. The man who had worked with him in eastern Siberia offered to go with him to Saint Petersburg. Meyer also heard from his Chinese interpreter, Chow-hai Ting, who was in Kashgar (Kashi). When his permits and passport finally seemed to be in order, Meyer left Berlin for Breslau (Wroclaw), Poland.

In the eight weeks following, he gradually learned that he could accomplish nothing quickly in Russia. With his former interpreter, he traveled across eastern Poland. At the Russian frontier, officials rejected their passports, but their baggage went on to Saint Petersburg. When Meyer returned to Breslau to ask the American consul for help, he learned that Russia prohibited possession of firearms and levied heavy taxes on cameras. Because he had packed both, he wired the authorities, requesting the return of his baggage. After six days with no reply, he left Breslau without his luggage.

At the customs house in Saint Petersburg, he found the vouchers, seed bags, and medicines that he had shipped from Liverpool, but three days passed before officials would release them. Between 10:00 A.M. and 3:00 P.M. on one day twenty-five different people handled his papers, requiring him to sign five documents and pay a twenty-ruble tax. He then spent five days having passports visaed by two branches of the Police Department, the civil authorities, and the Department for Foreign Travelers. "Russia is ridden by bureaucratic and autocratic rules," he observed. His lost baggage finally arrived after twelve days in transit from Warsaw.

Russian authorities repeatedly delayed approval of his application to undertake botanical exploration in Turkestan, to carry firearms, and to take photographs. They asked him to provide a detailed itinerary giving specific dates. He complied. After three more weeks, they requested his exact route from Andizhan to the Chinese frontier, even though only one road existed. A week later they wanted information about his guides. That they may have expected a bribe did not occur to him.

Though the bureaucracy made his trip difficult, individuals received Meyer graciously at the Imperial Botanical Garden, the Agriculture Department, and the Agricultural Museum in Saint Petersburg. Language posed no barrier, for many of the botanists and agronomists could speak either English, French, or German. The herbarium at the botanical garden offered a rich collection of the flora of Central Asia and provided valuable information about the products of the Caucasus. At the Imperial Botanical Garden he met men interested in exchanging seed lists with the USDA, and he began such a list by sending the department several pages of notes about desirable plants. From Saint Petersburg he also sent to Washington five packages of cuttings of trees and shrubs, accompanied by the customary inventory cards.

By December the daylight hours in the capital began at 9:00 A.M. and ended at 3:00 P.M. By Christmas Eve daylight lasted only five hours. Everyone felt the "deadening effect" of the long nights. Though many murders and robberies occurred, instead of patrolling streets the police searched hotels and residences for forbidden literature and weapons. Eighty people had already been arrested in hotels when a police officer questioned Meyer a few days after Christmas and made notes of where he came from, where he was going, how much money he had, and so on. "Russia is about a century behind time," he told Dorsett, "and one is subjected to all sorts of red tape."

As 1909 ended, authorities finally granted permission for Meyer to travel to Russian Turkestan with his interpreter and an assistant and to carry his revolver and camera. He left Saint Petersburg for Moscow (Moskva) on January 1. With the temperature at −20°F, he tried to "be careful of his ears" and to avoid touching metal because "one could leave his skin behind." But the strong wind did not keep him indoors. He visited the Kremlin where he saw cannon from the Napoleonic Wars and observed a strange mixture of old towers and onion-shaped domes beside modern houses and stores. Since the Russians did not permit him to move about Moscow freely, he could not venture farther. Snow and ice prevented his exploring the Moscow Arboretum, but the botanical garden and the agricultural college provided information that he needed about alfalfas. During his last few days in Moscow, he became aware of a "reign of terror," the police arresting people "right and left." His interpreter and his assistant "were held up by these guardians of the peace." He wondered, prophetically, how long the downtrodden people would accept this treatment.

Though he left Moscow on January 6, he did not arrive at Sevastopol until the ninth, "for trains go slow in Russia." After visiting the large military cemetery, in "mild 40-degree weather" he climbed rocky cliffs near the city searching for wild alfalfa. There he found a privet (*Ligustrum vulgare*) that has consistently withstood cold winters and drought, even at North Platte, Nebraska, and is one of the best adapted to the rigors of the upper Midwest.[2] Postal clerks in Sevastopol were puzzled about the location of Washington and bank tellers took two hours to cash Meyer's letter of credit, but he managed nevertheless to send the department a large package that contained seeds of the privet, millet, fodder plants, and a new Bulgarian cabbage.

He hired carts on January 14 and began the four-day trip to Yalta, collecting seeds and roots along the way. Though he traveled through hail and rain, at Yalta mild weather made his work pleasant, and he soon mailed nineteen packages to America. These included strange algae and a red fungus for W. A. Murrill at the New York Botanical Garden and herbarium material to be divided with the Arnold Arboretum. For the entomologists he sent scales, cocoons, strange galls, and caterpillar's eggs. This package created a small sensation when it reached Dr. L. O. Howard in Washington with live caterpillars escaping from their confinement.

At the Imperial Botanical Garden at Nikita, the head gardener agreed to exchange with the USDA. Meyer took a large quantity of olive cuttings there, soaking his clothes as he worked in heavy rain. Though Fairchild wanted more information about these large, cold-resistant olives, Meyer explained that the Russians knew only that these trees were survivors from ancient Greek plantations.

Returning to Yalta, he tried to mail eleven packages of olive cuttings to Chico to be tested by Robert L. Beagles, the newly appointed superintendent, who had worked with Dorsett from dawn to dusk to create the Chico Plant Introduction Garden in 1904. Postal officials in Yalta shocked Meyer by locating Washington in Germany. Three or four clerks conferred before they finally decided to accept his packages. That task completed, with his interpreter and assistant, he set out by steamer for Gagri under a full moon. After a beautiful three-day journey along the shore of the Black Sea, he reached the Russian province of Georgia in the Caucasus.

Bridge to Asia

The Caucasus
FEBRUARY TO MAY, 1910

ME Y E R enjoyed his four months in the Caucasus. He liked the friendly Georgians, admired the beautiful scenery, and collected a variety of fine fruits, nuts, and grains. On the shore of the Black Sea at Gagri (Gagra) "towering mountains rise splendidly back of us." The mountain peaks were snow covered, but wild cyclamen, violets, primroses, snowdrops, and scillas were blooming in the valleys. Professor von Waldheim of Saint Petersburg had asked Meyer to convey his greetings to the prince of Oldenburg, the most distinguished resident of Gagri. The prince took an interest in Meyer's work and offered two armed guards to accompany him on the four-day journey to Sukhum. Since Meyer had learned that "hold-ups and plunder" were common along his route, he accepted the prince's offer.

Traveling on foot with his interpreter and assistant, accompanied by the guards on horseback, Meyer encountered no brigands. They passed through varied terrain — wild and rugged regions, forests of beeches, and valleys full of alders. He found Georgia "a wonderfully beautiful land, rivaling California in its diversity." One night they slept at the celebrated monastery at Novai Avon where hundreds of monks maintained fine olive plantations.

Arriving at Sukhum in heavy rain, they dried their wet clothes at an inn. Meyer discovered that he could not cash his letter of credit at the local bank; he had difficulty even exchanging gold. But he had greater success at an agricultural experiment station near Sukhum where staff members were willing to exchange seeds with the USDA. He sent some of their bulletins to Washington along with nine varieties of pomegranates, five kinds of hazelnuts, seeds of Turkish tobacco, olives, and parcels of entomological material. In Sukhum he also found a promising ornamental, an evergreen hawthorn, now known as *Crataegus meyeri*. During a side trip to Sinape, Meyer collected grape cuttings and scions of pears and apples and persuaded growers to exchange their products for American pecans, hardy citrus fruits, cotton, corn, and sorghum.

Meyer's party took a steamer from Sukhum to Batum near the border of Turkey, arriving the next day in a drenching rain. Five successive rainy days followed, but for Meyer the clouds lifted when the American consul gave him letters from all over the globe, the first mail he had received since he had left Saint Petersburg six weeks before. While rain continued to pour, he packed his collection and sent the department twenty-eight bundles along with the usual notes. The grapes he considered the most important, but he also included apples, hazelnuts, almonds, raisins, chick-peas, and wheat. In addition, he mailed herbarium material to be "shared liberally" with Sargent, soil samples, and strange fungi.

He traveled by rail from Batum to the Imperial Domain at Chakva to see bamboo and tea plantations. Bamboo growing on the red clay hillsides yielded lumber, poles for scaffolding, and water pipes. Light but strong furniture already was being made from plants set out only fifteen years earlier, and the demand for bamboo products exceeded supply. The success of this enterprise raised his hopes that the bamboo he had brought from China would produce attractive furniture for children's rooms, sun rooms, and porches in America.

After he reached Tiflis (Tbilisi) at the beginning of March, he made the capital of Georgia his headquarters for two months. Situated where the Koer (Kura) River cuts through the surrounding high mountains, homes and beautiful churches perched on a mountainside high above the rocky shore of the river. Shops sold Persian and Armenian handwork made by craftsmen who worked in the streets, women carried water in jugs on their heads, and little donkeys brought fruits and vegetables to the markets. Though people of many nationalities lived in Tiflis, few spoke any Western language. As usual after a journey, Meyer's first task was mailing the department his collection including ten packages of scions and budwood of native apples and cherries, cuttings of grapes, and rooted wild almonds. The local post office seemed even less efficient than those in the Crimea, and he had to complete six or eight forms for each parcel that he mailed. "Privately the people are extremely kind," he told Fairchild, "but officially — I better be silent until some other time."

Both Dorsett and Fairchild wrote encouraging news. Additional acreage was being devoted to Meyer's Chinese persimmon and Sargent's prediction that it would be worth $100,000 to the American public promised to prove accurate. Fairchild suggested that Russian officials had delayed Meyer at Saint Petersburg for such a long time because they had thought that his name was Jewish. Meyer disagreed. Informed people had told him that he was delayed because he had failed to offer "some smaller and larger notes to those with whom I had to deal. I consider that such a low method that I never attempted it."

He described the bounty of the Caucasus with enthusiasm and wished that he could remain there a year to study the fine plants and to climb the mountains. A. C. Rollow, director of the Tiflis Botanical Garden, agreed to exchange seeds and publications with the USDA and helped Meyer to gather a fine collection. In addition to a large box of grains, Meyer sent the department beans, chick-peas, cuttings of fruit trees, melon seeds, dried apricots, and samples of coffee made from ground soybeans. He also included a new peony and a peculiar eggplant for Fairchild's uncle, Byron Halstead of Rutgers. At the Caucasian branch of the Russian Department of Agriculture, he had a lengthy conference in German with the director, followed by conversations with one botanist in French and with another in English. "To fly from German to French to English with a little Latin and Russian thrown in," he wrote Dorsett, "makes one a trifle tired."

After he had mailed his collection, he prepared for the first of several journeys beyond Tiflis. For a short trip southwest to Yerivan, the capital of Armenia, he needed both Armenian and Tatar interpreters. Near the borders of Turkey and Iran, he barely escaped being arrested by suspicious local officials "for looking with my field glasses at some scenery." When he returned to Tiflis, his assistant's passport had expired. "We are as usual in trouble with the authorities here," he commented. Despite these setbacks, his harvest from Armenia included thirty-one selections of grapes, plums, a rare black raisin, hazelnuts, black barley, and onions, as well as shells for the Smithsonian Institution.

On his ten-day trip to Elizavetpol in Azerbaidzhan, one of the wheels of his springless cart struck a rock and the cart overturned. "I am bruised here and there," he wrote Fairchild, "but will soon be all right again." Evidently his injuries were more serious than his description implied. Answering Fairchild's anxious query twelve weeks later, he admitted that his left shoulder still ached considerably when he moved his arm. People in Elizavetpol entertained him hospitably and gave him cuttings of various fruits, including the true Paradise apple (*Malus pumila*) from its native habitat. His journey yielded seven boxes of roots, six different alfalfas, and entomological material, in addition to the cuttings and scions.

Though he had been in Tiflis for weeks, Meyer had received no mail. When a large number of letters finally arrived in late April, he learned that the delay had resulted from a misunderstanding. The postal authorities at Tiflis mistakenly thought that the American consul at Batum had wired them to return Meyer's mail; therefore, they sent it back to Batum each time it came. "Now I find that the Russian postal officials mixed up the names of

Meyer and Schnaider, they resembling somewhat one another." One of Fairchild's delayed letters asked how he could secure ginger rhizomes from Shantung Province in China. Meyer sent him the names and addresses of six missionaries in Shantung, ranking them in order from the most likely to the least likely to succeed. The Seed and Plant Introduction bulletins that Fairchild had sent pleased him especially; he noticed with pleasure that "my observations occupy a good bit of space."

In reply to an accumulation of seven letters from Dorsett, Meyer revealed his thoughts about the nature of plant exploration: "Some day the work of an agricultural explorer will have to be split between a trained photographer, an economic botanist, and an administrative clerk. Such men have to have the knowledge of a few languages, besides being of hardy and happy dispositions. . . . My work is primarily pioneering work. One acquires knowledge by bits and pieces. We are only cutting out a few steps in the mountain of knowledge and others have to mount by our steps."

Before going to the northern Caucasus at the end of April, Meyer packed and mailed sixteen bags of seeds, long blue raisins, pistachio nuts for Swingle, wheat for Carleton, photographs, lichens, galls, and scales; then he left on foot with his interpreter for Pyatigorsk. As they moved north, at high altitudes snow covered the ground. Meyer admired the matchless scenery and collected herbarium material, alfalfas, and clovers. When he and his interpreter were caught in a snowstorm at seven thousand feet their whiskers froze, but soon afterward they descended to green valleys where wild pears, apples, plums, and cherries were blooming. After passing through Vladikavkaz, they reached Pyatigorsk, completing a splendid trip.

Meyer went to Pyatigorsk because he hoped to persuade Edward Ryssel, a plantsman who had traveled in Russian and Chinese Turkestan and parts of Mongolia, to act as his interpreter for the remainder of the expedition. After lengthy bargaining about salary and clothing allowance, Ryssel agreed to meet Meyer in Baku on June 1. When a week-long celebration of Easter ended and banks and post offices reopened, Meyer mailed the department twenty-eight packages of plant material collected on the journey from Tiflis. His otherwise pleasant trip was suddenly interrupted when authorities realized that he had been in Russia exactly six months and therefore must have his passport renewed immediately. Officials forced him to return at once to Vladikavkaz. After arriving there at midnight "against my wish," he was waiting for the government office to open early the next morning. Because the "necessary — or rather unnecessary — formalities" lasted the entire day, he had to remain there another night. After experiences like this, in reply to his father's inquiry about whether the people of the Caucasus were "better" than the Chinese, he answered emphatically, "No, not at all."[1]

During the next five days he and his interpreter traveled to Derbent to examine fine grapes and then followed the shore of the Caspian Sea to the port of Baku in Azerbaidzhan. At that point his interpreter had to return to Saint Petersburg because his permit was about to expire. As Meyer waited eight days for Ryssel to join him, he had leisure to consider his plans for the future. He was sure that he would never choose to live in Washington: "Too hot and humid a summer clime, too mild a winter, and too many government parasites," he wrote A. J. Pieters. "Some of these days I want to make me a home somewhere. There are so many places to choose from—Massachusetts for intellectual surroundings, Michigan for its kind people, California for scenic conditions. I am, like all of us, seeking happiness in my own way; not finding it, of course, but only trying to find it, like every other mortal soul."

News from Washington, as usual, combined "the sweet nut and the bitter shell." Dr. Walter Van Fleet considered Meyer's Tangsi cherry especially valuable and was attempting to combine its early-fruiting characteristic with the size and taste of American cherries. Meyer appreciated Dorsett's picture of the cherry tree in bloom, as well as two superb photographs of his hardy yellow rose. Fairchild requested twelve more tins of the roasted soybean coffee. He had served it to Mrs. Fairchild and Mrs. Bell without their realizing that it was not "the ordinary coffee used by our family."[2] On the other hand, some of Meyer's packages had failed to reach Washington, and both Dorsett and Fairchild wrote of a "beastly smut" that had developed on the Chinese bamboo.

From Baku Meyer dispatched five bundles of alfalfa and a large case containing grain, dried fruits, legumes, and sixty-nine herbarium specimens. He also sent the Smithsonian Institution a fossilized ram's horn, a fossil snail, a copper ornament from a prehistoric grave, and pottery from a grave in Samarkand.

Just as his Russian interpreter arrived in Baku, Meyer received a letter from his former Chinese interpreter, Chow-hai Ting. Ting had left Tashkent, planning to return to his home in Peking, but he had become ill at Khotan (Hoten). At the end of six months, he had exhausted his funds. Meyer sent him money and assured him that he might "be of value yet to me when I arrive in Chinese territory." On May 30 Meyer and Ryssel left Baku by steamer and crossed the Caspian Sea to Russian Turkestan.

Delay and Frustration

Russian Turkestan
JUNE TO OCTOBER, 1910

W H E N Meyer and Ryssel landed at Krasnovodsk in Russian Turkestan, police officers and "gendarmes" checked their passports and allowed them to proceed by rail to Kizyl-Arvat. Several days later, near Bacharden, Meyer hired Armenian cartmen who professed to know the countryside. After they had ventured into the mountainous region to the south, darkness forced them to camp not far from the Persian (Iranian) frontier because they had become hopelessly lost. Meyer collected a variety of unusual plants and a "goodly pile" of herbarium material before going on to Ashkhabad. By that time he realized that he had made a mistake in hiring his new interpreter. Though Ryssel knew plants and had traveled widely in Central Asia, he could no longer see clearly and he could not walk great distances.

Turkestan did not impress Meyer favorably after the verdant Caucasus. At 8:00 A.M. the temperature registered 100°F; by midday it could reach 120°F. In the hot and dry climate, trees required irrigation if they were to survive. Even water for bathing was not readily available, though dust, heat, and vermin made frequent washing a necessity. Because of hot summers and cold winters with high winds, the vegetation lacked variety. Caravans of camels brought cucumbers and apricots from Persia, but the local markets offered inferior vegetables and fruit.

Four days in Ashkhabad included one "lost" day, a Russian holiday, "of which they keep 38 a year." Meyer visited the local experiment station during the absence of the director, but a subordinate hesitated to allow a foreigner to look around without written permission from the police. The next day the police summoned Meyer to appear at their headquarters, delaying his departure for Merv. The captain asked whether he really was a botanist and warned that under no consideration would he be granted permission to go to the frontier of Afghanistan.

After an exceedingly hot trip, Meyer and Ryssel arrived at Merv (Mary) in time for the weekly market day. Fruits and vegetables growing at the edge of the desert were of poor quality, but "Turkomans, Afghanistanese, Kurghisians, and many other wild-looking inhabitants of this region" fascinated Meyer. In the town park he saw for the first time the Kashgar elm (*Ulmus carpinifolia*, formerly *U. campestris*, var. *umbraculifera*). He felt sure that settlers in the American Southwest would appreciate the dense foliage and the striking umbrella shape of this tree.

Meyer and Ryssel traveled by cart the following day to examine alfalfa and cotton that colonies of German immigrants were growing at the edge of the desert. By this time Ryssel's vision had deteriorated so greatly that he fell into ditches unless Meyer guided him. As they crossed the desert, Meyer observed tens of thousands of acres covered with camel's thorn (*Alhagi* sp.) that not only provided food for camels and fuel, but also acted as a sand binder and enriched the soil. Late that night they arrived at the German colonies where Meyer hired a young farmer who loved mountains to accompany him on his journey. The next morning he inspected fine fields of alfalfa and less successful plantings of cotton which had to be flooded in dry seasons. Ancient canals, said to be three thousand years old, irrigated the fields.

A few days later he left Merv with his two assistants. Near Chardchui (Chardzhou) they came upon some of the world's finest melons growing in almost pure sand. After arranging to send the USDA seeds of the twelve best varieties, Meyer traveled to Bokhara (Bukhara) where local officials questioned the validity of his permit to take photographs. The political agent grudgingly allowed him to photograph botanical subjects when accompanied by an official representative; however, Meyer had to pay the salary and expenses of that official. Faced with many restrictions, he limited his wanderings to the grain market in Old Bokhara before setting out with his two assistants for Samarkand.

When he reached Samarkand, though he spoke only a little Russian and had no knowledge of the Sart language, Meyer was traveling alone. His German assistant had returned home reluctantly because he received word that a horse had seriously injured the man he had left in charge of his farm. Ryssel had left for Pyatigorsk when his eyesight and general health completely failed in the intense heat. "To go with a stranger in some out-of-the-way places with the necessarily large amount of money I generally have with me is not a safe proceeding," he admitted to Fairchild. Despite problems in the field, he enjoyed the ancient and beautiful city of Samarkand and did not envy the "desk people" in Washington. "I would rather die than change places; I still shiver when I think of my forced captivity last summer in sultry Washington, writing away on a bulletin. Here I have a feeling I am of greater use to my fellow men than when sitting at a desk in a sweatbox of an office."

When Fairchild wrote that he missed Meyer's visits to In the Woods and described Meyer's Korean lily that had produced eight beautiful blooms in his garden, that beloved place seemed near for a few minutes: "I see Mori religiously weeding and you mixing cement for a permanent cold-bed, and Mrs. Fairchild tells us that tea is ready. . . . And then all of a sudden I look out of my window and there I am in quiet Samarkand. And a Turkoman passes by hawking black currants and cherries, shouting their names in Russian—'Achorny smarodnaia ee vishna!' Life is so very strange and none of us really knows for what we have to go all through it."

For more than a week he looked for an interpreter and a guide. He wanted to search the Hissar Mountains south of Samarkand for nuts, fruits, and leguminous plants, but he knew that he must have at least one reliable man with him. By the first of July he had found an interpreter who spoke German and Russian and was willing to "rough it" in the mountains. Three days later he hired a guide and secured permission from the chief of police to begin his journey.

He arrived at Pendzhikent at 10:00 P.M. the next evening. There he conferred with the acting chief of police and received a permit to proceed. Since no trails for carts existed in the Hissar Mountains, he hired three horsemen and six horses to carry baggage. In the morning they traveled across a dry plateau where hordes of locusts were devouring all the vegetation; by afternoon they were climbing the mountains; at 9:00 P.M. they reached a small village five thousand feet above sea level. After eating very little supper, they slept on the porch of a temple. The next morning, having passed through a wild valley where a river flowed from the mountains in a raging torrent, they scaled a dangerously steep mountainside. At sunset, at an elevation of ten thousand feet, they found a Sart encampment near a beautiful lake fed by snow from the mountains. Masses of junipers, mountain ash, barberries, and yellow roses grew near the lake. Though the mountainside was free of snow from May until September, the air felt cold to Meyer after weeks on the hot plains, and he gladly accepted an invitation to sleep in a tent made of carpets.

During the next two days they climbed mountains where descending proved more dangerous than ascending. Camping near a stream in the evening, the weary men found little food to supplement the canned sausages they carried. The few inhabitants of the mountains could sell them only sour milk and bread made of pea flour. Their guide, who was "addicted to strong drink," became sullen. Meyer nevertheless admired the wild rocky scenery as they traveled along precipices where each of the six horses had to be led by two men to prevent an accident.

While he was collecting the Siberian bush cherry (*Prunus prostrata*) at about 5:00 P.M. on July 11, Meyer was surprised to see a caravan of twenty people on horseback. These travelers over roads generally used only by natives happened to be the Russian adminstrator of the district, accompanied by the chief of police from Pendzhikent, local chiefs, guards, and scouts. The administrator asked to see Meyer's papers and commented that his pass was not sufficiently detailed, but he allowed Meyer and his party to proceed. Half an hour later a rider overtook them with a message. The administrator had decided that they should go no further. Meyer sent his interpreter to say that they had permission from Saint Petersburg to explore in that region; therefore, he would proceed and would report the incident to the embassy if he were stopped. The interpreter returned with a warning that the administrator would have him arrested in the next village and sent to Samarkand under guard. This time Meyer went to see the administrator personally and learned that the acting chief of police at Pendzhikent had failed to enter on his pass the date and number of his permit from Saint Petersburg. Instructed to remain where he was until a messenger could go to Samarkand to investigate, Meyer explained that he could not wait there for ten days because his caravan of men and horses cost him fifteen or twenty rubles a day. When he suggested instead that he return by another route, the administrator agreed.

The next morning Meyer and his men took the only alternate route north. The road, one of the worst that he had ever seen, wound along the roaring Zarafshan River, sometimes at water level and sometimes several hundred feet above. At unusually hazardous points, Meyer hired natives to act as porters because he could not risk losing baggage that contained passports, a thousand rubles in paper money, and his letters of credit. In the rich valley of the Zarafshan River they passed orchards of mulberries, apricots, and walnuts. Two days later they traveled across mountains again, climbing rocky cliffs and descending precipices. During the trip Meyer collected herbarium specimens of pistachio and almond trees, maples, and junipers. At night his party occasionally found shelter from a strong wind on the porch of a mosque. The inhabitants of the mountain villages spoke Sart, Uzbek, Kirghiz, Farsi, and many local dialects.

Though Meyer had planned to be away a month, he returned to Pendzhikent after an absence of just ten days. The acting chief of police had to accept the blame for the omissions that made Meyer's permit unacceptable. Since Meyer had paid the horsemen a hundred rubles in advance, he asked for a refund of the unearned balance. When the three men refused to return any part of the money, he enlisted the aid of the police and a judge and recovered all except twelve rubles of the unearned amount. In the meantime his guide became "dead drunk" and the whole affair turned out to be "tragi-comical."

As soon as he had settled matters at Pendzhikent, Meyer returned by cart to Samarkand. There the governor gave him a pass granting him "full rights to travel in the same district I had been closed out of," but his hope of exploring the Hissar Mountains ended when his interpreter declined to undertake another exhausting journey. Though Meyer had witnesses to their agreement that the interpreter would work for him for a month, he did not insist on enforcing the contract, remembering an old Dutch saying, "It is a bad job catching hares with an unwilling dog." For a week he looked for another interpreter, but rumors of his rugged journey hindered his search. As soon as he had engaged a replacement he left Samarkand, for he feared that his new interpreter would hear discouraging stories of "mountain climbing difficulty."

By the time he reached Tashkent a week later, his new interpreter had become intoxicated and had proved so incompetent that Meyer had discharged him. "I have had experiences with non-hardy fellows, with a swindler, with some hard drinkers, and with very incompetent help," he wrote Dorsett. He nevertheless sent the department herbarium material and seeds of wheat, millet, apricots, and legumes and mailed soil samples, dried citrus fruits for Swingle, and fungi, scales, and galls for the entomologists. For scientists at the Smithsonian Institution he added shells, a bottle of beetles, and a dried mouse from the desert. "A specialist at the Smithsonian will probably be delighted with it," he commented. Evidently his judgment was correct, for he received letters from two departments of the Smithsonian, thanking him for the fossils from Samarkand and the shells, beetles, and mouse from Tashkent.[1]

Two weeks later he was still looking for an "intelligent and hardy man of good habits." Most of the inhabitants of Tashkent were illiterate, and Meyer became discouraged as he worried about the waste of time and money. "I would like to fly off to regions where I can find more intelligent and social surroundings," he told Fairchild. "Before I appear somewhere in eastern China, I will have gone through many a lonesome day. This land could supply Western Europe with early melons, grapes, and minor fruits, but Russia sleeps as yet." Since he would soon be going to Chinese Turkestan, he decided to solve his problem by sending money to Kashgar (Kashi) to his former Chinese interpreter, Chow-hai Ting, and asking him to come to Tashkent.

Two more weeks passed before Ting arrived. In the meantime Meyer mailed his photographs and negatives to Washington, expressed concern about a missing warrant for $5,000 for his expenses, and mentioned that "cholera is at present among us, and maleria is rather strong." Though he had been in Tashkent for a month, he had not found an assistant. The prolonged delay had been depressing, and he did not feel well physically. When he finally hired a German-born assistant who spoke Russian and

Turki, he still could not leave the disease-ridden city because he was having difficulty securing the necessary papers for Chow-hai Ting. After two more weary weeks, he received the permits that he needed "with the assistance of loose cash," a method that he abhorred and a measure of his desperation.

Feeling that a journey through the countryside would restore his health, Meyer left Tashkent on September 12 with his interpreters and twelve hundred pounds of baggage. After three days of traveling through rice fields, fruit orchards, and deserts, they reached Khojent (Leninabad). There the inhabitants were celebrating a religious feast. Meyer's small party could not find food or even a cup of tea "as long as the sun is in the skies." They were forced to eat the main meal of the day at 11:00 P.M., an inconvenient hour for travelers.

For three days they journeyed across stony alkaline deserts, sometimes ankle deep in sand. Gray and brown coats of dust covered the men and their baggage when they came to Kokand. Russian innkeepers, mistaking them for "robbers returning with loot," at first refused to accommodate them. After surrendering their passports, they found lodging and bathed for the first time in seven days. Meyer then hurried to the market to inspect fruit and grain but was disappointed to find little that was new.

He and his men left Kokand by train for Margelan in Ferghana Province. Though he called on the chief of police and the governor there, he could not secure a permit for either his German-born assistant or his Chinese interpreter to accompany him on a journey to the adjacent mountains. Since cholera was prevalent in the town, they were unusually careful about their food and drinking water. Seventeen deaths from this dreadful disease had been reported in one day, but the natives concealed many cases and drank water from polluted places "as if there were not such things as bacilli." Under those conditions, they did not linger at Margelan.

The police promptly summoned Meyer when he reached Andizhan. After cross-examination, officials decreed that his German-born assistant could remain, but not Chow-hai Ting. "We had to whisk him away to some native inn," Meyer wrote Fairchild. "The moment one leaves the railroad, questions are asked, and for every little excursion special permits are necessary." Donald Culross Peattie must have been thinking of this phase of Meyer's travels when he wrote that "stout-hearted Meyer was insulted, assaulted, denied entrance, denied exit, and arrested more times, probably, than any other man in the service."[2]

By early October, Meyer felt eager to leave Russian territory where so many obstacles had frustrated his attempts at plant exploration. With Ting ill from a light attack of cholera, they left Andizhan for Osh, a town about fifty miles from the border of China. The $5,000 warrant for expenses had not arrived, but Meyer used his own money to finance his journey into an area far removed from highways and railroads. Despite intoxicated carters, the travelers reached Osh and prepared for the eleven-day journey to Kashgar. "Robbers on the road murdered some people these last two nights, but a botanical collector is generally exempted from these annoyances," he assured Fairchild. After hiring eight packhorses to carry their baggage, they left Osh on the ninth of October.

CHAPTER 15

Privation and Postponement

Chinese Turkestan
OCTOBER, 1910, TO FEBRUARY, 1911

MEYER'S party encountered no brigands during the eleven-day journey to Kashgar, but the weather was uncomfortably cold in the mountains and the arid countryside nearly devoid of vegetation. Except for artemisia and salt bushes, Chinese Turkestan appeared barren and desolate. (What then was called Chinese Turkestan is now the Sinkiang Autonomous Region, Xinjiang Uygur Zizhiqu, China's northwestern frontier.) When they reached the "dirty and shabby" town of Kashgar, Meyer applied for a Chinese passport, called on the English and Russian consuls, and visited Swedish missionaries who provided helpful information about local products.

After three days of negotiations he persuaded the post office to accept five large packages addressed to the American consul at Saint Petersburg. To mail parcels directly to Washington was impossible. Customs officials insisted that he pack "every little bit under the very eyes of the officials so that nothing could be smuggled in!" In addition to four packages of entomological specimens, he included five varieties of almonds for William A. Taylor, plums for U. P. Hedrick at Geneva, wild roses for Walter Van Fleet, twenty kinds of melons for testing in the Southwest, and a wild alfalfa for specialists in fodder plants.

The British consul at Kashgar, George Macartney, invited Meyer to join him on a trip to Yarkand (Shache). Meyer accepted at once, realizing that this journey would offer a fine opportunity to collect in an isolated area southeast of Kashgar. Traveling in a caravan of carts and horses, he seldom had a chance to enjoy Macartney's company. When oases occasionally broke the monotony of the journey through sandy or stony deserts, he noticed fields surrounded by hedges of Russian olives (*Elaeagnus angustifo-*

lia), "a glorious sight, the bright orange-red fruits contrasting beautifully with the silvery foliage."

At Yarkand, a more attractive town than Kashgar, the travelers found lodging at a good inn. Meyer called on the Chinese magistrate and visited Swedish missionaries, seed stores, gardens, and fruit markets where he saw fine nectarines and peaches. Chow-hai Ting decided that he did not feel well enough to undertake the difficult journey into the mountains south of Yarkand unless he could ride in a cart and have wood for a fire at night. Meyer could not guarantee these luxuries; therefore, he set out for Khotan (Hotan) accompanied by a native guide and his German-born assistant, who spoke Russian and Turki.

After leaving Yarkand, they spent several days crossing "a most abominable piece of desert — dreary expanses of sand and grit." The temperature plummeted at night and they shivered in the piercing cold. At the oasis of Guma (Pishan), they paused long enough to call on the Chinese magistrate and to receive him in return. During five additional days they crossed desolate gray-brown desert, varied occasionally at small oases by Russian olive hedges protecting fields from hot winds and blowing sand. Sometimes they passed ancient ruins of cities. Seen through the peculiar dusty haze that hung over the desert, they appeared unreal.

As they approached Khotan on November 20, the Akshakal, an Indian official, greeted them, for they were a little less than one hundred miles from the border of India and only a little farther from Tibet. Remembering the advice that Huntington had given him in New Haven, Meyer had brought with him a supply of watches of varying quality to present to the authorities that he met. He made the required calls on the Chinese magistrate, as well as on the Akshakal and other Indian officials, and received all their calls in return. When the local dignitaries offered him tea and sweets, he distributed gifts according to the importance of his hosts. Having discharged his obligations, he then explored Khotan. In an old cemetery he took cuttings of an ash (*Fraxinus potamophila),* hoping that it would thrive in treeless, arid, and alkaline regions in America. Near Khotan he also collected two wheats, *Triticum aestivum* 'Ak-Mecca Boogdai' and 'Kizil Boogdai'. The USDA, working with the Reclamation Service, planted thousands of seedlings of the Khotan ash on the high plains of Nevada; the wheats are still maintained in the USDA germplasm collection at Beltsville, Maryland.

After a week spent collecting grains and fruits, Meyer found a competent guide who was willing to accompany him on a difficult journey through a remote mountainous region. He left at noon with his Russo-Turki interpreter, guide, horsemen, and eight horses. The five-day journey to Khanaka exhausted them. Somewhere in the desolate region that they traversed, on November 29, 1910, Meyer's thirty-fifth birthday passed without celebration. At Khanaka, after calling on the Chinese magistrate and the Turki headman, he collected cuttings of ornamentals and fruit trees. The next day he made an all-day excursion on horseback to gather more cuttings and seeds in the surrounding countryside.

The rugged six-day journey across barren mountains from Khanaka to Karghalik (Qarghaliq or Yecheng) tested even Meyer's endurance. Though they slept in their clothes, a dense cold fog seemed to penetrate their bodies. The sun did not shine for eight successive days. Tea froze as soon as they removed it from the fire. Food was limited in quantity and poor in quality. Yet Meyer managed to collect many varieties of wheat and barley, as well as cuttings of fruit trees and ornamentals. Reaching Karghalik on a market day, he conferred with local dignitaries, bought seeds, and engaged fresh horses for the trip back to Yarkand.

When he returned to Yarkand on December 14, he paid the obligatory visits on the Akshakal and the Chinese magistrate and then packed his collection to go directly to Kashgar, for he was not planning to return by the main track. As soon as he had dispatched the seeds and cuttings, he and his men set forth again on horseback.

They plodded through heavy snow for two days and reached Yangi-hissar (Yengisar) on December 22. There Meyer took cuttings of grapes, peaches, and apricots. During three more days spent crossing a snow-covered desert under a dull gray sky, they lost count of time. All day they saw only leaden skies and falling snow; at night both the men and their horses suffered from the piercing cold. Meyer did not realize that Christmas day had come and gone until he reached Upal at 7:00 P.M. and made entries on his calendar. After receiving notables on December 26 and resting at the first good inn he had found in many weeks, Meyer hired a native guide, horsemen, and packhorses to go with him to the mountains beyond Upal.

He looked forward to leaving the snow-covered desert, but the horsemen delayed his departure until 11:00 A.M. Though the guide had hoped to reach an encampment of the nomadic Kirghiz by evening, when night fell they had to stop at the foot of Pustan Terek, unable to find any sign of an encampment. While an icy wind blew down the mountain, Meyer and his men unloaded the four packhorses and sent the two guides off on horseback to look for the Kirghiz camp. In the meanwhile they built a fire and melted snow to make tea. "You never had a cup of tea taste better than that brew we had that cold star-lit night," he told Fairchild. Since no better shelter was available, they gathered brush, built a barricade, and were about to "unroll our beds" when the native horsemen heard the sound of horses' hooves. Soon Meyer's guides arrived with a Kirghiz and fresh horses. Willingly repacking their baggage, the men sought the shelter of the nomads' tents.

After a wild ride through the night, they reached the Kirghiz camp at 11:00 P.M. The nomads kindled a blazing fire and helped their guests to brew tea. Meyer's guide managed to secure some mutton and, at 1:00 A.M., they enjoyed bowls of steaming soup. Meyer spent the following day exploring the rugged mountains in fine weather. He found the southern slopes bare, but he identified poplars, junipers, and groves of spruce (*Picea schrenkiana*) on the northern slopes. He also bought from the Kirghiz a sack of a superior variety of hull-less barley (*Hordeum vulgare*) and a yellow-flowered alfalfa that grew wild in the mountains.

They returned to the oasis of Upal in a heavy snowfall and prepared for the journey to Kashgar by way of trails used only by natives. On New Year's Day, 1911, they came to Kashgar again after an absence of two months. That holiday season had been a trying one not only for Meyer, but also for his parents, who had not heard from Frans for many weeks. Early in January Maria Hoogland wrote David Fairchild about the family's concern. Letters had come to Amsterdam from Kashgar by the time she received Fairchild's reassuring reply.

Meyer once admitted that he told Fairchild only half of the difficulties he faced on his expedition; the two-month journey through "the terrible dry mountains" south of Kashgar certainly was one of the periods when he omitted many of the unpleasant details. He was confined to bed for three days after his return to Kashgar as a result of "a good many privations" and exposure to "cold and inhospitable quarters." Though he found a large pile of mail waiting for him, he postponed writing letters and mailing his quarterly accounts and the first installment of his collection until January 18. Even when he completed his report on January 24, he admitted that "the cold and the discomfort and the troubles with men and animals are of too recent a date to give me any pleasure to describe."

After he had recovered from exposure and malnutrition, he packed nineteen bundles containing 117 parcels of cuttings, scions, and budwood and sent them to Washington through the American consul at Saint Petersburg. His parcels included hardy and drought-resistant peaches, nectarines, apricots, plums, and three kinds of pomegranates. In addition, he mailed several varieties of elms, rare poplars, and willows. Though he had found fruits, grains, legumes, and trees of possible value in Chinese Turkestan, he nevertheless concluded that this arid country was a dying land.

He had hoped to return to Russian Turkestan to collect material that he had spotted during the summer, but the Russian Consulate informed him that his pass to travel there had expired. He applied for a renewal of his permit and waited in Kashgar for an answer. Since even the best inns lacked the bare essentials for comfort, he rented unfurnished rooms for himself and his interpreters and guide, using his small trunks for tables and chairs. With a door taken off its hinges and covered with a sheet to serve as a writing table, he made himself as comfortable as possible. Snow fell nearly every day from a leaden sky. Most foreigners in Kashgar, including both of

Meyer's interpreters, became ill; he also "had a stroke of it." The native guide from Khotan felt homesick, the German-born interpreter decided to return to Tashkent at the earliest opportunity, and Ting announced that he could not continue to "rough it." Fairchild later wrote that the exploration of Chinese Turkestan "without doubt has been the most trying from the standpoint of privations that any explorer from the Department has had to endure."[1]

While Meyer waited for the Russian officials to reply, he considered the problem of choosing a route for the remaining half of his expedition. He had planned to travel to Kuldja (Gulja or Ining), then east to Lanchow, and down the Yellow River Valley to Peking. To go to Russian Turkestan, then across Siberia to Peking, and up the Yellow River Valley offered a second alternative. He also considered journeying from Kuldja to Chuguchak (Qo-qek or Dacheng) in Mongolia and then north to the Trans-Siberian Railroad. After he had selected the mountainous northern route and had reached Mongolia, he received Fairchild's letter confirming the wisdom of his choice: "In choosing routes, remember that wild forms from colder regions of the mountain slopes north of you will be extremely difficult for us to get. It will probably be many years before we get them if you do not push your exploration through into that region. . . . The work which you are do-ing is of quite as pioneer a character as that of any of the great world explorers."[2]

Though this advice came too late to help Meyer at Kashgar, other letters brought encouraging news. His October shipment of plant material had set a record because no one else had ever successfully shipped cuttings and scions from Chinese Turkestan to a foreign country. Among the issues of *Plant Immigrants*, a bulletin that reported the accomplishments of the Foreign Seed and Plant Introduction Section, Meyer observed with pride that one (no. 51) contained fourteen of his photographs. Fairchild also explained the fate of the missing $5,000 warrant for Meyer's expenses, sent to Batum on July 18 but somehow burned aboard a French steamer. Meyer hoped to cash the duplicate warrant if the bank at Kashgar "could handle such a big affair." For six months he had been using his savings to finance his expedition.

After waiting for several weeks for an answer to his request to reenter Russian Turkestan, he received a telegram saying that there were "political objections" to his returning. He had learned to expect delays, but a com-pletely negative reply surprised him. After this experience with Russian officials, he felt grateful to the Chinese authorities, who had treated him "with greatest courtesy everywhere." He therefore asked Fairchild to ex-press his appreciation to the Chinese government for the consideration shown him. In addition to his failure to secure a permit from the Russian officials, he faced other problems. His interpreter of Russian and Turki had contracted malaria, and earthquakes were causing "heavy movements" in Kashgar. The only good news he heard came from P. H. Dorsett and Peter Bisset, the department's two expert plant introducers. Bisset's report that the Central Asian herbarium material had arrived in good condition and Dorsett's expression of confidence in the success of the Chinese jujube in semiarid regions of America helped to relieve that gloomy January.

With leisure to think about his future, Meyer wondered what he would do when he could no longer explore remote regions. He asked Adrian Pieters, now at the University of Michigan, to let him know of any suitable opening in a plant breeding station or a botanical garden. "Agreeable people weigh heavier with me than salary or a spectacular position. To start a plant breeding station somewhere in the Rocky Mountains appeals to me, but the funds are not there."[3]

Early in February he packed his final shipment from Kashgar. Having noticed that the natives ate apricot kernels like almonds, he sent the department eleven varieties of sweet kernels (*Prunus armeniaca*). He also included herbarium material and seeds of alfalfa, melons, walnuts, almonds, nectarines, and plums, accompanied by the usual inventory cards. For the entomologists and pathologists he mailed lady beetles, cocoons, swellings on a poplar, fungi on a willow, puff balls, and a ground fungus from the desert. Because he had no more oiled or paraffin-coated paper for packing, he made some by mixing linseed oil with heated stearine from candles, applying the liquid to paper, and then drying it in gentle heat.

Lacking wooden cases, he mailed the twelve hundred pounds of seeds that he had collected in kerosene cans, cleaned with hot wood ashes and lined with felt. At the customs house, where the authorities watched to be sure that he did not smuggle contraband into the cans, he sewed a felt covering over each container and submitted each one to be sealed officially. Though they were badly battered when they reached Washington months later, the contents arrived in good condition. The cans contained wheat for Mark Carleton to test under irrigation in the desert; naked barleys, "beauties of their sort," for H. B. Derr, the specialist Meyer had met in South Dakota; ten varieties of rice identified in English and in Turki; and seeds of Russian olives and alfalfas.

With his collection on the way to America, he sent Fairchild a request along with news of other plant hunters in Asia. He asked Fairchild to repay the courtesies shown him by the magistrate of Yarkand, Chu-ting Wang, by receiving Wang personally when he visited Washington. In addition, he reported that MacGregor had written from Shanghai about E. H. Wilson's serious injury "when a big boulder fell on his leg." He had heard also that George Forrest had returned to England after only a year in the Salween Delta, "a bad thing to do for a good collector."

In preparation for the next phase of his expedition, Meyer obtained letters of introduction to officials in Kuldja and Chuguchak and paid fare-well calls on members of the diplomatic corps. Though Chow-hai Ting refused to attempt the dangerous trip across the Tien Shan range, the Ger-man-born interpreter of Russian and Turki agreed to go. Meyer had been treating him with quinine and he was recovering from malaria. Unable to find a competent Chinese interpreter, Meyer hired "a specimen who says he knows enough Chinese to help us out. He will be our cook also." With these companions, Meyer hoped to reach Kuldja in a month.

By February 9 he had hired a large Turki cart, a carter, and four mules, and had packed his twelve hundred pounds of baggage. He regretted the condition of his luggage, which had been "badly ruined" when the pack-horses "fell a few times in the mountains," but he could not replace broken trunks in Kashgar. As he started a challenging journey into a remote region visited by few outsiders, he reminded Fairchild that no post offices existed in the hundreds of miles between Kashgar and Kuldja or between Kuldja and Chuguchak in Mongolia. "If you do not hear from me in three months, have the British consul, George Macartney, find what has become of me. I don't expect anything bad, but a man never knows and this part of the world is very secluded."

CHAPTER 16

The Tien Shan

Chinese Turkestan and Mongolia
FEBRUARY TO MAY, 1911

F O R six monotonous days Meyer and his party traveled across the desert. At the oasis of Maral-Bashi (Maralwexi or Bachu) on February 15, all of them became violently ill from eating contaminated fish. After resting for a day, everyone except the guide recovered. Meyer used the extra time there to collect two fine winter melons. Traversing the desert seven more days brought them to Aksu (Aqsu).

They remained in Aksu for a week while Meyer completed preparations for the most challenging segment of his expedition. He hired as a guide "a rough-looking but hardy chap" who had traveled in Mongolia. The guide's dog, Shamrah, would accompany them. Since they were leaving the main road east to China and taking a rough trail north, they replaced their carts with packhorses. No supplies would be available along the way; to his twelve hundred pounds of baggage, Meyer therefore added a three-week supply of food. While he was negotiating at length with horsemen, he also received and paid "various necessary and unnecessary visits" and collected tamarisk and desert poplars that might be useful as sand binders and windbreaks in the Southwest.

He left Aksu on March 2 with his interpreter, guide, horsemen, six packhorses, and a mounted guard that the prefect of Aksu had sent to escort them. For three days they gradually ascended to an elevation of 6,650 feet. Meyer then hired a seventh horse to carry enough barley and maize to feed all the horses in snow-covered mountains for ten days. After crossing a stony plain, they entered a narrow valley surrounded by towering mountains. Even there, in the Tien Shan, Meyer collected two wheats (*Triticum aestivum* 'Kara Boogdai' and *T. turgidum*) that the USDA still maintains in the germplasm collection at the Agricultural Research Center at Beltsville,

Maryland. At eight thousand feet Meyer bought from the natives an unusual black hull-less barley, their only crop. He and his party spent one night in a mud hut encircled by rocky mountains and heard the cold wind howling between boulders. The men stopped the next evening at a rest house where nothing covered the open windows. Wind whistled into the hut from the snow-covered peaks all around them, and they did not consider undressing in the bitter cold.

On March 7 they crossed a broad icy plain formed by a river that had overflowed into a valley and reached the foot of the great Mussart Glacier. Since they carried firewood with them, they did not suffer from the cold, even at an altitude of 9,700 feet. Their thoughts focused not on the temperature but on the climb across the awesome glacier the next day. Even the mounted guard worried about ascending the dreaded Muz-dawan or Ice Pass. "The glacier is a moving one," Meyer later wrote Fairchild, "and the trail across it changes perpetually; where yesterday a good crossing existed, there may be tomorrow a gaping chasm. It really is a pretty bad piece of climbing." The Chinese government maintained a small force to keep the trail in passable condition.

They ascended the glacier the next morning, using steps that the Chinese detachment had cut into the frozen surface. "One finds skeletons of horses, donkeys, and camels strewn along the trail. Our horses got over all right, but a small caravan a few hours before saw one of their horses fall into an abyss." Meyer's party risked delaying and helped to rescue the horse. Though he found the setting awe-inspiring, he admitted that "the cracking and moaning sounds heard at intervals made one feel anxious to get on terra firma." Wild pigeons and finchlike birds living on the glacier were so tame that they approached Meyer and ate crumbs of bread that he threw to them. After six hours on moving ice, at 3:00 P.M. they were on solid earth again.

Beyond the pass they scaled the steep ascent, reaching thirteen thousand feet. From that height they gazed on a panoramic view of snowy peaks, glaciers, and deep abysses. Meyer recognized the towering and unconquered twenty-four-thousand-foot Khan Tengri in the distance. At 4:30 P.M. they began the descent in deep snow. Though they knew that a rest house would provide shelter somewhere ahead, they had to stop at dusk and camp in the open. With the little remaining wood, they kindled a small fire, but the cold was fierce, "an icy wind chilling us to the bone." That night their shoes froze to their feet. No one could sleep because of the thin air and the piercing cold. At daybreak they made a two-hour forced march to the rest house. There they paused to enjoy hot tea and protection from the biting wind.

Until they descended to the timber line and entered a splended grove of towering spruce trees, the reflection of the sunlight on the snow nearly blinded them. Meyer nevertheless agreed with the Chinese who named the

Tien Shan "Heavenly Mountains." To him the forests "acted as a tonic after the dreary wastes of Central Asia." Two days later they left "the glory of the Tien Shan" behind, but he would always remember the panoramic view from the mountaintops and the splendor of the forests.[1]

Heavy snow alternated with sleet, rain, and hail for several days as they crossed a snow-covered plain. In a howling hailstorm, the guide became confused and led them in a circle until he finally located a nomad settlement at midnight. The next day Meyer scratched the snow away and "grubbed out" roots of climbing asparagus and a rare alfalfa (*Medicago platycarpa*) that the Sarts used as a food for their cattle. Though the rough trails ruined his boots, he tramped about in rain and hail gathering scions. After finding refuge in another Sart settlement, they paused for a day because of a heavy snowfall. The horses could not travel, but Meyer managed to collect scions of extremely hardy apples, apricots, and willows.

After three days in a barren region, they crossed the Tekes River by a primitive ferry and arrived at last at Kuldja (Gulja or Yining). The faithful dog, Shamrah, as well as the men, had walked every step of the way from Aksu. Though spring had begun when they left Kashgar, winter lingered on the north side of the Tien Shan. People of many nationalities speaking ten or eleven different languages inhabited the ill-kept town, nominally Chinese but really Russian. As soon as Meyer had settled at a dirty inn and called on Russian and Chinese officials, he hired horsemen and a local guide to go with him to collect in the mountains nearby.

At the end of March he mailed to the American consul at Saint Petersburg fifty-two packages of roots and cuttings with the corresponding notes and inventory cards. He included two rare poplars, willows, a hawthorn for the Arnold Arboretum, two alfalfas, and the rare climbing asparagus. For the hybridizers he sent currants, scions of hardy apples, and wild apricots "of great promise."

Meyer remained at Kuldja for a month because heavy rains and wet snow made roads impassable; nevertheless, he continued to collect whenever he could explore the countryside. As soon as buds began to swell and a few tulips, fritillarias, and corydalis bloomed, he decided to move on. Before leaving Kuldja, he sent the department herbarium specimens, ornamentals, and seeds of apples, apricots, melons, rice, barley, and alfalfas. He also mailed diseased twigs, fungi, puff balls, algae, and spider egg bags, as well as shells for a specialist at the Smithsonian and thirteen curious soil samples for E. C. Free of the U.S. Bureau of Soils.

Having shipped his collection, Meyer hired a guide and negotiated for horses in preparation for a two-week journey to Chuguchak. Accompanied by his interpreter, his guide, a caravan leader and his helper, and a mounted guard, on April 19 he left Kuldja with a caravan of six horses. Small green leaves on the trees and butterflies fluttering over the fields offered evidence that spring had begun at last. By afternoon the road had dwindled to a trail. The next day they followed a stream into the mountains where yellow tulips made the landscape bright. Meyer also noticed alfalfa, wild apricots, gnarled apple trees, and white crocus growing at six thousand feet among patches of snow. That evening they camped among spruce and aspens beside a Kirghiz settlement. At midnight Meyer woke to the sounds of dogs barking, horses neighing, sheep and goats bleating, cows bellowing, and Kirghiz shouting because a wolf had approached the encampment.

Persuading a native to guide them to the next village delayed their departure. As they followed a mountain trail later that morning, two of the packhorses slipped and fell into a stream, soaking bedrolls, clothing, paper money, medicines, and a number of watches that Meyer had intended as gifts for local officials. In the afternoon they climbed a steep mountain to a pass at an elevation of eight thousand feet. Though they had waded through icy slush earlier, the snow lay three or four feet deep on the mountaintop. Camping that evening in a sheltered nook, they dried their wet boots beside a fire of juniper and spruce. Rain fell during the night. After they broke camp at 7:00 A.M., they tramped through ice and snow and waded across a swift stream many times as they struggled to gain the 9,800-foot crest of a steep mountain. Descending the north side in deep snow caused the horses more difficulty than ascending. Several times they fell, damaging the baggage and losing the irreplaceable teakettle and a bottle of brandy carried for medical emergencies. By the end of the fourth day of the journey, they reached a village on the shore of a frozen lake. Shivering in an icy wind, they found an inn and dried their clothing, bedding, and baggage.

Hiring a guide who was willing to go with them into "a robber district" posed a problem. A Kirghiz finally agreed to accompany them, and they started their journey in a cold wind. After a few hours, the guide became frightened by his own gruesome stories of atrocities committed by outlaws in the area and "fell on his knees before me and cried and spoke about being slaughtered." When Meyer remained adamant about proceeding, the guide quietly slipped away. Meyer felt glad to be rid of him because the man had demoralized the caravan leader. The guide, however, took with him the letter of introduction from the magistrate at Kuldja. Meyer now found himself without credentials and without any companion who knew the roads "in a district considered dangerous." He nevertheless continued to "march along," guided by a map and a compass.

That afternoon they scaled a pass at 9,250 feet and found beautiful groves of spruce trees on the northern side of the mountain. In the labyrinth of mountains and valleys, they came to a Kalmuck guard house and hired a guide for the rest of the day. In the late afternoon Meyer selected a campsite in a protected ravine on the mountainside above the trail in order to avoid "dreaded robbers." As a precaution he made only a small fire for cooking supper and extinguished it before dark. Though he and his German-born interpreter from Tashkent felt secure, the caravan leader and his helper, as well as a Sart merchant who had joined them, were "in deadly fear."

About four o'clock the next afternoon, they reached a Kalmuck settlement in the region called the Bogh-dâlâh (Bogdo Ula). The chief and the head lama welcomed them and served tea, bread, butter, and sweets. When the chief invited them to his tents nearby, Meyer accepted; however, "nearby" proved to be a hard two-and-a-half-hour ride on horseback through a heavy shower. They arrived in the dark, tired and wet, wishing that they had declined this invitation. But they soon changed their minds. The chief ordered a felt tent erected for his visitors and had a sheep killed in their honor. While they waited for dinner, tea was served in the chief's tent. Meyer was surprised to see not only chairs, tables, a Russian samovar, and candles, but also beautiful Tibetan silver and embroideries. With the lamb they ate a peculiar sort of cheese and drank tea with salt, fat, and milk in it. The meal ended with brandy distilled from milk. In appreciation of his host's hospitality, Meyer gave the chief conserved fruit and a silver watch. Later he wrote Fairchild, "And that was in the dreaded Bogh-dâlâh where the Kirghiz guide had told us that men are sometimes butchered like sheep for sacrifice. These things may have occurred twenty-five years ago, but now I hardly think anything like that would happen."

The usual difficulty in finding a guide delayed their departure until the next afternoon. That night rain interrupted their rest at 3:00 A.M. After traveling in wet clothes until afternoon, they dried their clothing at a Kalmuck military post. Rain continued to pour, but Meyer climbed between boulders in order to collect a bush cherry (*Prunus prostrata*) that might prove useful in dry regions in America.

Warned by the Kalmucks of bad roads and a lack of water on the Chinese side of the frontier, he decided to cross to the Russian side even though he lacked a permit. After following a winding valley, his small party crossed arid plains, saw Lake Ebi-nor in the distance, and turned northeast into the desert. Late that afternoon they had found no water. Far away, to their surprise, they saw two men. When the men drew close, Meyer realized that they were customs guards patrolling the border. The guards, who seemed glad to meet company in that lonely area, guided Meyer and his men to a spring and spent a pleasant evening talking about the severe winters in that region. Meyer's party continued to trudge north across an alkaline plain for several days. Only artemisia and tamarisk grew in this desert country, and the mountains on their right appeared appallingly barren.

On the last day of April they left the desert and entered rolling country. Camping near Kirghiz tents that evening, they heard of robbers nearby and therefore posted a guard throughout the night. At 5:00 A.M. the brigands appeared. As soon as they learned that Meyer had "made arrangements to receive them," they left hastily before anyone fired a shot. After that adventure, Meyer's party traveled through hilly countryside for a day and then crossed a dry alkaline plain. They had found little food for a week and were hungry when they camped that evening beside the Emil River and feasted on fine fish.

Knowing that they were approaching their goal, they rose at 4:30 the next morning. For breakfast they ate leftover fish and potatoes, but the milk in their cups froze before they could drink it. After traveling until noon, they saw in the distance the tall poplars and the Chinese towers of Chuguchak. About 3:00 P.M. they reached the town and found rooms that provided such luxuries as a table and a lamp. Meyer promptly called for his many letters and read "until the wee hours of the next day."

As soon as he felt settled, he wrote Fairchild a summary of his journey from Kuldja: "Of the fourteen nights we were on the road, I was under cover only four of them, and out of the other ten, one night we were disturbed by a wolf, two nights by rain, four nights by robbers prowling about, and the remaining three we made the most of. Still it was on the whole not a bad journey, for the sheep and goats had just lambed and whenever we struck a Kalmuck or Kirghiz settlement, we were able to obtain a goodly quantity of either sweet or sour milk." He had collected herbarium material, wild apples and apricots that would tolerate excessive cold, and a bush cherry for semiarid parts of America, but he had looked in vain for promising grains. Nevertheless, at the end of this challenging trek across Chinese Turkestan he felt fortunate. "I personally have very little bad luck on my journeys," he assured Fairchild. "It seems as if the good wishes from so many people who take an interest in my work keep some sort of protective atmosphere around me."

The Altai Mountains

The Mongolian Border of Siberia
MAY TO JULY, 1911

DESPITE his rigorous journey, Meyer's enthusiasm for his career as an agricultural explorer remained unabated. "I love this work very dearly," he wrote Fairchild, "and am possessed of good health to stand the hardships connected with it. I am blessed with a good memory that enables me to live on accumulated knowledge without having access to many books or cultured people. I think I was born for the work I am engaged in now."

His long-awaited bulletin, *Agricultural Exploration in the Fruit and Nut Orchards of China*, reached him at Chuguchak (Qoqek) or Tacheng (Dacheng).[1] On the inside cover, heading the staff of the Plant Introduction Section, were the names of David Fairchild, Agricultural Explorer in Charge; P. H. Dorsett and Peter Bissett, Expert Plant Introducers; George W. Oliver, Expert Propagator; and Frank N. Meyer, Agricultural Explorer. In the ten years since he had found his first job in America in the USDA greenhouses, he had achieved recognition among the men whom he respected most. He felt "a peculiar pleasure to look at the pictures I am so familiar with and to read the text upon which I plodded so many a month."

Often a deluge of mail brought unpleasant news along with encouraging letters; at Chuguchak all the news was good. Meyer not only received word of a promotion, but also William A. Taylor's praise of the Chinese persimmon and W. F. Wright's expression of appreciation for the large quantity of herbarium material that had reached Washington. Meyer asked Fairchild to file this letter "as showing the world I really have made contributions to various herbaria and did not stick to the seeds, roots, and cuttings only, as I was accused of the first years." In addition to supportive letters from Washington, C. W. Janssen, the Dutch philanthropist, praised

Meyer and the USDA for "far-sightedness in exploring far corners of the globe for useful products and putting those things at the disposal of the world."

Perhaps it was Janssen's letter that caused Meyer to ponder the value of agricultural exploration: "It really is a noble work we are doing, Mr. Fairchild. You in an office directing things, I out in the wilds, others in propagating gardens, some keeping records; it is all good work. And the ultimate results farther reaching perhaps than we ourselves now realize. While the original cost of introducing Durum wheat didn't exceed ten thousand dollars, the present annual value of this crop alone is estimated to be thirty million dollars. Who knows what greater marvels may be found among our introductions?"

To the Janssens he confided his thoughts and hopes. After having trouble with passports or interpreters or suffering privations, he confessed thaț he would sometimes say to himself, "Is it not enough now?" But sunny days always followed and then he said, "Well, it was not that bad." After his fortieth birthday he planned to take a long trip to the Netherlands and the Dutch East Indies, and then he hoped to supervise a plant testing station in the American West "where blue lakes and snow-covered mountains will give me inspiration." If the United States government would subsidize his work, he could develop new varieties of fruits to fill the needs of people who lived in dry or cold regions.

Replying to Fairchild's comments on the "medieval restrictions" on his movements in Russian Turkestan, Meyer expressed his belief that "the intense fear of the English to have Russia as a neighbor to China keeps the whole of Central Asia in an absurd state of seclusion. All these little bits of buffer states minimize the danger of possible Russian invasion considerably, but...some day that part of the world will be properly opened." He deplored the existence of Baluchistan, Kashmir, Nepal, Sikkim, and Bhutan because they separated India "from normal intercourse with the rest of the world" and "from the benefits of the progress of civilization." If mountains alone barred his way instead of political restrictions, he felt sure that he could travel farther and accomplish much more in Asia.

A talk with the Russian consul at Chuguchak ended his lingering hope of returning to Russian Turkestan. Russia had mobilized because of a conflict with China, and the military administration would not allow foreigners to wander freely through the countryside. Several thousand Russian soldiers were camped at the frontier, ready for action. "Rumors have it that Russia wants Mongolia," Meyer wrote Fairchild. "Let us see!" With that route closed, he planned a two-month trip through the Altai Mountains to Omsk. Thereafter he proposed traveling on the Volga before crossing Siberia to Peking in the autumn. During the winter and spring he hoped to collect in China, returning to Washington in June of 1912. Nepal, Bhutan, Assam, and upper Burma had not been explored yet, he reminded Fairchild. "I personally will stick to Asia the rest of my life in the field."

After two weeks in Chuguchak, Meyer left on May 18 for the remote Altai Mountains. During the six-day journey across the Mongolian border to Zaysan in Siberia, Meyer and his interpreter traversed barren and uninhabited country. Most of the people they met were Kirghiz or Tatars, bold men who "lacked pleasant manners and habits." As Meyer's party climbed a steep incline in a cold rain on the fourth day, the large cart that he had hired to transport their baggage overturned. Worse than that, a bucket of tar that they carried to grease the axles spilled over their baggage and bedding. At sunset they found shelter in a yurt, a round tent made by stretching felt over a wooden frame. There they dried their wet clothes, but fleas, mice, bleating lambs, and crying children interrupted their rest. Despite a diet limited to bread, wurst, and tea, Meyer felt well; however, he never could become accustomed to the vermin encountered in nomad encampments. Regardless of difficulties, he and his interpreter tramped across desolate countryside to their destination.

Willows, poplars, elms, and rowans at Zaysan offered a pleasant contrast to the semiarid region that they had passed. Meyer and his interpreter immediately presented themselves to the police and to customs officials. They also found an inn that appeared to be clean; however, Meyer wrote his sister a week later that he had been bitten so often by "nocturnal visitors" that he felt ill. Remembering how much his mother and Dutch people generally valued cleanliness, he lamented having to live with "numerous vermin" in Siberia. He had caught twenty lice before he could sleep the night before, and he knew that the coming night would be no better. During the day, however, he enjoyed excursions into the nearby mountains and admired the varied flora—masses of forget-me-nots, primroses, iris, bellflowers, anemones, peonies, and clematis. He also collected currants, hawthorns, cotoneasters, and a daphne (*Daphne altaica*) that he had never seen elsewhere.

Various matters delayed his departure from Zaysan. As usual in Russian territory, he had difficulty with his passport; in addition, rain fell constantly for three days while he searched without success for packhorses. He eventually hired two men who owned mountain wagons with wheels set far apart to give balance, but he had to wait while they repaired their carts and harness. At the end of ten days he and his interpreter prepared to start north through little-known territory.

They left Zaysan on June 2 in heavy rain and a shower of large hailstones. On the second day of their journey a primitive ferry carried them over the swift Irtysh River (Ertix He). For several days they saw only a few poplars and aspens growing in sandy soil. One evening, finding no wood in the monotonous desert, they collected dried cattle dung to use as fuel for a fire to cook their food and to drive mosquitoes away. The next morning, efforts to pull the carts out of the black slush exhausted their horses. That afternoon they entered rolling country where they found water and tall grass for the horses. While the tired animals grazed, Meyer collected poplar, white birch, cotoneaster, daphne, and herbarium specimens.

Climbing a steep mountain exhausted the horses, but Meyer enjoyed the cool air and the absence of the mosquitoes that had plagued them in the lowlands. At five thousand feet he found masses of flowers — *Iris sibirica, Trollius asiaticus,* and *Daphne altaica,* which covered whole mountain slopes with tiny white flowers and perfumed the air with a scent reminiscent of hyacinths and lilacs. Patches of snow remained in the pass at six thousand feet, but even there he saw in bud primroses, anemones, and peonies. As they descended, they walked through meadows full of golden trollius and dense masses of pansies, buttercups, and violets. They camped that evening beside a gurgling mountain stream near a Russian settlement where all the houses had been built "log cabin style" from larch and spruce trees.

After climbing a mountain the next day, they found themselves in a forest of spruce and firs. Though the scenery was picturesque, the rough road caused the heavier cart to "turn topsy-turvy with all the baggage on it." Everything had to be repacked and tied securely again. Later, a mountain stream rushing past big ice-covered boulders barred their path. Abandoning their carts, they balanced on fir logs as they carried hundreds of pounds of baggage across the stream. Soon afterward they reached their immediate goal, a Russian settlement on the shore of beautiful Lake Markakol. There Meyer dismissed the carters, since the road ahead narrowed and became dangerous for carts.

He and his interpreter spent the next two nights at the home of a dairy farmer. Solitary larches and clumps of graceful white birches sloping down the hills to the edge of the lovely lake reminded him of Switzerland. Even in a pouring rain, he admired the scenery while he collected red and black currants and herbarium material. He also spent hours arranging to hire packhorses to take his baggage into the wilderness ahead.

After leaving Lake Markakol, Meyer enjoyed climbing snowcapped mountains and tramping through groves of larch, spruce, and fir trees. When he and his party camped beside a mountain stream that evening, their fire attracted a group of peasants carrying leather bags of flour to Markakol. In answer to their questions about his country, Meyer showed them some American magazines. They marveled at pictures of twenty-story skyscrapers, wondering how people dared to live in such buildings and asking whether the wind ever blew them down as it did big trees in the Altai. Touched by their longing for knowledge of the outside world, Meyer gave them pictures, which they accepted eagerly. "Those isolated Russians," he told Fairchild, "are like children, so natural, so unsophisticated."

Early the next morning they scaled a steep mountain, following a narrow trail along the edge of a precipice. Meyer nevertheless enjoyed seeing deep blue gentians, pansies, and three species of primroses. Trees near the mountaintops in the Altai remained in leaf only ten weeks in the year, for snows began in late August. Meyer saw birches and willows that never exceeded a height of twelve to twenty-four inches because of the short growing season. As the men trudged past banks of snow at the 8,600-foot summit, a thunderstorm broke and icy rain and hailstones pelted them. After descending the mountain and passing through dense forests of larches and pines, they arrived at a Kirghiz settlement where they dried themselves and their clothes in a yurt. Neither rain, hail, nor wind troubled Meyer, but a diet usually limited to bread, tea, and occasionally a few eggs made him long for fresh vegetables, fruits, and meat.

During the next three days they followed the beautiful Boochtarma River Valley, journeying past meadows where wild flowers bloomed. At a Cossack village Meyer dismissed the horsemen from Markakol. He and his interpreter lodged with a Cossack family for two nights while they looked for experienced moutaineers to accompany them on the difficult journey ahead. Unable to find competent assistants, Meyer decided to travel by cart northeast along the Boochtarma Valley to Berel where he could hire packhorses and guides. Traveling through the valley toward the border of Mongolia, he responded to the beauty of the surrounding mountainsides covered with forests and the snowcapped mountaintops. He also noticed that the local farmers grew everything they needed except tea, sugar, and salt; they even distilled tar from white birches to grease the wooden axles of their carts.

After two and a half days disturbed only by an overturned cart and further damage to their baggage, they reached Berel at noon. There they stayed with a prosperous farmer and learned about the industry that made him wealthy. Since ancient times the Chinese had believed that stag antler restored lost youth and virility; therefore, they were willing to pay high prices for powdered staghorn. Russian hunters previously had killed stags and marketed their antlers in China. About forty years before Meyer's visit, the Russians near Berel had learned that stags would multiply in captivity and that their antlers could be removed each year without injuring the animals. Each stag grew antlers worth seventy rubles annually, and some farmers owned as many as four hundred stags.

When he had gathered herbarium material in the beautiful wild countryside near Berel and had found two men and six packhorses to accompany him on his journey, Meyer left the Boochtarma River and headed north over a steep mountain. Even heavy showers of cold rain did not dampen his pleasure when he came upon masses of golden trollius and blue pansies. He and his men dried their clothes around a campfire in the evening and were surprised to find mosquitoes active at 6,300 feet. The next morning they climbed over fallen tree trunks in a "desolate and appalling" burned forest with "here and there a naked limb pointing to the blue and silver sky as if imploring pity." After they reached the eight-thousand-foot summit of the mountain, they began to descend through meadows filled with dark blue gentians, dogtooth violets, and alpine buttercups blooming in several inches of snow. Camping that evening under a majestic pine near an icy stream that flowed down the mountain in a torrent, Meyer reveled in the wild beauty of the scene.

Though one mountain range followed another, Meyer enjoyed a feeling of freedom in this untamed region. After scaling two high mountains, they waded through snow and icy bogs. Meyer found no fruit trees, but he did see currants, raspberries, blueberries, and small strawberries, as well as a crimson primrose blooming in the snow. The following day proved to be even more strenuous. They plodded through deep snow alternating with swamps, rocky level stretches, and barren mountainsides. When they came to alpine meadows gaudy with rose, orange, yellow, blue, and violet flowers, Meyer rejoiced because "fear and wrong disappear in such surroundings." Rising early the third morning, they crossed two more mountain chains. On a plateau at 8,200 feet, dark blue gentians and light blue pansies made walking a joy. They noticed paw prints of bears in a valley but "missed the chance of having some adventures." From the valley they ascended to an elevated plain where fiercely cold and windy winters limited the height of willows to a few inches; yet graceful birches and tall larches three or four feet in diameter thrived in the valley below.

Though Meyer had enjoyed hiking across three mountain ranges in three days, his companions were glad to reach villages at lower altitudes. The horsemen were eager to return home and the interpreter from Tashkent was exhausted and becoming morose. Meyer therefore released the horsemen and hired a carter and two carts. This region normally was fertile, but black dust whirled through the air as a result of a lengthy drought. Only a few Kalmucks inhabited the arid countryside. On their third day in the lowlands they came upon wheat and rye under cultivation. When they camped that evening, they scrubbed themselves to remove the black dust that made them look like coal miners.

Just three days before they reached a city, the Russo-Turki interpreter from Tashkent announced that he could not stand the discomfort and monotony of traveling any longer and threatened to leave at once. Meyer was puzzled when his companion complained that he was enslaved night and day. "If a man does not get satisfaction out of being in free nature," he wondered, "what shall one offer them?" The weather made the situation worse, for rain fell "by tubs full." Meyer and his men covered the baggage with oilcloth and spent a miserable night in their wet clothes with dry bread and "half-boiled tea" for supper. At 4:00 A.M. they gladly packed the carts and moved on past fields of grain. The villages they saw disgusted Meyer with their dilapidated houses and neglected yards with cows, pigs, ducks, chickens, and manure everywhere. Abandoned carts, barrels, boxes, and rubbish surrounded homes and cluttered the landscape.

The following day they ferried across the Katoun River to rolling country and across the Biya River to the town of Biysk. There Meyer noticed several stores selling American agricultural machinery bearing the familiar names of Deering, Osborne, and McCormick. After searching a long while, he and his interpreter found one available room. Having reached a town with a telegraph at last, Meyer estimated his accounts for the fiscal year which would end in just three days and reported an unexpended balance of three hundred dollars.

They left Biysk early in the morning on a wood-burning steamer, going north down the Ob river. A day later they transferred to another steamer at the busy city of Barnaul. All that day they floated past a monotonous landscape in sultry weather, reaching Novonikolaevsk (Novosibirsk) at 7:00 P.M. The next day they took the Trans-Siberian Railroad across swampy land to Omsk, arriving on July 2 after a four-month journey.

The Alfalfa Project

Omsk, Tomsk, and Semipalatinsk
JULY TO OCTOBER, 1911

A F T E R scouring the rough city of Omsk for rooms, Meyer found lodging and claimed a large accumulation of mail. His journey through the Altai Mountains had yielded no useful fruits or grains; however, he hoped that his currants and forage plants might be of value in cool parts of the United States. Siberian farmers, he concluded, could benefit far more from American introductions than American farmers from Siberian introductions. Within the next two weeks, he dispatched four packages including twenty pounds of hardy alfalfa seeds, ninety-eight photographs, and the corresponding negatives. He then labeled his herbarium material and tried to replace his interpreter, who planned to return to Tashkent.

Replying to Fairchild's twenty-one letters, he indignantly denied that the white bark of a certain Chinese persimmon tree resulted from whitewashing. The leaves were more lanceolate than those of other persimmon trees, he insisted. "When back in China, I will collect herbarium material of this white-barked fellow." He was pleased that Fairchild considered his almonds and apricots of value and his Kashgar elm potentially the best shade tree ever introduced into the Southwest. Answering Fairchild's inquiry about wild alfalfas that he had seen, he wrote, "I surely would not have believed these plants to have been the ancestor of our luxurious tall alfalfa, but they are just the same and who of us mortals will be able to say what possibilities are latent in some of these Central Asian alfalfas and in the hybrids and selections that we may obtain from them." Though many of his cuttings had not survived the two-month trip to Washington, some had arrived in good condition, "the first time in history that someone has sent cuttings so far." Thanking Fairchild for sending him clippings, he added,

"Scientific items are especially welcome; politics not; they tire one too much of man at large."

He also kept in touch with relatives and friends, continued his scientific correspondence, wrote business letters to shipping agencies, banks, photographic suppliers, and consuls, and continued to search for a scientifically trained interpreter who would not object to hardship. Still uncertain about his route for the remainder of his expedition, he considered going to eastern Siberia and Manchuria or to the Yellow River Valley of China; either route at that time would be "a confounded gamble."

Weighing the alternatives open to him, he decided that most people would not enjoy the difficult journeys that he undertook—certainly not "those in love, those loving home life, or those liking ease. This agricultural explorer work is a mighty great education to the man who is able to stand it," he wrote Fairchild. "Pushing on and that feeling to conquer new worlds is the great spring that drives us on." After spending more than four months walking most of the thousand-odd miles across deserts and mountains from Kashgar to Biysk, he concluded that plant exploration "often knocks a man hard and steady, but if he has resistance power enough, he comes out strengthened and is often grateful he went through his experiences."

As he was replying to mail at Omsk, a telegram from James Wilson, secretary of agriculture, abruptly changed his plans: "Collect 500 pounds red clover and *Medicago falcata* seed." He had objected when a directive from Secretary Wilson had brought him from Harbin to Shanghai in 1907, interrupting his expedition. This time he did not protest, although he was not sure that he could find such a large quantity of the yellow-flowered alfalfa. Four days later he sent all the alfalfa and clover seeds that he could assemble immediately. This shipment also contained ninety-five photographs, including pictures of the Mussart Pass to be shared with Dr. Erwin Smith.

Instead of proceeding to the Volga as planned, Meyer had to remain in Omsk. He asked farmers to supply the clover and alfalfa that he needed, but "none will bite." Later a few signed contracts and broke them. Even in Siberia he complained about the heat and humidity in July, but an outbreak of cholera posed a more serious threat. Since he could not collect alfalfa seeds before late August, he decided that he would go to Tomsk to study herbarium material at the university. If he could find an interpreter there, he could work his way south to the region around Semipalatinsk where he hoped to find a quantity of wild alfalfa. Though he longed to go to the rich Yellow River Valley in China, he admitted that "the northern things" might be of greater value to the United States.

Letters from England, Holland, America, and China prevented his feeling forgotten at Omsk. When the distinguished amateur botanist, Augustine Henry, complimented him on his bulletin about fruit and nut culture in China, he told Fairchild that such praise compensated for "all that plodding I did in a dingy room in a shaky building on B Street." Further encouragement came from Howard Dorsett, who wrote that he had contracted with Harold Hume's nursery in Florida to propagate five thousand persimmon trees from varieties that Meyer had introduced. An article in a plant introduction bulletin that Fairchild had sent amused Meyer. The author explained that he planned to place sphagnum moss under trees on mountainsides in the Andes to receive falling seeds. "My own experience of mountains is that they are pretty stern subjects where violent winds blow," Meyer commented. "The man who wanted to cover the ground with moss would have to sit on it to keep it in place." A letter from the daughter of S. P. Barchet of the American Consultate in Shanghai brought news of the death of one of Meyer's good friends. He was touched to hear that almost the last words that Dr. Barchet had spoken were of him and the wonderful work he was doing.

Before leaving for Tomsk, Meyer wrote at length to Hugo de Vries. He agreed with de Vries that such a small country as Holland was remarkable in supporting six universities and four botanical gardens, a record that must be "unique in the whole world." He then revealed conclusions he had reached after "lonesome thoughts in deserts and forests" about conditions he believed necessary for the advancement of mankind. First, he advocated wise laws to prevent the accumulation of enormous amounts of capital in the hands of a few. Second, education, even at the university level, should be free. Third, the state should own all land and rent it "for shorter or longer duration." Fourth, railroads and utilities should be 45 percent private property and 55 percent state owned. Fifth, the mentally defective and criminally insane should not be allowed to reproduce. Sixth, use of birth control should be limited in Europe and America "where the most progressive people live." Finally, people must recognize that the existence of many different languages and nationalities in Western Europe forms "an obstacle for the future." The world should have one language, a single currency, and a central capital.[1]

Meyer left Omsk alone on August 14, traveling east by rail to Tomsk where faculty members at the university received him kindly. For several days he studied herbarium material and made notes of promising forage and fodder plants. Though he spent "pleasant and profitable hours" with various professors, no one could tell him where to gather a large quantity of *Medicago falcata* seeds. Wild alfalfa plants were widely scattered, but the greatest concentration appeared to be in the region around Semipalatinsk. Russian indifference to wild forms of useful crops appalled him. When he tried to discuss Siberian forage plants with a Russian agronomist at Tomsk, the agronomist simply said, "You Americans work it out and then we buy them from you."

After spending ten days at Tomsk, Meyer took a steamer up the Ob River, arriving at Barnaul three days later. There he employed an intelligent young interpreter, Svend Lange, who knew local conditions well. Traveling by cart, they collected alfalfa, vetches, and clovers in small quantities, as well as "wonderfully vigorous" raspberries. After a week near Barnaul, they moved on to Zmeinogorsk.

Though people there were unfriendly and suspicious, Meyer remained near Zmeinogorsk for ten days, finding small quantities of alfalfa here and there. He soon learned to hide his camera and field glasses, for the peasants regarded them with a mixture of curiosity and awe. Because people thought that he and his interpreter were spies, Meyer repeatedly had to show the police his passport; however, many of the "so-called police were drunk already in the early morning." Even when Meyer offered two rubles a pound, the peasants refused to collect alfalfa seeds for him. Meeting many "vicious drunken fellows" and seeing intoxicated men in muddy ditches beside the roads surprised him. Each village had a government-sponsored vodka shop "where the devilish stuff is sold to everybody over sixteen years of age." In one town the people warned him that robbing and beating travelers was common. For the first time in Central Asia he wore his revolver in order to be prepared for intoxicated troublemakers.

Working southeast of Semipalatinsk in falling rain, Meyer and his interpreter reached Ekaterinskia, Krasnoyarsk, and Ust-Kamenogorsk. In the distance they could see the Altai Mountains draped with black clouds, and they knew that many miles away a fearful storm was raging. A storm also howled through the trees at Ust-Kamenogorsk and icy rain and hail blew into their faces. Constant rain that summer had caused crops to rot in the fields. As Meyer prepared his quarterly intinerary report, he could hear the church bells tolling "to induce Jupiter Pluvius to abstain." He had met "lazy, dirty, vicious specimens" in that part of Siberia, as well as decent working people, and he had stayed in filthy houses. The local inhabitants aroused feelings of "disgust and pity mingled together." After much work, he had gathered only small amounts of *Medicago falcata*, clover, and vetches. Though he searched near Semipalatinsk in snow and rain, the quantities of alfalfa seeds that he sought were not available. He had, however, collected leguminous plants (*Hedysarum* and *Astragalus*) that should help in propagating forage crops in stony, semiarid land in America where no other forage could survive.

Returning to Omsk, he packed three large parcels containing the results of six weeks' work in the field. These packages included three sacks of alfalfa seeds, promising forage crops, legumes, and various grasses for dry pastures. In addition, he shipped samples of wheat, conifer cones for Sargent, pathological and entomological material, and herbarium specimens, the results of "a very great amount of painstaking work."

Letters waiting for him at Omsk explained the chain of events that had caused Secretary Wilson to instruct him to collect such large quantities of wild alfalfa. In 1898, before he had authorized Fairchild to form the Foreign Seed and Plant Introduction Section, Wilson had sent Niels E. Hansen to Siberia for grains. Hansen had continued to travel widely and to collect, although Fairchild had never asked him to work for the Plant Introduction Section. In 1911 Hansen bypassed Fairchild and wrote directly to the secretary of agriculture, asking Wilson to send him to Siberia for large quantities of urgently needed alfalfa. Wilson summoned Galloway and Fairchild to discuss Hansen's suggestion. Fairchild stated that Hansen had received a large appropriation and had collected a small amount of seed. He felt confident that Meyer, who was already in Siberia, could make better contracts. "Many of Hansen's things were dead when they were unpacked," he argued. Dr. Galloway and Secretary Wilson agreed to entrust the alfalfa project to Meyer.[2]

Meyer was surprised to learn that Hansen had written that "seed will have to be gathered by the ton," for *Medicago falcata* grew in Siberia only as a wild plant. When Meyer tried to make contracts for seeds, Russian farmers laughed and said, "We don't want to gather weeds." Knowing that Galloway and Fairchild had endorsed him, he was determined to justify their confidence if he could possibly do so. At least, he knew that he could work more economically than Hansen, whose salary alone had been three thousand dollars. Meyer eventually did succeed in collecting the greatest quantity of *Medicago falcata* that ever had been brought to the United States by any plant explorer.[3]

In response to a request for information about Russia, Meyer sent Fairchild a concise prescription for the problems that he had observed: "Restrict the sale of vodka, build more schools, make education compulsory, teach the people cleanliness, select better men for the police and pay them better, make bribe-taking a penal offense and enforce that law. After these have been carried out, a new Russia may arise out of her present medieval condition."

Rumors that China was in convulsion reached Meyer at Omsk. He had intended to ship some of his baggage to Harbin, but he read that revolutionaries were "taking over the reins" in Manchuria, and "in Shansi Province just where those persimmons grow, there is great unrest." He asked Fairchild to consult the State Department to learn whether foreigners actually were leaving Peking and whether conditions were as serious as reports indicated. Turning away from China with regret, he left Omsk to work along the Volga.

The Volga to the Potomac

Russia, Holland, and England
NOVEMBER, 1911, TO APRIL, 1912

A F T E R traveling nearly one thousand miles by train, Meyer visited the agricultural station at Samara (Kuibyshev) on the Volga. There Professor Tuliakoff shared the results of his work with drought-resistant grains and forage plants. A week later, Meyer went to Syzran to inspect Woeikov's nursery and horticultural school. Since both men spoke French, Meyer was able to discuss breeding hardy fruits and exchanging hardy American cherries for Woeikov's hybrids. Woeikov also contracted to supply up to five hundred pounds of clean *Medicago falcata* seeds at two rubles a pound. With his search for alfalfa completed, Meyer proceeded to the horticultural school at Penza and then to the new university at Saratov.

Leaving Saratov, he reached Krasny Kut at midnight. Early the next morning he visited Mr. Bogdan, director of the agricultural experiment station, who had assembled fifteen cultivars of the wonderfully variable *Medicago falcata*. At first Bogdan was "somewhat cool about exchanging things," Meyer told Fairchild, "for he told me he had given Professor Hansen some selected strains of watermelon seeds. These same things had recently been brought back to Russia as American products and he had never received even a bulletin from Mr. Hansen for thanks! One hears so many things here in Russia about Mr. Hansen that I have to tell you them." After Meyer reassured him, Bogdan gave Meyer ten pounds of *Medicago falcata* seeds in exchange for USDA bulletins on grasses, alfalfa, and clover. He also showed Meyer one of his treasured possessions, a USDA bulletin called "Pasture, Meadow, and Forage Crops in Nebraska." Seeing Bogdan's work, Meyer felt ashamed that Hansen had "put in the Russian papers that he was willing to supervise for the Russian government the collection of great quantities of *Medicago falcata* in cold Siberia."

After he returned to Saratov, Meyer arranged an exchange of wheat samples and spent several days in the hills taking cuttings of wild apples and pears. In a ravine on a dry hillside near Saratov he collected samples of *Coronilla varia*, never guessing that some day propagators at the Soil Conservation Service and the Iowa Agricultural Experiment Station at Ames would use it to develop the Emerald crownvetch that controls soil erosion on steep banks along interstate highways in cooler sections of the United States.[1]

When he took a steamer south, he could purchase a ticket only to the point where the Volga became completely frozen. He reached Tsaritsyn (Stalingrad, now Volgograd) on November 27 after a thirty-hour trip, and the Volga was closed for the winter three hours later. From Tsaritsyn he went to Sarepta and found lodging at a German inn—"for the first time a bed without bugs." After adding the famous Sarepta mustard to his collection, on sandy slopes he gathered seeds of crested wheat grass (*Agropyron cristatum*). Continuing to search for useful plants in snow and icy wind, he found little except curious fossil sponges. A severe cold anchored him for two days; then he left by train for Rostov-on-Don.

After ten days at Rostov, he considered his plans in relation to conditions in China and his own health. Although Fairchild had written on November 22 that the State Department considered China safe for foreigners, Meyer had read newspaper reports of fighting, looting, and massacre there. In addition, strange as its seemed to him, he had developed typhus malaria during bitterly cold weather. (Actually this was not strange because typhus malaria is carried by lice, not by mosquitoes.) As soon as Fairchild received this news, he sent Meyer a new letter of instruction: "Unsettled conditions prevailing in China at the present time preventing you from carrying out the work authorized in the original letter, you are now authorized to reach Washington about February 15."[2] Realizing that he could not attempt to go to China while the country was in a state of revolution and his own health was poor, Meyer planned to work his way toward Saint Petersburg (Leningrad) where he could study the rich collection of herbarium material from the Kansu Province of China; then he would travel to England to talk to Augustine Henry about the flora of Kansu and Szechwan.

He spent a week swallowing quinine and Santogen and then, thinking that he was "over the worst," he visited an experiment station in icy winds. He also mailed six packages of grasses, alfalfa, apricot scions, dates for W. T. Swingle, and walnuts and hazelnuts for W. A. Taylor, as well as two heavy cases containing forty elm trees and fifty apricot trees. Leaving Rostov on December 20, he inspected the Kharkov Botanical Gardens, the Agricultural Selection Station, and the Seed Bureau of the Kharkov Agricultural Society.

After working at the Seed Bureau on Christmas day, he left for Koslov (Michurinsk) and spent the next two days with Gregori Mijurin, who was called the Luther Burbank of Russia. Mijurin had tested thirty thousand peach trees for resistance to cold; after three years only fifteen had survived the bitter winters and late spring frosts at Koslov. Meyer sent two parcels of Mijurin's valuable cuttings and scions to Washington, warning Fairchild to place these items with expert propagators only, for they included some of the hardiest cherries, apricots, plums, and quinces in existence.

By the time Meyer reached Moscow on New Year's Eve he felt ill, but he managed nevertheless to go to the Moscow Agricultural Institute and to arrange for a shipment of seeds and cuttings of Vladimir cherries. Despite several feet of snow, he traveled to Torchek to promote an exchange with the owner of a private arboretum and herbarium. He reached Saint Petersburg by train three days later, confident that his health was improving because his temperature rose only in the afternoon.

At Saint Petersburg he found a quantity of mail awaiting him; he also consulted a doctor who diagnosed his illness as recurring malarial fever resulting from exposure and exhaustion. Since Secretary Wilson and Galloway were eager to hear how the alfalfa project was progressing, Meyer spent some time indoors preparing a thirty-eight-page report with six accompanying photographs of wild alfalfa. Fairchild had written that the Office of Forage Crops had gratefully acknowledged receiving two new pasture crops from the Altai, *Lathyrus pisiformis* and *Vicia megalotropis*. In his reply Meyer noted regretfully that "anarchy reigns" in many parts of China; collecting in the Yellow River Valley that winter would have been impossible, even if the alfalfa search had not delayed him.

Though the temperature fell to −25°F, Meyer enjoyed the "bracing" weather; however, he had to walk constantly to keep warm and to rub his nose and ears so that they would not freeze. Despite heavy snowstorms, bitter cold, and few daylight hours, the Russians stayed up late at night. When he visited friends, he did not return to his hotel until 1:00 or 2:00 A.M. If only the Russians could become "wiser," he told his sister, they had the potential to make great advances. In answer to her comments about saving his money, he replied that he did not want to become rich but did intend to prepare for his old age because the USDA had no insurance or pension plans. Referring to his mother's terminal illness, he expressed his sorrow for her suffering.[3]

By mid-January he contracted a cold and malarial fever recurred; though he complained that it was hard to recover in such a raw climate, remaining indoors did not occur to him. At the end of January he sent the department a superior strain of flax, ten pounds of wheat seeds, herbarium specimens, and botanical material including cones of a hybrid pine for Sargent and three smooth-awned barleys for H. B. Derr. In February he conferred with specialists at the Bureau of Applied Botany, the Saint Petersburg Seed Testing Station, and the Imperial Academy of Sciences. He also replied to a letter from Roy Chapman Andrews, curator of mammalogy at the Museum of Natural History in New York, who wanted to consult him if he had actually traveled in the mountains of northern Korea. Since Andrews was planning to make a zoological collection there, he expected to "run down to Washington" to talk to Meyer in the spring.

Instead of leaving Saint Petersburg at the beginning of March as he had planned, Meyer, who had drained his strength, spent a week in bed. Though he still felt ill, he left for the Latvian port of Riga on March 11. At Riga he received letters from his family urging him to come to Amsterdam at once because of "the sad state of health of my dear mother." After spending three days in bed and resting several more days, he boarded a train to Berlin and Amsterdam.

When he reached Amsterdam he not only saw his family but also visited Hugo de Vries at his experimental garden. He was disappointed to hear that the Janssens were out of the country, for he had not seen them since his days at Walden. This homecoming was not a happy reunion with his relatives because of his mother's illness. Everyone knew that this was a farewell visit. Several days after he arrived, his malarial fever recurred and he spent three days resting and gathering strength to go to England. On March 28 he left Amsterdam, arriving exhausted in London the next day.

April in England seemed to be the remedy for Meyer's illness. No more entries of "unwell" or "unwell in bed" appeared on his yellow itinerary records. After many months in Siberia, he enjoyed seeing the lovely gardens surrounding modest and large homes. At Cambridge he conferred with Augustine Henry and learned that he had become engrossed in his second career as a lecturer on forestry. When Dr. Henry failed to find his field notes on plants that grew in the interior of China, Meyer was disappointed and Henry embarrassed. Meyer also visited Veitch and Sons and Kew Gardens, where he studied fine collections of rare trees and shrubs, especially E. H. Wilson's introductions from China. When officials at the Royal Botanic Gardens at Kew sought permission to publish some of his photographs, Meyer felt gratified. As he enjoyed the mild weather and the congenial atmosphere, his health improved rapidly.

At Fairchild's request, he traveled to Cambridge again the following week to form an opinion of Frank Kingdon-Ward as a collector and to make him an offer. Meyer decided that the young plant explorer, who was to spend more than forty years in the field, loved exploration "strictly for botanical reasons" and that he was not at all concerned about economically useful plants. He showed no interest in Fairchild's invitation to come to Washington to discuss collecting plants for the USDA. Meyer judged accurately that the young man would never stay long in such a small country as England.

"He feels here as much at home as a fish out of water," Meyer wrote, perhaps remembering how unhappy he had felt in Holland when he was twenty-three.

His assignments completed, Meyer returned to America on the *Mauretania*, leaving Liverpool on April 10. But his voyage home did not lack drama. During the crossing he wrote that his letter about his conferences with Augustine Henry and Kingdon-Ward may have left England on the *Titanic*. "In that case, it is now at the bottom of the sea as this splendid new boat went down with the majority of its passengers and crew. We here are under the influence of that terrible accident. We ourselves almost came in collision yesterday with another boat in a dense low fog hanging all around." Haunted by the fate of the *Titanic*, the passengers on the *Mauretania* did not enjoy the Atlantic crossing.

Since he could not go to the Yellow River Valley in China, Meyer was returning from barren regions without a collection of living plants. He had concentrated on sending the department material that would tolerate extreme cold, drought, and alkaline soil. His harvest had reached America ahead of him—olives from the Crimea; fruits from the Caucasus; the Kashgar elm, Khotan ash, sweet-kerneled apricots, and soil-binding plants from Turkestan; hardy apricots, cherries, and currants from the Altai; and alfalfas and wheats from Siberia and European Russia. Unfortunately, inadequate postal facilities in Russian Turkestan and Siberia had caused the loss of tamarisks, desert poplars, Russian olives, and many of his fruit trees. On April 19 the *Mauretania* docked in New York. After the familiar train ride past Philadelphia and Baltimore, Meyer's long journey ended in Washington.

Interlude in America

The United States
APRIL TO OCTOBER, 1912

ME Y E R enjoyed a reunion with friends at the plant introduction office as soon as he reached Washington. David Fairchild was out of town, but he had suggested that Meyer call on the Alexander Graham Bells, "who will be very glad indeed to see you and have frequently asked when you expected to return." Though everyone wanted to hear details of his expedition, he found time to complete his accounts and to file his itinerary at the end of April. For the first time he saw *Chinese Plant Names* by Frank N. Meyer, a publication naming hundreds of plants that he had sent from China between 1905 and 1908. Each name appeared first in roman letters, then translated into Latin, and finally printed in Chinese characters. Published in 1911, the book represented a compilation of all the inventory cards that Meyer had sent to the department from China.[1] Fairchild had urged Meyer to return to America in time to go with him to the Chico Garden in the spring to check the progress of his introductions. Meyer missed this opportunity and spent May at the office working on records of his introductions and identifying his photographs.

Late in May he submitted a brief bulletin and a memorandum. In "A Popular Name for *Medicago falcata*," he proposed adopting the Kirghiz word *Sholteek* to identify this particular alfalfa. He also pointed out that *Medicago falcata* varied widely in the wild and that it exhibited many objectionable qualities. Though he believed that it would be important in hybridization, he felt that it should not be distributed until it had been subjected to extensive field tests in various localities.[2] His memorandum recorded his feeling about having anything named for him: "I wish to put on record that I personally object to having anything called after me. Mr. Burbank called a spineless *Opuntia* that I discovered in Mexico after me. Mr. Marlatt named a pernicious insect *Aspidictus meyeri*. Mr. Oliver calls the semi-double rose from North China *Meyer's Yellow.*" Instead of naming introductions for him, he suggested finding a name that would give information about the source of a new plant or about its characteristics.

While aboard the *Mauretania*, he had wondered where he was going to "recuperate entirely." His vacation lasted all of June. Perhaps he returned to Cape Cod during the tourist season, or he may have accepted A. J. Pieters's invitation to visit him at Ann Arbor, or possibly he chose some other place where he could find companionship and an opportunity to relax, swim, and take long walks. By this time he had received word of the death of his beloved mother. As a result, he felt "a great emptiness that never will be filled. My own life has less value to me because there is no hope ever to see her again."

After his vacation ended, he worked many hours on various assignments in his hot office in Washington. He reviewed George Oliver's bulletin on alfalfa, listed trees and shrubs that should survive at the testing garden at Mandan, North Dakota, and began an article on plant exploration. Every day he wrote reports and dictated letters "while my heart longs for mountains and clear cool lakes." He also outlined his proposed itinerary for the next three years. He planned to cross Siberia and Manchuria en route to Peking; in China he wanted to explore Shantung, Honan, Shensi, Kansu, and Szechwan provinces. While he waited for Congress to appropriate the necessary funds for his next expedition, he and his associates suffered through moving from the old brick building to the partially completed new headquarters of the Department of Agriculture.

He spent much of his free time that summer at the Fairchilds' home, In the Woods. Impressed by the amount of new and valuable information that Meyer had stored in his memory, Fairchild urged him to record his accumulated knowledge permanently in a government bulletin. But formal composition was not congenial to Meyer, even though he was unusually articulate in conversation. During the summer of 1912, he often stretched out on the floor of Fairchild's laboratory and talked while Fairchild took notes, fearing that otherwise important observations might be lost. Though Meyer complained about the heat and humidity in Washington, Fairchild enjoyed his company. They shared an abiding interest in all flowers, shrubs, and trees, especially those growing around Fairchild's home. If Meyer noticed an unfamiliar plant, he approached it "with the eager interest of a child," looking, feeling, smelling, and tasting in his attempt to identify it. Once acquainted with a new plant, he never forgot it.[3]

He escaped the confining quarters of the office in September with his friend, Howard Dorsett, when Fairchild asked them to study the problems facing the new experiment farm at Mandan, North Dakota. They spent several days with Canadian agriculturists at Ottawa before inspecting experiment stations and farms near Winnipeg and Indian Head. After arriving at Mandan, they assessed the prospects of the new testing garden. Meyer then traveled alone to the plant introduction garden at Ames, Iowa, arriving at 1:00 A.M. Since the only hotel in Ames was full, he slept for a few hours in the bus driver's room. Later that morning he gave a talk to four hundred students at Iowa State College. After a brief stop in Chicago, he returned to Washington.[4]

When October came, he was impatient to begin his expedition; however, preliminary paper work delayed him. In the meantime, Fairchild advised him that "those interested in *Medicago falcata*" did not want more seeds; therefore, Meyer would have to discourage Woeikov from collecting more. After he had spent six months searching for a large quantity of alfalfa, this news disturbed him because it meant that he must renege on his contract with Woeikov. Secretary Wilson evidently had failed to investigate the need for the tons of seeds that Hansen had considered indispensable. Compared to this development, the auditor's review of Meyer's expenditures was only a minor irritant. Once during the preceding quarter, he had exceeded the five-dollar total allowed for three meals and lodging in any twenty-four-hour period; the auditor had disallowed the extra eighty cents.

Meyer said good-bye to his friends in Washington on October 10 and traveled to Massachusetts, where he enjoyed the cool weather and the glorious autumn colors. He devoted most of his first week at the Arnold Arboretum to studying the herbarium, but he also had frequent discussions with Sargent and E. H. Wilson, who received him cordially. They looked at plants together and talked about the work that Meyer might be able to accomplish in the Kansu Province of China. Sargent suggested that he should consult William Purdom in England because Purdom was the only Western collector to have worked in Kansu, except for the Russian Potanin. "People here are treating me very nicely," he wrote Fairchild, "and they take a keen interest in my remarks and observations about plants and conditions I saw. The prospect of all this travel makes me feel exalted, and I just wish I could fly from here to those Nan Shan Mountains."

A transformation had gradually occurred in the relationship between Meyer and Wilson since their first meeting in Shanghai five years earlier. Meyer now respected Wilson's accomplishments, while Wilson had learned to value Meyer's enthusiasm, tenacity, and practical knowledge. Though Wilson had the reputation of being uncommunicative with strangers and reserved with casual acquaintances, with friends he lost his diffidence.[5] He took Meyer to see newly introduced Chinese plants at Farquhar's Nursery near Boston, and together they studied Wilson's collection of *Prunus* from China and decided that western Hupeh Province might be the home of the wild peach.

During his second week at the arboretum, Meyer spent much of his time talking to Jackson Dawson, Wilson, and Sargent, and taking extensive notes in the arboretum's twenty-five-thousand-volume library. He read Franchet's *Plantae Davidianae* and "learned the mountains" of Kansu. To his surprise, he found that the arboretum lacked herbarium specimens of common Chinese plants and that Sargent wanted examples of "ordinary" trees. Sargent wondered whether Meyer would find the ginkgo tree in the wild in China and told Meyer to expect "to meet it somewhere" in the mountains of Shensi Province. In such pleasant surroundings, Meyer did not object when he learned that his dwarf lilac had been named *Syringa meyeri.* "They consider it here a remarkable little lilac," he wrote Fairchild, adding that Sargent, Wilson, and Jackson Dawson had asked for copies of his bulletin, *Agricultural Exploration in the Fruit and Nut Orchards of China.*

Sargent believed that Meyer should send all rare woody plants directly to the Arnold Arboretum, where they would have a better chance to survive than at the USDA facilities. Fairchild could not agree to this suggestion because the department had to inspect and number foreign introductions before distributing them. Meyer proposed as a compromise that he label rare plants for the arboretum and send them by way of Washington. After two stimulating weeks at the arboretum, he left Boston for New York.

Only a few days remained before his departure. Russian officials visaed his passport after he paid two calls at the Russian Consulate. He then devoted one day to visiting Dr. W. A. Murrill and Dr. Britton at the New York Botanical Garden and another to conferring with Roy Chapman Andrews at the Museum of Natural History. Meyer and Professor Vladimir Kamarov, a Russian botanist, were the only white men who had traveled through the mountains of northern Korea ahead of Andrews.

As Meyer prepared for an expedition that would encircle the globe, only the department's unwillingness to buy the alfalfa that he had contracted for clouded his horizon. "I will face the music there in Russia," he wrote Dorsett from New York. "This whole falcata subject has been a pretty sore topic with our Department. A little more firmness would have facilitated matters considerably. Then the Hansen affair would not have assumed such big dimensions." Meyer spent his last two days in America on Long Island visiting Henry L. Hicks, the nurseryman who had taken him to see President Roosevelt. On November 2 he boarded the SS *St. Louis* for the voyage to Southampton.

The Third Expedition

Meyer about to set out
on his third expedition.
October 10, 1912.

*"My mule and donkey
caravan, with assistant and
interpreter, on the top of a
pass, about 4000 ft.,"* in
the mountains near
Yingtau, September 13,
1913.

Main road, worn into a gully by centuries of traffic by carts and pack animals, near Sian, Shensi, February 1, 1914, where Meyer's carters fought earlier for the right-of-way.

Meyer's caravan, Shansi, China, August 1914.

Meyer's *"carts in the courtyard of the inn where we stopped; the weather was exceedingly hot and sticky and man and beast had to move about slowly."* Pai-hsiang, Shansi, China, August 10, 1914.

Meyer holding a heavily loaded branch of the Taiyuan jujube tree, Shansi, August 1914.

"At the Shansi side of the Yellow River, our carts being pushed onto the boat that will take us across," near Taching, August 15, 1914.

Meyer's carts landing on the Shensi side of the Yellow River, August 15, 1914.

"When we left Siku in search of wild almonds and Potanin's peaches, we had to cross this rickety bridge, decidedly risky in windy weather," near Pantsai, Kansu, October 1914. (A wonderful example of Chinese engineering ingenuity. Note second part of caravan waiting to attempt a crossing after the first donkey makes it.)

Wild and rugged mountain country where Meyer found many of Potanin's peaches, near Paodji, Kansu, November 9, 1914.

Johannis de Leuw (left), Meyer's assistant throughout the third expedition, with Meyer, who captioned the photo, *"Together we stand or fall."* February 6, 1915, after returning to Peking.

"A large and old white-barked pine at the Princesses Tombs, near Peking. Note how the Chinese have cut away pieces of bark and made incisions to obtain resin, which all helps to build a fire to cook a meal or some tea water." May 16, 1915.

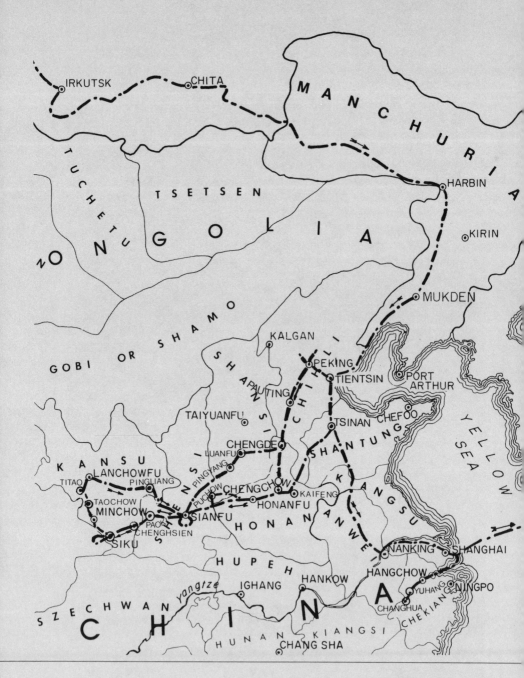

THIRD EXPEDITION, 1912–1915

Peking (Beijing) via Siberia

Russia, Manchuria, and Peking
NOVEMBER, 1912, TO SEPTEMBER, 1913

ME Y E R arrived in London intending to learn about William Purdom's experiences in the Kansu (Gansu) Province of China. Purdom, who had returned from a troubled and unsuccessful expedition, evidently was not eager to meet Meyer. Replying to Meyer's letter, he wrote that he was out of town and gave an incomplete address. Apparently unconscious of Purdom's reluctance to confer with him, Meyer called on Purdom's sister in London and learned that he was at Ambleside near Windermere, seven hours away by train. Since Purdom was the only Western botanist who had penetrated certain parts of Kansu, Meyer wired that he was coming to Ambleside.

He spent only a day and a half in the Lake District, but he did glean some valuable information. Purdom appeared reluctant to discuss his expedition; in fact, Meyer reported that he acted "like an officer who had lost a battle." Working in a relatively unproductive region in China, he had suffered a series of misfortunes including the loss of his baggage and collection and a fall that caused a serious injury. He had survived only because a little Taoist nun who lived in the woods like a hermit had nursed him back to health.[1] Meyer sympathized with him, not only because both he and Purdom had made their first expeditions without extensive preparation, but also because Purdom had incurred Sargent's displeasure by agreeing with Meyer that the Wu Tai Shan offered nothing more to a plant explorer.

Meyer's family had hoped that he could visit Amsterdam after he had seen Purdom; however, he explained to his sister that he must go to Saint Petersburg immediately. To stop in Holland would be difficult when he was traveling with a tremendous amount of baggage. He expressed his concern because thousands had died that year in the conflict between Turkey and the Balkan League. "The differences in the Balkans could start a world war," he predicted.

Once more his arrival in Russian territory spelled delay and frustration. He had hoped to find an assistant at Saint Petersburg (Leningrad) and to proceed to Siberia ahead of the coldest winter months; however, a prolonged search for a competent helper proved unsuccessful. The December weather varied from freezing rain to snow, heating and ventilating systems recirculated stale air, and sunlight lasted only five hours a day. The long hours of darkness and the lack of fresh air made Meyer feel lethargic. By mid-January, when he had not seen the sun for three weeks, he found the weather "sorely depressing" and the number of suicides daily shocking.

As he continued to search for an assistant who would be willing to cross Siberia in the winter, he also called on Colonel P. K. Koslov, an Asian explorer who had been in Kansu, and studied the herbarium material at the Saint Petersburg Botanical Garden, especially the bush almonds, cherries, and wild peaches. Though he dreaded discussing "the disagreeable *Medicago falcata* subject," he settled his accounts with Woeikov and informed him that the department could not buy more alfalfa at the time. He did order some of Woeikov's hardy shrubs and trees for testing at Mandan, North Dakota.

Meyer felt concern about the effect of the recent American election on the USDA. Woodrow Wilson had defeated William Howard Taft and Theodore Roosevelt. James Wilson, who had served as secretary of agriculture under the Republican administrations of McKinley, Roosevelt, and Taft, would certainly be replaced after having served sixteen years, the longest tenure of any secretary of agriculture. Meyer wrote Dorsett that he hoped for the appointment of a "scientific man," not a politician.

Late in January he abandoned his search for a resourceful and scientifically inclined Russian assistant, deciding to look instead for a Chinese helper at Harbin. He shipped most of his baggage to Manchuria and left "the dark, uncongenial city" of Saint Petersburg. After he and his interpreter had traveled by way of Moscow to Koslov (Michurinsk), he engaged a sleigh in order to visit Mijurin to consult him about unusually hardy plants that might succeed in North Dakota.

Leaving Koslov, Meyer journeyed by rail over the Ural Mountains to Chelyabinsk and then to Kyshtym and Tyssel-Vul in Siberia. At Tyssel-Vul he hired a sleigh and traversed the steppe in a biting wind in order to meet I. M. Karsin, a potential correspondent for the department. Karsin agreed to exchange grain and forage crops for drought-resistant wheats and short-season sorghums. Another train ride took Meyer to Novonikolaevsk (Novosibirsk). There, in snow and piercing wind, he conferred with his former interpreter, Svend Lange, about collecting seeds of wild forage plants for the department. At Tomsk, where the temperature registered $-30°F$ and a fierce wind howled, driving clouds of fine snow before it, he stayed long enough to arrange for the collection of seeds for the USDA.

Boarding a train at 4:00 A.M. on February 4, he continued eastward across Siberia and stopped at Krasnoyarsk. He spent hours there studying herbarium material and talking to a specialist who agreed to trade seeds of hardy crab apples and Ussurian plums for American apples, plums, and grapes. Riding in a droshky, he visited an English fur dealer and saw "fierce and cruel" sables. Since hunting sables had been prohibited for three years in order to save the animals from extinction, furs from sables bred in captivity had become extremely valuable. Meyer therefore suggested to Fairchild that this would be a profitable industry for the USDA to introduce in the northern Rocky Mountains. At 3:00 A.M. on February 8 he left Krasnoyarsk for Irkutsk. With the temperature at −20°F, he reached the Department of Management of Imperial Domains and arranged to have the foresters collect seeds of larch, pines, poplars, and birches for the USDA.

After traveling by train for two more days across picturesque mountains and valleys, he reached Chita in the Trans-Baikal. The weather remained cold but Meyer enjoyed the blue skies, shining sun, exhilarating air, and mountains covered by pine forests, "so different from the dreary gloom of St. Petersburg." At Chita he conferred with the government agronomist and persuaded a collector of wild plants to sell the USDA seeds of unusually hardy varieties of crab apples, bird cherries, currants, gooseberries, and dwarf almonds. Though he had collected little plant material in Siberia, he hoped that the new correspondents whom he had enlisted would furnish valuable seeds for propagating cold-resistant fruits and ornamentals.

Leaving Chita by train, he crossed the Manchurian frontier and reached Harbin two days later. Despite a severe cold, he visited V. F. Ladigine, who had been in Kansu with Colonel Koslov. Ladigine entertained him for two days "with real Russian hospitality" and supplied helpful information about Kansu. He warned Meyer that robber bands roamed that wild and unmapped area, few people lived there, and little food would be available.

Meyer had to remain in Harbin almost three weeks because of a severe recurrence of malarial fever. His illness probably resulted from the hardships he had encountered as he crossed Siberia in midwinter. After spending a week in bed and taking a quantity of medicine, he recovered. Though he minimized the extent of his illness when he wrote to his family, his letters revealed that physical weakness had been accompanied by a feeling of irretrievable loss: "I think often of Mother. I never can see her again and never can talk things over with her. As we get older, we know we understand little. We must accept without questioning."

On March 9 Meyer journeyed to Mukden (Shenyang) alone, having failed to find a Chinese assistant at Harbin. As a jinrikisha took him from the train station to the Astor Hotel, he was surprised to see city parks and imposing buildings. Since his last journey, the Japanese had transformed

Mukden. With the consul general, an acquaintance from Peking, he visited the agricultural experiment station and called on a Japanese naturalist who was writing a book about the flora of southern Manchuria.

Four and a half months after leaving New York, he reached Peking (Beijing) on March 14 and observed many changes that had occurred since he had come there as an untested plant explorer ten years earlier. Revolutionaries led by Sun Yat-sen had overthrown the corrupt Manchu dynasty and established the first Chinese republic. Wealthy Chinese gentlemen, their queues shorn, imitated Westerners by wearing high hats and patent leather shoes, eating in European hotels, and listening to American music. When the gates of the Forbidden City were opened for the funeral of the widow of the former emperor, Meyer was one of hundreds who took advantage of the first opportunity for Occidentals to enter that area.

What surprised him most was the reception that he received in Peking. As soon as he went to the embassy to pick up a large stack of mail from several continents, people began to call on him. Even the new Chinese government sent a representative to invite him to become an adviser on forestry and agriculture. He was glad to learn that E. T. Williams of the American Legation, with whom he had spent many pleasant hours, had become American chargé d'affaires. He even escaped the usual tiring search for assistants. Five days after he arrived, he had hired Chow-hai Ting, his interpreter on his first two expeditions, and Johannis Josephus Cornelius de Leuw, "a young Hollander who is out here on his own." Though Ting sometimes drank and borrowed money from Meyer, he spoke excellent English and Chinese and his experience was invaluable.

Dorsett wrote that Mrs. Fairchild had been ill and David Fairchild had taken her to Florida for the winter, leaving him in charge of the office. The trees and shrubs that Woeikov had sent to be tested at Mandan had arrived safely. Dorsett also reported that Hansen was still trying to promote his proposed journey to Siberia for *Medicago falcata*. "I have been instructed to cancel orders for seed of this plant," Meyer replied. "The Russians will think the U.S. Department of Agriculture chases soap bubbles."

Soon after receiving Dorsett's letter, Meyer mailed him twenty-eight lots of seeds including *Pinus cembra* var. *sibirica* "for the forestry people," a larch (*Larix leptolepis*) for Mandan, a fir (*Abies firma*) for Henry Hicks of Long Island, *Cryptomearia japonica* to form windbreaks around the bamboo at Brooksville, *Zelkova acuminata* for testing in Texas, and *Chamaecyparis obtusa* to be used as an evergreen windbreak in the South. He also sent a Buddhist rosary carved from wild peach stones, "too interesting to be lost," suggesting that Dorsett photograph it and then send it to a museum.

After dispatching his collection, Meyer decided to take a trial trip to Shantung (Shandong) with his "new crew." Making Tsinan (Jinan) his headquarters in Shantung, he sent three packages of scions and cuttings of large seedless jujubes to Robert L. Beagles, who was in charge of the Chico Garden. He also mailed Dorsett seeds of rare local varieties of cucumbers, a dozen different melons, a white eggplant, a "flat" walnut (*Juglans cathayensis*) for Sargent, and nuts from a large walnut tree (*Juglans regia*).

Upon his return to Peking, he felt disturbed because his overdue luggage sent from Saint Petersburg to Harbin had not arrived and, for the first time in his seven years as an agricultural explorer, his accounts showed a deficit instead of a surplus. The deficit of two hundred dollars resulted from the high cost of transporting his baggage across Asia. Meyer offered to pay the amount himself, though he had not charged the department for medicines or for the heavy clothing that he had needed in Siberia; he had not even reserved a berth in a sleeping car. Fairchild ended discussion of this subject by authorizing Dorsett to send Meyer a warrant for two hundred dollars.

In May Meyer suffered another recurrence of malarial fever. After he learned that the baggage that had left Harbin on February 27 had not arrived in Peking, nervous strain complicated his physical symptoms. For two weeks he had been unable to sleep. The missing luggage contained his reference books, most of his photographic equipment, and dozens of other items not available in China. To replace twelve hundred pounds of carefully selected items by mail would have been impossible; yet he could not carry out his assignment without his equipment. Fever, lack of sleep, and mental stress combined to produce a condition approaching delirium. When he heard that his baggage had reached Tientsin safely, he was able to sleep at last. Three days later he had regained enough strength to ship seven parcels containing forty-eight kinds of seeds and eight samples of different kinds of persimmons and walnuts, all identified by names written in Chinese characters. He also sent a large quantity of seeds of the Chinese bush cherry, stones of the northern wild peach, live seedless jujube plants, and samples of the datelike preserved fruit.

Both Dorsett and Fairchild wrote Meyer the surprising news that Hansen was going to Russia for *Medicago falcata* on behalf of the state of South Dakota. Fairchild wrote about this new development with exasperation: "He had the gall to get his friends to write the new Secretary, urging him to grant him five thousand dollars and *carte blanche* so that he would not have to take out any vouchers. The present Secretary of Agriculture will handle this matter differently from the previous one." When Meyer learned that South Dakota was paying an unprecedented amount for this expedition, he felt bewildered.

During the spring, changes had occurred at the USDA. Fairchild wrote about President Wilson's "extremely fortunate" choice of David F. Houston, formerly president of Texas A & M and the University of Texas, to succeed James Wilson as secretary of agriculture. Two thousand people had attended a reception for "Tama Jim" Wilson at the Smithsonian Institution. Beverly T. Galloway had been named assistant secretary of agriculture and William A. Taylor, Meyer's companion during his tour of the northern states in 1908, was replacing Galloway as head of the Bureau of Plant Industry. The new adminstration had already authorized an increase of fourteen thousand dollars for plant introduction.

Fairchild was more concerned about the terrible blight that was threatening American chestnut trees than about the reorganization that the new secretary of agriculture was initiating. The blight had already caused losses amounting to twenty-five million dollars. Dr. C. L. Shear and Dr. Haven Metcalf of the Office of Forest Pathology believed that the fungus (*Endothia parasitica*) must have a foreign origin. They wanted Meyer to search for evidence of the disease in the Orient. Though Meyer had no training as a pathologist, Fairchild felt confident that he could find the disease if it existed in northern China. Shear sent Meyer a fragment of affected bark and a description of the fungus. "If you discover the same fungus over there," Fairchild wrote, "it will affect the whole chestnut blight situation in this country."

Soon after he received Fairchild's letter, Meyer made a four-week trip to the mountains north of Peking to look for fungi on chestnut trees. Despite heavy rains, he enjoyed his journey. He stayed in a lovely valley surrounded by "mountains clothed in pines." On June 4 he wrote from an old Chinese inn that he had collected specimens of the chestnut bark disease and had taken photographs as well. Though he believed that the same fungus was killing American chestnut trees, the Chinese chestnuts did not die as a result of the blight. On some trees he had observed dead limbs and on others old wounds had healed. He enclosed in his letter a tiny piece of affected bark. He also sent a box of chestnuts with the suggestion that the trees grown from these nuts might be immune to blight.

Meyer's letter containing the two-inch-square piece of bark reached Fairchild early in July. When he looked at the tiny specimen, he wondered why Meyer had cabled so confidently; he nevertheless took it immediately to Haven Metcalf. With a magnifying glass, Metcalf could see the familiar fungus strands, but he had to develop cultures in order to establish its identity beyond question. After ten days C. L. Shear reported that they had found the characteristic ascospores of the fungus in the culture. Within three months of Meyer's discovery, pathologists had inoculated trees with cultures made from the fungus that he had sent from China and had proved beyond doubt that the American chestnut blight had been introduced from the Orient.[2] Metcalf later wrote Meyer that his efforts in relation to the origin of the chestnut bark fungus had been the most important work done in plant pathology in the past ten years. When Fairchild assured Meyer that everyone in the office was "pleased and excited about your discovery,"

Meyer replied, "Haven't you any more such problems to solve in China? They do not involve so much labor and trouble as, for instance, bamboo culture or jujube problems."

While Fairchild's duties kept him away from his office, he assigned his secretary, Grace Cramer, the task of writing Meyer a weekly letter to keep him in touch with the plant introduction office and with news in general. Fifteen years earlier, when Fairchild had become head of the new Plant Introduction Section, he had chosen Grace Cramer as his secretary though she was still in her teens and had just arrived in Washington from Kansas. His friends laughed because he had selected a girl still in short skirts with her hair in a braid down her back, but Fairchild had not made a mistake. He had recognized the enthusiasm, intelligence, and industry that made Grace Cramer his invaluable helper for many years.[3]

During the spring of 1913 she accepted her new responsibility enthusiastically. Meyer soon learned from her that his Feicheng peach had set fruit at last and that his photograph of a Russian sable was to be published soon. Grace Cramer also told of floods in the United States, revolution in Mexico, the illness of the pope, and lengthy congressional debates about tariffs. Replying to her inquiries, Meyer explained that he was not interested in hearing about competitive sports, "too great a waste of human efforts, with very little practical outcome." Later he received a letter revealing her vigorous support of women's suffrage. When women pay taxes, she reasoned, they should be able to vote as well. "I am taking it for granted that you are in favor of votes for women. If you are not, don't dare to say so until you get back here and then I will convert you, if necessary calling on the assistance of Mrs. Fairchild."

In late June Meyer mailed his accumulated collection. One box contained grains – winter barley, sorghum, soybeans, and cowpeas, "a wrong name for a bean." He also sent several thousand walnuts to Chico and 42,000 stones of the promising bush cherry (*Prunus tomentosa*) to be tested in North Dakota. Despite excessive heat, a week later he mailed seeds, botanical specimens, fungi, entomological material, herbarium specimens, and photographs, as well as his quarterly accounts and itinerary report. That the government had refused to reimburse him for insurance on his baggage surprised him. He felt that Treasury Department officials should not expect him to send valuable equipment across Asia uninsured or to pay the fees himself.

When the temperature reached 103°F in late July, Meyer and de Leuw could not sleep at night. Neither de Leuw nor Ting felt well. Since he had not received clearance for his trip to the interior, Meyer decided to go to the mountains beyond Peking for the remainder of the summer. Before he left the capital, he mailed five packages that contained eleven kinds of seeds, including about 150,000 stones of the Chinese bush cherry, a valuable variety of Chinese cabbage, a winter radish, and a rare soybean, in addition to diseased chestnut bark, galls on twigs and leaves, and herbarium material.

His duties completed, he set off with de Leuw and Chow-hai Ting for the Western Mountains. There he lived in a Buddhist temple while he finished his accumulated correspondence. At an elevation of five thousand feet, his helpers soon felt well again. He enjoyed climbing the 11,500-foot mountain near his lodging. He told his father that he felt well in these botanically rich surroundings where he had no new correspondence to worry about, no ambassadors or "big-shots" to visit, and no occasions to dress in fine clothes and wear a stiff collar. He also suggested that he and his father might enjoy taking a trip to the mountains together when he returned to Europe in 1916. After pleasant weeks spent adding to his collection, investigating the problem of variation in the Chinese persimmon, and making eighty herbarium specimens of woody plants, he returned to Peking in mid-September.

CHAPTER 22

A Delayed Journey

Peking, Honan, Shansi, and Shantung
SEPTEMBER, 1913, TO MARCH, 1914

T H O U G H Meyer had hoped to travel to Kansu during the summer, in September authorities still had not approved his trip. With garrisons in mutiny and robber bands active in Kansu, Chinese government officials warned him that they could not guarantee his safety there. While he waited to hear that conditions in the interior had stabilized, he labeled, described, and packed his collection.

News of his promotion with an increase in salary from $2,200 a year to $2,500 pleased him. (His salary had been increased from $1,000 to $1,400 in 1907, $1,600 in 1908, $1,800 in 1910, and $2,200 in 1912.) Fairchild had advocated this raise because Meyer was "a man of extremely rare qualifications for pioneer exploration" who was underpaid "for the services rendered and the results obtained." On a USDA form Fairchild rated him *Excellent* in originality and adaptability, efficiency and energy, and executive capacity; *Exceptionally* or *Extremely good* in training and skill in investigation, ability to organize, and ability to present information; and *Very good* or *Unusually good* in ability to cooperate with others and success in addressing gatherings. Fairchild added, "Speaks and reads Dutch, German, French, English, Italian, Spanish and Russian; slight knowledge of Chinese."[1] Though Meyer appreciated his promotion, at the same time his subsistence allowance had been reduced to $125 per month because the law provided that the sum of salary and subsistence could not exceed four thousand dollars. He noted "the welcome news of my promotion" without mentioning that he would receive a net raise of only twenty dollars a year. As he had written earlier, he considered "an interesting life of higher value to man than a large salary."

When Fairchild relayed Sargent's continuing criticism of Meyer's failure to make an adequate collection of herbarium material on his first expedition, Meyer protested that the department had not shown any interest in herbarium specimens at that time. "I saw Professor Webber's Florida plants in a basement on B Street," he pointed out, "and mice and moths had played such havoc with them that most had to be burned." He planned to concentrate on herbarium material on this expedition and to absolve himself from further criticism, even though drying and pressing specimens and writing descriptions required many hours of confining work.

"What a nuisance it is to become somewhat known! I have been asked to dinners and teas by some very eminent people here," he lamented. "These affairs eat away one's valuable time." While he was busy "cornering the market" on over fourteen hundred pounds of stones of the northern wild peach, his advice had been sought by the secretary of the Asiatic Institute, the agent of an importing firm, an archaeologist, and George E. Morrison, an adviser to the Chinese government. Meyer was not optimistic about the future of the new republic that Morrison served. The expenditures of huge sums of borrowed foreign money, the apathy of the masses of Chinese people, and the lawlessness of army troops "form dark clouds on the horizon of Republican China."

Peking seemed quiet without the noblemen and "hangers-on" who formerly surrounded the Imperial Court. Much that had been picturesque was disappearing as China concentrated on attempting to modernize. Chinese ladies of the higher class followed the latest Paris fashions, Meyer wrote Grace Cramer. He had seen one woman wearing high-heeled gold shoes "of which she seemed remarkably proud." By the year 2000, he predicted, the whole world might look and dress alike.

Though he appreciated Grace Cramer's letters, he occasionally offered criticism. After hearing that Professor Bailey Balfour of Edinburgh University had said that George Forrest's introductions of valuable plants from China had revolutionized English gardens, he wrote, "And I didn't even know of this, and I am supposed to be a specialist on Chinese horticulture." Undaunted, Grace Cramer continued to write frequently, filling her letters with a combination of scientific information, world affairs, and personal items about Meyer's friends in the department. When she wrote about the militant suffragettes in England, Meyer did not hesitate to warn her about "some of the red-hot suffragette literature. . . . Some very degrading proposals are being made by 'advanced' authors, some even going so far as to advocate absolute liberty as regards indulgence of the pleasures of the flesh." Though his attitude now seems chauvinistic, he was flouting the mores of his time by discussing such a subject with a young lady.

Meyer was glad to hear from Miss Cramer that P. H. Dorsett was about to head an expedition to Brazil to study the problem of variability of the navel orange. A. D. Shamel, who had been working with oranges at the Riverside Citrus Station in California, and young Wilson Popenoe would accompany him. Fairchild had recruited Popenoe when he was just twenty years old, but his extensive knowledge of tropical fruits and his enthusiasm made him invaluable to the Plant Introduction Section. Meyer wished Dorsett the best of luck in his first venture into the field and admitted that he almost envied his opportunity to see the flora of southern Brazil.

As October began, planning his long-awaited journey to the interior absorbed Meyer's attention. He decided not to take a cook or any other servant with him, since Chow-hai Ting was experienced, de Leuw was hardy, and "I am not too fastidious in my demands." When he consulted E. T. Williams, the American chargé d'affaires, about beginning his journey, he received discouraging news. Powerful bands of brigands still terrorized all of Honan (Henan) Province. They had seized a high government official as a hostage and had "relieved a Belgian engineer of all his baggage." Outlaws in Hupeh (Hubei) Province had held Swedish and American missionaries for ransom. Near Kalgan (Zhangjiakou, formerly Changchiakou) a British citizen had been murdered along with his companions. Considering these developments, Meyer bought a rifle and an additional revolver from an American army officer. "The process of leaving this globe is, after all, not such a big thing; we all have to go some day," he conceded. "But when one's belongings are taken, one cannot work any longer."

Obliged to delay his departure, he mounted and labeled herbarium specimens until late at night and shipped seven large wooden cases containing sorghums, walnuts, 250 pounds of fresh chestnuts, and 1,500 pounds of wild peach stones, the greatest quantity of *Prunus davidiana* that ever had been gathered together. He urged Fairchild to give Merton Waite a quantity of the peach stones to use in his research, but Waite already was testing four hundred wild peach trees that he had grown from an earlier shipment of stones. Meyer also sent seeds of evergreens, a dwarf cherry (*Prunus humilis* Bunge), a giant sixteen-pound kohlrabi, asparagus, inventory notes, and photographs.

Early in November he shipped nine more bundles containing twenty thousand persimmon seeds, seeds of a rare striped soybean, and jujube scions. Botanical specimens identified with Chinese names included dried fruit, burrs, seed capsules, and catkins. Diseased chestnut bark, rust on a blue spruce, and a fungus on a poplar were among the pathological specimens for L. O. Howard, head of the Bureau of Entomology. He also mailed five wooden whistles designed to be tied to pigeons. "When the birds sail through the skies, these whistles produce the queerest of tunes." The whistles, a product of painstaking and imaginative craftsmanship, are now in the bamboo collection at the National Arboretum.

He received clearance for his trip to the interior when C. L. Williams, the son of his friend at the American Legation, returned from Sian in Shensi Province and reported that the main roads were fairly safe. Since silver by weight was the only currency in use in Kansu Province, bank officers advised him to take cash with him; however, he objected that the weight would be too great to carry and the cash could make his small party a target for robbers. He arranged instead for native banks to supply drafts in Sian and Lanchow. The new American minister to China, Dr. Paul S. Reinsch, who had met Meyer when he spoke to the University Club in Madison in 1908, took special interest in his journey and asked to be informed of his progress.

Early in December Meyer packed his last bundles and mailed five hundred labeled sets of herbarium specimens, the result of many hours of indoor work. He explained that the cost of obtaining, preparing, and shipping that single wooden case had amounted to $1,200 including salaries, making herbarium specimens "the most expensive item of my work." He also shipped a large tin of persimmons, pears, jujubes, crab apples, and grapes, which he had cured in alcohol and packed in alcohol-soaked shavings, and four packages of cuttings, "insects, rusts, and monstrosities." The cuttings included *Viburnum farreri* (*V. fragrans*), a beautiful shrub that had grown under cultivation only in the gardens of the Imperial Palace before the Revolution.

During his final week in Peking he completed his correspondence, acknowledging a copy of the *Gardeners' Chronicle* containing Purdom's description of his work in Kansu, an article from *World's Work* on E. H. Wilson's accomplishments in China, and a USDA bulletin, *Plant Immigrants*, that described a number of his own introductions. Fairchild's request for seeds of "the variety of hemp from which hashish is made" puzzled him. He wrote George Macartney, the British consul at Kashgar, asking him to ship twenty pounds of seeds to the United States, but he wondered "what use the American public can make of this hashish." He also thanked Grace Cramer for sending him a consular report on new railroads in China and fifteen photographs. He especially enjoyed seeing a picture of Dorsett, Popenoe, and Shamel as they left for Brazil, but a snapshot of Miss Cramer evoked brotherly criticism: "Of your own self I should say the scales must tell a different tale from some year or so ago; it is not *too* bad, however!"

In mid-December Meyer, de Leuw, and Ting finally left Peking by train with their twenty heavy pieces of baggage. After waiting so many months to travel to the interior, Meyer found "fearful" conditions at Honanfu (Luoyang). As a result of famine, he saw beggars everywhere. "They cling to one and throw themselves at one's feet in the middle of the street." In the somewhat milder climate, he waded through "a slushy mess" of ankle-deep melted snow, but he still needed his fur-lined coat and felt boots for warmth. The town appeared indescribably dirty. On the south gate he saw the heads of robbers, reminders that gave him "a creeping sensation."

He hired carts for the next phase of his journey, but the Chinese magistrate and the missionaries persuaded him to change his plans. The magistrate warned him that the large bands of robbers operating near the city made travel on foot in any direction unsafe. Swedish missionaries compounded his frustration by describing a district south of Honanfu that had never been visted by a Western collector. Bamboo plantations, lacquer trees, and monkeys lured him, but the missionaries had been unable to go there even in peacetime without an escort of armed soldiers. Meyer reluctantly abandoned any hope of collecting in that part of Honan. With de Leuw and Ting, he journeyed by train to the end of the railroad at Tiemen, where coolies used five wheelbarrows to haul their baggage to an inn.

Though Meyer later assured Fairchild that he had encountered little trouble, actually he experienced a challenging trip across Shensi. He used carts at first, but he had to depend on donkeys in the mountains. In the rugged Ta hua Shan range, coolies carried the baggage for several days because trails were too steep for donkeys. Meyer considered the inns in rural Shensi the worst that he had ever seen. Leaking roofs, broken doors, and windows lacking the usual paper covering inconvenienced the travelers; furthermore, previous occupants had used corners of the room "for water closet purposes." Fuel was scarce, but the cold temperature prevented attacks by bedbugs and other vermin. As they traveled on foot, they noticed a few "suspicious looking specimens of humanity armed with old flintlocks and big rusty knives." At rare intervals they met forlorn Chinese soldiers on patrol. During the cheerless journey, Meyer and de Leuw must have observed Christmas and exchanged good wishes for 1914 at some wretched inn. On January 3 they reached Sian (Xi'an), the capital of Shensi Province.

In the Ta hua Shan, Chow-hai Ting had fallen and sustained an injury. Meyer took him to the English Baptist Mission Hospital at Sian, where Dr. George Carter advised an operation. Ting demurred. Meyer felt that the trauma of an operation would cancel the benefits; he therefore decided to let Ting rest for a while and then to limit his activities to "plains and lower mountains." To enter an area known to be unsafe with a partially disabled interpreter would have been foolhardy. Meyer did not record his anguish when he realized that he must abandon his cherished plan to proceed to Kansu Province, the goal of his expedition.

He spent four weeks in Sian, calling on officials, receiving visitors, and exploring the region around the city. *Nandina domestica*, winter jasmine (*Jasminum nudiflorum*), pagoda trees (*Sophora japonica*), soap-pod trees (*Gleditsia sinensis*), and paulownia flourished in the mild climate. While Chow-hai Ting rested, Meyer collected nine named varieties of persimmons, including some that produced excellent juicy fruit. He also sampled persimmon vinegar, persimmon brandy, persimmon pie, and persimmon paste stuffed with walnuts and pressed into square cakes. From Sian he shipped nine bundles including bamboo, a large apricot, four jujube varieties, persimmons, and inventory notes.

Late in January he made a short journey to the mountains south of Sian. There he examined chestnut trees (*Castanea mollissima*) that had scarcely been affected by the bark fungus and cut scions from those that appeared to have resisted the blight. In the mountains he also collected scions of six named varieties of rare persimmons and discovered among rocks a dense, slow-growing privet (*Ligustrum quihoui*) bearing masses of small black berries. This fine privet was widely distributed by the USDA for use as a hedge and border shrub in mild-wintered, semiarid regions. In the Southern states it produces panicles of creamy-white flowers and remains evergreen all winter. Though it has been neglected elsewhere, a hedge planted many years ago at the USDA Plant Introduction Station at Glenn Dale, Maryland (Test block 2, item no. 207), is thriving. About one hundred feet long, it is maintained by pruning at four feet in height and six feet in width.[2]

Instead of complaining because his long-awaited trip to Kansu had to be postponed, Meyer wrote Fairchild enthusiastically about the prospects for his return to Peking by way of Shansi, Honan, and Shantung. He had heard of fine persimmons and of jujubes nearly as large as hen's eggs in Shansi. He planned to see "if these hens lay not perhaps some rather small eggs." He also told Fairchild about the botanical garden that C. W. Janssen was founding on the east coast of Sumatra and asked Fairchild to exchange with the new Dutch garden. After negotiating with carters, Meyer, de Leuw, and Ting left Sian on February 1.

Despite wind, sleet, and snowstorms, they pursued their route. At Puchow (Puzhou) on the north side of the Yellow River in Shansi Province, Meyer collected one of the best persimmons (*Diospyros kaki*) in China, a favorite of the former Imperial Court. Traveling northwest, he entered the Tshehsien and Anyihsien districts which had been famous for centuries for large jujubes (*Zizyphus jujuba*) of fine quality. "I saw indeed some as large as hen's eggs," he admitted. At Anyihsien on February 14 he collected cuttings of 'Li'—one of the largest and best of all jujube cultivars. Having found the fruits that he sought, he began the journey to the nearest railroad. As snow, hail, and cold rain fell, the loaded carts stuck in mud every few minutes. Everyone lost his temper in the beastly weather, and all were glad to reach Honanfu and board the train for Kaifeng, the capital of Honan Province.

From Kaifeng, despite bad weather, Meyer and his party traveled south by cart to Chiningchow (Jiningzhou). There he shipped nine bundles to Washington and two to Chico. Though he had trouble completing the labels and inventory notes in a dirty and noisy inn, he sent four varieties of large jujubes and various kinds of persimmons. A few days later he mailed six parcels of seeds including an elm (*Ulmus parvifolia*) suitable for use as an ornamental in semiarid regions. This is the tree now known as the Chinese elm, though Fairchild and Meyer used that name for the dry-land elm, *Ulmus pumila*, now called the Siberian elm.

A twenty-four-hour rain delayed the beginning of Meyer's trip from Kaifeng to Shantung. The interior of China had suffered drought from January until October of 1913, but snow, hail, sleet, and rain had fallen frequently during the winter. While the rain poured, Meyer reported to Fairchild that he expected to be able to "push through" to Tsinan, though he had heard that there were "bad characters" in the area. He had spent most of the money that he had carried, reducing considerably the cost of being robbed. The delay in leaving Kaifeng also gave him time to write the Janssens about his three months in the "hinterland." He admitted that he felt "not twenty any more," but he was satisfied with the work he had accomplished.

After an uneventful trip, Meyer and his assistants arrived at Tsinan (Jinan). Shantung Province proved bountiful once more, and Meyer packed and shipped twelve packages to America. He sent scions of many fruit trees—pear, apple, haw, quince, and jujube, as well as root cuttings of *Paulownia fortunei*, the silk tree (*Albizia chinensis*), and the white poplar (*Populus tomentosa*). Of the poplar he wrote Fairchild, "The more I see of this tree, the more I like it; I will not rest until I see it established in America."

The next day he left Tsinan on foot with wheelbarrows, hoping to collect some budded specimens of the famous Feicheng peach tree (*Prunus persica*). This assignment proved difficult because the inhabitants of Feicheng were aware that their trees produced the finest peaches in China. They allowed Meyer to collect scions but refused to sell trees unless he would pay forty to fifty dollars per tree. Ting solved this problem "by diplomatic dealing" when he paid a farmer forty dollars for a plot of ground containing eight trees. Meyer and his party removed the trees promptly; however, they had to leave Feicheng hurriedly because the farmer's relatives, who had not been consulted about the sale, tried to recover the trees. Unwilling to risk transporting all eight peach trees together, Meyer managed to circumvent postal regulations and mail one tree and twenty-six scions to Washington and another set to Chico.[3] At 3:00 A.M. on March 30, Meyer and his assistants left Tsinan by train with the plant material that he could not send abroad from the interior.

From Tientsin Meyer shipped the live material and submitted his accounts and itinerary for the quarter. He had limited his expenses by paying for his medicine, laundry, tips, and camping outfit from his own funds. Unable to foresee the fate that would befall his precious collection in Japan, he carefully packed a large wooden case containing six grafted trees of the famous Feicheng peach, ten budded quinces, six budded large-fruited haws, five *Paeonia lactiflora*, and twelve *Paeonia suffruticosa*. Chinese growers had told him that these tree peonies would have yellow and green tints. Even though he had not reached Kansu, he had obtained useful varieties of persimmons and jujubes, the Fei peach, scions of an apparently disease-resistant form of the Chinese chestnut, and the tree peonies, as well as 120 photographs. With his shipments, accounts, and itinerary completed, he felt "like a free man again" when he boarded the 8:00 A.M. train "to Peking and mail."

CHAPTER 23

The Long March Begins

Peking, Honan, Shansi, Shensi
APRIL TO AUGUST, 1914

MEYER was determined to try again to reach Kansu; however, he had much to do before beginning another journey. Though he enjoyed a cordial welcome from friends in Peking, he had little time for social obligations while he was facing an accumulation of 175 pieces of mail. Two packages sent to Washington in September had been returned to him "through error on the part of some clerk at the State Department." After having been boxed for several months, most of the collection had died. Meyer reacted to the loss of his time and effort with wry resignation, suggesting to Fairchild that "some gentle inquiries might be made as to the sanity of the party who mixed up this business."

Letters from Grace Cramer, David Fairchild, and Peter Bisset brought news from Washington. By mid-January, Meyer learned, Dorsett and Popenoe had gone into the interior of Brazil and were navigating the rapids of the São Francisco River, a decided change for Dorsett who had been office-bound for years. Harold Hume was puzzled by the astringency that Meyer's "puckerless" persimmons had developed in America. Bisset assured Meyer that nurserymen were using his northern wild peach successfully as a stock and sent photographs of a seedling Feicheng peach and three Chinese persimmon trees bearing heavily. "We have been carrying out your suggestion and sending Professor Sargent one-fourth to one-half of all seeds you are sending," Bisset added. "Couldn't we propagate first and then share?"

But discouraging news came from Kobe in late April. Japanese authorities had detained the large wooden case containing Meyer's six Feicheng peach trees because inspectors had found insects on some of the plants and had decided to fumigate the entire lot. Meyer feared the possible loss of the budded quinces and haws, the rare tree peonies, and especially the peach trees that had cost him several days' travel with wheelbarrows and much negotiating. In May Beagles reported that the case had reached Chico, looking as if the contents had been removed for fumigation and simply "dumped in" thereafter. All the trees were in bad condition.

The stringency of the Japanese inspection may have resulted from the passage of America's long-deferred Plant Quarantine Act of 1912. This act permitted the importing of nursery stock from countries maintaining an inspection service. The Japanese had become painfully conscious of the importance of inspection because so many insects had infested their original gift of two thousand flowering cherry trees to be planted around the Tidal Basin in Washington that the trees had to be burned. Whatever the reason, Japanese officials notified Meyer that they could no longer forward live material to America because American laws had become very strict.[1]

Despite this setback, by May 13 Meyer had mailed sixty-three bundles to the department. These lots included chestnuts, large haw fruits, stones of the Feicheng peach, a large "saucer" peach, and different types of jujubes. Meyer suggested that a member of the office staff preserve some of each variety in bottles in order to create the only collection of named jujubes in the world. Neither reference books nor the herbarium at Kew could help to clarify the confusion about jujubes, for at least three hundred cultivars flourished in commerical culture in northern China and many more in private yards.

Early in April Grace Cramer wrote that she had paid the five dollar fee for the rent of Meyer's safe-deposit box and that he could either "remit this to me in money or buy me some blue china in Peking—a little vase of blue and white or a bowl." After thanking her and enclosing his check, Meyer replied, "Your suggestion as to spending this on some blue porcelain has been considered, but the chances are you might have to pay a pretty large amount as duty; therefore, I will bring something with me, and payment will be out of the question, of course." According to Fairchild, Meyer always selected gifts from China with discriminating taste and an apprecia-tion of beauty in form and color. An incident that he related suggests that Grace Cramer did indeed receive her "little vase of blue and white." After Meyer returned to America, he accepted an invitation to dinner and pro-ceeded to rearrange his hostess's living room, removing all the ornaments that cluttered the surfaces and featuring in appropriate settings two or three good pieces of Oriental porcelain. Fortunately, she liked the effect that he achieved.[2]

Although Meyer had planned to leave Peking for Kansu early in June, failure to find a qualified interpreter and unsettled conditions in the interior presented difficulties. The men whom he interviewed in an effort to replace Chow-hai Ting lacked either the required knowledge and experience or the courage necessary for plant exploration in western Shensi and Kansu. A band of outlaws headed by an infamous "monster-robber" called White

Wolf had been terrorizing Shensi Province. The government had sent soldiers to Sian to limit the activities of roaming bands of brigands, but Meyer learned that "the brutal and merciless White Wolves" were marching across Kansu. By the end of May, White Wolf had advanced almost to Lanchow, having looted all the towns between that point and Sian. One of the victims of the robber band was the little Taoist nun who had saved William Purdom's life when he was seriously injured during his first expedition.[3]

In May Meyer shipped ten more bundles to the United States. He described the roasted soybeans that he included as hard enough to develop jaw muscles and possibly to damage teeth and warned, "I will under no circumstances be held responsible for any damage to various parts of the anatomy of any party who eats them." Three packages contained negatives and prints, "scenic as well as scientific," for he could not resist photographing Chinese landscapes, gardens, and architecture. He also sent quantities of seeds of pears, quinces, persimmons, blood-red carrots, and ornamentals. In addition, he mailed rooted wild rice plants, mosses and lichens, and, for specialists at the Smithsonian Institution, fossils, a mole, and a cricket in alcohol.

Though he wished that he could leave his desk and "run away into the wilds," he finished answering the sixty letters that he had received from Fairchild that spring. One item had impressed him: "I notice your remark *re* the discovery of lipins and vitamins in food. I have no idea what they are and how they work. I will make it a point to find out more when in America." He felt pleased because the *Journal of Heredity* had published some of his letters from Turkestan in March and April, 1914. But the best news of all brought a cheer: "Messrs. Dorsett and Popenoe back again safe and sound; hurrah!" He wished that he could have joined the festive celebration the staff held in their honor. He also rejoiced to hear that his large box of five hundred lots of herbarium material had arrived safely and that Fairchild had sent Sargent part of the collection. Replying to Fairchild's request for beans that would produce edible sprouts, he recommended Mung and Adzuki beans. Instead of agreeing to send samples from China, however, he suggested that the department buy some for analysis from a Chinese restaurant on Ninth Street in Washington.

Though he sought new introductions constantly, he continued to express interest in the plant material he had already sent to America. Fairchild had written that water remained standing on the bamboo plantings at Brooksville long after rain had fallen, because of the red clay subsoil. Few new bamboo canes were developing and the older ones were only fifteen feet high. Though this news was disappointing, Meyer rejoiced because Fairchild believed that the Chinese chestnut would replace the American chestnut, not as a timber tree, but as a source of nuts. Fairchild also reported that Jackson Dawson had succeeded in grafting cuttings of Meyer's

Viburnum fragrans (now called *Viburnum farreri*) at the Arnold Arboretum, and Sargent had declared that such a handsome new shrub had not
been introduced into America for a long time.

Despite a "frightful" dust storm that tore the new green leaves from the
trees, Meyer's preparations for his journey to Kansu continued. Buying
medicine for the entire party was essential. He paid three dollars for
quinine, two dollars for anticholera tablets, four dollars for one hundred
headache tablets, and a dollar and a half for a bottle of citric crystals. The
search for a qualified interpreter consumed much of his time. Prospective
employees were deterred by stories of looting, atrocities, murder, and corrupt officials who accepted bribes to deliver whole cities to the White
Wolves. Meyer heard that William Purdom had been ill with fever at Sian.
"The poor fellow has had bad luck," he wrote. "I am sorry not to have seen
him." Never having heard of Reginald Farrer, he reported that Purdom was
going to Kansu "with a Mr. Collier?, a specialist in alpines."

Anticipating his departure, Meyer completed his correspondence and
shipped his collection. Grace Cramer reported that Dorsett had taken and
developed over eleven hundred photographs in Brazil and had packed the
negatives so carefully that only two of the glass plates were broken when
they reached Washington. Meyer answered that Dorsett's accomplishment
amazed him; "I could not have done it." In June he shipped fifteen cases of
stones of the bush cherry (*Prunus tomentosa*) and eight boxes containing
herbarium specimens, plant material used in making dyes, botanical specimens, and dried jujubes.

Though Fairchild believed firmly that the jujube would become an
important agricultural product because it would grow in barren regions that
would not support any other crop, Meyer never shared his confidence.
When he sent preserved jujubes to Washington, he predicted correctly that
the Bureau of Chemistry would find them less nutritional than dates. The
wife of the American minister at Peking served candied jujubes (Mitsao)
stuffed with walnuts and "most delicious they tasted"; yet Meyer cautioned
Fairchild not to encourage growers to plant jujubes on a large scale.
Though Fairchild offered candied jujubes to Alexander Graham Bell's
guests at his Wednesday Evenings and to members of the National Geographic Society at their annual banquet, he could not develop a wide market
for a new food because the Plant Introduction Section lacked funds available to promoters of commercial products.[4]

In mid-June when Meyer was about to leave Peking, he realized that
the well-educated interpreter whom he had tentatively engaged could not
bear the hardships of a journey to Kansu and possibly south to Chungking
(Chongqing). Desperate at his failure to find an interpreter who was both
educated and robust, he placed an ad in the Peking *Daily News* and considered each of nineteen applicants. Many were competent translators but

none had experience in the field. Meyer chose the man who appeared best suited for an arduous journey; however, the interpreter's mother persuaded him not risk his life in an area roamed by White Wolf. At last Meyer selected Chi-nian Tien and made a contract with him in the presence of two witnesses.

Before setting out, Meyer described his proposed itinerary, his goals, and three difficulties that he might face. He listed brigandage as the first potential problem. Next he wondered whether his well-educated but un-tested interpreter would prove satisfactory in the interior. His final worry concerned having enough money available to pay his expenses. "When I do not get robbed, I think we will be able to manage," he told David Fairchild. His Peking bank had sent drafts to banks in Sian and Lanchow. He also had advanced $300 to Chow-hai Ting to enable him to buy seeds near Peking. He was taking with him $300 in government notes, $300 in silver, and $50 in copper cash, as well as a $3,200 letter of credit. "Robbers roam every-where," he admitted. "We will trust, however, to our usual good luck."

Accompanied by de Leuw, Chi-nian Tien, and a servant, he bought second-class tickets, boarded a train with thirty bulky pieces of baggage, and traveled to Changde (Anyang) in the northern tip of Honan (Henan) Province. Early in July he wrote Fairchild from a dark room in an inn so infested with flies that he had been forced to drape a mosquito net around him and his small writing table. Though he had suffered several attacks of "this accursed fever," he was preparing to enter a wild mountainous region.

Two days later he and his small party began their two-week journey across Honan and into Shansi Province. At first their inexperienced carters had difficulty loading the two carts securely, and their baggage kept working loose. By the end of the week they had replaced the carts with twelve pack animals in order to cross the Linhsien Mountains. As they traveled, Meyer took photographs and collected and dried herbarium specimens. In such humid weather, green, succulent material molds if it does not dry thor-oughly within a day or two; therefore, this task could not be postponed.

When they reached Luanfu (Changzhi), they rested for a few days while Meyer searched for pack mules, dried the herbarium specimens, and enjoyed the company of Roman Catholic missionaries. Monsignor Timmer of Haarlem invited him to dinner and showed him the large garden that the missionaries were cultivating. Meyer wrote his father that he enjoyed having a glass of beer or wine with Dutch people again. He sent good wishes for his father's coming birthday and hoped that he could deliver his congratula-tions personally in 1916. He did not mention that the missionaries had warned him about a band of thirty or forty robbers who had been pillaging along the route that he planned to take.[5]

Meyer and his party left Luanfu in heavy rain and traveled toward Pingyang (Linfen) with ten pack mules. In the rugged mountains they had no encounters with brigands, but they did battle flies by day and fleas by night. Meyer hired five soldiers as a convoy "over a bad place" near the border of Shansi; however, they saw only a human head in a wooden cage hanging in a large apricot tree as a warning to other bandits. Along the way Meyer noticed many beautiful white-barked pines and collected "quite a stack" of herbarium material despite heavy thunderstorms. A few days east of Pingyang, he found in a ravine a small green peach the size of a marble. "Looking up I noticed several bushes clinging to the edge of a steep loess wall and having fruits on them. Here at last was the original wild peach, from which probably most, if not all, of the cultivated strains have been developed."[6] Excited by this discovery, he did not mind trudging through heavy rain until he reached Pingyang at 8:00 P.M. on July 25.

From Pingyang Meyer sent Fairchild news of his journey. During the hard trip from Changde he had seen much wild alfalfa growing far away from men or animals and had concluded that the spreading strain of *Medicago sativa* was native to China, though he was not sure about the upright forms; much more significant was his discovery of the "real wild peach" (*Prunus davidiana* var. *potaninii,* formerly *P. persica potaninii*) at an altitude of four thousand feet. As he traversed Shansi, Shensi, Kansu, and the Tibetan borderland, he continued to find this peach occurring in the Tsingling range, both as specimen trees and in thickets. His untried interpreter was "holding out fairly well," though he was "by far not as clever" as Chowhai Ting. Villagers had beaten Chi-nian Tien and the coolie, but "we are negotiating with the local magistrate to have this beating business returned to the proper parties." Remaining in Pingyang for a week, Meyer dried his herbarium specimens, received visits from Roman Catholic missionaries and native Christians, and negotiated with carters for the next segment of his journey.

On August 4 he and his party began the difficult journey to Sian, the capital of Shensi Province. Even in the mountains candles melted and sealing wax "fraternized with lead pencils and rubber bands." High temperatures spoiled their food, and the humidity made drying specimens almost impossible. Finding enough to eat became a problem; the noodles they carried did not furnish much nourishment and they met few natives from whom they could buy food. Extremely poor roads, made worse than ever by heavy rains, impeded their progress. At a village along the way, Meyer was shocked to hear rumors that war had been declared in Europe.

As the travelers approached the Yellow River (Huang He), which was in flood, they became confused because their maps showed neither roads nor villages and Chi-nian Tien could not understand the local dialects. Either the natives deliberately misinformed him or else he misunderstood their directions. In any case, they wasted several days making a wide detour before reaching the river. After maneuvering their carts along liquid mud flats, they attempted the treacherous crossing despite swampy areas and quicksands. Two and a half hours passed before boatmen succeeded in landing the two carts and eight mules on the west bank of the river. The next day they intersected the main road to Sian. As they trudged on four more days in sultry weather, they felt tired, dirty, and hungry. After ferrying across the Lo and the Wei rivers, on August 19 they finally reached Sian.

Even in the provincial capital, the best accommodations were uncomfortable; however, devastating news of the outside world made physical hardships seem relatively unimportant. Though fatigue and "exceedingly bad sanitary conditions" caused Meyer, de Leuw, and Tien to feel "not quite well," Meyer was more deeply troubled by reports of war in Europe and by rumors of a Japanese declaration of war against China. "Has hell broken loose on earth? There seems to reign darkness over the Earth now, and this after nearly twenty centuries of Christian teaching," he wrote bitterly. "Well, we must keep our heads together, although the misery suffered there in Europe among those of our race and kin seems to cry out to us here in China even." From the first he perceived the war in terms of the waste of promising young lives and the destruction of valuable crops and forests.

His own work continued nevertheless. From Sian he mailed the department bundles containing hemp for fiber specialists, castor beans with spineless burrs, apricot stones, galls, scales, and a bottle of insects, "some new monsters among them." Most important of all, he sent samples of the wood, dried fruits, and seven hundred stones of the "real wild peach" (*Prunus davidiana* var. *potaninii*), inquiring eagerly, "Are they new? Bretschneider even thinks *Prunus davidiana* might have been the original peach."

During his ten days in Sian, Meyer faced several problems. He and de Leuw, Tien, and their coolie had arrived tired, hungry, and "not in very good health." He soon learned that many of the inhabitants of the capital were dying as a result of a severe dysentery epidemic. Furthermore, officials had placed the city under military rule because of the threat posed by the White Wolves, and farmers had hidden the mules that had not already been commandeered by the army. As a result, Meyer could not hire pack animals in order to go into the mountains to search for new plants.

On August 24 he had an audience with the governor of Shensi Province about his proposed trip to Kansu. At first the governor insisted that the roads were unsafe. He apparently believed that "it would make trouble for him if something happened to me; perhaps he finds it convenient to tell me terrible things, hoping I won't go. I *will* go, however." When the governor eventually realized this, he helped Meyer to find eight mules and muleteers. Looking forward to "exciting adventures ahead," Meyer began his challenging trip, accompanied by de Leuw, Tien, their servant, and the muleteers.

The Border of Tibet (Xizang)

Kansu Province
SEPTEMBER, 1914, TO FEBRUARY, 1915

MEYER later admitted that the journey from Sian to southwestern Kansu Province presented major difficulties including rain and fog, mountainous terrain, trouble with muleteers, and dreadful accommodations. When the White Wolves had passed through this region during the preceding summer, plundering and burning as they marched, they had either stolen or killed all the pack animals they could find and had terrified the villagers. Incompetent muleteers and "fearfully inquisitive" local inhabitants added to Meyer's problems. Tien and de Leuw felt ill after leaving Sian, but Meyer continued well and worked until late at night drying and pressing the specimens he was collecting.

No inns existed in the region between Sian and Paoki (Baoji), but the travelers usually found shelter in old temples. "How we lodged I ought not to say," Meyer told Fairchild later. "We have shared stables with our mules, oxen, and other creatures; in old temples the idols were our companions; and how we slept some nights I hardly know." On one occasion they could not sleep because the moon was in eclipse. All night long the natives made hideous noises in order "to scare away the monsters that were eating the moon." They spent the next night in a ruined temple but left by 5:00 A.M. because of the hostility of the inhabitants. Again they ferried across the Wei River. Later they passed over a deep and dangerous torrent. Meyer continued to collect herbarium material and to take photographs until they stopped at Paoki to seek replacements for their "obstinate muleteers."

After leaving Paoki, they ferried across the Wei River again and saw for the first time wetland ginger plantations. In the mountains beyond Paoki Meyer found wild peaches, plums, apricots, crab apples, grapes, walnuts, and chestnuts. He collected a large amount of herbarium material, cleaned the stones of wild peaches, and dried his herbarium specimens above charcoal fires. While cold rain fell at Fenghsien (Fengxian), he and his party spent several nights at an inn with a leaking roof. He searched for two days before finding eight pack mules to carry their baggage westward. On September 22 they set out in a heavy rain, wading along trails filled with liquid mud that made progress slow for men and mules. The next night not even a ruined temple provided shelter. "Slept with four mules and eight other people as company," Meyer noted in his itinerary report.

After crossing a mountain range the next day, he forgot the discomforts of the night because he was entering Kansu Province at last. Neither the weather, the terrain, nor the primitive living conditions dampened his enthusiasm for this opportunity to collect in an area visited by few foreigners. In heavy rain he and his party climbed steep mountains and crossed high mountain passes. The muddy trails became slippery and dangerous as rain continued. Yet he collected many specimens, admired beautiful white-barked pines and pistachio trees sixteen feet in circumference, studied chestnut trees affected by bark fungus, and noticed wild peach trees everywhere. Until this time, botanists believed that *Pinus bungeana* occurred wild only in Hupeh (Hubei) Province; Meyer discovered it scattered and in groves not only in Kansu but also in southern Shansi and central Shensi.[1]

Continuing across southwestern Kansu, he stopped at Huihsien (Xuixian) where he dried his herbarium material above charcoal fires and searched for mules and muleteers for the next phase of his journey. He also visited Roman Catholic missionaries, admired the fine garden they had cultivated, and received helpful information about the region and its products. After spending the next night at a dilapidated temple in a village where they were mistaken for robbers, Meyer and his men traveled to Chenghsien (Chengxian). They paused there four days while they sought and then negotiated with another relay of muleteers. Again Meyer spent his time collecting plants, cleaning seeds, drying herbarium material, and exchanging visits with Roman Catholic missionaries. After they left Chenghsien and found shelter for the night in a neglected temple, they realized that one of the muleteers had disappeared. They searched for him until midnight when they realized that he had deserted and had taken his mule with him. With the remaining mules heavily loaded, they spent the next several days traversing mountainous country in rainy weather and ferrying across a river. After following slippery trails and climbing precipitous mountains, on October 10 they reached Chiehchou (Jiezhou).

Meyer searched for accommodations for two hours before choosing the best inn available at Chiehchou. He had hoped to complete his overdue accounts there, but he wrote Fairchild that his financial report would be late because he could not concentrate. "Imagine an overcrowded inn, with merchants and coolies shouting and having angry disputes; with partitions between the rooms so thin as to make them almost transparent; with people gambling with dice and cards all night long; others smoking opium; hawkers coming in, selling all possible sorts of things from raw carrots to straw braid hats; and odors hanging about to make angels, even, procure handkerchiefs. Here you have a picture of the best inn in town." But he had to remain at that inn for six days while, as usual, he dried his herbarium material above charcoal fires and looked for muleteers willing to accompany him to the wild Tibetan borderland. By this time Chi-nian Tien and the coolie had suffered enough hardships; both gave notice that they were not willing to continue the journey beyond Lanchow.

After leaving Chiehchou, both Tien and the muleteers objected to entering Tibet in search of wild peaches and bush almonds. Rumors of vats of boiling oil waiting in Tibet influenced the muleteers more than the extra strings of copper coins that Meyer offered as an inducement. (In 1914 Tibet was independent and its boundaries extended farther north and west than at present. Meyer did not plan to enter the Tibet Autonomous Region, Xizang Zizhiqu.)

Entries in his itinerary report presaged the confrontation that was developing: "October 20 — Arrived Siku. Muleteers afraid to go into Tibetan country; October 21 — Difficulty with muleteers and interpreter. Discharged four muleteers; October 22 — Difficulty with interpreter and coolie. They do not want to go with me any further. Afraid."

At this point one of those coincidences that is stranger than fiction occurred. Two plant-hunting expeditions happened to meet in the remote town of Siku (Zhugqu) in the fall of 1914. An Englishman, Reginald Farrer, headed the other party. In 1913 Farrer, a well-to-do amateur botanist with a special interest in alpines, had met William Purdom in London. Both men were thirty-three years old; otherwise they presented a striking contrast. William Purdom was tall, lean, blond, handsome, quiet, and reflective, while Farrer was short, stout, dark, talkative, and excitable. When Farrer asked Purdom to manage the practical details of a plant hunting expedition to Asia with no salary but with all expenses paid, Purdom accepted eagerly because he was longing to return to the Orient.[2] After narrowly escaping death in Tibet, Farrer and Purdom had retreated across the border into China. From Siku Farrer had been sending the *Gardeners' Chronicle* a series of articles describing his "state of perfect isolation and blockade, no postman ever daring to affront the terrors of the road." Into this solitude came Meyer's small party. Farrer later wrote that he had heard the news of the arrival of another plant collector "in a tempest of surprise, by no means wholly pleasurable." When he learned that the intruder was an agricultural explorer, he felt "able to greet him with all the joy the occasion warranted and to take a first installment of delight in Mr. Meyer's flow of conversation."[3]

The three plant hunters met on October 23 under less than ideal circumstances. Meyer had spent three days trying to overcome the fears of his muleteers, interpreter, and coolie in an effort to salvage the remainder of his expedition; Farrer still felt inclined to resent "the unthinkable freakishness of fortune" that brought Meyer to Siku; and Purdom's financial dependence on Farrer made it impossible for him to receive Meyer cordially. Farrer reported in the *Gardeners' Chronicle* that he and Purdom and Meyer "gathered gleefully and ungrudgingly,"[4] but Meyer wrote Fairchild that Farrer and Purdom "do not seem to be inclined to tell a fellow much."

The following day Meyer sought the help of the local magistrate in an effort to prevent Tien from breaking his contract and withdrawing from the expedition. Tien had heard "all sorts of horrible stories" about the terrifying people who lived across the mountains in Tibet. When Meyer repeated his intention of going south despite warnings of certain death, Tien refused to go, saying, "I will stay here and take home your body when it is recovered." Meyer reminded Tien that he had promised in Peking in the presence of witnesses not to desert him. Without an interpreter he could scarcely hope to continue his journey though Kansu and across Szechwan.

When Farrer and Purdom returned to Siku from a short trip, they found that the situation had reached a climax. According to Meyer's itinerary report, he had "great difficulty with the interpreter and coolie. They left the inn and hid themselves." Farrer wrote two accounts of the events that took place during his absence. In the *Gardeners' Chronicle* he related that "Mr. Meyer had been ill-advised enough to bring up-country with him a very expensive fine gentleman of an 'interpreter' from the coast, of lily hand and liver to match." When the interpreter refused to go south of Siku, an altercation resulted, followed by "a rapid descent of the stairs by the interpreter. . . . There is poor Mr. Meyer, perfectly helpless . . . as many years in China have not led him to like the Chinese well enough to learn their language." Farrer's second account in his book *On the Eaves of the World* is consistent with the first: "Meyer maintained so rooted a repulsion for everything Chinese that he had successfully avoided any acquaintance even with the language . . . and therefore had an interpreter." After the interpreter refused to so south into Tibet, "words flew until the interpreter descended the stairs with more precipitation than he would have chosen, followed by a coolie." Farrer also implied that Meyer's conduct had antagonized the townspeople to such an extent that his life was in danger. "We meditated lending him rifle and revolver for immediate need," he wrote, "until we discovered he already had both, loaded and ready to discharge at any moment on any provocation."[5]

Both accounts contain misrepresentations that reveal a lack of understanding of Meyer's character, motives, and goals. He did not feel "a repulsion for everything Chinese," he had not "avoided any acquaintance even with the language," and he had tried for months to avoid hiring an "office

man" as his interpreter. Furthermore, Farrer portrayed Meyer as belliger-
ent, stubborn, and bungling when he said that Meyer was ready to shoot "at
any moment on any provocation." Meyer consistently depended on discre-
tion and courage rather than firearms. Farrer carefully avoided writing that
Meyer struck or shoved Tien, but two recent accounts based on Farrer's
description add that Meyer "threw him and a coolie downstairs."[6] These
versions suggest to Westerners a fall down a Western staircase instead of the
one or two steps leading to a remote Chinese inn. Unfortunately for Meyer,
the half-truths told by an unsympathetic author (who was not a witness)
recorded these events permanently for Meyer's contemporaries and for posterity.

After Tien and the coolie left the inn, Meyer returned the visit of Farrer
and Purdom. Both Englishmen then accompanied him to confer with the
magistrate about enforcing Tien's contract. Since Farrer spoke Chinese and
was acquainted with the officials at Siku, he helped Meyer to present his side
of the case. Tien had already "influenced the local officials," Meyer later
told Fairchild, "and there were some very angry scenes." When he realized
that he could not prevent Tien's desertion, Meyer insisted on recovering the
money that he had advanced to Tien and the coolie. Farrer's account of
these events is more dramatic: "On his moving appeal, we put ourselves at
his disposal....Had it not been for our presence, indeed, it is not easy to
imagine how the American party could have extracted themselves from the
present predicament....Thus we were able to overcome the lack of sympathy for Mr. Meyer's troubles, interview the Governor for him, discover
him a servant and send him on his way rejoicing."[7]

Instead of going "on his way rejoicing," Meyer spent the next two days
in Siku preparing for his trip south. Storing his excess baggage at the inn, he
and de Leuw set out on October 28 with a guide, muleteers, and four pack
mules. For several days they worked in the mountains near Lantsai (Lan-
cai). Just one day south of Siku, Meyer found both the wild peach (*Prunus
davidiana* var. *potaninii*) and the bush almond (*Prunus tangutica*). He then
climbed "steep mountains" and reached Ga-hoba on the Tibetan frontier,
where he collected wild plums and peaches. After working there for two
days, he decided not to go farther because he had obtained the peach stones
and the almonds that he sought and because of the increasing danger of
becoming snowbound.

Meyer and his party returned to Siku briefly before following the Siku
River westward. During this four-day journey he collected scions of
peaches, pears, apricots, plums, cherries, crab apples, and hazelnut trees
(*Corylus tibetica*). In tree-covered mountains he gathered seeds and specimens at altitudes up to ten thousand feet. By this time, he realized that the
guide Farrer had found for him was addicted to opium and was too lazy to
be helpful. Though Farrer and Purdom with their large escort had already

sought winter quarters, Meyer returned to Siku once more. He evidently did not share Farrer's belief that he was not safe there, for he used the town as a base for another week. During that time he collected, cleaned, and labeled seeds, worked on herbarium material, took photographs, and negotiated with muleteers. When he finally managed to hire eight mules, he had difficulty with the muleteers. Discovering that the guide "was also in the game," he discharged him "for crooked dealings, he being caught on the spot."

On November 19 Meyer and de Leuw started their three-week journey across the mountains of southern Kansu to Lanchow, the provincial capital. This was a difficult journey so late in the year. To attempt it without an interpreter, guide, or helper of any kind increased the challenge. Yet Meyer had little choice. Exploring the mountains of Kansu had been the chief aim of his third expedition. With that purpose in mind he had conferred with Wilson and Sargent at the Arnold Arboretum, with Purdom in England, with Colonel Koslov in Russia, and with Ladigine at Harbin. He could not abandon his plan now. His itinerary contains only the barest description of the week after he left Siku: "November 20 — Snowy weather; November 21 — Much snow on trails. Climbed slippery mountain; November 22 — Left at 7:30. Freezing hard. Climbed mountain pass at 8,700 feet. Arrived Minchow [Minxian]; November 23 — At Minchow; November 24 — Cold. Stayed at mountain settlement 8,800 feet; November 25 — Crossed pass at 10,400 feet; November 26 — High country. Crossed four passes 11,000, 11,250, 11,500, and 11,700 feet. Reached New Taochow at 9,000 feet."

Traveling through the mountains with only the muleteers for company, Meyer and de Leuw endured primitive living conditions. "We have to cook our own food, wash our own clothes, and whatnot else — truly quite troublesome and taking much time which could be better spent." Whether they were climbing slippery mountain trails in freezing snow, attempting to communicate with the few local inhabitants, or sharing the tasks of food preparation, fire building, and laundry, de Leuw proved to be an invaluable assistant because he was "much better able to deal with those rough Kansu people than I am myself and he understands the various dialects much better than I do."

But the journey did not lack compensations for the hardships they faced. In regions never before explored by foreigners, Meyer saw groves of magnificent spruce trees 150 feet tall with trunks twelve to fifteen feet in circumference, as well as splendid red-barked birches nearly one hundred feet high. He also observed clumps of a hardy reedlike bamboo (*Sinarundinaria nitida*), which was used for matting, basket-weaving, and for cables to guide ferry boats across swift mountain streams. On one mountain the tall firs, a treelike rhododendron, and the small bamboo formed what resembled a jungle.

At Taochow (Lintan) on the Tao River, American missionaries received

Meyer and de Leuw cordially. The Reverend C. F. Snyder of Reading, Pennsylvania, and his wife, who was from Goshen, Indiana, represented the China Inland Mission. Mr. Snyder readily agreed to act as a correspondent for the USDA and promised to ship the department seeds of the bush almond, hull-less barley, oats, broad beans, flax, and spring wheat grown at eight to ten thousand feet. He also planned to send his native helpers to collect tree peonies in wild mountain valleys across the border in Tibet, where white men could not travel. In return, the Snyders were eager to have winter wheats and vegetable and flower seeds that would grow in a semiarid area at 9,400 feet.

In the mountains near Taochow Meyer found many bush almonds (*Prunus tangutica*); however, only spoiled seeds remained on the ground. Squirrels had carried off all the sound nuts that had fallen. Meyer offered the villagers one cent for each good seed that they brought to him. Soon so many boys, women, and old men were searching that he had to reduce his offer to one cent for two seeds. One boy demonstrated a remarkable knowledge of the location of squirrel caches. Again and again he brought Meyer handfuls of nuts. When "bad local people" began to buy the seeds from little boys and sell them at a profit, Meyer withdrew his offer.

To botanists interested in the evolution of stone fruits, the most important result of Meyer's expedition was his discovery of the late-flowering bush almond (*Prunus tangutica*) and the genuine wild peach. Plant propagators expected these hardy, drought-resistant plants to be valuable for breeding, but they had a different significance to scholars. Since the peach had not been found in the wild when Darwin was writing, Darwin had contended that the peach and the almond were from the same stock and that the peach was a modification of the almond. Neither the wild peach nor the almond had been collected since the Russian plant hunter, Potanin, had found them in Kansu in the spring and summer of 1885. Both Meyer and Potanin secured proof that the peach and the almond had evolved from separate stock and that both were natives of a semiarid region of China; Meyer alone attempted to introduce them into cultivation in the Western hemisphere.[8]

When Meyer and de Leuw left Taochow, their accumulation of seeds, scions, and herbarium material had become so bulky that they needed ten pack animals to carry their baggage. For several days they climbed a high chain of mountains, crossing passes at over 11,000 feet. Available food was both scarce and coarse, and the scattered houses they passed were crudely built. Since they were following the route of the White Wolves again, the few inns were in ruins, the doors, chairs, and tables burned. Nevertheless, Meyer admired the rugged mountain scenery and took many photographs. Along the way he collected herbarium specimens, wild cherries, apricots, plums, pears, and walnuts, as well as the lovely *Daphne tangutica*. After traversing a deserted mountain valley, on December 2 they came to a pontoon bridge across the Tao River. There Meyer dismissed the muleteers and crossed the river to Titao (Lintao). Stopping at an uncomfortable inn, he consulted English missionaries about the products of the region and negotiated with carters for the five-day journey to Lanchow.

As they traveled toward the capital of Kansu, they crossed a series of mountain ranges in a wild and desolate region. Along the way they had "difficulty on the road with some rascals," but Meyer related no details of this encounter. The next day they trudged through a mountain gorge while an icy wind blew and snow fell. The terrible condition of the roads made progress difficult for the carters. When they crossed a mountain pass at 8,600 feet, they saw whole mountainsides of the bush almond.

They reached the gates of Lanchow on December 7. Though Meyer had hired relays of pack animals and carts, he and de Leuw had walked every mile of the approximately one-thousand-mile trip from Sian "except when crossing some rivers." After several hours of searching, he found a passable inn and went to the post office to collect correspondence that had traveled from Holland via Siberia and from Washington via Shanghai. He received 120 pieces of mail, his first letters since the end of August. Able to relax at last, he read his mail until dawn.

Lanchow (Lanzhou) and Return

Kansu, Shensi, Shansi, Honan, and Peking
DECEMBER, 1914, TO MARCH, 1915

MEYER'S account of reaching Lanchow (Lanzhou) borrowed imagery from his boyhood memories of the harbor at Amsterdam: "At last I have arrived here and I feel like an old-time sailing ship that has come into port loaded with good things. But the ship has weathered some storms and it is with the loss of the mainsail that it is berthed here now. My interpreter and coolie deserted me cowardly in Siku, for fear of being killed by Tibetans! My Dutch assistant has stuck faithfully to me; without him I would not have known what to do." He had much to tell Fairchild because he had not written for two months. In a city at last, he felt that he dared to entrust a letter to the postal service.

Time had not tempered his indignation toward Chi-nian Tien; in fact, he felt angrier than ever when he thought of being unable to return to Peking by way of Szechwan (Sichuan) Province, "the California of China." Tien had been educated by American missionaries in Peking, his family had been protected by the American Legation during the Boxer Rebellion, and his brother had been sent "by charitable American people" to take his Ph.D. at Columbia University. Meyer therefore considered his desertion doubly culpable and planned to sue him for damages "for having frustrated all my plans." (He did not realize that the most serious consequence of Tien's desertion would be Farrer's unsympathetic account of the incident; today it has become the chief source of information about Meyer's character and personality.) Though he hoped to punish Tien's disloyalty, he also planned to reward Johannis de Leuw for his faithful service. Two years later he wrote his will and included a one-thousand-dollar bequest to de Leuw, a generous legacy equivalent to about ten thousand dollars today.[1]

Despite cold weather and snow, within three days of his arrival he called on several missionaries and other members of the small foreign colony at Lanchow. "Here in this city there is a station of the China Inland Mission with several workers; also a Roman Catholic Mission; also an English postmaster with whom I am acquainted from Sian already; and last but not least, Mr. Farrer, an alpine amateur, and his assistant, Mr. William Purdom, are here," he wrote Fairchild. "These last two, however, are somewhat out of order."

On December 18 a telegram from Fairchild informed him that his discovery of the wild peach had created great excitement. In his reply Meyer pointed out that the department might be the only place in the world with ripened seeds of both the wild peach and the wild almond, for Potanin's material that he had seen at Saint Petersburg was not "ripened off." He believed that the original peach might occur in the wild from southwestern Tibet and the Himalayas to Afghanistan and Persia. With the enthusiasm of his youth he added: "I think I ought to travel someday from Asia Minor through Persia, Baluchistan, the Pundjab, Kashmir, Nepal, Bhutan, Upper Assam, and Upper Burma into Yunnan and Szechuan, and I think that I would find wild peaches for the greater part of the way." All the peaches that he had found were freestones; he had never seen a clingstone growing wild.

The holiday season did not bring a respite from responsibility. On December 24 he sent thirty-one parcels to America and on January 2, fifteen more bundles, inventory notes, quarterly accounts, and his itinerary report. His packages included wild peaches, bush almonds, apricots, cherries, plums, pears, persimmons, walnuts, and hazelnuts, as well as a "first-class decorative," *Daphne tangutica*. In addition to seeds and herbarium specimens, he set a record by successfully sending living plant material the great distance from Kansu Province to Washington. His shipments had to be mailed to the coast as registered letters in order to ensure safe transit.

After talking at length to informed people in the capital, Meyer became distressed by the news that had filtered into the interior from Europe. On several occasions he exchanged visits with a Roman Catholic missionary who was a Belgian. He also had an official audience with the governor of Kansu. Afterward he wrote Grace Cramer, "We live here in an atmosphere of suspense as regards this terrible war in Europe. When will mankind be ready to inaugurate the United States of the World and do away with armies, navies, etc.? Some centuries to come, people will know how horribly senseless we were!"

Though Lanchow was the capital of Kansu, living conditions there were primitive. Meyer and de Leuw did not dare to eat in the unsanitary places that served meals. They were forced to buy and cook their own food and to clean and heat their own rooms. No hot water was available. Furthermore, all water used in the city came from the Yellow River in wooden buckets and, "horrible to say, in these very same buckets all the waste water is carried again to the river and thrown out." Both Meyer and de Leuw felt unwell several times during the month they spent in Lanchow.

Early in January Meyer acknowledged Dorsett's letter of authorization for six thousand dollars and a check for four thousand. Unfortunately he could not cash a check for such a large amount in the interior. For months he had been paying all the expenses of the expedition with his own money. Dorsett also informed him that the auditor of his accounts had disallowed his expenditure of one Yuan dollar (fifty cents in American money) for his newspaper advertisement for an interpreter.

Meyer tried in vain to locate a qualified interpreter to go with him to Szechwan Province. In Lanchow he could not find even an intelligent servant to accompany them. Neither he nor de Leuw knew enough of the language or the customs of the region to travel without an interpreter. He therefore decided that he must return to Peking with the bulk of his collection. Frustrated by Tien's desertion, he filed a claim for damages amounting to five thousand taels. "Even if no money comes foreward," he wrote Fairchild, "it will teach him how to behave next time."

On January 5 Meyer and de Leuw began the three-week journey to Sian with three mules, two drivers, and a large cart filled with baggage that included botanical and pathological material, as well as a great quantity of rare herbarium specimens from the interior. He believed that Sargent could no longer complain that he had neglected this aspect of his work. (Fortunately he could not foresee that most of this herbarium material would be lost in a cyclone at Galveston, Texas.) Several days after leaving Lanchow, they climbed a wind-swept mountain while a bitterly cold dust storm raged around them. Despite temperatures below freezing, each morning they rose at daybreak and started their journey at 7:00 A.M. Around ten or eleven they stopped for breakfast. Early one morning they climbed a steep mountain, had breakfast at eleven, crossed a treacherous pass at 4:00 P.M., and then spent the night in a drafty room. The next day their cart stuck firmly in the ice for several hours before the mules could pull it free. By 3:00 P.M. they were forced to stop to let the exhausted animals rest. On the following morning the cart remained stuck in ice for an hour. That afternoon they faced an exceedingly cold dust storm before reaching Pingliang, where they spent an hour searching for suitable shelter for the night.

Four days later they encountered serious difficulty at Changwuhsien (Changwuxian) on the Kansu-Shensi border. Just an hour after leaving an inn, they met four soldiers who stopped them and attempted "to search us on our bodies" for contraband. When Meyer objected, one soldier blocked his way and "spat me in the face." Johannis de Leuw reacted to this outrage promptly by "giving the soldier a few kicks" with the butt of his Springfield rifle. (De Leuw was a small man but his courage matched his name which means *the lion*.) The other soldiers joined the fray, beating the foreigners with heavy sticks. Meyer and de Leuw returned their blows "with our fists, a walking-stick, and the above-mentioned rifle. After the fight was finished, we left."[2] Meyer failed to realize that the four soldiers who had accosted him were stationed near the border to prevent the smuggling of opium out of Kansu. When the patrol spotted foreigners with carts loaded with seeds and plant material, they reasoned that legitimate businessmen did not travel without a retinue; these men therefore must be smugglers. Meyer had broken E. H. Wilson's rule: "Any white man who travels in the more remote sections on foot loses caste."[3]

Satisfied that the fight had settled the incident, Meyer and his party continued their journey until "a rabble of fifteen soldiers on horseback came flying after us and, under the most vile curses and oaths, ordered our carters to halt." Lacking an interpreter to explain their mission, Meyer and de Leuw insisted vainly that they were collecting plants for the United States government and that their baggage contained no poppy seeds or opium. No one could read their passports and their denials failed to impress the "rowdy" soldiers who forced Meyer and de Leuw to stand against a wall and threatened them with immediate execution. Eventually the men compelled them to return to Changwuhsien. During the hour's journey, the soldiers "freely cursed us and indulged in all sorts of insulting remarks, like foreigners being cowards, dogs, etc." Hoping to provoke an incident that would justify shooting the Westerners, the soldiers repeatedly pointed loaded carbines and revolvers at them and challenged de Leuw to aim his rifle in return.

When the procession reached Changwuhsien, the soldiers "exhibited us to bystanders as criminals and made very coarse and dirty remarks about us to make the townspeople laugh and sneer." At the headquarters of the customs inspector, an army officer observed the behavior of his men with apparent approval. He asked Meyer and de Leuw to show their passports and their permit to carry firearms. Then he delivered a "haughty and disrespectful lecture" about the treatment of the border patrol and yielded his prisoners to a civilian inspector in charge of the customs station. The inspector asked whether they were carrying opium, poppy heads, or poppy seeds. When Meyer answered each question in the negative, the inspector wanted to know whether he was willing to open some of his baggage. Meyer consented and the inspector chose a trunk. Inside he found clothes, a few books, and some lump silver. Satisfied that Meyer and de Leuw were not smugglers, he thanked them for their cooperation and released them.

Though Meyer's entry in his itinerary report merely noted, "Difficulty with Chinese soldiers. Compelled to return to the town," he filed a strong protest with Paul Reinsch, the American minster at Peking. He told Reinsch that he wanted an apology from the haughty officer and from the soldier who "spat me in the face." The Chinese Foreign Office eventually reported that "the soldiers implicated" had been severely punished and that the officer in charge had been ordered to apologize.[4]

During the next five days Meyer and de Leuw and the muleteers passed through deep loess ravines and climbed steep mountains. For one entire day they traveled in a severe dust storm; the following day they tramped through deep dust. After ferrying across the Wei River, on the twentieth day of their journey from Lanchow, they reached Sian at noon. Though they were still eight days from the railroad, the most difficult phase of their trip lay behind them. Before continuing across Shensi and Shansi to Honan, Meyer paused in Sian long enough to report to the American consul and to hire two drivers, a cart, and three mules.

During the last five days of January, he and his party started at 6:30 each morning and traveled along roads covered with deep layers of dust. By January 29 they had traversed the imposing Ta hua Shan range, encountered another dust storm, and crossed the border of Honan Province. Eager to reach the railroad, they passed the "difficult Chinese Customs" at Tungkwan (Dongquan) and then had the axles of their cart changed to fit the narrow track ahead. Three days later they hired an escort of four soldiers as they traveled through a region where robbers had been especially active.

Realizing that they were approaching the railroad, the next day they started their journey at 5:30 while an icy cold wind blew a fierce dust storm around them. In the morning they crossed deep loess ravines and barren hills; by afternoon they ascended a mountain and encountered sleet and snow. Advancing as rapidly as they could, they did not stop for breakfast until 2:00 P.M. When evening came they "plodded through darkness," arriving at Menchi at 9:00 P.M. Weary but triumphant, Meyer recorded in his itinerary, "Marched forty miles this day" – a day that had included fifteen hours on the road, traversing ravines and mountains through dust, sleet, and snow.

At 7:30 A.M. on February 4, Meyer and de Leuw carried ten large pieces of luggage aboard a train. Express service did not exist in China. At Honanfu (Luoyang) at 10:30 A.M. and again at Chengchow (Zhengzhou) at 5:30 P.M., they changed trains. The following day at 5:00 P.M. they reached Peking, passed the Chinese Customs, and had their first opportunity in many weeks to bathe and rest at a comfortable hotel. Meyer found a large accumulation of mail waiting at the American Legation. Just as he had done at Lanchow, he read his letters until daybreak.

He and de Leuw felt "fearfully tired" for two weeks after their journey ended, but conditions in Peking allowed little time for relaxation. While they tried to rest, "hosts of visitors" called and others wrote for information. Much more disturbing was "all this horrible war news!" In mid-February Japan had sent China an ultimatum known as the Twenty-one Demands. Meyer had difficulty sleeping while the Chinese reaction to Japan's threatened aggression remained in doubt and "everybody held himself ready for a revolution or worse." In addition, he learned that Chow-hai Ting had spent the three hundred dollars advanced to him for the purchase of peach stones and chestnuts to pay his personal expenses. Though Meyer deducted part of this sum from Ting's wages, the amount was so large that he had to share the loss. As he labeled herbarium specimens and photographs and prepared to ship bundles to America, his thoughts kept returning to the conflicts in Europe and in Asia: "A dark cloud hangs over all humanity. . . . If only we are not at the threshold of another dark age. The sun of human progress has certainly set for a while. When will she rise again?"

Letters that David Fairchild and Grace Cramer had written eight months earlier awaited Meyer in Peking. Fairchild feared that William W. Rockhill, who had been serving as an adviser to the president of China, may have been planning to lure Meyer away from the USDA: "I am beginning to fear lest China will gobble you up. Should an offer come to you, my dear Mr. Meyer, do not accept it until you have given us a chance to come back with a counter-proposition." After hearing that Meyer had secured a quantity of seeds of the wild peach and the wild almond, Fairchild commented, "Mr. Swingle will nearly stand on his head when I tell him this." Grace Cramer explained that Beverly T. Galloway was leaving his position as assistant secretary of the department to succeed Liberty Hyde Bailey as dean of the Cornell College of Agriculture. To the consternation of the staff of the Plant Introduction Section, Fairchild was one of the men being considered to head the Bureau of Plant Industry. "It would be a calamity to the Office of Foreign Seed and Plant Introduction for him to leave it," Grace Cramer wrote. For the first time she mentioned her fiancé, Winfield Scott Clime, who had "put motion photography on its feet in the Department." [5]

During the four weeks after he returned to Peking, Meyer mailed thirty-four packages to America. Fruits and nuts constituted the largest segment of his harvest — seven hundred pounds of peach stones, persimmon seeds, a valuable jujube, and large chestnuts. Ornamental trees, shrubs, and flowers included the weeping elm, a beautiful flowering plum (*Prunus triloba*), a viburnum, a lilac, roses, and a new lily. He also sent hull-less barley, huskless oats, broad beans, soybeans, and hardy alfalfas that might succeed in North Dakota. Other parcels contained cones for Sargent and dried and candied jujubes to be shared with Mr. Kellogg of Battle Creek, Michigan. Among pathological specimens were wilt disease on tobacco leaves and scales, cankers, and galls. E. R. Sasscer, a USDA entomologist, found a rare scale on one of the twigs from Kansu. Photographs, inventory notes, a

After finishing his official correspondence, Meyer disclosed his concerns to his sister. Though the war in Europe grieved him most, everyone in Peking was living under tremendous tension because Japan might declare war against China. Political conditions had caused the rate of exchange to drop; he would lose 20 percent of his money if he converted it at this time. In addition, he did not look forward to the long trip to America with so much troublesome luggage. Even after he reached Washington, he would be living in a boardinghouse among strangers. Anchored at Peking, he found sedentary life uncongenial and longed to be in the field again.[6]

CHAPTER 26

Departure via Chekiang (Zhejiang)

Peking, Shanghai, Hangchow, and Yokohama
APRIL TO OCTOBER, 1915

A S April began, anxiety in Peking continued to delay Meyer's plan to travel south of Shanghai. Everyone was wondering what move Japan would make if China refused to grant her Twenty-one Demands. If China should agree to accept the Japanese ultimatum, informed people expected a revolution. Though Meyer was eager to explore Chekiang (Zhejiang) Province, the American minister had advised him to wait for at least three weeks. "Worries of war produce a bad effect," he wrote Fairchild. "My own nerves are not what they ought to be, and I have not been able to sleep for four nights now." Too many visits to be paid and received and too much correspondence added to his burdens. He nevertheless sent the department his itinerary report and his quarterly accounts, commenting that he felt better after a forty-mile walk than after two days of desk work.

Still waiting in Peking a few weeks later, he wrote his family that the situation in China remained critical, but he deplored the depressing news of the war in Europe most of all. Some of his German acquaintances had died when Japan bombed Tsingtao (Qingdao) in Shantung Province; others were prisoners of war in Japan. He no longer knew what had happened to many of his German, French, Russian, and Belgian friends. In Peking he saw old friendships shattered. "Is there really no other way to get along? Do all these young lives have to be sacrificed to prove who is more powerful? A wild animal in the forest is not more murderous than modern people." For the first time he admitted missing the consolations of a home and a family of his own: "In another life hereafter, I have to take it more quietly. . . . I have to have my own family. Yes—so one starts to daydream."

He blamed intelligent people of all nations for allowing militarism to grow until it had culminated in world conflict. Considering measures that might prevent wars in the future, he explained to his family that people who were cosmopolitan believed that differences between nations could be settled by arbitration. "For us, it is doubly hard to see this war, and I personally cannot justify it. When it is over, most problems will appear again. Why didn't these nations unite into a United States of the World — or at least Europe? Is it necessary to destroy each other to reach agreement?" In the future, heads of government must abolish secret diplomacy and strictly control munitions manufacturers. "I have seen much in my travels of agents of Krupp, Maxim-Vickers, Creusot, etc." In order to make large sales, these people "bribe and swindle to get inside information." They had sold the munitions used to kill Europeans when Japan bombed Tsingtao.

Early in May a letter from C. F. Snyder, the missionary who lived where the bush almonds grew, reminded Meyer of the wild and beautiful mountains of southern Kansu. "It must be nice out in western Kansu and Szechuan," he wrote Fairchild, "and I have not been there except autumn and winter!" He envied Farrer and Purdom their opportunity to explore the Sining Alps in Kansu that spring. "Re your being disappointed that I could not penetrate into Szechuan, believe me, Mr. Fairchild, if there is one person who regrets this, it is certainly I myself. Had I been able to ship my bulky baggage and the herbarium material, I still would have done it."

Others letters brought good tidings, as well as a number of requests. E. H. Wilson's safe return from Japan with an interesting collection pleased Meyer, and he was glad to see that a USDA bulletin of new plant introductions included a number of his own contributions. C. W. Janssen offered to pay his expenses if he could visit the new botanical garden in Sumatra. Fairchild requested fifty pounds of seeds of *Prunus davidiana*, a bushel of *Pistacia chinensis*, several bushels of *Pinus bungeana*, at least twenty-five pounds of *Ulmus pumila*, and one thousand pounds of jujubes. Meyer protested that no one knew which of dozens of jujubes would perform best in America. The department would be taking a risk, he warned, if they released seeds to growers before extensive testing.

Though the critical political situation in China troubled him, he continued to plan further journeys. When he thought about "the Japanese war cloud over the land," at times he suffered from "nervous fever." Walking was the best cure. As he waited for the Japanese ultimatum to end in invasion, revolution, or compromise, he felt the need of "a big change to shake all the worries to the four corners of the earth." An expedition from Constantinople to Chengtu in Szechwan Province, he pointed out, would offer him an opportunity to work in Asian countries that he had never seen — Turkey, Iran, Afghanistan, India, Nepal, Sikkim, Bhutan, and Assam. "I know now that I won't stay here in China very long anymore," he wrote Fairchild. "I almost hate to leave the country, however; it is such an interesting land! I really do wish I could have started this exploration work at an earlier age! Now a man soon will be old and there is so much to be done yet!"

When the situation in China stabilized at the end of May, he sent twenty-two packages to the United States and prepared to leave for Nanking, Shanghai, and Hangchow. The boxes that he shipped included seeds of the dry-land elm, 40 pounds of wild peach stones, 220 pounds of jujube seeds for the Chico Garden, and herbarium material. Fur coats, heavy boots, herbarium frames, ropes, and other impedimenta, "some official, some personal," he stored at the American Legation before setting out.

Meyer and de Leuw reached Nanking (Nanjing) on May 30 and spent a week visiting the Purple Mountain reforestation area, where the original vegetation remained only around the temples. Joseph Bailie of the University of Nanking showed Meyer the Chinese government's reforestation experiments. Concluding that dense growth could be reestablished, Meyer recommended that the United States government continue to offer assistance to this project. Bailie promised to send the department seeds of the Chinese pistachio, the Chinese elm (*Ulmus parvifolia*), and the ornamental silk tree, *Albizia chinensis*. Before ending his visit to Nanking, Meyer spoke at the American consulate about his work in China.

When he reached hot and humid Shanghai, he called on the consul general and surveyed the new plantings in the parks with his old friend MacGregor. A cable from the department directed him to stop in Japan on his way to America in order to duplicate E. H. Wilson's collection of cherry budwood and to seek evidence of the chestnut bark fungus there. A few days later W. T. Swingle joined him for a tour of the fruit markets in Shanghai, where they examined litchis, mangoes, golden loquats, plums, peaches, and apricots. They also conferred about the problem of duplicating Wilson's cherry budwood collection and Swingle's recent discovery of a canker that was attacking citrus fruits.

In Shanghai, Meyer saw a newsreel of French troops storming a height and thoughts of the war raging in Europe disturbed him: "It was sickening to see how many figures dropped out of the ranks; . . . and the others moved on, just as if it was the most common everyday affair. . . . Shame on our so-called Christian civilization which has led us into these dark canyons of destruction." He deplored "confined nationalities" with "painfully staked-off territories" that existed instead of a "Federated Earth" with a supreme council of government and no armies or navies. He hoped that America would not become involved in the war. "It is a sore enough thing that American capitalists and American workingmen are earning blood money by making ammunition for the Allies; for humanity's sake, let us stay out!"[1] Referring to Holland's continuing neutrality, he commented, "Holland is like a bright little fox terrier watching the fierce fight of some powerful bulldogs and mastiffs. Shall they leave the little thing alone?"

During his two weeks in Shanghai, Meyer bought eighty pounds of litchis and prepared twenty pounds of clean litchi seeds for mailing to

Washington, spoke to fifty American businessmen about plant exploration, and gave interviews to newspapers and to W. H. Donald, editor of the *Far Eastern Review*.[2] He also enjoyed reading E. H. Wilson's new book, *A Naturalist in Western China*. As usual he had difficulty finding an interpreter for his trip south; nevertheless, he intended to make the trip and to ship scions of the white-barked persimmon to Washington in order to prove that he had not seen persimmon trees that had been whitewashed, as several people had claimed.

He arrived in Hangchow (Hangzhou) during the rainy season and was drenched by heavy showers that alternated with sultry heat. Yet his first week in Chekiang (Zhejiang) Province yielded an exciting discovery that enabled him to forget that his clothing and his straw hat were covered with mold. In the markets he noticed what seemed to be hickory nuts, although the natives called them "mountain walnuts." He knew that the hickory never had been reported in China; Wilson had commented on this fact in his recent book. Meyer asked two missionaries, Dr. Duncan Main and the Reverend Henry W. Moule, to investigate the source of this nut. Local inhabitants told them that it came from Yuhang in the Pan Shan southwest of Hangchow. Meyer decided to search for hickory trees in this region as soon as he completed his work near Hangchow.

Despite continual rain, in the lowlands he found the white-barked persimmon that he sought and arranged for Dr. Main to send seeds of this unusual variety to the department. Unlike other persimmons, it grew in deep shade. Henry Moule promised to mail hickory nuts to the USDA in the fall. Alexander Kennedy, the missionary who had helped Meyer find the Tangsi cherry in 1906, agreed to ship bamboo plants. Near Hangchow Meyer collected herbarium material and observed wild tea bushes, camphor and tallow trees, hollies, junipers, oaks, and chestnuts seriously attacked by the bark fungus.

Instead of returning to Shanghai after ten days as he had planned originally, Meyer and de Leuw left Hangchow on what became a month-long journey through the Pan Shan in sultry Chekiang Province. Traveling by train, by rowboat, and on foot, they reached Yuhang (Linping), an old city on the shore of a "canalized river." There Meyer learned that the hickory trees that he was seeking grew three days' journey to the west at Changhua. For two days he botanized in intense heat near Yuhang while he arranged for a guide and men to carry his baggage. Local authorities insisted on assembling a sedan chair, two bearers, three carrying coolies, and an escort of eight armed soldiers to accompany him. With this convoy, Meyer and de Leuw set out.

As they were approaching Changhua, Meyer saw hickory trees from forty to sixty feet in height and no more than a foot in diameter. He spent three days in that area despite mosquitoes, humidity, and intense heat, and he observed whole groves of hickories. They grew in sheltered valleys in the mountains at altitudes of eight hundred to twelve hundred feet. Natives used the strong wood for making tool handles, and the wealthy fried cakes in hickory nut oil. Sargent later wrote Meyer that finding the hickory was "by far the most interesting thing you have accomplished in China, that is, from the botanical point of view."[3] Meyer also gathered many herbarium specimens in this region and noticed that the ginkgo tree grew semiwild there.

As he and de Leuw returned to Yuhang in mid-July with an escort of five soldiers, the fierce heat made them feel ill. A terrific thunderstorm disturbed their rest while they lodged overnight in a temple; however, it failed to bring relief from the sultry weather. After stopping briefly at Yuhang, they traveled by boat to Moganshan.

For three weeks they stayed with missionaries while Meyer explored the mountainous region, collected herbarium material, and studied bamboo culture. He sent the department a detailed account of his observations, explaining that workers held the bamboo canes over a hot flame and applied hot cloths as they bent the canes gently. He felt sure that Americans would like bamboo baskets, vases, and furniture. In the intense heat he continued to feel unwell and de Leuw contracted a fever. As Meyer prepared to mail his accounts and his itinerary report, the humidity was so great that he had to dry the ink on his paper over a burning candle. He enclosed a specimen of the Chinese hickory, asking that it not be named for any person. Two days after American missionaries in Moganshan gave a reception in Meyer's honor, a typhoon struck, damaging homes and destroying crops. While Meyer watched, tree branches and stones hurled through the air, the windows blew in, and rain poured into the house that he was occupying. During the following week, de Leuw's health improved. On August 6 they left Moganshan with a sedan chair, three bearers, and six carriers. The next night they traveled by boat in heavy rain and then boarded a train for Shanghai.

Meyer spent several weeks in Shanghai before going to Japan. He was appalled by the effect of "the fearful war" on the port. Slackened business activity had resulted in much unemployment, and the poor appeared on the verge of starvation. On August 11 he went to the harbor to see Johannis de Leuw off to Chefoo (Yantai). The Netherlands Harbor Works Company there had offered him a good position. "My faithful assistant, Mr. J. J. C. de Leuw, has left me," he told Fairchild. "I miss him a good deal since we have shared the difficulties and the pleasures of life here in China for about two and one-half years." Sultry and oppressive weather made sleeping difficult. "My nerves are not what they have been," he admitted, "and my health not of the best."

He expressed his concern to his family about personal problems and about reports of death and destruction in Europe. Next he must go to Japan, he explained—"a country that in the future will cause us a lot of problems." In the fall he would return to the United States where he feared that Americans would be divided about the war. If the conflict continued, he might have to postpone his long-awaited trip to Holland in 1916.

Despite the weather, Meyer mailed ten parcels to the USDA in August. Five contained ornamental shrubs, forage crops, hickory nuts, dried fruits, the bark of the white-barked persimmon, entomological material, and inventory notes. He also sent soil for analysis from a thriving bamboo grove, as well as photographs of the white-barked persimmons, the "noble white-barked pines," diseased chestnuts, and the new hickory.

On September 7 he boarded the *Hakuai Maru* and left Shanghai. By 3:00 P.M. his ship was caught in a violent typhoon that lasted thirty-six hours. The boat rolled continuously, causing even the crew to become seasick. After landing at Kobe, he took an express to Yokohama. From the train he viewed the Japanese countryside—"like China but everything smaller and *clean*." He enjoyed seeing tobacco, tea, and mulberry plantations, as well as pears, pomegranates, loquats, and figs, but new factories were beginning to spoil the beauty of the landscape. On Sunday he visited parks in Yokohama and was surprised to notice young Japanese playing baseball and drawing large crowds of spectators. The bracing air in Japan soon made him feel much better than he had felt in Shanghai.

After passing customs with his bulky load of baggage, he traveled to Tokyo and called on Ambassador Guthrie. When he visited the Imperial Botanical Gardens, he learned that their funds were limited because "Japan spends every spare sen on enlarging her army and navy, sad to contemplate." He also called on Eliza R. Scidmore, an American writer who had interested Mrs. William Howard Taft in planting the Japanese flowering cherries in Washington.[4] Miss Scidmore, who was one of Fairchild's dollar-a-year "collaborators," agreed with Meyer that the microscopic spores of the chestnut fungus could have come to the United States on infested Japanese nursery stock.

Returning to Yokohama, he consulted Fairchild's acquaintance, H. Suzuki of the Yokohama Nursery Company, and confirmed his own opinion that it was too early in the season to collect cherry scions. He and Suzuki traveled to Kamakura where Suzuki showed him immense *Gingko biloba*, colossal *Juniperus chinensis*, and other botanical curiosities. Along the way they stopped at several nurseries that grew flowering cherries, but they found the wood far too green to cut scions.

The next day Meyer left Yokohama for Nikko, arriving late in the afternoon. The following morning he explored the nearby hills and mountains, photographing and collecting "plenty of evidence" of the chestnut blight. After a late lunch, he "gave some long looks" at the beautiful avenue of cryptomerias and wished that he could have stayed longer. Leaving Nikko at 3:30 P.M., he reached Yokohama late that night. His brief trip had yielded vital information: the chestnut blight was well-established, though unrecognized, in Japan.

With only a few days remaining before he left for America, he visited the quarantine station and discussed inspection problems with Professor S. T. Kuana. When Meyer told Kuana that he had found chestnut blight at Nikko, both Kuana and Suzuki went with him to Okuba near Tokyo where Meyer pointed out the characteristic fungus. After the harsh treatment of his crate of Feicheng peach trees, he may not have expected a Japanese quarantine official to be a congenial companion; nevertheless, he thoroughly enjoyed being the guest of his new Japanese friends at a supper of unfamiliar Japanese delicacies. Suzuki agreed to collect the cherry scions for the USDA and ship them to America after Kuana had inspected them.

Meyer spent many of his remaining hours in Japan with his friends. He studied the trial gardens at Suzuki's nursery and promised Kuana a pound of American chestnuts for testing, as well as literature on the bacillus that caused the blight. After making a hasty trip to the American Embassy at Tokyo to arrange for the shipment of the cherry scions, he found Suzuki waiting at his hotel to escort him to his ship. At 2:30 P.M. on July 20 he boarded the SS *Minnesota*. He had enjoyed his eleven days in Japan and regretted leaving. His health had improved considerably; he now felt "pretty near the same as some years ago." Looking back, the hot and humid summer in Chekiang Province seemed like a nightmare.

Since the crossing lasted nineteen days instead of the scheduled twelve or fourteen, Meyer had leisure to read, write, complete his quarterly accounts, and finish his itinerary report. After eighteen days at sea he complained about the slow voyage, a result of having left Yokohama "without the right kind of stokers," and predicted that "some day we are going to have a railroad from Seattle to Khabarowsk with a tunnel underneath the Bering Straits." On October 8 the *Minnesota* entered Puget Sound at last. As Meyer stood on the deck holding a rare dwarf cycad in a green porcelain urn, a gift for Fairchild that he would not entrust to anyone else, he had a pleasant surprise. Not at his desk in Washington but on the dock waiting to greet him was David Fairchild himself.[5]

CHAPTER 27

Home by a Southern Route

The United States
OCTOBER, 1915, TO AUGUST, 1916

H AVING spotted Fairchild as the *Minnesota* docked in Seattle, Meyer hurried to disembark, but immigration officers and newsmen besieged him. Before he could leave the ship, he stood at the rail shouting the news that the chestnut bark fungus apparently had come to the United States by way of Japan. As soon as Meyer had discharged his duties, David Fairchild and his companion, David Whitcomb, loaded Meyer's luggage into an automobile and took him to the Seattle experiment station and then to Whitcomb's home. Along the way Meyer learned that Fairchild had decided to combine a business trip across Canada with the opportunity to meet him in Seattle and to go with him to the Chico Garden in California to inspect his introductions. Fairchild and Meyer spent half of that night talking.

The next day, Meyer traveled to San Francisco to attend the Exposition. For a week he studied the Chinese and Japanese exhibits, inspected agricultural, horticultural, and botanical displays, looked at camping outfits, and explored the Golden Gate Park. These days would have been completely satisfying if he had not received word that his large shipment from China had been caught in a cyclone in Galveston. "If the herbarium specimens are really seriously damaged," he wrote Grace Cramer, "then the loss is very great indeed—and more than a year's work has gone to the dogs. In personal effects I also may be out a great deal. Well, such is life!"

At midnight on October 18 he returned to the Chico Plant Introduction Garden after an absence of seven years. Fairchild enjoyed showing him his dwarf lemons producing a high yield, grafted jujubes bearing dozens of fruits, drought-resistant almonds from Chinese Turkestan, wild olives (*Olea europea,* formerly *O. ferruginea*) from Central Asia, rows of tung tree seedlings, and Van Fleet's hybrids of Chinese chestnuts. Seeing his Asian introductions thriving in America delighted Meyer. He observed Tangsi cherry orchards, as well as other cherry trees growing on his northern wild peach stock in soil so alkaline that even alfalfa would not thrive there. Proof that his introductions had actually made possible the cultivation of stone fruits on soil that previously had been considered almost useless gave Meyer a greater feeling of the importance of his work than anything else.

During the ten days that Meyer remained at Chico, he worked on his Chinese collection, gave interviews to reporters, and spoke to several local groups. "Life is so much easier here," he wrote Dorsett, "a revelation." Robert Beagles was doing an excellent job as superintendent. Most of the plant material that Meyer had sent from Asia was living, the jujubes bearing more heavily in Chico than in China. The enthusiasm of fruit growers for the remarkably drought- and alkali-resistant *Prunus davidiana* as a stock for stone fruits pleased Meyer most of all.

In contrast to the success of his former introductions, news of the destruction of his large shipment in Galveston was hard to accept. At first he hoped that some of the herbarium material representing almost eighteen months of hard work might be salvaged; however, Dorsett wrote that the herbarium specimens "are a total loss and the personal effects are in very bad condition." Remembering the long journey to Kansu — nights spent in makeshift shelters, inadequate food, and hours of drying herbarium material over charcoal fires — Meyer grieved because many specimens new to science had traveled halfway around the globe safely, only to be destroyed so close to their destination. Though he valued the crate of specimens at five thousand dollars in terms of salaries and traveling expenses, the impossibility of duplicating the collection made the loss even more serious. The staff eventually did salvage many of the woody specimens but all the herbaceous material was ruined. This loss left a wound that never healed.

At the end of October Meyer left Chico on a tour of nurseries and USDA experiment stations from California to Florida. He first inspected jujube and bamboo plantings at Bakersfield before arriving cold and sleepy at the Riverside Citrus Experiment Station at 1:45 A.M. Later that day he conferred with H. J. Webber, who had worked with Swingle to develop the tangelo, and A. D. Shamel, who had gone to Brazil with Dorsett and Popenoe. Continuing south and east, he reached the Indio Experiment Garden where Bruce Drummond showed him fine jujubes, nectarines, and dates. At the Yuma Experiment Farm at Bard, California, where the Chinese peach stock had succeeded under irrigation, he suggested that the department test the jujube, persimmon, Tangsi cherry, and globular-headed willow. The following day he inspected the Arizona Experiment Station at Tucson and spoke to the Businessman's Luncheon Club.

After a hot and uncomfortable journey, he spent four days at the USDA Experiment Farm at San Antonio, working intermittently because he was suffering from fever and chills. Moving on to Austin, he enjoyed three days at F. T. Ramsey's home and nursery. Ramsey asked for more jujubes, a thousand pounds of seeds of the northern wild peach, Chinese walnuts, and the globular-headed willow. The Ramseys entertained Meyer cordially, giving him "a glance at the everyday life of an average American household which, to a fellow coming from China, is worth fully as much as seeing nurseries."

Leaving Austin at 11:00 P.M., he traveled to College Station, Texas, arriving at 4:00 A.M. The town offered only a boardinghouse, but he found no vacancies and had to spend the remainder of the night sleeping on the floor of the office. In the morning Bonney Youngblood, superintendent of the Texas A & M Agricultural Experiment Station, arranged for him to speak to an audience of four hundred students gathered in the chapel. For three days he inspected grounds and nurseries, discussed plant introductions, and held conferences. "This station is getting on its feet," he assured Fairchild.

On November 19 Meyer departed for Houston, nearing Washington "at a snail's pace." After visiting a Japanese nursery where the terrible storm a few months before had damaged pecan trees and live oaks, he made a pilgrimage to Galveston to see for himself the destruction "in which I also am no small loser." Though several months had passed since the cyclone had struck, the area looked as if it had been shelled. Alone, he mourned the lost herbarium material before returning to Houston.

"A step nearer you all," he wrote Dorsett when he reached New Iberia in the Mississippi Delta. Stopping at the home of Fairchild's friend, Edward McIlhenny of Avery Island, Meyer saw experimental orchards and a fine grove of bamboo which McIlhenny had propagated from plants sent to him by the USDA.[1] When Meyer traveled to Glen Saint Mary in Florida, he inspected Chinese persimmon orchards that Harold Hume had been testing for ten years. "With most pleasant recollections," he left Glen Saint Mary for the USDA station that he had been responsible for locating at Brooksville.

During four days at Brooksville, Meyer enjoyed being greeted as an old friend, despite the disappointment of seeing that the bamboo planting had not been successful. The leading citizens of Brooksville nevertheless offered him ten acres of good land free of charge if he would stay there as an adviser. After meeting many people who had followed his career with interest since his visit in 1909, Meyer realized that he had become "much more known than I imagined when I was out in old China." He thought that the problems at Brooksville could have been averted. The land was waterlogged, he admitted, but it should have been ditched deeply, and the plants should have been allowed more space. He suggested importing a team of Japanese workmen experienced in manufacturing bamboo products to teach young men at a nearby industrial training school the techniques for making bamboo baskets and furniture.

On his fortieth birthday Meyer wrote Dorsett, "Now in old Brooksville and the charm of the South has come upon me." Among the gnarled live oaks, slender pines, and vivid green palmettos, he admitted that "the call gets stronger, but I feel my time has not come yet to settle down for good." He had repeatedly said that he would end his travels when he was forty and begin a career at a plant propagating station, after visiting his family in Holland. Since war in Europe had spoiled his plans, he did not feel ready to give up agricultural exploration; yet his lack of a real home troubled him increasingly.

After completing his tour at the Gainesville experiment station, he reached Washington on December 5, following an absence of three years and three months. Friends welcomed him cordially, and he soon found bachelor quarters at 821 C Street not far from his office. Except for a trip to New York in January, he remained in Washington all winter. His first official act was to gain approval for his suspended accounts by sending a fifty-cent piece to the Treasury Department to repay the cost of his advertisement for an interpreter to accompany him to Kansu. Most of his days he spent writing reports, preparing notes and slides for lectures, and working on an article for the *Yearbook of Agriculture*.

When he received the audit of his accounts for the third quarter of 1915, he readily conceded the amounts that the auditor had subtracted for tips to baggage masters, table stewards, and bath attendants, but he questioned deductions for the escorts of soldiers provided by local authorities. These soldiers could not be dismissed and they expected to be paid. "I do not understand the use of the words 'improper charge,' " he responded. "No charges are included in my accounts that are not considered proper and authorized."

Throughout February, March, and April, Meyer corresponded with friends on three continents and delivered a number of lectures. In addition to speaking to civic and professional groups in Washington, on March 25 he addressed the Massachusetts Horticultural Society in Boston. Before he showed his hand-colored lantern slides, he described his journeys into the interior where glorious blue mountains and lovely valleys rewarded him for the hardships that he sometimes endured. His photographs included Chinese scenes — mud-roofed greenhouses, grafting techniques, and the beautiful gardens of the Summer Palace, as well as his own introductions.[2]

While he was in Boston, he spent pleasant days at the Arnold Arboretum with E. H. Wilson, Jackson Dawson, and Camillo Schneider, a distinguished Austrian botanist rescued by the Arnold Arboretum when he was about to be interned as an enemy alien by the British at Shanghai. After he returned to his office, Meyer submitted a memorandum to Fairchild:

"Knowing the peculiarities of Professor Sargent and how little he is inclined to part with things too easily, I suggest we have a list made up of desired plants and then have a handy person go up to the Arnold Arboretum with packing materials and have him collect things they will allow him to take. Since Professor Sargent has gotten so many things from us, he cannot (or at least ought not) to object to us getting a few cuttings of some plants. But the person who goes *must* be some sort of diplomat." In the fall of 1916, Fairchild sent Walter Van Fleet and H. H. Skeels. They returned with a generous quantity of cuttings. Some of these plants still grow at the USDA Plant Introduction Station at Glenn Dale, Maryland.

From Boston Meyer went to New York to lecture to the Society of American Florists at the annual flower show. People crowded into the auditorium and stood in the corridor outside to hear his talk on horticultural exploration in China. Before returning to Washington, he also spoke at the University of Pennsylvania in Philadelphia.

During the winter and spring of 1916, Meyer's most enduring accomplishment was an article published in the *Yearbook of Agriculture*, "China, A Fruitful Field for Plant Exploration." His emphasis on the importance of having a competent interpreter suggests that he may have read Farrer's critical article in the *Gardeners' Chronicle*. The twenty-two different languages and the four hundred dialects of China presented no problems on the beaten track, he wrote, but an agricultural explorer had to visit isolated communities where the rural Chinese would not talk to a foreigner. A good interpreter could sit by the fire at a country inn, exchange news with the local inhabitants, and gain necessary information about the agricultural products of that region.[3]

Late in May Meyer left Washington. After attending E. H. Wilson's lecture at the New York Botanical Garden, he spent several days at the Museum of Natural History, Columbia University, and the New York Public Library. During the next three weeks at the Arnold Arboretum, he conferred frequently with Sargent and Wilson about his next expedition. He also enjoyed discussing plant propagation with Jackson Dawson, who was so skilled in various methods of budding, grafting, and growing plants from cuttings that anything he put into the ground seemed to take root instantly. Meyer urged Fairchild to accept Sargent's invitation to join their conferences about future agricultural and botanical exploration in China, but Fairchild declined. Though he said that he had learned "to enjoy the Professor's sarcasm and the pitfalls he sets for my ignorance about some species," Fairchild nevertheless considered Sargent's remarks "rather severe and almost brutal." He could not forget Sargent's statement that botanists at the USDA were interested only in plants they could eat.

After he had returned to Washington, Meyer submitted his proposed itinerary for his fourth expedition. First, he wanted to survey Colorado,

Utah, and Idaho in order to select a place to establish an experiment station for the propagation of hardy cherries, plums, peaches, and almonds. He planned to reach Peking by way of Japan, Korea, and Manchuria and to spend the fall collecting in northern China before going to the south. During 1918 he hoped to stay in fertile Szechwan and to return home in 1919 by way of the Yangtze. Among the changes that department officials made in this proposed itinerary was the deletion of the Rocky Mountain area where he had hoped to look for a site for his plant breeding station.

When Meyer started his third expedition in 1912, he had hoped that it would be his last long journey; yet in July of 1916 he was preparing "to roam for many more years, primarily in China." He had often said that, after his fortieth birthday, he expected to settle down and "create plants and shrubs there is a need for," but the USDA showed no interest in anchoring him at an experiment station. Though he confessed to Dorsett that "the spectre of a lonely old age looms up larger and larger, and the spectacular office of an agricultural explorer does not hold it down any longer," he was as far as ever from ending his wanderings. Dorsett's suggestion that Meyer's friends would be glad to comfort "any special young lady" whom he was leaving behind suggests that his friends were concerned about his loneliness; if they attempted matchmaking on his behalf, they did not succeed.

In the past he had often found refuge at In the Woods, but in February of 1916 David and Marian Fairchild had bought "The Kampong" in Florida. Since Fairchild had been suffering from bronchial colds and had been forced to spend weeks in bed each winter, in the future he planned to live at The Kampong as much as possible. By 1918 President Wilson's secretary of war, Newton Baker, had rented In the Woods and the Herbert Hoovers became the next tenants.[4] Meyer must have known that he would not have the forty acres of Maryland woodland as a retreat when he returned from China.

In addition, the war had prevented his long-awaited visit with his family and friends in Holland. He had hoped not only to see de Vries and the Janssens but to travel by way of India to the Dutch botanical garden in Sumatra. Since the war continued to separate him from his family and old friends, only his time-tested formula for escaping periods of restlessness remained, but the prospect of travel did not seem as enticing as it had in the past.

Dorsett thought that he stood summer heat and humidity in Washington better than usual, but Fairchild noticed that Meyer was leaving "with a certain reluctance and an expressed doubt as to whether he should ever return." He attributed this to long years of solitary living in China; Meyer's "sensitive character," he said, "had been touched by the fatalism of the Orient."[5] Knowing that he would not see his relatives for a long while, Meyer sent them photographs. The one that he mailed to his sister Alida, who had retired as the trusted maid of a wealthy family on the Keizergracht in order to care for her father, bore this affectionate inscription: "To my sister Alida Wilhelmina Meyer, who always gave me good advice and has been a great example for me!"[6]

Before his departure Meyer had his attorney prepare his will, including a bequest to the office staff. "It isn't much," he told Fairchild, "but I feel grateful to them for all they have done for me." On August 15 he finished packing and set out to visit western experiment stations. From Minneapolis he wrote to Dorsett, betraying the tension that he was experiencing: "The long and lonely journey has commenced, and I feel the weight of it. Is there rest and permanency somewhere?"

The Fourth Expedition

Meyer, summer 1916,
before leaving on his
last expedition.

"In an old Chinese garden there is far more imagination, more mystery, and more detail than in any Western garden," Changsha, Hunan, May 16, 1917.

Grave of Frank N. Meyer in Bubbling Well Cemetery, Shanghai. Photo taken August 15, 1924, by P. H. Dorsett, who erected this granite headstone. Vertically, above Meyer's name, are the Chinese characters that appear on the Meyer medal, "In the thousand plants he takes delight." The stone is no longer standing; however, the two arborvitae at the head and the *Pinus bungeana* at the foot of the grave may have survived to mark this spot.

Obverse and reverse of the Meyer medal. This particular medal was awarded to P. H. Dorsett in 1936.

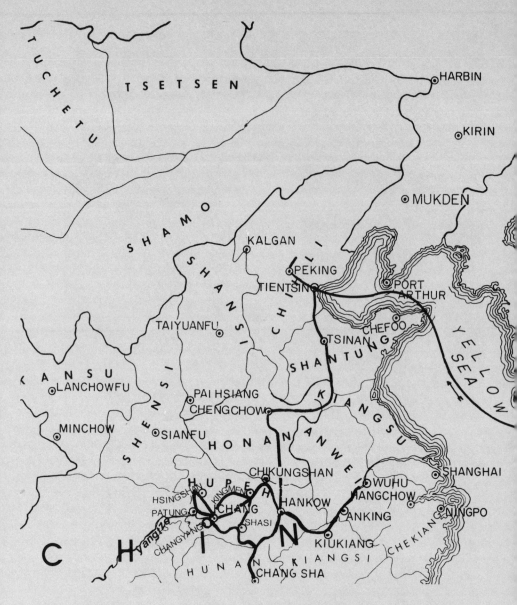

THE FOURTH EXPEDITION, 1916–1918

Peking (Beijing) via Japan

The Northwest, Yokohama, and Peking
AUGUST, 1916, TO FEBRUARY, 1917

MEYER'S fourth expedition began with "a few rumblings of thunder." When he reached the agricultural experiment station at Minneapolis on August 17, the weather was extremely hot and sultry, 96°F in the shade. Three days after inspecting fruit tree hybrids in the burning sunlight, he suffered fever, loss of appetite, and sleeplessness. As his temperature rose, he became delirious. Afterward he wrote Fairchild that "for a few days I was in that strange borderland when sanity has slipped away and insanity is entering. . . . The visions I have had are too strange to describe; just fancy yourself visiting the earth a million years ago when *Pithecanthropus erectus* and all the strange beasts were around. Well, I went through it and marvelled. When I began to get better, the animals and fishes went away and landscapes and forests came in succession. I cannot explain these matters!" After he had swallowed "quite some medicine," he improved rapidly. His doctors believed that sunstroke and fatigue had caused this recurrence of malarial fever; possibly his emotional state made this illness unusually severe. On August 28 he felt strong enough to leave Minneapolis for Mandan, North Dakota.

When an agricultural explorer became ill in the field, his daily allowance stopped and he paid all the expenses incurred in connection with his illness. From August 21 through August 27 Meyer entered in his accounts, "Sick and unable to attend to official duties. No charge for meals and lodging." After he had claimed his nine hundred pounds of baggage, he entered the storage charge as an official expense. The Treasury Department disallowed this $10.40 because "it appears that the charge for storage August 21–27 was occasioned by the illness of the traveler."[1] It is not surprising that Meyer worried about his future if he should be seriously injured or permanently disabled.

215

He felt much better when he reached North Dakota and enjoyed seeing the remarkable progress that had been made at the Mandan Experiment Farm since he and Dorsett had inspected the new testing station in 1912. Where he remembered only a barren tract of land, he observed "thriving little forests" of poplars, ash, willows, and elms. Fine tomatoes, eggplants, corn, and beans grew where people had told him four years earlier that no vegetable could survive. The threat of a railroad strike forced him to hurry to Oregon after one day at Mandan.

In Portland he received Dorsett's answer to his statement that "the long and lonely journey has commenced." Dorsett wrote, "What on earth is the trouble—a longing for dear old Washington and the personnel of the Office of Seed and Plant Introduction, or are you in love and pining for the loved one left behind? Dear Friend, I am afraid that rest and permanency are not to be found in this life. We know your ability and have faith in your being able to accomplish what you are undertaking; we will help you when we can." In his reply Meyer expressed surprise because Dorsett had not realized that he always felt lonely during his expeditions. "There are times that my loneliness may destroy me," he admitted. Dorsett's prompt answer revealed his concern: "You refer to lonely old age looming larger and larger. Why should such a ghost appear to disturb your active mind? You are too young a man with too bright a prospect to become so despondent."

Despite Dorsett's encouragement, Meyer continued to sense "rumblings of thunder." He had great difficulty securing a stateroom on a steamer bound for Japan. After a week spent sending a series of cables, he found accommodations on a small steamer, the *Inaba Maru*. Logistic problems faded to insignificance, however, when he heard of the death of his friend, Jackson Dawson. Their acquaintance had not been limited to sharing an interest in plant propagation at the Arnold Arboretum; Meyer also had visited the Dawsons at their home on Center Street in Jamaica Plain. "I was a good friend of his," Meyer wrote Dorsett, "and knew many members of his family."

After observing plantings of filberts and walnuts at Vancouver, Washington, and studying fire blight (*Bacillus amylovarus*) in pear orchards along the Hood River, Meyer traveled to the Southern Oregon Experiment Station at Talent. There he conferred with Professor F. C. Reimer about his experiments with the fire blight that was destroying large branches and even killing entire pear trees. Meyer had come to Talent feeling skeptical about Reimer's claims, but several days in the Rogue River Valley convinced him of the validity of Reimer's work. Reimer estimated that the value of a congenial immune stock for pears would amount to millions of dollars. He had tested all available varieties of pears and had discovered that only the wild pears that Meyer had sent from China resisted blight. Meyer agreed to try to collect large quantities of seeds of the wild Chinese pears (*Pyrus ussuriensis* and *Pyrus calleryana*) for testing at Talent. His spirits rose as he saw proof once more of the importance of his introductions, and he referred to his coming expedition as "a great trip in tumultuous times."

With only a few days remaining before his ship sailed, he hurried north to the Bellingham Garden in Washington to confer with Beverly T. Galloway. Meyer had met Galloway many times, but he had never had an opportunity to know him well. In 1916 Galloway had returned to the USDA after serving briefly as dean of the College of Agriculture at Cornell. Meyer thoroughly enjoyed the two days they spent discussing the problems at Bellingham. He wrote Dorsett enthusiastically, "This is the first time in my life I became somewhat intimate with him and is it worthwhile!!"

Fairchild heard about Meyer's illness and loneliness when he returned to Washington and wrote immediately to tell him to return to the United States if he did not feel well in China. "I am sorry you feel forebodings with regard to this trip to the Orient. You are too valuable a man for the government to take chances on your health." Knowing that this letter might not reach the coast before Meyer left, he also sent an encouraging wire: "What other man has behind him such appreciative people eager to try whatever you find? Success from us all. Bon voyage." Meyer's answer was reassuring: "I feel quite all right now except that I have a touch of 'Heimweh.' That's no crime. Even wanderers find it hard to break ties of friendship!"

On September 20 he boarded the small *Inaba Maru* "with this ungodly lot of nearly 900 pounds of baggage." The ship, selected in desperation, proved a poor choice. He endured a rough seventeen-day crossing with high winds, rain, and heavy seas. Cramped quarters, a lack of entertainment, and cockroaches even in the food made him miserable. In addition, "racial feeling" among passengers of several nationalities, intrigues, and "little scandals" made the atmosphere unpleasant. By the time Meyer landed at Yokohama and passed customs on October 7, he was suffering from digestive trouble, fever, and insomnia.

He spent two weeks in Yokohama, his attack of "nervous sleeplessness" persisting most of that time. Though he called at the American Consulate and conferred with Suzuki at the Yokohama Nursery, he dreaded the long nights when he could not relax. Long before stress-management techniques became familiar, he developed methods for reducing tension, avoiding coffee and tea and taking long walks. He also tried to remember that "what has to come must come; the more fatalistic one becomes, the easier things pass off." When he went to the American Embassy at Tokyo on October 19, he was feeling energetic again.

After reaching Kobe, he confided his concerns to his family. Most of all, he regretted that the "depressing war" had prevented his coming to Holland and had postponed his trip to Indonesia. Remembering the loss of his baggage when he had shipped it ahead four years earlier, he was enduring the burden of keeping the entire nine hundred pounds with him; "I think one does not travel in heaven, and there is no luggage to take care of there." He hoped that his current expedition would last no more than three years because he wanted to live "among my own race before I get too old."

Though the trip from Kobe to Peking (Beijing) lasted a week and he was the only passenger aboard, Meyer relaxed as soon as he stored his twenty-nine bulky pieces of luggage safely on the small Japanese steamer, *Santo Maru*. His itinerary report recorded his relief: "Left Kobe for north China at 10:15 A.M. Thank heavens!" On October 31 he reached Tientsin (Tianjin), paid his obligatory call on the American consul, and left for Peking the next day.

As soon as he had called at the American Legation, he began his work. Despite having received many visitors, he mailed six boxes containing seeds of the white-barked pine, weeping elm, walnuts, and chestnuts. Twelve more packages including preserved jujubes and clumps of wild rice followed. He suggested that soil samples from the rice clumps might be given to Dr. Nathan A. Cobb for analysis, for "strange creatures might be found in it." He also wondered whether the fermenting organism in the fine soybean cheese that he was sending would prove to be a new one.

In the stack of mail waiting for him at Peking, Meyer found letters from Washington, as well as C. W. Janssen's offer of employment as agricultural adviser at the Dutch botanical garden in Sumatra. He assured friends at the office that he felt quite well again and sent his greetings to the staff for a merry Christmas and a prosperous 1917. Declining Janssen's offer, he explained, "I have so much to do in China, I can never finish. Time flies so fast and one gets old before you know it."

His letters to Dorsett revealed renewed confidence and understanding of his previous difficulties. "I have no fears of laying my hands on almost anything we want," he wrote, "but one cannot rush things. Important matters are discussed with a cup of tea in one's hand." After thanking Dorsett for writing him "often and voluminously" during the weeks when he had not felt well mentally or physically, he explained, "It is purely and simply a psychological problem. When advancing in years, one cannot adjust oneself as readily as when young. By the time I return, I may be old and gray and no longer able to jump from the floor onto a table. . . . I am without a home and when suddenly separated from old friends and acquaintances, one does not know how to adapt."

Three weeks after arriving in Peking, Meyer negotiated with carters for a trip to the wild pear groves in the Shinglung Mountains "near the wild monkeys." Chow-hai Ting, the interpreter who had worked with him on all his previous expeditions, had joined him once more. Before he departed for three weeks in the country, he purchased a few essential articles: one enamel teapot, $1.50; one copper washbasin, $2.00; one steel frying pan, $1.50; two enamel plates, $0.80; one bamboo provision basket, $0.35; quinine, $1.60; aspirin, $0.75; anti-cholera tablets, $1.20; and castor oil, $0.60.[2]

He set out from Peking on November 22 with a caravan of donkeys. Near Malanyu he obtained some seeds and samples of the northern wild pear (*Pyrus ussuriensis*). About eighty miles northeast of Peking, he reached the rugged Shinglung Shan. Though he collected wild pear seeds and bought pear tree roots there, he did not overlook ornamentals. In the mountains he observed a tall-growing species of spruce and added it to his collection. Alfred Rehder and E. H. Wilson later named it *Picea meyeri*. He also sent the department seeds of a stately wild walnut tree (*Juglans mandshurica*) that might be of value as a shade tree or as a stock for Persian walnuts in cold regions. After a week had passed, he hired a large cart and searched for pears near Ling Shan for five more days. On December 13 he returned to Peking laden with his harvest.

During the following month he mailed many boxes of plant material to the United States. Fifteen large cases contained about 200,000 peach stones (*Prunus davidiana*), several hundred pounds of dried jujubes, Chinese walnuts suitable for the Rocky Mountains, and seventy-five pounds of *Juniperus chinensis* berries for nurserymen. After pausing to enjoy Christmas day with friends and to exchange visits on New Year's Day, on January 3 he dispatched twenty more packages by diplomatic pouch. These included several varieties of fresh pears and wild pear seeds and scions "for very capable people only." Though he forwarded fourteen pounds of seeds of cultivated pears, he was unable to obtain a quantity of the wild form because farmers had destroyed the pear groves as land was opened to cultivation. He also submitted his itinerary report, referring to the yellow forms as "inquisitorial sheets comprising my police record for October 1 to December 31, 1916."

In January ice a foot thick formed on the canal at Peking, floating ice at the mouth of the Yangtze delayed shipping, and even the Yellow Sea (Huang Hai) froze; yet he continued to collect, pack, and then wait for an opportunity to mail material to America. Six boxes for F. C. Reimer in Oregon held roots of *Pyrus ussuriensis* and seeds of both cultivated and wild pears packed in damp sphagnum moss. Another bundle included lichens for Elizabeth Britton, fungi for W. A. Murrill, acorns for Sargent, grasses for C. V. Piper of Forage Crops Investigations, and entomological material for L. O. Howard, head of the Bureau of Entomology. A few days later he sent negatives, prints, and seeds of Chinese cabbages that sometimes weighed as much as twenty pounds. "I wish I had seven bodies," he wrote Fairchild. "China is too big for one person to cover it all."

Because the war had disrupted shipping lines between Peking and Holland, mail spent several months in transit; Meyer nevertheless sent his best wishes to his father on his eightieth birthday and regretted that he could not

be at home to join the celebration. He had met many Germans and Aus-
trians who were stranded in China without money or employment; they too
were wishing that the war would soon end. "We hope for better times and it
is this hope that keeps us living. I used to think that, of faith, hope, and
love, love is the strongest. Now I think hope is the strongest." He admitted
to his father that he felt discouraged sometimes after he had packed cases
and no ships arrived to take them to America. "If I ever give up this work,
men cannot say that I have not done my best to help the world. It seems to
me sometimes that I have lived more than one life, but I will never be able to
see the whole world. At eighteen one thinks that one can see everything. At
forty you know that the world is too big and life is too short. You reduce
your plans and wishes."

His many letters from around the globe and from missionaries in many
parts of China had become a burden. He could not fail to respond to the
missionaries because they had offered him hospitality and assistance, but
"looking after all my correspondence could only be settled by a Buddha
with forty-eight arms."

As usual he followed the work of other plant hunters with interest.
When he heard that E. H. Wilson had begun a journey to Formosa (Taiwan)
and Korea, he wrote that Wilson deserved "all success" in the interesting
task of linking Chinese and Japanese flora. Once more he expressed his
bitter regret because he had failed to collect herbarium material in Korea in
1906. Fairchild had sent him the current issue of *Plant Immigrants,* a publication of the Plant Introduction Section, commenting that young Wilson
Popenoe's work in Guatemala had "captured the field." Meyer replied,
"Why not give the boy a chance also to become a celebrity? It will be a race
between Wilson Popenoe and me to see who will leave to posterity the
greater number of introductions." Meyer also heard news of William Purdom, who had entered the forestry service of the Chinese government.
Purdom was receiving five thousand dollars in gold annually but was dis-
heartened by the failure of the republican government to support reforestation.

Meyer admitted to Fairchild that he did not feel quite well. He blamed
loneliness, the burden of his work without an assistant, and especially "the
paralyzing effect of this never-ending horrible war" for "robbing me of my
sleep and making me feel like a ship adrift." Germany's "ruthless undersea
warfare" filled him with apprehension. "Did civilization reach its highest
point on August 3, 1914? Let us hope not. Surely those who believe in an
Almighty, All-good, All-wise Creator must feel themselves strongly shaken
by events." In lonesome hours he often read Walt Whitman's Civil War
poems including "Come up from the Fields, Father," but he must have
found scant comfort in contemplating the death in battle of the farmer's
only son.

Overenthusiastic enforcement of quarantine laws by entomologists and pathologists who knew more about insects and diseases than about plant material also troubled him. All specimens, scions, seeds, and plants now had to be shipped to Washington for inspection, even if their ultimate destination was Chico or Oregon. Dorsett and Fairchild had planned an elaborate "quarantine hospital" in Washington, but Congress granted only five thousand dollars for this project. While congressmen voted hundreds of thousands of dollars for matters of special interest to their constituents, Dorsett supervised construction of an inadequate structure to receive all plant material from abroad.[3] Fairchild warned Meyer that the Federal Horticulture Board would destroy the seeds and nuts that he was sending if inspectors discovered fungus or insects in his shipments. Plant material must be free of even universally common pests such as aphids, red spiders, thrips, and mealy bugs. Meyer replied that the board was "throwing out the baby with the wash water." Without facilities for fumigation, he could not be absolutely certain that no insects were lurking among seeds or on plants. Fear that his collection might be destroyed haunted him. Knowing that his plants, cuttings, and scions had to survive shipment, not only from China to Washington but also from Washington to the West Coast, added to his concern.

As he prepared to leave Peking for the interior, Meyer missed de Leuw's companionship and wondered how much longer he could endure hardships alone. "I may return in 1918, sooner than I expected," he warned Fairchild. A few days before his departure, he packed fifteen pieces of baggage and stored the remainder at the American Legation. While a cold dust storm blew "with remarkable violence" for twenty hours, he wrote Stephen Stuntz, Fairchild's botanical assistant, that he planned to follow the Yangtze into central China where the southern wild pears occurred in sufficient numbers to enable him to collect a large quantity of seeds. "Some time yet and then I will leave this work in the hands of younger men."

Terra Sancta

Ichang and Hankow
FEBRUARY TO AUGUST, 1917

BEFORE beginning his major project in central China, Meyer intended to try once more to introduce the famous pound peach of Shantung. Twice he had collected scions at the remote town of Feicheng, but the department had not succeeded in establishing any quantity of this desirable tree. "This Feitcheng peach is a sore affair with me," he told Dorsett; "it is a black sheep in plant exploring work." Leaving Peking with Chow-hai Ting, he reached Taian just before midnight. The next day he hired "wheelbarrow coolies" and traveled for eight hours in a cold and dusty wind. At Feicheng he cut the scions. After returning on foot to Tsinan, he packed and mailed two bundles of peach scions to the USDA. With that task completed, he and Ting left Shantung.

During the next two weeks he covered many miles. His route at first led south to Suchow (Suzhou) where he visited missionaries before taking the newly built railroad west to Kaifeng and then to Chengchow in Honan Province. There he and Ting boarded a train and traveled south for twelve hours until they reached Hankow (Hangou). During the week he spent there, he called on the American consul general, visited Boone College below the Yangtze (Chang Jiang) at Wuchang, and engaged a guide for his trip west. When he boarded a steamer to go up the Yangtze, he entered territory new to him. During the next four days unfamiliar plants along the shore tantalized him because he could not disembark to examine them. Each evening the steamer moored at sunset because large sandbanks made progress at night hazardous. On March 18 it docked at Ichang (Yichang).

"I am now on *Terra Sancta*," Meyer wrote Fairchild a few days later. "Mr. Wilson and Dr. Henry had Ichang as headquarters for many years. I feel like a Christian in Palestine or Mohammedan in Mecca." In the rugged countryside he had seen primroses, lovely purple-blue daphne, and strange citrus fruits—"big, warty, orange-red things." Chow-hai Ting was learning the local dialect quickly, while Meyer was seeking the southern form of the wild pear (*Pyrus calleryana*), learning how to make soybean cheese, collecting seeds and herbarium specimens, and drying his herbarium material over charcoal fires. He was disappointed to find that the wild pear trees were widely scattered. To assemble at least seventy-five pounds of seeds would require months of toil.

After ten days in Ichang, Meyer stored his excess baggage, hired six coolies, two bearers, and a sedan chair, and set out with Ting and a guide on a sixteen-day trip across the mountains and plains of Hupeh (Hubei) Province. Though he "did not sit for one minute" in the sedan chair, his interpreter and guide found it useful. The weather varied from hot and sultry to windy and rainy. Despite this drawback, he enjoyed being in the field again. He intended to find quantities of seeds of the wild pear that Reimer needed to produce trees immune to blight, but he also took many photographs, gathered herbarium material, and dried the specimens over charcoal fires. In one district he discovered thousands of pistachio trees in bloom. Natives boiled and ate the young shoots and used oil from the nuts for illumination.

Conditions in Hupeh Province distressed Meyer. In filthy and overpopulated villages he saw scores of children with no chance to grow into healthy adulthood. Generations of intermarriage had produced entire villages populated by people who were syphilitic or who demonstrated some obvious hereditary defect. Blindness and deafness were common. At "dreadful inns" the travelers slept three abreast on one broad bench under "stinkingly dirty bedcovers that never were laundered." Meyer commented that it was no wonder that 80 percent of the local population suffered from skin diseases. He found fleas, lice, and bedbugs so "exceedingly plentiful and blood-thirsty" that he slept in his hunting boots for protection.

In this isolated region he came upon wild pear trees in quantity and learned that they grew on dry sterile slopes, in standing water, on ledges in the burning sun, in low bamboo jungles, or on the burned-over slope of a pebbly hill. He therefore believed that they would have great value as a stock. The trees did not occur in groves; however, he discovered a concentration around Kingmen (Jingmen), four or five days' walk northeast of Ichang. After negotiating at length, he paid one hundred dollars in advance to a merchant who promised to collect several thousand pounds of ripe pears and to bring them to Kingmen in September.

As he was returning to Ichang in a steady rain, he visited Swedish and Roman Catholic missionaries and later collected plants in the mountains near Tangyang in a heavy downpour. He found the trails in "fearful condition." His coolies amazed him by looking beneath stones for large centipedes that were sheltering there and by catching the insects to use as ingredients in medicines. When he reached Ichang, a quantity of mail awaited him. Walking eight hours a day for two weeks had made him feel much better than he had felt before his trip; however, he saw no way to escape a sweltering summer, since he hoped to travel to Hankow and Canton before returning to Kingmen for the pears in September.

Two days after his arrival at Ichang, he received a cable from Fairchild: "Ship immediately 100 pounds viable poppy seed." In his indignant response, Meyer reminded Fairchild that Chinese farmers who raised poppies were beheaded. He and de Leuw had barely escaped execution simply because they had been suspected of smuggling opium. "One hundred pounds is enough to sow half a province," he commented. "British India should be able to furnish some if the Department needs poppy in a special hurry." Fairchild later admitted that he had responded too readily to concern about a shortage of opium, needed to alleviate suffering in army hospitals.

Letters from the States brought gratifying news. Bisset wrote that the Plant Introduction Section had distributed 17,234 dry-land elms that year. They had grown twelve feet in one season at Riverside, California, and five and a half feet at Mandan, North Dakota. He wanted an additional fifty pounds of seeds because settlers in the northern plains were clamoring for more. A department report justifies this unprecedented demand: "Trees when received (May 1, 1918) were not over three feet high and about the size of a lead pencil. On November 1, 1921, by acutal measurement, they were 16 to 19 inches in circumference and from 15 to 25 feet high."[1] In addition, W. A. Murrill acknowledged two valuable fungi that Meyer had sent, while the distinguished editor, botanist, and author, Liberty Hyde Bailey, wrote that he planned to confer with Meyer in China in August.

In contrast with this good news, Meyer heard about America's impending declaration of war. "Let us hope that, by some means not now apparent, we may be spared this Hell on earth," Dorsett wrote. "It all appears to me as wanton butchery." Knowing that Meyer would be devastated when his adopted country joined the combatants, Fairchild revealed his concern in a message sent from Brooksville: "This may be the last letter written to you before we rush into the horrible flame of this world conflict. . . . Good night, my dear Meyer, and may the spirit of goodness watch over you through the coming months which look so full of uncertainty."

After news of America's entry into World War I reached Ichang, Meyer had an attack of "nervous prostration" and could neither eat nor sleep. Dr. A. Graham of the Scottish Mission at Ichang explained that many people found the humid climate of the Yangtze Valley depressing and advised him to leave his desk and walk as much as he could. With the aid of exercise, cold baths, and sedatives, Dr. Graham believed that Meyer could continue to do a reasonable amount of work; however, he warned that continued overwork, loneliness, and worry about the war could cause a repetition of such nervous attacks. If that should occur, he recommended that Meyer give up plant exploration.

The timing of Meyer's depression suggests that it was the result of overwork and worry about America's involvement in the war. Without an assistant, he was hoping to fill department requests for large quantities of seeds of the northern wild pear from the Shinglung Shan northeast of Peking, fifty pounds of seeds of the dry-land elm from Manchuria, fifty pounds of Chinese cabbage seeds from Shantung, one hundred pounds of seeds of the southern form of the wild pear, one hundred pounds of pistachio seeds, and a few hundred pounds of chestnuts. "Is it strange that a man gets very tired? And more so now that my adopted country has seen fit to join in this monstrous war. We too will get our lists of wounded and killed regularly." Hoping for help with his work, he asked John H. Reisner of the University of Nanking to try to find a student or graduate of the College of Agriculture who would be willing to act as his assistant. "I have so much to do," he explained, and China is *so* awfully large."

Meyer probably wrote the penciled notes headed "Proposed Resignation" at this time. Because paper was scarce in the interior, he slit the ends of three old envelopes and used the inside to outline his reasons for considering resigning. No other item in the fifteen large document boxes at the National Archives is as poignant as these notes on three tattered envelopes:

Not feeling as well as formerly — sleeplessness — less energy
Mentally soon tired; not being able to do as much work as formerly
Paralyzing effect of this terrible everlasting war
Loneliness of life and very few congenial people to associate with
Travel with all this enormous amount of baggage
So much squalor and dirt in China
The destruction of my one and one-half years' work over herbarium
    material has given me a much deeper blow than I ever admitted.
The new plant quarantine laws; the difficulties of shipping
No garden to study the plants one has collected
Assistants have no real interest in this work.

The burden is becoming too big. I propose the following:
    That I should attempt to finish various problems here until spring,
        1918
    That I should return to Washington some time in June, 1918
    That I will probably resign from the service on July 1, 1918, so as to
        be able to enjoy some comparative rest
    That a young fellow should be selected to take over my labours
    Such a young man should, if possible, come out to China a few
        months before I return so that I can give him a lot of advices and
        turn over my official exploration outfit to him, as well as much
        of my personal effects which I am using in this work.

It may seem strange that a person of my age, 41, should already become weary, but my long travels in so many uncongenial parts of the world, the fact that I have so much absolutely unnecessary indoor work to do, and that one is unable to associate himself permanently in this sort of

life with congenial people—all these slowly but surely have been mold-
ing my mind in this state.[2]

By the first week in May his health had improved sufficiently for him to
prepare to go to Hankow by way of Changsha. On May 8 he and Ting
boarded a steamer, leaving Ichang at midnight. During the week that he
spent south of the Yangtze at Changsha, he called at the American Consulate, toured a soybean factory, visited the Changsha Experiment Station,
and lectured to students at the Yale Mission and at the Presbyterian Mission
School. "They have a rainy climate but an enthusiastic lot of Americans,
especially in the Yale Mission," he commented. "They roped me in for three
lectures in the seven or eight days I was there."

He reached Hankow by steamer at 6:00 A.M. on May 21 and began to
respond to the fifty letters that awaited him. He was glad to hear that F. C.
Reimer was coming to China to study the wild pear trees in their native
habitat and sent him a twelve-page letter offering detailed advice. He wrote
the Janssens that, since America had entered the conflict, he could not feel
happy "with so much misery in the world"; his only remaining hope was that
mankind might learn from this experience to end wars. Writing more cheer-
fully to de Vries about a number of mutations that he had observed, he
described his work with the wild pears. Collecting several thousand pounds
of pears, he explained, might result in the development of pear trees that
were immune to the bacillus that was destroying orchards in America. The
department had also assigned him the task of learning how the Chinese
made cheese from soybeans. "I never can finish my work," he concluded.
"Even if I had seven bodies, I could use them all."[3]

By the end of May he realized that he could not travel to Canton
(Guangzhou) that summer. Grave rumors about the political situation in
China were circulating in Hankow. He regretfully decided that the Chinese
were not ready for a republican form of government. China first needed to
develop "the four cornerstones of life, purpose, honesty, discipline, and
cooperation." Lacking these cardinal principles, the nation was fractured by
internal dissension and "anarchy may be at hand."

As the United States mobilized, the Foreign Seed and Plant Introduction Section was challenged to help feed America and her allies. After
describing the planting of backyard vegetable gardens, Fairchild asked
Meyer to suggest other ways to produce more food. Meyer replied promptly
that the government could drain swamps to gain more arable land, close
distilleries and breweries in order to use all grain for food, stock fish ponds,
encourage the raising of guinea pigs, and promote the growing of bean
sprouts. In addition, women should learn how to preserve and pickle. But
Americans should not uproot flowers and shrubs to grow food, he warned;
people must have beauty in their lives or humanity would revert to the Dark

Ages. He advised his countrymen to prepare for a lengthy period of misery as long as people continued to believe in "narrow nationalism, yellow-journal patriotism, military and naval glories, secret diplomacy, and other such clap-trap."

In contrast to such pessimism, he anticipated with pleasure Liberty Hyde Bailey's arrival in Hankow. "Professor Bailey is near," he told Dorsett, "and at last again I will meet somebody who is my superior in knowledge of plants." Early in June he guided Bailey on a tour of markets and gardens. During the several days they spent together, they had "some solid talks" and Meyer marveled at the energy of the fifty-nine-year-old professor. "It does one good," he told Fairchild, "to meet a man *interested* in our work and one who *knows* something besides!" Early in June Bailey returned to Hankow to confer with Meyer for several more days.

After Bailey had departed, Meyer mailed hardy walnuts and soybean curd and indignantly defended the bean cheese that he had sent earlier, insisting that it was no more spoiled than Limburger or Camembert. Concerning complaints from inspectors that the odor of his twenty-pound cabbage had been offensive when they unpacked it, Meyer replied without sympathy that people who used so much carbon disulphide "might congratulate themselves that their olfactory nerves have not struck work yet."

Fear of sending harmful insects or diseases to America troubled Meyer at the same time that rigid quarantine enforcement frustrated him. He read that R. Kent Beattie of the USDA had told the Botanical Society that 157 different diseases had been found on plant material imported by the department in 1916. Meyer wondered how many of these he had sent to America. He nevertheless believed that entomologists were creating antagonism by excessive preventive measures; as a result, agricultural exploration was becoming increasingly difficult.

Only Meyer's dogged determination enabled him to work in sultry Hankow during the summer, while missionaries were escaping from the heat of the valley into the cool mountains. He felt obliged to remain in the lowlands until he had shipped beans, rice, and vegetable seeds, translated Chinese plant names, and completed his desk work. He suggested that Fairchild ask Wilson Popenoe whether he would like to work in southern China. "I wish I could talk to you," he told Fairchild. "I often think the life I am leading here is perhaps not the thing I ought to continue much longer. This strange land fascinates and repels me at the same time. . . . If only I could nurse some of my own plant introductions! Perhaps later in life it may yet come."

As the temperature rose to 99°F in the shade at the end of June, "a prelude of hell," he fought loneliness by writing to half a dozen friends at the plant introduction office. "When one has to sleep at night in inns infested with vermin and have syphilitic people all around, observing one's habits, one does not always feel happy," he told Stephen Stuntz, Fairchild's botanical assistant. After twelve years of working seven days a week or spending Sundays at botanical gardens or parks, he felt tired and asked, "What is a fellow supposed to do on a Sunday? I can't find any regulations as to that."

In addition to temperatures ranging from 95° to 100°F, financial worries troubled him. In February of 1917 the American gold dollar had dropped from a high of $2.40 to a low of $1.56 in relation to the Yuan dollar. At the end of June he was losing the difference between the actual rate of $1.48 and the official government rate of $1.60 every time he exchanged a gold dollar. By August he was receiving only $1.36 for an American gold dollar that had been worth $2.00 in silver when he first came to China. "Grave thoughts come up from time to time," he wrote Harold Chandler, who was handling his accounts. "If I become ill, would my salary stop entirely?" Since the Dutch government provided insurance and pensions for employees, he found it hard to understand the failure of the United States government to offer similar coverage.

While he endured the heat, humidity, and vermin-infested inns in July, he had to search for a new interpreter. Chow-hai Ting, who did not like the climate, people, or food in the Yangtze Valley, decided to return home. "He has simply left me, never thinking about his employer's difficulties," Meyer wrote Fairchild. "The easiest way is to quit, of course, and he did so. What would become of our social structure if we all did the same?" Meyer spent days seeking a new interpreter before engaging a man who proved to be "of the sponge variety, absorbing all and giving back little or nothing."

Despite his lack of competent help, at the end of July he shipped a 260-pound crate via Wells Fargo at Shanghai. The contents, all marked with the proper Chinese characters, demonstrated once more the breadth of his interests. His harvest contained walnuts, ginkgo nuts, citrus specimens for Swingle, early-maturing rice, sugared and roasted soybeans, soybean cheese, and late-maturing soybeans for W. J. Morse to test in the South. For N. L. Britton's museum of vegetable products at the New York Botanical Garden, he sent articles made from bamboo and palm fibers—a teapot cover, a shoebrush with pig's bristles, a scrubbing brush, a fly whisk, a goat's-hair hat brush, and a back scratcher. L. O. Howard of the Bureau of Entomology and W. A. Murrill of the New York Botanical Garden were to share aphids, scale, borers, snails, bagworms, and a lizard preserved in alcohol. He also included a basket of shells for Dr. Paul Bartzog at the Smithsonian Institution, lichens and moss for Elizabeth Britton, soil for nematode analysis for Dr. Nathan Cobb, a growth similar to a crown-gall on wisteria for Erwin Smith, and cones for Sargent.

His collection dispatched, he remained in Hankow for another week in "extremely hot and humid weather" while he bought supplies, engaged a guide, packed his baggage, and completed his correspondence. Despite Dr. Graham's warning that he must not risk extended periods of loneliness and overwork, from late May until early August he had functioned efficiently in the uncongenial atmosphere of Hankow without an assistant. "I long to have a garden of my own in a cool, bracing region," he wrote Fairchild, "but I'll first try to finish a few pieces of work that have been entrusted to me. . . . I am not going to leave China until I have at least one hundred pounds of clean *Pyrus calleryana* seeds." On August 4 he left Hankow by steamer for the mountains of northern Hupeh.

The Wild Pears

Kingmen and Northern Hupeh
AUGUST TO DECEMBER, 1917

R E L E A S E D at last from his long confinement in the Yangtze Valley, Meyer lost no time before beginning to explore the mountains of Hupeh. He arrived with his interpreter and guide at 3:30 P.M. and climbed one mountain before dinner. During the next ten days at Chikungshan (Zhigongshan or Yingshan) near the southern border of Honan Province, he botanized with missionaries in the delightfully cool mountains, collecting plants, insects, and herbarium specimens.

When this pleasant interlude ended, he resumed his travels. Hiring fourteen coolies, he departed on a rigorous sixteen-day journey with his untried guide and interpeter. The first night they slept "amongst debris and centipedes"; on the second, they camped in a dry river bed. At Suichow on the third evening Meyer found an inn, dried his herbarium material, and hired twelve coolies for the next phase of the journey. After sleeping the following night with twenty people in one room, he and his party reached the remote Tahung Shan, where no inns existed. Often they slept at temples among the idols; one night they camped in a river bed on a plot of zoysia grass. After ascending the steep Tahung Shan, they stayed in a thousand-year-old temple before plodding on through a cloud of dense mist. Arriving dripping wet at a village, they lodged in an empty shop. Near the Han River Meyer found wild peaches, plums, apricots, grapes, and a few cherries. Best of all, the air was delightfully cool in the mountains and beautiful springs supplied him with ice-cold water. Traveling from 8:30 A.M. until 8:30 P.M. the next day, he reached Anlu (Zhongxiang), dismissed the coolies, and paused for several days to dry his herbarium specimens. For almost two weeks he had not seen another white man, and he longed for the companionship of someone like de Leuw as he drank tepid tea at a filthy inn.

En route to Kingmen, he and his party crossed the Han River, trudged all day in the rain, and at last went to sleep "amidst the stench of pigs, the grinding of a squeaking bean mill, and the wailing of several babies." At 7:30 the next morning they departed in continuing rain. A third rainy day left the trails in terrible condition. The men were not only soaked but also were covered with sticky mud; nevertheless, they reached Kingmen at 4:00 P.M. on the last day of August. Since they could not find a suitable inn, Meyer rented a private house which he shared with mice, mosquitoes, and a cricket. By this time he knew that the interpreter who had replaced Chow-hai Ting had no interest whatsoever in his work. The guide had proven to be so lazy that Meyer sent him back to Hankow.

After unpacking and drying the herbarium material, Meyer inspected the pear trees in the countryside near Kingmen. He soon realized that the wild pears that he sought would not ripen for three or four weeks. He bought hundreds of pounds of cultivated pears in order to obtain twenty-five pounds of seeds; however, he could not be certain that they would be immune to fire blight.

At Kingmen (Jingmen) he received letters that Fairchild had written two months earlier in response to the news of his "nervous prostration." After expressing concern, Fairchild wrote, "If you get to a point where you think you should return to this country and take up quieter work, do not hesitate to let me know and we will arrange for your return. The information which you have in your head is the most important thing to consider and that means your health. Be guided by the best doctors you can get." Meyer could become a breeder of plants in America, Fairchild added, but he doubted that "a man of your restless disposition" would be contented with the quiet life of a plant breeder. "There will always be a place for you here," he assured Meyer, "and I will do my best to make arrangements so that you can move from place to place in connection with the development of any of your 'pets.' " Meyer replied that "being unwell happens like periods of bad weather." Because plant exploration required solitary work, he admitted that it "gets pretty hard on one's nerves. Some day the world will be in a happier condition and it will reflect on us."

While he waited for the wild pears to ripen, he visited missionaries, made overnight trips to inspect pear trees at some distance from Kingmen, dried herbarium specimens, and answered letters from six associates in Washington. He asked Harold Chandler to file his protest concerning the government's medieval sick-leave and annual-leave policies for travelers abroad. The existing rules, he argued, were neither liberal nor humane. In response to a query from Robert A. Young, he answered that the Chinese did know how to make a rubber substitute from tung oil. One of the missionaries at Moganshan had been about to discard a pair of cracked boots when his servant offered to mend them. The missionary explained that repair would be impossible because China had no rubber. A few days later the servant returned the boots completely waterproofed with a tung oil product.

As October began, Meyer filed his quarterly reports and shipped packages to America. Once more the rate of exchange had fallen. Though the Treasury Department had pegged the value of a gold dollar at $1.60, he was receiving just $1.35; therefore, he was losing about $285.00 for the quarter. "To lose a thousand or so a year gets a little bit too much," he protested. His letters to Bisset, Beagles, Chandler, and Dorsett also reflected his mounting frustration because the slowly ripening wild pears were anchoring him at Kingmen, causing him to miss the opportunity to collect fruits and nuts in the mountains north of Ichang.

F. C. Reimer wrote that he had reached China and would soon come to Kingmen. En route to the Yangtze Valley, he had been studying wild and cultivated pears in Japan, Korea, Manchuria, and northern China. On October 6 Meyer wrote him that "the wild Calleryana pears refuse to ripen quickly or uniformly. I may have to wait another couple of weeks before I get my hundred pounds of clean seeds. Please be not disappointed when you see my humble abode where we have no bedbugs at least."

Throughout October the middlemen whom Meyer had employed were delivering pears to Kingmen from outlying districts where the scattered trees grew. Meyer inspected the trees periodically to decide when the pears would be ripe enough to harvest; he also hired natives to split the tiny pears, remove the seeds, and clean them thoroughly. Since he needed five thousand pounds of pears the size of marbles, this project represented a major undertaking. To complicate matters further, he found *Pyrus betulaefolia* mixed with *Pyrus calleryana*. Unless leaves were attached, it was impossible to distinguish between these two pears until they became fully ripened. At that point *Pyrus calleryana* turned brown, but *P. betulaefolia* became black. Meyer personally supervised culling *P. betulaefolia* from the five thousand pounds of small pears. By October 24 he had just twenty pounds of clean seeds. Bad weather and illness had impeded his progress. Both malaria and dysentery had taken a toll in Kingmen; Meyer had dysentery but the kindness of the missionaries helped him to recover rapidly.

In addition to the pear project, he became involved in several other undertakings. He hired natives to harvest a large quantity of seeds of a wild grass that later became one of the finest lawn grasses in the Gulf States. He also collected quantities of pistachio seeds. Late in October he received a cablegram from Fairchild announcing the government's immediate need for one-hundred-pound lots of castor oil and several million bushels of castor beans for the aviation industry. Though Fairchild must have realized that Meyer could not supply tons of castor beans, he knew that he would be able to tell him where to look. Meyer answered promptly that Newchwang and Dalny were the chief sources of this product. Weeks later Meyer learned that castor oil, the heaviest of all oils, was insoluble in gasoline. Using it as a lubricant would give American aviators an advantage over the enemy.[1]

Meyer missed Fairchild's frequent letters and felt increasing concern for the future. "When one's chief is busy with other things, then one gets that loose feeling of a homeless child in the street." He could find little comfort in China. Civil strife was making many parts of the country unsafe for travelers, robber bands roamed Szechwan, and Canton was in a state of rebellion. "I feel the evening of life slowly descending upon me, and the fearful sorrow that hangs over the earth does not make life the same as it used to be. The loneliness and responsibilities therefore seem to me to become heavier and heavier, and some time, not too far distant, I'll lay down this heavy cloak." When that time came, he wondered what he would do. "One thing is sure. The office life is not in my line. I must have plants around me and be able to visit collections of living plants for study and inspiration." In the meantime, he hoped that Fairchild could find a young man who wanted to make plant exploration in China and the Himalayas his life work.

Merton Waite's encouraging news that the Feicheng peach had fruited brought an enthusiastic response: "Is it really so? Was it one of the eight trees I sent in 1914? I *am* glad I have succeeded in getting it introduced into the United States." He had feared that America never would have this large clingstone peach; now he wondered whether it would become as highly regarded at home as it was in China.

His solitude ended on October 26 when F. C. Reimer arrived in Kingmen. Meyer spent the next week showing him the wild pears in their natural habitat and demonstrating the seed-cleaning process. Reimer had been able to collect only a few ounces of seeds of the northern wild pear, *Pyrus ussuriensis*, in the Shinglung Shan north of Peking. Not until he had reached Kingmen had he appreciated the immensity of the project that Meyer had undertaken. Meyer was shipping forty pounds of pear seeds to Washington, and he felt confident of accumulating one hundred pounds. Reimer believed that these seeds would be worth hundreds of thousands of dollars to pear growers in America, but Meyer cautioned that long and painstaking testing would be necessary to determine whether the wild pear would become a suitable stock for cultivated pears. Furthermore, he was concerned because *Pyrus ussuriensis* might not adapt in the South and *Pyrus calleryana* could winterkill in the North. If the two types became confused after they were released to the nursery trade, or if they were planted close enough to other pears to cross-pollinate, all his work could end in failure. His fears were unjustified, for *Pyrus calleryana* has remained for sixty years the best source of resistance to fire blight.

Though he shared with Reimer "unreservedly" all the information that he had gathered and showed him "special trees that it took weeks to spot," he could not suppress a twinge of regret when he realized that Reimer would publish these findings and receive credit for the research. "He is taking many photographs and his observations will appear in print before mine," Meyer told Fairchild. "It is somewhat painful to give away all one's information, but pioneer work is missionary work; one is a sower and others are the reapers. It is all for a good purpose and the benefits fall to all humanity!" Reimer appreciated not only the work that Meyer shared with him, but also the price that he was paying in loneliness and fatigue. "Few people," Reimer later wrote, "ever realized the tremendous battle that was raging within his soul."

Heavy rains delayed their departure for the mountains northwest of Ichang. The condition of the trails defied description after the deluge. In addition, the revolution raging in neighboring Szechwan and Hunan threatened to spread to Hupeh. After storing his excess baggage and his collection with Swedish-American missionaries and arranging to return for the remaining pear seeds, on November 3 Meyer left Kingmen with Reimer, the interpreter "of the sponge variety," his competent guide, and nine carrying coolies. After a four-day journey on foot, varied by a night at an exceptionally poor inn and by difficulties with the coolies, they reached Ichang where Meyer mailed an additional twenty-five pounds of clean pear seeds to Washington.

Three days sufficed to prepare for their journey to the Chinkang Shan in northwest Hupeh. "We expect to have a pleasant and successful trip," he wrote Fairchild on the eve of their departure. After leaving Ichang by boat, at Sanyutung he and Reimer hired coolies to carry their baggage and climbed steep mountains. After ten weeks of working constantly with pears, Meyer welcomed a change, for "an all-around man gets at times fed up with the same dish served morning, noon, and night." For five days he and Reimer botanzied, collected herbarium specimens, and took photographs in the rugged Chinkang Shan. Reimer found *Pyrus serotina* and *P. serrulata* there, as well as *P. calleryana* and *P. betulaefolia*; however, he and Meyer had to return to Ichang because Reimer's leg became infected. Thereafter he spent three weeks in a hospital in Hankow.[2]

During their journey to the mountains Meyer learned that Reimer wanted the USDA to send the entire lot of pear seeds to the Southern Oregon Experiment Station. Solving all the problems connected with the development of an immune stock, Meyer thought, would require more time, acreage, and labor than Reimer's station alone could offer. Reimer eventually justified his request, for the Southern Oregon Experiment Station and the Oregon Experiment Station not only pioneered but remained dominant in pear stock research.

After Reimer's departure, Meyer visited a bean curd factory, selected samples of bean cheese to send to the USDA, negotiated with carrying coolies, and bought supplies for a seventeen-day trip. A week later he described Hsingshanhsien (Xingshanxian) "six days march" west of Ichang: "Here I am in a small hole of a town surrounded by high mountains. The flanks of these mountains are brown with withered vegetation, but here and there a tallow tree stands out as a bit of flaming red and purple; some scrub of *Rhus cotinus* [*Cotinus coggygria*] is a blazing carmine and a few bushes of *Rhus javanica* are an indescribably warm hue of orange-red. Indian summer is speeding to its close." Between Ichang and Hsingshanhsien he had made an important discovery. He had found *Ginkgo biloba* growing "undoubtedly wild" for the first time. He felt content as he visited citrus orchards, collected herbarium specimens, took photographs, and observed his forty-second birthday in this mountainous region. With his spirits refreshed by climbing mountains, he planned to return to Kingmen in a few weeks for the pear, pistachio, and grass seeds and then to proceed to southern China.

From Hsingshanhsien he mailed a wooden box containing two items of unusual interest. He sent twelve Ichang lemons (*Citrus ichangensis*) for Swingle, who had requested seeds of the relatively hardy citrus fruits from this region. He had found only three hardy lemon trees in the wild near the border of Szechwan and only one of those bore fruit. His other treasure was the smooth Yang tao (*Actinidia chinensis*), the Chinese gooseberry or kiwi. This fruit had an unusual and delicious flavor. The Yang tao could not tolerate freezing temperatures, but Meyer thought it would thrive wherever loquats flourished.

On November 28 he set out in the rain for the Wantiao Shan, accompanied by his interpreter, guide, seven coolies, and a guard. In those mountains Wilson had found the dove tree (*Davidia involucrata*) and other unusual plants. Meyer gathered chestnuts as he scaled steep and slippery mountain trails. Early December brought snow while he collected seeds at an elevation of 8,800 feet. On December 4 he returned to the Yangtze and ferried across to Patung (Badong). The next day he hired rowboats and spent a day and a half working his way down the Yangtze to Ichang.

Though he heard that the revolution had spread to Hupeh Province, he nevertheless made the disastrous decision to risk another week's travel in Hupeh instead of leaving for Kingmen at once. With his interpreter and guide, he traveled by boat to Yidao (Itao) on the south shore of the Yangtze and set out with seven coolies for Changyang. He spent two days in this region, cutting citrus scions and studying large bamboo groves. On December 13 he and his companions climbed the Tienchu Shan and collected seeds. For several days his interpreter had been suffering from an inflammation of his eyes. This condition rapidly became worse until someone had to lead him down the precipitous trails of a 5,700-foot mountain. After having been delayed by this handicap, they reached the Yangtze on December 15 and crossed to Ichang.

By the time Meyer took his interpreter to Dr. Graham at the Scottish

Mission for treatment, the political situation had become serious. He later wrote Fairchild that "we might possibly have skipped through and obtained my stored baggage and cleaned pear seed at Kingmen" if his interpreter had been well enough to travel. Instead, he collected more scions, cleaned seeds, took photographs, and lectured at the American Church Mission while he waited for his interpreter to recover. On the afternoon of December 23, fighting between government troops and revolutionaries began near the city. War had engulfed Frank Meyer at last.

Impasse in Ichang (Yichang)

Hupeh Province
DECEMBER, 1917, TO MAY, 1918

T H R O U G H O U T late December and early January, Meyer tried to fill his days with useful activities while troops fought sporadically near Ichang. On Christmas Eve he spoke at the Anglo-Chinese school; on Christmas day he paid visits and wrote letters; two days later he talked to students at the Church of Scotland Mission School. He also continued to collect and pack seeds, scions, and chestnuts. Early in January he sent eighteen parcels to the American consul general at Shanghai. While revolutionaries and bandits harassed the neighboring region, he advised the American Church Mission about the maintenance of their grounds, called on Roman Catholic missionaries, arranged his herbarium specimens, and translated Chinese plant names.

"We are living in the midst of a revolution here; soldiers everywhere, looting and burning," he wrote Fairchild. "Of course we are under strict martial law." He hoped that the seeds and baggage he had stored with the Swedish-American missionaries at Kingmen would be safe from brigandage. Though he needed his notebooks and inventory forms in order to record and describe plant material, the revolutionary troops surrounding Ichang prevented him from going to Kingmen. "I have worried a great deal and sleep stays away from me," he admitted. "All foreigners here have been living under a strain." At the end of January he joined other members of the foreign colony to discuss the increasingly serious situation. Fighting took place close to Ichang on February 1, but he went out into the country the following day and observed *Primula sinensis* in bloom. Though his official itinerary sheets were stored at Kingmen, he nevertheless submitted his itinerary report, as well as his quarterly accounts.

While he listened to rifle fire as troops fought a mile north of the city, he wrote Fairchild about the flora of Hupeh, enclosing a letter to Swingle about *Citrus ichangensis*. The province of Hupeh was the size of Montana with the climate of Georgia, but the terrain was extremely rugged—high mountains intersected by deep valleys. No roads or public accommodations existed in the countryside. Even if there were no civil war, "no one man can cover the province on foot and one cannot travel otherwise."

Early in February Meyer described his situation to John Reisner at Nanking and to Liberty Hyde Bailey. "We are here in a sort of trap," he told Reisner. "Fighting between Northern and Southern troops takes place at intervals around this city and east of here." Brigandage was common. Soldiers and bandits committed atrocities, looted mails, and murdered mail carriers. Though he longed to move on, he did not dare to travel to Kingmen. Some day the war in China would end, "just like this terrible slaughter in Europe," he wrote Bailey. "How the world will be when peace has come again, that's a question! Hatred has gone so deep now that it may take a few generations before it has been bred out again." In the meantime, chaotic conditions were upsetting all his plans. "I never get through with my work here. China is too big a land, too rich, and at times too unsettled to allow one person to cover it all. And the worst is that the country attracts and repels one alternately. When in China one often wants to get out, and when one is out, one wants to go back again. It is tantalizing."

Though Meyer worried because he could not continue his exploration, for the first time during his expeditions he became a part of a group of Westerners who were united by common problems. Edward Gilchrist, commissioner of customs at Ichang, said that Meyer nearly "fretted his heart out" because he was unable to travel west of Ichang where Wilson had worked. While he was "cooped up" at Ichang, he continued to be productive by assisting members of the foreign colony with their horticultural problems. His projects began modestly when he spent several days helping Roman Catholic missionaries to prune their vineyards and trees. Commissioner Gilchrist then asked him about transplanting trees on the grounds of the customs compound. As a result, Meyer spent much of the rest of February supervising the moving of a dozen tea-olives (*Osmanthus fragrans*), which had been planted too close together many years before. Twenty-five coolies helped to lift each of the large trees. Nothing like this had ever been attempted in Ichang. "Should all these trees pull through," he commented, "my work will be tied up with this city for a hundred years to come."

While troops fought nearby, Meyer's itinerary report shows that he alternated walks into the countryside with work in the city:

February 17   Went out into the country
February 18–23   Assisted in transplanting trees in Customs Compound and in various gardens

February 24	Out into the country
February 25	Assisted transplanting trees. Fighting between soldiers of various factions around the town
February 26–27	Transplanting trees
February 28	Snowed hard
March 1	Advised people re their grounds. Heavy snow
March 2	Assisted in transplanting trees. Fighting occurring near the town
March 3	Fighting going on all day near town
March 4	Assisted in transplanting trees. Fighting within the city; foreign residents holding emergency meetings
March 5	Assisted in transplanting trees in various gardens. Took a walk in the country to see fighting.

Early in March he wondered whether the letter and cuttings that he was mailing would ever reach Fairchild. He had not received any communications for several months, food had become increasingly scarce, and all commerce had ceased. Occasionally a Japanese steamer made its way up the Yangtze as far as Ichang, but Meyer would not consider leaving Hupeh without his collection. "Fighting occurs almost hourly around the city these last weeks," he wrote Fairchild, "and everyone feels depressed from this long-drawn state of suspension." He had joined other foreigners in forming a defense committee; however, he realized that "a mere handful of white residents can do nothing against brigands in uniform, and there are thousands around us. I saw last week how some of them took out the hearts of fellows they had shot and mutilated the corpses in unspeakable ways. They were going to eat those hearts to get courage." Regardless of atrocities, Meyer noticed that plum trees were blooming and cherries were budding after the mild winter.

As he supervised the transplanting of trees on March 8, he heard heavy cannonading all day; a few days later he walked into the country and found soldiers camped ten miles west of town. On Good Friday he enjoyed "a long tramp out into the country with several people." As he walked, he searched for hardy citrus fruits which had cross-pollinated to produce a variety of hybrids. Edward Gilchrist later remembered his returning with an armful of branches "which even he could not determine definitely to be oranges, lemons, or grapefruit. He would show me one and say, 'Dis is pappa,' and of another, 'Dis is mamma,' and of a third, 'Dis is baby.' "[1] At times these walks into the country may have involved some risk of personal safety, but he must have weighed that danger against the greater risk of feeling totally imprisoned in Ichang.

Since he had been unable to work, the expenditures that he reported to Chandler for that quarter were meager. "We are virtually prisoners of war," he explained. Soldiers were drilling with machine guns in the streets of

Ichang, and no one dared to travel even one day westward to the mountains because "uniformed bandits" were plundering the countryside. He had dismissed the interpreter who had failed to take any interest in his work and had retained only his faithful guide, Yao-feng Ting. He wondered how the auditor would react to his work on the gardens of the customs commissioner and other Westerners. He could not do desk work because paper was scarce, and he did not dare to venture into the mountains as he wished to do. An active person would become mentally unbalanced, he told Chandler, unless he could find a project to absorb his energy.

The temperature had begun to rise in the Yangtze Valley on May 2 when Meyer and his guide finally began the four-day journey to Kingmen. Meyer was not sure that it would be possible to reach his destination, pick up his baggage, and then make his way safely to Shashi, a port on the Yangtze below Ichang. He and Yao-feng Ting walked the trails eighty miles northeast to Kingmen, experiencing difficulty finding food as they passed through looted and burned villages. At one inn the walls as well as the beds were covered with lice. Sleep was impossible. By morning even Meyer's straw hat was infested. Several times soldiers stopped them. "Some unpleasantries were indulged in, but we could have fared far worse," he commented. At Kingmen he paid for the last lot of pear seeds and repossessed the baggage and seed collection that the Swedish-American missionaries had kept for him. After a sixty-mile journey on foot, he and Yao-feng Ting reached Shashi and boarded a riverboat bound for Hankow.

He arrived on May 14 and rested at the Hankow Hotel. "At last I have been able to break though the lines of soldiers around Ichang," he told Fairchild. "I am awfully glad that I got away; the situation began to depress me. One can't live for months in an atmosphere of suspension without feeling the effects. And, as I had cheerless, uncomfortable quarters and lacked substantial food at times, there were both mental and physical discomforts." He told John Reisner that he had decided to leave the Yangtze Valley as soon as possible because the winter in Ichang had been "worrisome" and the warm spring weather made him feel lethargic. He planned to go to Shanghai and ship his collection to the United States before moving to Shantung Province, where he would label the herbarium material that he had collected during the past year. "China is surely in a sad plight right now," he concluded. "Oriental character and republicanism do not seem to agree."

Fairchild's response to his October letter about leaving plant exploration in China to a younger man reached Meyer at Hankow. Fairchild wrote that his fondness for Meyer "makes me wish at times that you could be here with us. If you should come back, we could arrange for a place where . . . you could carry on your work in a way that would make your knowledge available to the country and prevent what I am always afraid might happen, the loss of your great store of sifted observations and reflections. You really owe it to your adopted country to make this information available, putting it on paper so that it would be a source of information to the next generation." In reply, Meyer thanked Fairchild for his concern, but he did not promise to record his store of information; the prospect of being confined to a desk in an office was one of the worst fates that he could imagine.

Fairchild also conveyed news from the Plant Introduction Section. The Tangsi cherry was "doing splendidly" at Brooksville, Swingle was finding the citrus material from Ichang of great interest, and the Feicheng peach apparently had come true from seed. The USDA was planting three hundred acres in soybeans at the Yarrow Garden near Rockville, Maryland; this would be the largest acreage in America devoted to soybeans. In his reply Meyer regretted the need to displace ornamentals at the Yarrow Garden. More distressing to him was the news that Paul Popenoe, Wilson Popenoe's brother who had edited the *Journal of Heredity,* was enlisting in the armed forces. Meyer hoped that Wilson Popenoe would not follow Paul's example. "I trust that he will see that in developing new supplies of food . . . he assists his fellow men more than by going to try to kill a few who happen to be from somewhere else on this globe and who are not at all in sympathy with those driving them."

Sad news came from Grace Cramer Clime and from Fairchild during the influenza epidemic of 1918. Mrs. Clime wrote of the death of "our chum," Charles Mansfield, who had left the USDA to become a veterinary surgeon. Remembering camping and fishing trips with Mansfield, Meyer answered that this information "affected me most sorely." Fairchild wrote of the death of his botanical assistant, Stephen Stuntz, who had joined the staff when Meyer was in Central Asia. A good linguist as well as a botanist, Stuntz had studied the botanical literature of many countries and furnished information about little-known plants to Meyer and others. Two years earlier Meyer had given him a wolfskin as a present for his new baby, and it had occupied a place of honor on the window seat of his home. Meyer felt shocked by the untimely death of "our friend Stuntz, only a young man yet."

In reply to Fairchild's request for information about the diet of the Chinese people, Meyer sent what Fairchild later called "a masterly analysis of the Chinese food situation." In central China, Meyer explained, the poor lived chiefly on rice, which formed three-quarters of their diet. Meat and fish constituted only a small fraction of their food. The remainder consisted of beans, peas, lotus rhizomes, roots, tubers, and leafy vegetables. "The Chinese love best of leafy greens the cabbage and mustard group." They also enjoyed spinach, apparently comprehending instinctively that these green vegetables supplied nutrients. Instead of meat and dairy products, "the hundred and one different manufactures of the soybean supply protein." Americans, however, would not willingly accept this substitute for meat.

Unsettled political conditions had caused the outlook for plant exploration in southern and western China to become "decidedly gloomy." In Fukien (Fujian) Province brigandage was so prevalent that farmers were joining robber bands instead of sowing rice; in Honan and Shantung outlaws had kidnapped Americans; brigands had molested and even killed missionaries in Shansi and Szechwan. Sporadic traffic going up the Yangtze stopped at Ichang. No shipments of tung oil or hides or silk were reaching Hankow, and the merchants were suffering gigantic losses.

Though these conditions made any plans uncertain, Meyer explained his immediate goals. He expected to take a steamer down the Yangtze, possibly stopping at Kiukiang (Jiujiang) to inspect tung oil plantations. When he reached Shanghai, he would spend several weeks packing and shipping his bulky collection. As the heat became more intense in late June, he hoped to move north to Chefoo (Yantai) and to find some quiet place on the coast of Shantung where he could work on his large accumulation of herbarium specimens. His choice of Chefoo possibly was influenced by de Leuw's residence there, as well as by the cooler climate. In the fall, he planned to collect several hundred pounds of chestnuts and a quantity of seeds of the northern form of the wild pear near Peking.

Once more he expressed concern about a world that appeared determined to destroy itself. "Uncontrollable forces seem to be at work among humanity and final results, or possibly purposes, are not being revealed as yet, so far as I can look into this whole titanic catacylsm. Times certainly are sad and mad, and, from a scientific point of view, so utterly unnecessary."

A week later Meyer told his family that he did not enjoy the Yangtze Valley in June; he had become less able to tolerate high temperatures and suffered loss of appetite and inability to sleep during hot weather. Political unrest, insects, disease, and generally unsanitary living conditions made him feel weary. Traveling might seem a pleasure to someone who stayed at home; however, a traveler often longed to have a home and a garden. As soon as peace came, he promised to visit his family in Holland. Unaware that the war would end in less than six months, he expressed fear that civilization might collapse in exhaustion if the conflict continued too long.[2]

He had postponed leaving Hankow because he had contracted a digestive disturbance, "stomach trouble accompanied by vomiting." While he felt too ill to be sociable, Western naval officers at the Hankow Hotel kept asking him to have a drink with them. He therefore moved to the native

Tierhpin Hotel on May 28. After three days there he seemed better, but Yao-feng Ting noticed that he looked thinner than when they left Ichang.[3]

At 7:00 P.M. on Friday, May 31, Meyer and his guide boarded the Japanese riverboat, *Feng Yang Maru*, for the trip down the Yangtze to Shanghai. Practically all foreigners except missionaries traveled first class, but Meyer as usual chose the less expensive first-class-Chinese accommodations. On Saturday morning he ate only gruel for breakfast. Though he told Yao-feng Ting that he was feeling somewhat better, he did not disembark and examine the tung oil plantations at Kiukiang that morning. A British insurance man, Islay Drysdale, boarded the steamer at Kiukiang. Meyer shared his cabin with Drysdale and spent most of the day talking with him until he left the riverboat at Anking at 4:00 P.M.[4]

During the afternoon, in response to Captain Inwood's inquiry, Meyer replied that he was well except for a headache. That evening he ate a normal Chinese dinner. Afterward Yao-feng Ting served tea in his master's cabin, and Meyer assured his guide that he was better. About 11:20 P.M. he left his cabin, presumably to go to the water closet which was near the rail. Possibly he lingered at the railing to enjoy the fresh air. Before midnight the cabin boy reported to Captain Inwood that he could not find Mr. Meyer. The captain ordered a search of the small steamer, but Frank Meyer was not on board.[5]

Journey's End

Aftermath

I shall not wholly die. What's best of me shall
'scape the tomb.

HORACE *Odes* 3.30

A T midnight, as the *Feng Yang Maru* navigated the Yangtze below
Anking, no one could search for Frank Meyer. When the riverboat
docked at Wuhu on June 2, Captain Inwood asked the harbor
master to wire the American consul at Nanking that Meyer was missing;
however, the *Feng Yang Maru* departed from Nanking before the telegram
reached the consulate. When the steamer reached Shanghai on June 3,
Captain Inwood took Meyer's baggage to the Japanese Consulate because
the *Feng Yang Maru* sailed under a Japanese registry. On June 4 Japanese
officials delivered Meyer's effects to the American consul general. At last the
news of his disappearance had reached people who knew him personally.
Action followed promptly. The consul general at Shanghai wired Samuel
Sokobin, vice consul in charge at Nanking, instructing him to "spare no
effort in ascertaining Mr. Meyer's whereabouts." He also cabled the State
Department in Washington that Meyer was missing. A telephone call from
the Consular Bureau of the State Department brought Fairchild the first
news of the catastrophe at 4:00 P.M. on June 4.

The consul general assigned R. P. Tenney, a young consul who had
known Meyer, to direct the investigation at Shanghai. On June 5 Tenney
boarded the *Feng Yang Maru*, interviewed the officers and the deck steward,
and secured an affidavit signed by the officers. The deck steward remembered having seen Meyer cross the saloon at about 11:20 P.M. on June 1,
apparently on his way to the water closet, which was only a few steps from
the rail. The ship's log showed that the steamer had been abreast of the
Barker Island light-boat at that time. Though the officers had searched
along the guards and rails, they had found no mark or trace that could
explain Meyer's disappearance. He had given Hotel Kalee in Shanghai as his
address.

After Samuel Sokobin at Nanking received the telegram from Shanghai instructing him to organize a search, he wired the Consular Service in Washington that he was "proceeding upriver" to look for Meyer and that he had sent for W. T. Swingle who was in Japan. The Consular Bureau telephoned this message to Fairchild on June 7. On that same day Sokobin and his interpreter reached the home of a Standard Oil executive at Wuhu. The executive could offer no information to help Sokobin in his search; however, Sokobin's interpreter talked to the Chinese servants and learned that a boatman had recovered the body of a bearded white man from the Yangtze on June 5 and had taken the body to a customs officer nearby.

The following day, Saturday, June 8, Sokobin completed his grim task. At 7:00 A.M. he interviewed the crew of the Socony launch, learned that they had witnessed the recovery of the body, and went with them to the customs station at Tikang (Digang), thirty miles above Wuhu. There the customs officer related that about noon on June 5 a boatman named Yu-yuan Chen had seen a swollen body floating in the river. Chen had towed the body to the shore at the customs station. The officer sent for Chen, and Sokobin questioned him about marks of violence on the body. Possibly because the face had been "black with dirt," Chen and other witnesses agreed that they had not seen evidence of any injury. In order to verify identification of the body, Sokobin took possession of the victim's shoes and suspenders, which the customs officer had given to the boatmen as a reward for recovering the body.

The officer then showed Sokobin the spot on San To Miao Hill about one hundred yards from the shore where workmen had buried the body under a mound of turf. When Sokobin persuaded three reluctant laborers to open the small mound, he saw the body resting on two wooden planks. A third plank had covered it, but there was no sort of coffin. Sokobin had never met Meyer; however, he had seen him at the American Consulate at Shanghai. Though the head had decomposed, he recognized the beard and felt sure that he had accomplished his mission.

Sokobin purchased a coffin and then hired two men to prepare the body and place it in the casket. At 6:00 P.M. they carried their burden to the shore and loaded it on a sampan. By 10:00 P.M. the Socony launch had towed the sampan to Wuhu. Early the next day Sokobin embarked on a steamer, accompanying the casket as far as Nanking. There he wired the Consular Bureau in Washington, "Found Meyer's body thirty miles above Wuhu." He then boarded a train in order to reach Shanghai in time to make arrangements for burial before the steamer docked.

A telephone call from the State Department on June 10 brought the Plant Introduction office the news that Sokobin had found Meyer's body. Everyone there shared feelings of shock and loss. Staff members found it difficult to realize that they would receive no more messages from remote villages in Asia. As they waited for the consular report to bring some explanation of the circumstances surrounding Frank Meyer's disappearance, Fairchild faced the task of writing to his father.

In the meantime Samuel Sokobin completed his investigation by interviewing Meyer's guide. Yao-feng Ting of Ichang related that he had worked for Meyer for ten months. Recently his master had been suffering a minor stomach disorder, but he had appeared and spoken as usual when Ting served his evening tea on June 1. Apparently in response to Sokobin's questions, Ting testified that Meyer had not offended anyone, that there were "no bad characters to my knowledge" aboard the ship, and that his master had never shown any symptoms of insanity. He also identified the shoes and suspenders as those that Meyer wore when he disappeared from the steamer.

Meyer's body reached Shanghai on June 10. Sokobin had consulted Meyer's acquaintances there about funeral arrangements, for he did not know whether Meyer should be buried in the Protestant, Catholic, or Jewish cemetery within the international settlement. On June 12 the Reverend John Hykes, a popular American clergyman, conducted the funeral service, which was followed by burial in the Bubbling Well Protestant Cemetery. The consul general, members of his staff, and Meyer's old friends in Shanghai attended the funeral.

Sokobin's task was nearly complete. He had inventoried Meyer's baggage and valued the contents at five hundred dollars in gold. On June 12 he wrote his report on the investigation and filled out consular form 192 on the death of an American citizen. By this time, an employee of the consulate had interviewed Islay F. Drysdale, who remembered that Meyer had been "very much depressed because of the war." On the basis of this statement and Yao-feng Ting's description of Meyer's illness, Sokobin stated on form 192 that "Mr. Meyer had been ill for some time and seemed depressed at the time of his disappearance." Though death had apparently resulted from drowning, it was impossible to determine whether by accident or suicide.

When Swingle reached Shanghai, he took charge of Meyer's valise and three trunks containing his personal effects and his collection. The bulk of the baggage consisted of seeds of the wild pear and the grass that Meyer had found near Kingmen. C. V. Piper of the USDA later identified this grass as *Eremochloa ophiuroides* and named it centipede grass. Among Meyer's personal effects was the stout walking stick that he had carved and carried many miles. His family thereafter cherished this staff, which he had fashioned to look like a snake curled around a stick. At the bottom of a trunk was the dinner jacket that Fairchild had given Meyer when he came to Washington from Saint Louis in 1905. Though it had been covered with mold when Meyer had unpacked it in 1908, he continued to treasure it as a symbol of the friendship that Fairchild had offered when the two men first met.[1]

On June 14 David Fairchild sent a long letter to Jan F. Meyer expressing his sympathy and promising details of Frank Meyer's disappearance as soon as the consular report reached Washington. "I need not tell you that your son's death brings to all who knew him here in Washington a keen feeling of personal loss," Fairchild wrote. "He had endeared himself to all those with whom he came in contact by his rare personality and kindliness and generosity." Fairchild then described Meyer's service to the USDA: "Of his work for the government it would be difficult for me to speak in too high terms. I consider that he has done the best pioneer exploration work in agriculture that has been done for the Department by any of its explorers. The thousands of plants which he has brought in and which have been increased to hundreds of thousands by propagating them in this country, have been scattered throughout the length and breadth of America." After expressing regret because Meyer's "remarkable fund" of knowledge had not been published and "spread broadcast," Fairchild assured Jan Meyer that his son's introductions would not be confined to the United States but would be given to foreign countries as well.

When Jan Meyer thanked Fairchild for this letter, he requested copies of any articles that might be published about his son and added, "That his life has been so useful for the agriculture of the United States in particular and that of the world in general will always be some consolation for us." A week later he acknowledged Fairchild's second letter containing "full particulars as to the death of my son." After thanking him for his kindness, he offered Fairchild any of Frank Meyer's books that might be of use to the department.[2] Fairchild accepted this offer and later identified each volume with a plate naming the donor.

Speculation as to the underlying cause of Meyer's death soon appeared in obituary notices, private correspondence, and published accounts of his work. *Horticulture* reported that Frank N. Meyer, "an expert of worldwide reputation, mysteriously disappeared from the riverboat *Feng Yang Maru* Saturday evening, June 1. . . . It is believed that he fell overboard and was drowned in the Yangtze a short distance out of Wuhu. . . . Captain Inwood said that Mr. Meyer appeared in normal health and spirits before his disappearance." The death notice in the *American Nurseryman* began more dramatically: "In the wilds of Siberia and Korea this bewhiskered scientist took his chances, single-handed, in search of plants that might be adapted to the soil and climate of the United States. . . . Several times he avoided death by murder, but he pursued his way quietly. Finally it came. He disappeared from a steamer on the Yangtze and his body was found later with no marks to show what had caused his death. It is one of those mysteries of the white man in the Orient, which, in all probability, will go unsolved."[3]

What was being said privately is reflected in Sargent's letter to E. H. Wilson on June 19, 1918: "I hear from Fairchild that Frank Meyer disappeared one night from a boat between Hankow and Nanking and nothing further has been heard of him. He may have committed suicide or some of the Chinamen may have thrown him overboard. This is certainly bad news, for he was getting to be a useful collector." Sargent's grudging admission of Meyer's worth seems particularly ungracious because Meyer had often sent items in his collections for the Arnold Arboretum. Possibly S. B. Sutton, author of *Charles S. Sargent and the Arnold Arboretum*, was justified in concluding that Sargent was secretly jealous of the success of Fairchild and Meyer.[4]

Fairchild considered a variety of explanations for Meyer's disappearance before admitting in his autobiography in 1938 that "Meyer's death will remain a mystery to his friends." Evidently he had mentioned the possibility of murder to Sargent before Sokobin's report reached Washington. That report did not even consider the possibility of foul play. No one wanted to find evidence of murder—evidence which may have created an international problem. As a loyal employee of the United States government, Fairchild accepted the results of the formal investigation. The condition of the body when it was disinterred made it almost impossible to ascertain whether or not there had been a head injury. Certainly the visual examination by Sokobin was not sufficient to eliminate that possibility. No motive for murder existed; yet men have been killed for the change in their pockets and opportunity did exist in the darkness at the rail of the riverboat near midnight.

With foul play ruled out by the consular report, Fairchild wrote in "An Agricultural Explorer in China," that either a recurrence of nervous prostration or vertigo might have been the cause of Meyer's death. Fairchild apparently thought of vertigo beause Meyer could have suffered an attack of nausea after eating a normal dinner for the first time in many days. If he had become ill and had leaned far over the rail, dizziness could have caused him to fall into the muddy Yangtze. Knowing Meyer's physical strength and remembering all the dangers that he had survived, Fairchild evidently did not find this explanation satisfying.

If he eliminated the possibility of murder and accident, only the theory of depression leading to suicide remained. In an article entitled "A Hunter of Plants," Fairchild wrote that Meyer's confinement at Ichang and his concern about the war could have combined with loneliness and overwork to precipitate a recurrence of nervous prostration. "Before he could reach the encouraging companionship of people of his own class," Fairchild said, "he was drowned in the waters of the Yangtze River." This theory had its faults too, for Meyer had enjoyed the company of educated Westerners at Ichang and had not been overworked there. Even more important, Fairchild realized that Meyer's creed included devotion to duty and scorn for a quitter. He knew that Meyer was determined to ship his collection, prepare his herbarium specimens, and return to Peking for chestnuts and seeds of the northern wild pear. Meyer considered it dishonorable to quit until he had completed all the tasks that had been entrusted to him. Once more ambivalence resulted from failure to find a satisfying explanation for Meyer's death, and Fairchild concluded that "the real cause of his death will always be a mystery."

Whether or not Meyer was experiencing a depression of any severity at the time of his death is a key question. Available evidence is tenuous because laymen used that term to mean anything from a temporary feeling of unhappiness to an acute clinical condition. Meyer had written Fairchild that he left Ichang gladly because he had begun to feel depressed there. He did not mention nervous prostration but simply the effects of "cheerless quarters, lack of wholesome food, and confinement." After his difficult twelve-day journey to Kingmen and Shashi, he admitted feeling miserable because he had suffered lack of sleep and loss of blood as a result of having been bitten by many insects. Six days before his death he wrote his family that he felt weary because of the debilitating climate in the Yangtze Valley, unsanitary conditions, and political unrest. Drysdale said that he seemed "very much depressed" about the war on the day of his death, but the war continually made him unhappy. Only Yao-feng Ting, who had been with him at Kingmen and Ichang, could have testified to a progressive or acute depression; yet Ting told Sokobin that Meyer seemed "as usual" except for a digestive disturbance. To decide on the basis of this limited evidence whether or not he was suffering a severe depression is impossible.

The perplexity that Fairchild felt years ago cannot be dissipated today. F. C. Reimer, who lived and worked with Meyer for several weeks, said that "a tremendous battle was raging within his soul," a conflict between devotion to duty and longing for rest and companionship. Could these pressures have mounted beyond the limits of endurance? Meyer considered discipline and purpose "cardinal principles" of life; for him to plan suicide consciously when he had not finished describing and shipping his collection seems entirely uncharacteristic of a man who never was a quitter. It is possible to imagine his suppressing increasing tensions until those stresses built to an insupportable degree. If, as he stood at the rail of the *Yang Feng Maru* just before midnight, his will to continue the struggle faltered, could he have sought rest in those muddy waters in a temporary lapse of rational consciousness? Since one cannot know the truth with certainty, no one can justify a final judgment; as Fairchild wrote, Meyer's death will remain a mystery to his friends.

When the editor of the *Far Eastern Review* interviewed him in Shanghai in 1915, Meyer expressed his feeling about the death of a plant explorer: "He considers it as easy to die in the open in China as it would be to die while tending money in a bank. So long as his collections are saved and contribute their quota to the world's wealth, the passing of the explorer does not matter. In Mr. Meyer's creed, it is the work, not the man, that counts."[5]

His Contemporaries Speak

His life was gentle, and the elements
So Mix'd in him that Nature might stand up
And say to all the world, "This was a man."
SHAKESPEARE, *Julius Caesar,* Act 5, Scene 2

W H E N accounts of Meyer's death appeared in newspapers, friends on three continents mourned for him. Many people wrote to Fairchild, their letters reflecting the affection and respect that Meyer had earned among those qualified to judge his work. Messages came from distinguished horticulturists, from supervisors of plant introduction gardens and experiment stations, from expatriates who had known him in China, and from fellow Americans who had grown the plants he had introduced. Professor J. Russell Smith of the University of Pennsylvania was one of many who asked whether the newspapers had "irrefutable confirmation" of Meyer's death. "I hope it is not true. If it is, I shall feel that it is a double loss—to the economic welfare of the world and to my personal welfare. One of the great adventures to which I had looked forward was the plan of some day knocking around with him in some corner of the world just as a hanger-on."

Liberty Hyde Bailey and E. H. Wilson felt the loss both personally and professionally. Bailey wrote, "I shall never cease to regret his untimely end; and I am more than ever glad that I had the two opportunities to be with him last summer, not only because I liked him personally, but also because he gave me so very many points of view and so much interesting information about China." From the Chosen Hotel in Korea Wilson wrote Fairchild, "I am much distressed over the sad end of Meyer and also deeply puzzled. By his untimely death plant exploration has lost one of the most energetic and enthusiastic servants it ever had."

From all sections of America came letters of condolence and statements about the loss that American agriculture had suffered. A. B. Connor and Bonney Youngblood of Texas A & M, Robert L. Beagles of the Plant

Introduction Garden at Chico, and J. E. Morrow at Brooksville expressed their shock and grief. J. C. Upholf of the Missouri Botanical Garden and F. T. Ramsey of Austin, Texas, felt sure that "the good he did will be a blessing on our country for generations to come." Most deeply touched of all, perhaps, was F. C. Reimer of Oregon: "Nothing has affected me so in a long time as this sad news. . . . Mr. Meyer possessed a great brain and also a great heart. The remarkable new field that he opened up and the vast quantities of materials that he has introduced will always remain as a great epoch in American agriculture and horticulture. I am certain that future generations will appreciate his work even more than we can today."

Meyer's friends in China understood best the difficulties that he had faced. Letters from D. MacGregor of Shanghai, Joseph Bailie of the University of Nanking, and George F. Mitchell, supervising tea examiner for the Treasury Department in Hankow, conveyed essentially the same message. "He undoubtedly knew more about the economic vegetation of China than any other man," his old friend MacGregor wrote. "Further, he was such a slave to his calling that he never knew what it was to rest when he thought there was another chance to acquire further knowledge. Living in China, I understand better than people at home the amount of hard work he put in to be able to traverse such a large section of the country as he did."

To Fairchild the letters from people who had never known Meyer personally were especially touching. One came from L. E. Stoddard, a newspaperman in Alamo, California, who wrote that he and his wife had seen Meyer's name on tags attached to trees they had received from the Chico Garden and they had great admiration for him. After looking at their orchards in the evening, they would wonder where he was traveling and try to imagine the difficulties that he had encountered in collecting certain trees. Now they too grieved for him.

The Alexander Graham Bells offered the use of their home in Washington for a memorial service in honor of Meyer. In preparation, Fairchild selected 58 lantern slides from the 1,740 photographs that Meyer had taken during his expeditions. When he received a copy of Meyer's will, he had an additional reason for calling together the employees of the Foreign Seed and Plant Introduction Section. On July 31 a group of Meyer's friends and colleagues including Beverly T. Galloway, Howard Dorsett, Peter Bisset, Grace Cramer Clime, and Robert A. Young gathered in the Bells' paneled library.

After reading highlights from Meyer's letters and showing his slides, Fairchild disclosed the pertinent provision of Meyer's will: "Unto David Fairchild . . . the sum of One Thousand Dollars which I desire to be divided equally among all of the persons then connected with said Office, or else, if such persons shall so prefer, to be used for some outing or entertainment for them."[1] Fairchild remarked that Meyer had come to America without any financial resources and had "so regulated his life" that he was able to save a number of thousands of dollars; furthermore, he was so devoted to his work and to "those of us who were associated with him in it, that he left a portion of this money to us as a token of appreciation." Since the settlement of the estate would take at least a year, the staff would have ample time to consider the best use of the bequest. The memorial service ended with appropriate music sung by Grace Clime.

In addition to this bequest to his fellow workers, Meyer's will directed his executor, the American Security and Trust Company of Washington, to convert his entire estate to cash and to pay legacies to his brother, Jan Martinus Meyer of Schiedam; his maiden sister, Alida Wilhelmina Meyer; his married sister, Maria Meyer Hoogland; his niece Maria Hoogland Kersch; and Johannis de Leuw of Chefoo. The remainder he instructed the executor to pay to his father; if his father failed to survive him, this amount was to be shared equally by his brother and his two sisters.

Fairchild sent Meyer's family a detailed account of the memorial service, copies of the letters of condolence, newspaper clippings, and Meyer's published articles. When Jan F. Meyer asked for a picture of Fairchild with his son, Fairchild chose the snapshot taken in Seattle as Meyer disembarked from his third expedition, as well as a photograph of himself seated at his desk. "The large albums shown on the top shelf of the book-case directly behind me," he explained, "contain photographs taken by Mr. Meyer on his exploration trips."[2] In July, 1919, Fairchild wrote Jan F. Meyer to acknowledge several issues of *De Aarde en Haar Volken* containing Frederike van Uildriks's account of Meyer's life and work, "De Reiziger-Plant Kundige Frans N. Meyer en Zijn Werk" (The Traveler-Botanist Frans N. Meyer and His Work). At the same time he sent to Amsterdam a copy of his summary of Meyer's career, "A Hunter of Plants," which appeared in the July, 1919, issue of the *National Geographic*.

Earlier, Erwin F. Smith had written an essay and a poem in memory of Meyer. *Science* magazine printed this memorial and it appeared also as a booklet. Smith wrote, "Meyer was one of the most friendly men I have ever known and one of the most interesting. He was also a just and upright man. His knowledge of plants was phenomenal. . . . He was an entertaining public speaker . . . a good conversationalist, and a copious letter writer." Because he had known Meyer best when he first came to America and was interested in ideas that he had absorbed at Our House and Walden in Holland, Smith added, "In philosophy he was a follower of Schopenhauer; in politics a Marxian socialist; in religion a Buddhist."[3] This often-quoted summary appears to be inaccurate. Meyer had discussed these ideas with Smith during his first year in America, but they did not represent lifelong commitments. Meyer never alluded to Schopenhauer and pessimism after 1901, he showed only a general interest in Far Eastern religions, and his

acceptance of some utopian aspects of socialistic theory in the period preceding World War I did not constitute an endorsement of the application of
socialist theories thereafter. Fairchild apparently perceived the possibility of
misinterpretation of Smith's statement when he wrote succinctly in "An
Agricultural Explorer in China" that "Meyer was not a socialist."

No one else who knew Meyer ever suggested that he was a Buddhist.
Meyer always identified himself as a Protestant. In only one of many hundreds of letters did he discuss Buddhism. In reply to an inquiry, he told A. J.
Pieters that the Chinese were too materialistic and too practical to be deeply
religious. In addition to statues of Buddha, they venerated "scores of other
gods of rain, war, prosperity, or wisdom, as well as Lao-tze, Kwan-yin, and
Kwang-fu-tse or Confucius," apparently believing that "what one can't accomplish, the other may." There were Buddhists of purer character, he
added, but he had not met them. Neither Meyer's letters, his Protestant
burial at the direction of his friends, nor any other evidence, supports
Smith's identification of Meyer as a Buddhist.

What then was Meyer's creed? As he traveled in China, he often
stopped at Buddhist temples, Taoist monasteries, Roman Catholic missions,
or at the homes of Protestant missionaries; however, he said that he did not
discuss religion with his hosts. After World War I began, he wondered how
people who believed in a kind and loving God could maintain their faith. He
never expressed hope based on the benevolence of God. In the midst of
dangers in China, he wrote that he was protected from harm by his own
courage and by the good wishes of his friends. No specific denominational
viewpoint bounded his philosphy of life; however, serving his fellow human
beings did form a vital part of his creed. Like others who have observed the
life cycle of plants intently, he believed in reincarnation, referring occasionally to his previous and his next life. After living close to nature for so
many years, he may have become a pantheist. Ambassador Nelson T. Johnson supported this view when he wrote, "Meyer had lived alone with plants,
grasses, and trees so long and so intimately that I verily believe he believed
that his spirit was just a part of the great spiritual background of all life.
. . . I think he felt that he was merely leaving this life for another as grass,
flower, or tree, or perhaps as another human being."

Despite his somewhat mystic identification with nature, Meyer had
been an astute investor. Concerned about financial security in his old age
because the government did not provide a pension, he had sought protection by buying stocks and bonds. He invested in utilities, railroads, and
industrials, as well as in Liberty Loan bonds. In addition, he had made
three large personal loans that were due in 1919 when he expected to return
to America. His executor promptly liquidated his American assets, which
totaled over $28,000, but the U.S. Court at Shanghai did not administer on
his property in China until 1922. Legatees received $12,000 in 1920, $15,000
in 1921, and $3,000 in 1923. In Holland at that time this estate seemed quite

large; a Dutch journalist commented that Meyer had sought neither fame nor fortune but had achieved both. While the settlement of Meyer's bequests continued, Dorsett repaid the Treasury Department the balance of Meyer's appropriation, conceded the $31.74 that the auditor had disallowed, and closed the account.[4]

The staff of the Foreign Seed and Plant Introduction Section voted unanimously to use their bequest to create a medal honoring Meyer and to present it to any man or woman who made an especially meritorious contribution to plant introduction. Since the law did not permit a government agency to give such an award, the American Genetic Association agreed to present it. Theodore Spicer Simpson, a sculptor who was Fairchild's friend and who had known Meyer personally, offered to design the medal. On the right of the obverse is a fruiting branch of the Chinese jujube and, on the left, a cone-bearing branch of Meyer's favorite white-barked pine. The inscription in the center, written in Chinese characters, is a quotation from a poem by Chi K'ang of the Tang Dynasty: "In the glorious luxuriance of the thousand plants he takes delight." The reverse of the medal depicts Queen Hatshepsut's plant expedition in 1570 B.C. Copied from a bas-relief carved on the wall of a temple at Thebes, it shows men carrying aboard a ship bags of seeds and trees with their root-balls in woven baskets.[5] The original of the reverse is now at the National Arboretum; the obverse is displayed at the Fairchild Tropical Garden in Coconut Grove, Florida.

When the Meyer Medal was awarded for the first time in May of 1920, Fairchild wrote to Jan F. Meyer describing the medal and the ceremony. A few weeks later he received a black-bordered envelope containing an engraved card announcing the death of Frank Meyer's father at the age of 84. Since 1920 the Meyer Medal has been presented to men and women from Algeria, Australia, Brazil, Cuba, England, France, Italy, Tripoli, and the United States. Among Americans who have earned this honor are Charles Sprague Sargent in 1923, P. H. Dorsett in 1936, David Fairchild in 1939, Walter T. Swingle in 1947, and F. Wilson Popenoe in 1950. (See appendix C for complete list.) Beginning in 1983, the Meyer Medal will be awarded by the Crop Science Society of America, an affiliate of the American Society of Agronomy, Madison, Wisconsin.

In addition to the medal, Fairchild and others felt that a permanent memorial should be erected to Meyer, either in China or in Washington or at the Chico Garden, where so many of his introductions were growing. Fairchild submitted a proposal for a bronze plaque and a bench—"a seat made of rough stone brought from the mountains along which would be put some of his ornamental white-barked pines and over which would climb some of his Euonymus and perhaps leading to it a few trees might be planted to make an avenue or a group of his Chinese pistaches. . . . I think the fact should never be lost sight of that Meyer did this work because of his love for plants and his belief in free American institutions."

Beverly T. Galloway approved this plan and added that those who designed the tablet should remember that Meyer was "the soul of simplicity." He suggested the wording and spacing that he considered appropriate for a bronze plaque:

IN REMEMBRANCE OF

FRANK NICHOLAS MEYER

AGRICULTURAL EXPLORER

UNITED STATES DEPARTMENT OF AGRICULTURE

OFFICE OF FOREIGN SEED AND PLANT INTRODUCTION

NOVEMBER 29, 1875   JUNE 1, 1918

BY HIS COLLEAGUES

IN TOKEN OF AFFECTION AND APPRECIATION OF HIS WORK

FOR AMERICAN AGRICULTURE AND HORTICULTURE

Henry L. Hicks suggested that the memorial to Meyer should be erected at the proposed National Arboretum in Washington, for Meyer had been an ardent proponent of a national arboretum. "Surely his work is worthy of recognition by a memorial tablet or something of that kind," E. H. Wilson commented. Liberty Hyde Bailey added, "He was worthy of anything that we can do to perpetuate his memory."[6]

In order to accumulate material for an account of Meyer's life and work, Erwin F. Smith collected copies of letters that Meyer had written to Bailey, John Reisner, and F. C. Reimer. During the 1930s, Knowles A. Ryerson, Fairchild's successor, assembled copies of Meyer's personal letters to P. H. Dorsett, A. J. Pieters, and Charles M. Mansfield, as well as his official letters to his colleagues. Pieters withheld the letters that Meyer had written to him during his last two expeditions because he considered them entirely personal and not of botanical interest. When B. Y. Morrison headed the Plant Introduction Division, he wrote that "sooner or later some record of Mr. Meyer's work and personal activities should be published," but he had observed that the older men who had known Meyer seemed "less and less inclined" to complete such an account.[7]

Despite enthusiasm for a permanent memorial and a formal account of Meyer's work, time passed without either idea becoming a reality. It was P. H. Dorsett who placed a headstone on Meyer's grave at the Bubbling Well Cemetery in Shanghai. Carved on the four-foot marble slab were the inscription, "Frank N. Meyer, Agricultural Explorer of the United States of America, November 29, 1875 – June 1, 1918," and the Chinese characters used on the Meyer Medal, "In the thousand plants he takes delight." Probably MacGregor planted the arborvitae at each side of the headstone and, at the foot, Meyer's favorite white-barked pine.[8] Since the establishment of the People's Republic of China, the former Bubbling Well Cemetery has become part of a public park. Somewhere in the northwest sector Meyer's now unmarked grave may still be shaded by the white-barked pine.[9] In his autobiography, David Fairchild expressed the hope that "some day perhaps the beneficiaries of Meyer's life-work will erect a monument to him in America." More than sixty years after his death, this memorial has not materialized.

Meyer's Legacy Today

No work begun shall ever pause for death.
BROWNING, *The Ring and the Book,* 7

F R O M the perspective of the late twentieth century, the significance of Frank Meyer's work appears in sharper focus than his contemporaries could command. Some of his introductions that promised to be important are no longer useful; others have contributed in ways that were not immediately apparent. What is the permanent value of Meyer's work? First of all, he introduced plants that are still treasured because they are useful, beautiful, or new to botanical science. In addition, as a result of his efforts to find in remote areas "the rudimentary and long-forgotten parent stock or the as yet unused wild plant that may be adapted to man's profit by cultivation," he furnished new germplasm for the development of improved varieties of fodder plants, grains, fruits, nuts, shrubs, and flowers.[1] That his career represented pioneering work is equally significant. He opened the field of agricultural exploration in Asia; because of political upheavals since his lifetime, few Western plant hunters have returned to the outlying districts that he explored. His contributions also include his investigation of methods of dry-land farming in China, his development of the earliest USDA seed exchange lists, his establishment of a system of USDA correspondents and missionary-collectors, his techniques for shipping live material across great distances, and his collection of thousands of herbarium specimens. A set of his documented specimens is deposited at the National Arboretum Herbarium in Washington, under the supervision of Dr. Frederick G. Meyer. According to Dr. Theodore R. Dudley of the National Arboretum, other specimens are preserved at the Arnold Arboretum; the University of California Botanical Garden at Berkeley; the California Academy of Sciences, Golden Gate Park, San Francisco; the Philadelphia Academy of Sciences; and the New York Botanical Garden.

A survey of Meyer's hundreds of introductions would be impractical, but examples illustrate the significance of his work. People who lived on the arid plains and the windswept prairies of the United States during the early years of the twentieth century were pathetically eager to find any shade tree that would grow there. The most widely used of all Meyer's drought-resistant trees has been the Siberian elm (*Ulmus pumila*). This dry-land elm now thrives from Canada to Texas, breaking the searing winds on vast prairies. In the late 1930s a doctor from North Dakota told Fairchild that he had gone as a boy to the USDA experiment station at Mandan and begged a handful of elm seedlings. The tiny plants were no larger than knitting needles, but they became magnificent trees before many years had passed.[2] Multiplying this experience by thousands offers some conception of the extent of Meyer's contribution to life in America through a single introduction. When prolonged drought threatened to turn the prairie states into a permanent dust bowl, Meyer's elm helped to form the shelterbelt, a system of 17,000 miles of windbreaks planted between 1935 and 1942 by the Prairie State Forestry Project in order to reduce wind erosion and to conserve soil moisture.[3] The Chinese elm (*Ulmus parvifolia*) also was used in the 17,000-mile shelterbelt. Though experts consider it a more desirable tree than *Ulmus pumila*, it has not been as popular.

Meyer's introductions include other useful shade trees and unusual ornamentals. His Chinese pistachio (*Pistacia chinensis*), for example, has become an outstanding tree for street plantings in the Southwest. The Kashgar elm (*Ulmus carpinifolia* 'Umbraculifera', formerly *U. campestris* var. *umbraculifera*) also has succeeded as an ornamental in hot and dry regions, while the Khotan ash (*Fraxinus potamophila*) survives in southern and western Nevada. Other introductions, including some of Meyer's favorites such as the white-barked pine (*Pinus bungeana*), the spreading Chinese horse chestnut (*Aesculus chinensis*), and the Siberian larch (*Larix sibirica*) are still cherished as rarities in the United States. They grow in botanical gardens but have never become commonly available in the nursery trade.[4] Perhaps the striking white-barked pine has not attracted wider attention because it does not achieve its full beauty until it is at least one hundred years old. Though botanists were aware of the existence of all these trees, Meyer's distinctive contribution was introducing them into cultivation in America.

Meyer also discovered some trees and shrubs that had not been known previously by botanists. The true Chinese hickory (*Carya cathayensis*) is the most important of this group. In addition, he introduced the hybrid Korean flowering cherry (*Prunus* × *meyeri*), a spruce (*Picea meyeri*, first collected by Purdom in 1910), two new junipers (*Juniperus squamata* 'Meyeri' and *Juniperus chinensis* 'Columnaris'), and the dwarf lilac (*Syringa meyeri*). No plant hunter in modern times had found the maidenhair tree (*Ginkgo biloba*) in the wild until Meyer discovered it west of Ichang. Potanin had identified the original wild peach (*Prunus davidiana* var. *potaninii*, formerly *P. persica potaninii*) and the wild almond (*Prunus tangutica*) in 1885, but Meyer rediscovered and collected both of these botanically important species. According to Dr. Dale Kester of the Pomology Department, the University of California at Davis has maintained two of these wild almond trees in their almond germplasm collection for many years. Experimenters have produced first-generation hybrids and have retained several selections for future breeding because the species has potential as the source of late-blooming almond genes.

Though USDA plant hunters collected ornamentals only "when encountered," Meyer introduced a number of shrubs and flowers that previously had not been grown in America. Among the most important of these was his *Rosa xanthina*, which had never before been cultivated in Western gardens. Both the semidouble and the single forms of this pale gold rose were remarkable for hardiness, drought-resistance, and vigor. No other yellow rose could survive New England winters or grow on the great northern plains; therefore, *Rosa xanthina* became useful as a grafting stock. It can be found in the ancestry of all yellow roses that bloom early and freely in cold climates and in arid soil. Meyer's pale pink *Rosa odorata* also was widely disseminated after Edward Goucher of the USDA discovered that it is unusually successful as a grafting stock for greenhouse roses.[5] His *Viburnum farreri* (formerly *V. fragrans*, renamed for Farrer, though Purdom collected it in 1912, Meyer in 1913, and Farrer and Purdom in 1914) remains a favorite of many gardeners. *Ligustrum quihoui* from Shensi Province never has received the attention that experts at the USDA believe it deserves, but the *Ligustrum vulgare* that he found on a dry mountainside in the Crimea has successfully tolerated adverse conditions in the upper Midwest.[6] Meyer also sent to the United States the Beauty Bush (*Kolkwitzia amabilis*), a popular flowering shrub, while his scarlet lily enabled breeders to add new color to improved varieties of lilies.

Some of Meyer's fruit trees, as well as the hawthorn and bush almond, have proved useful in breeding ornamentals. The 'Bradford' pear, considered one of the finest street trees in America, emerged as a dividend from his wild pear, *Pyrus calleryana*. In 1950 Dr. John L. Creech, then superintendent of the Plant Introduction Station at Glenn Dale, Maryland, selected a dense-foliaged specimen of the Callery pear, grafted buds onto *Pyrus calleryana* seedlings, and established them in 1952 in a Washington suburb for a street tree study. After testing revealed that these trees were resistant to urban pollution and were beautiful in all seasons, Dr. Creech named this ornamental for F. C. Bradford, a former Glenn Dale superintendent, and the USDA released it to the nursery trade. In the three decades since he cloned the Bradford pear, 300,000 have been planted. During the spring and summer their abundant flowers and glossy green leaves present a pleasing picture, while the claret leaf color and numerous small fruits make it attractive during the fall and winter months. Dr. Creech, himself a plant explorer of international reputation, regards the Bradford pear as a living memorial to Frank Meyer.[7]

Other plant propagators more recently have used *Pyrus calleryana* to produce cultivars such as Aristocrat, Chanticleer, Whitehouse, and Capital. These will soon be available to the nursery trade. Dr. William L. Ackerman, research horticulturist at the National Arboretum, developed Whitehouse to fill a need for a less robust and more columnar form of the Callery pear, suitable for use where space is too restricted for the Bradford. He named it for Dr. William E. Whitehouse, retired senior horticulturist at the USDA Agricultural Research Center, because of his early work with this Chinese pear at Glenn Dale. Dr. Ackerman's Capital, while retaining the attractive features of Bradford, has an even narrower crown than Whitehouse, making it useful as an ornamental screening tree or in places where space is extremely limited.[8]

Meyer's inestimable contribution to the development of improved stone fruits and blight-resistant pears has largely been forgotten, except by the men and women who work with these fruits at the USDA and state experiment stations. His northern wild peach (*Prunus davidiana*) turned out to be a good rootstock for apricots and plums as well as for peaches. In dry or alkaline soil and in the cold northern states, it produced orchards that tolerated drought, alkali, and low temperatures. Because this stock also was resistant to root-knot nematodes, it was tested at the Chico Plant Introduction Garden, as well as at Fresno and at Beltsville, throughout the 1950s. Root-knot nematodes at this time had become a major problem affecting peach rootstocks in many areas. Dr. John Weinberger of the USDA Hunt Field Laboratory at Fort Valley, Georgia, also was working with selected seedlings of *Prunus davidiana*. After the USDA released his seedling called the Nemaguard peach in 1961, it became a leading rootstock and promises to remain important for many years.[9]

Meyer hoped that the Feicheng peach, the pound peach of Shantung, would justify his three arduous journeys to Feicheng, but the crosses that were made have not become a significant factor in breeding. When the Forest Service took over the former Chico Plant Introduction Garden in the early 1970s, bulldozers probably uprooted any remaining Fei peaches that Beagles had grown from Meyer's scions. The New Jersey Agricultural Experiment Station at Rutgers University has used the Fei peach in its breeding program because of its late-blooming characteristic. Recently, interest in this large white clingstone has reawakened and commercial nurserymen have asked the USDA for the Fei peach. Dr. R. E. C. Lavne of the Harrow Research Station in Ontario is introducing an ornamental developed from material sent to him by the New Jersey Agricultural Experiment Station.[10]

Meyer's Tangsi cherry (distributed as *Prunus pseudocerasus*) blossomed ten days earlier than any other cherry at the Chico Garden and has been valuable in breeding earlier fruit; however, tracing its contribution is no longer possible. After the USDA released this valuable stock to the nursery trade, commercial breeders developed improved hybrids. When they marketed new varieties of cherries, they did not acknowledge the USDA plant introductions that they had used.[11] According to Dr. William Beres of the Department of Genetics at the University of California at Davis, the Tangsi cherry was crossed with the Montmorency cherry at Davis. Dr. Robert Anderson of Michigan State University has received one selection from this cross (520–12), but further testing is necessary to determine whether it will be of value in the sour cherry orchards of Michigan. Though others tested, propagated, and selected the fruit trees that derived from Meyer's introductions, the basic debt to Meyer's pioneering work remains.

The USDA has used Meyer's wild pears extensively in its breeding program, and propagators are still experimenting with many crosses in an effort to use this stock to breed a substitute for the Bartlett pear. At the Southern Oregon Experiment Station scientists have repeatedly inoculated thousands of seedlings of wild and cultivated Chinese pears with the fire blight organism and have studied growth habits, adaptability, and resistance to blight over a period of many years. These test plantings became especially valuable in the late 1950s and early 1960s because of the growing problem of pear decline. *Pyrus calleryana*, the pear that Meyer collected in the Yangtze Valley, is not only highly resistant to blight and root aphids, but also resists decline in growth and productivity. The collection formed by F. C. Reimer is now maintained as a Western Regional Project W-6 by the Southern Oregon Branch Station, the Oregon Agricultural Experiment Station at Corvallis, and the USDA. Meyer's introductions, made useful by the work of F. C. Reimer, P. B. Lombard, M. N. Westwood, P. H. Westigard, and H. R. Cameron, continue to benefit the Rogue River Valley in Oregon and pear growers everywhere.[12] Though E. H. Wilson first collected *Pyrus calleryana* in 1908, it was Meyer's tremendous collection of seeds in 1917 that made this tree available for use in America.

Both Meyer's large seedless persimmons and hawthorn fruits as big as crab apples appealed to Fairchild; though he failed to promote the haw, delicious persimmons appear in American markets every autumn. Fairchild considered the round Tamopan persimmon most promising; however, other varieties known by their Japanese rather than by their Chinese names have become more important commercially. According to Dr. Howard Brooks of the USDA Agricultural Research Center, these persimmons are not the product of breeding and selection but are a direct result of Meyer's pioneering work in Asia. (Dr. Brooks points out that the lingering trace of astringency in the Oriental persimmon disappears when it is stored for several days in a closed bag with a ripening apple, banana, or pear.) In addition to the cultivated persimmon, Meyer's wild persimmon (*Diospyros lotus*) performed so well as a rootstock that orchardists substituted it for the native American persimmon that they previously had used for grafting.

Though jujubes were tested in California, Texas, and Oklahoma, they did not become the valuable crop that Fairchild had envisioned. In the 1930s the Tennessee Valley Authority used Meyer's jujubes in reforesting the flood plain behind Norris Dam. Several varieties he introduced are still growing there. As a result of a jujube breeding program the USDA initiated at Chico in 1952 under the direction of Dr. William L. Ackerman, a few small orchards were established in California; however, the project was abandoned in 1959. Despite its lack of success as a commercial crop, thousands of jujubes are growing as ornamental dooryard trees in the Southwest, and a commercial nursery in California that sells Meyer's 'Lang' and 'Li' has difficulty in keeping pace with demand. Property owners in Florida and adjacent states have recently recognized the usefulness of the jujube, for it tolerates heat and drought and does not require spraying to control insects or disease; furthermore, the fruit ripens in September when few other fruits are available in the Southeast. A fifty-tree planting, including at least nine of Meyer's original eighty-three cultivars, is growing at the University of Florida at Gainesville under the direction of Dr. Paul M. Lyrene. He believes that Meyer's 'So' has special value as an ornamental because of its attractive branch-forking and twig-twisting pattern, which Meyer described as "gnarled and zigzag."[13]

Recently, the International Tree Crops Institute, U.S.A., has focused attention on the high sugar content of the jujube. Working in the Southern Appalachian Region under a contract from the Department of Energy, the institute has begun research on tree crops that will grow on hilly, marginal land and yield alcohol fuel. Gregory Williams, director of the institute, has secured scions of the remaining jujubes at Chico in order to test them as sources of fermentable carbohydrates. Thus Meyer's long-neglected Chinese jujube still has potential, not only as a dooryard fruit but also as a source of energy. Because it bears heavily in almost any type of soil despite adverse climatic conditions and does not require spraying, experts believe that the jujube could help to solve the food and energy needs of the Third World.

Specialists tested the dwarf lemon (*Citrus* × *meyeri*) that Meyer discovered in China at the USDA gardens at Chico, California; Brownsville, Texas; and Brooksville, Florida. Because it is hardier than most other lemons, withstanding temperatures as low as 22°F, it has become popular as a dooryard or potted ornamental fruit tree, especially in California. Though it is too tender to ship well, it bears heavily and is unusually juicy. One bushy plant can produce a quantity of fruits that are slightly larger than most commercial varieties of lemons. It has been grown commercially in

Florida, Texas, South Africa, and New Zealand for local markets and for processing.[14] In 1981 orchardists were growing at least one thousand acres of Meyer's lemon trees for the production of processed lemon juice.

Meyer's introductions of grains, forage crops, and grasses are difficult to trace. His hardy and drought-resistant wheats, barleys, sorghums, alfalfas, and clovers went to Mark Carleton, Harry B. Derr, and others who were developing improved varieties. Though many of his introductions simply entered the department's program of testing, crossbreeding, and selection unrecorded, a few are stored at the Agricultural Research Center at Beltsville and the National Seed Storage Laboratory at Fort Collins, Colorado. There they are available for use in breeding crops adapted to America's changing needs. On sandy slopes at Sarepta in the Saratov district of Siberia, Meyer found crested wheat grass (*Agropyron cristatum*), previously introduced by Hansen and now an important forage crop in the mountain states. In a ravine near Saratov he gathered a spreading plant, *Coronilla varia*. From this modest introduction, the Soil Conservation Service and the Iowa Agricultural Experiment Station developed Emerald crownvetch. It now forms a hardy, vigorous, and attractive ground cover that controls erosion on the banks of the interstate highway system in cooler areas.[15] In addition, only twenty years after Meyer's death, the grass seed that Swingle found in his baggage had formed dense, wiry turf on lawns from South Carolina to Florida and the Gulf States. Though few people know its history, thousands enjoy lawns of Meyer's centipede grass.

His Chinese vegetables and bamboo generally did not interest Americans as much as his other introductions did. Though the Virginia Trucking Experiment Station used his Manchurian spinach to develop a cultivar called 'Virginia Savoy' that saved the spinach industry when it first was threatened by wilt and blight, employees of the USDA had discarded it as valueless before they observed that neglected seedlings resisted disease. According to Dr. Ramon Webb, chief of the Vegetable Laboratory at the USDA Agricultural Research Center, propagators have bred this ability to resist wilt and blight into spinach cultivars that are also resistant to downy mildew and white rust. Meyer's introduction therefore is one of the building blocks inherent in most multidisease-resistant cultivars of spinach grown in the United States today. Meyer hoped that the huge Chinese cabbage, the celery-cabbage, and the winter radish would become popular in the United States, but Americans were slow to accept Chinese vegetables. After more than half a century, American markets stock the bean sprouts, alfalfa sprouts, and bean curd that he recommended long ago, and American stores sell fine furniture made from bamboo.

The pioneer nature of Meyer's work is especially apparent in relation to his introductions of soybeans, chestnuts, and zoysia grass. Only eight varieties of soybeans grew in America before 1903. Between 1905 and 1908

Meyer collected forty-two more. Since that time thousands of additional varieties have been introduced into the United States, but Meyer remains a pioneer in this field. He collected the first oil-bearing soybean, source of an important ingredient of many industrial products. He also contributed careful studies of the uses of soybean products, especially as a protein substitute. Meyer laid the groundwork for future accomplishments when he collected nuts and scions from Chinese chestnut trees that appeared resistant to the blight that was killing the American chestnut and suggested that blight-free chestnuts could be bred from that source. In Korea in 1906 he made one of the first collections of zoysia seed ever sent to America. Because of his pioneering work, the USDA later named 'Meyer' zoysia in his honor, though it is a result of selection from a collection made in Korea in the 1930s. Other men returned to places that he had explored to collect the Feicheng peach, wild pears and peaches, soybeans, chestnuts, and zoysia, but Meyer's initial exploration revealed the source and the value of these plants.

Fairchild wrote in Meyer's obituary in *Plant Immigrants* that his plants were "scattered all over this country and other countries as well, growing into avenues, orchards, broad cultivated fields, and flowering borders." But even that is not the end result of Meyer's work. Men and women at the USDA and at state experiment stations have cared for his introductions and used them repeatedly. Having entered the mainstream of American agriculture, they will continue to make their unrecognized contribution. It is not possible to trace each introduction, to identify each use made of specific plants, or to predict their future value. What is significant is that all the developments from his introductions are based on his initiative and his discrimination.

Much of the work that the USDA accomplished in China between Meyer's death in 1918 and the closing of China in the mid-thirties followed his footsteps. From 1927 to 1930 R. Kent Beattie of the USDA searched Japan, Formosa (Taiwan), Korea, and China for blight-resistant chestnuts. He returned with scions of 90 selections, as well as 250 bushels of other kinds of seeds including rhododendron and azaleas. In February of 1929 P. H. Dorsett and W. J. Morse began a two-year expedition to China, Manchuria, Korea, and Japan to seek additional soybean cultivars that might be useful in America. They possessed a valuable tool that Meyer lacked, a carefully indexed eighty-two-page translation of the Chinese agricultural literature concerning soybeans, prepared by Michael J. Haggerty under the direction of Swingle. Instead of buying seeds of promising strains from farmers in remote areas as Meyer had done, Dorsett and Morse could search for specific cultivars that the Chinese had already recognized as valuable. They returned to America with almost three thousand kinds of soybeans, as well as other field crops, cherries, persimmons, rhododendrons, azaleas, and lilacs.[16]

Ever since its founding in 1898, the USDA plant introduction system has served as a model for agricultural exploration programs in other countries. In 1972 department reorganization eliminated the New Crops Research Branch, successor to the Plant Exploration and Introduction Division, dispersing the valuable store of information and expertise that Fairchild began to develop and Meyer helped to build. But the department's plant introduction work continues, with emphasis on gathering small amounts of targeted germplasm from a limited area to fill a specific need. For example, Dr. Melvin N. Westwood, director of the Northwest Germplasm Repository, and Dr. Paul Li of the University of Minnesota are concerned because many of the wild fruits and nuts collected in Asia by Meyer and others have been hybridized to the extent that their genetic composition is in doubt. With the reopening of the People's Republic of China for agricultural exchange, they have proposed an expedition to collect cold-resistant fruit and nut species from designated locations in northern China and Manchuria.[17] In contrast, when Meyer sought hardy fruits and nuts there in 1906, he roamed over a vast area, collecting large quantities of any useful plant that he encountered.

The early years of the twentieth century have been called the Grand Age of plant exploration. In addition to Meyer, five well-known British plant explorers, all born between 1873 and 1885, chose working areas in China and along the borders of Burma and Tibet. E. H. Wilson launched the new era at the turn of the century with his expeditions for Veitch and Sons. George Forrest and Meyer followed in 1904 and 1905, William Purdom in 1909, Kingdon-Ward in 1911, and Reginald Farrer in 1914. While the British collectors generally searched limited areas for ornamentals for private institutions or individuals, Frank Meyer covered great distances in his effort to find plants of economic importance for the United States government. Forrest, Meyer, Purdom, and Farrer returned to the East until they died there, all but Forrest between the ages of forty and forty-two. Kingdon-Ward alone continued to work in the field for more than forty years. At the end of World War I, Fairchild sent Joseph Rock to join the British collectors remaining in Asia. From 1922 until 1933 Rock traveled for the Arnold Arboretum and for the National Geographic Society. His work, however, was chiefly ethnological, not botanical.[18] China remained open to collectors for less than half a century; Kingdon-Ward alone of the giants of the Grand Age — Wilson, Forrest, Meyer, and Ward — lived and worked beyond that period.

China still lures plant explorers. In 1980, at the invitation of the People's Republic of China, the first Westerners to collect there in more than thirty years joined the Sino-American Botanical Expedition to western Hubei. This jointly planned, cooperative venture included eight Chinese and five American botanists, who worked under the auspices of the Chinese

Academy of Sciences and the Botanical Society of America, with grants from the National Geographic Society and the American Association of Botanical Gardens and Arboreta. The American members of the team were Dr. Theodore R. Dudley of the USDA's National Arboretum, Dr. Stephen Spongberg of the Arnold Arboretum, Dr. Bruce Bartholomew of the Berkeley Botanical Garden, Dr. David Boufford of the Carnegie Museum, and Dr. James Luteyn of the New York Botanical Garden. During three and a half months, in the Shennongjia Forest District, they collected 2,082 herbarium specimens in multicate (a total of 26,000) and over 620 vouchered germplasm introductions, many never before introduced into America. Dr. Dudley's observations of western Hubei parallel Meyer's in many respects.[19]

In the future, most efforts to preserve earth's threatened store of germplasm probably will be internationally sponsored. In 1980 the International Board for Plant Genetic Resources held a symposium in Japan on genetic resources of the Far East and Pacific Basin. Dr. John L. Creech, an American member of the board, visited China for the IBPGR in 1981 and commented, "How different an approach from Meyer's day. Now it is a worldwide effort organized at the international level, and China is still the most sought-after center of genetic resources. There never again will be the dramatic journeys taken by Frank Meyer, driven by the unknown and fired by the excitement of encountering new plants in forbidden lands — just the organized objective team approach with clear-cut goals."[20]

One must turn to British authors for an appraisal of Meyer's standing among plant hunters. Euan H. M. Cox, who accompanied Farrer on his second and last expedition, wrote, "It is unfortunate that much of Meyer's work has been forgotten in comparison to the more showy introductions of other collectors who specialized more in ornamentals than in economic plants. . . . To most gardeners he is not even a name, but he has done more toward helping the economic life of a country than most plant collectors and his name should be a household word among American farmers." B. J. Healey praised Meyer's "prodigious" and "incredible" journeys, while Tyler Whittle concluded that American farmers "from Cape Flattery to Florida and from the Bay of Fundy to San Diego ought to keep an annual Meyer festival in grateful remembrance of his work in Asia."[21] No American author has paid adequate tribute to Frank Meyer since Fairchild wrote in 1921.

Envoi

He was a man, take him for all in all,
I shall not look upon his like again.
SHAKESPEARE, *Hamlet,* Act 1, Scene 2

ME Y E R ' S record as a successful agricultural explorer has not been challenged, but his character and personality have been misunderstood. One explanation is that relatively little accurate information about Frank Meyer has been generally available. Another reason is that Meyer's complex character combined qualities that at first appear difficult to reconcile. His kindness, gentleness, and sensitivity contrast with his physical courage, strength, and stamina; his tendency to dream and his love of beauty do not seem appropriate to a man who was also practical and realistic; his enthusiasm and love of adventure are not qualities that one would expect to find in a person who often experienced loneliness and occasionally felt depression.

People who knew Meyer best had no trouble reconciling his physical courage and his inflexible code of ethics with the qualities that Erwin Smith called "tenderness of soul." Fairchild remembered especially his kindness and generosity. Toward his family he was always tender and loving, and his gentleness extended even to animals and plants. Yet he performed remarkable feats of endurance and defended himself aggressively when he was attacked by ruffians. He himself admitted that being prepared for trouble in regions inhabited by outlaws evoked the samurai spirit in him. Nevertheless, he was happiest sitting under the scarlet foliage of an oak in the Ming Tombs Valley, camping beside a waterfall high in the Altai Mountains, or hiking across an alpine meadow filled with golden trollius and masses of violets and pansies. He loved beauty not only in nature but in fine craftsmanship and in Oriental art. Chinese architecture, mysteriously beautiful old gardens, and lovely porcelains nourished his soul.

Responding to beauty and dreaming of places beyond the horizon are characteristic of a romantic, but Frank Meyer could be intensely practical.

270

He planned and directed his expeditions efficiently, managed his own and his employer's financial resources economically, and perceived war realistically as death and destruction, not as patriotism and heroism. Yet, despite his gift for succinct analysis of complex situations and his ability to cope with practical problems, he seemed to be constantly in search of a dream that eluded him. De Vries recognized this when he said that Frans Meyer never really felt at home in this world.

Meyer failed to find the inner peace that he sought, but his friends did not consider him taciturn or morose. E. H. Wilson remembered his energy and enthusiasm as his dominant characteristics, and C. G. Pfeiffer of the USDA said that his death was incredible because he was "so full of life and activity and the spirit of adventure." Though Meyer did suffer occasional periods of depression, acquaintances like Peter Bisset considered him "a robust and vivid personality." As a younger man he sang Dutch songs beside a campfire at Fairchild's home and "danced for pure joy" in the first snow of the winter in eastern Siberia. After the United States joined the combatants in World War I, he never again felt completely happy; nevertheless, at the Fourth of July celebration in Hankow in 1917, less than a year before his death, "Mr. Meyer, with his characteristic enthusiasm," George Mitchell wrote, "joined in the singing of all the patriotic songs to such an extent that he was hoarse when I saw him the next day." Mitchell, Reimer, and Liberty Hyde Bailey associated closely with Meyer and recorded their impressions of him during the final year of his life. None had known him well before that time, but all three commented on his enthusiasm and his appealing personality.

In *Plant Hunters* B. J. Healy refers to Meyer as "excessively bad-tempered," but Meyer's reputation for being ill-tempered rests entirely on Farrer's inaccurate account of the events at Siku. Meyer's behavior toward Chi-nian Tien does not illustrate ill temper as much as inflexibility in a situation involving a matter of principle. That Tien broke his word and quit in the middle of an endeavor was dishonorable conduct according to Meyer's creed. Meyer was committed to completing the project that he had undertaken; to him dangers lurking along the Tibetan border seemed irrelevant. He attempted to enforce Tien's contract, not because he was being vindictive, but because Tien's desertion threatened the success of his entire expedition.

Recent accounts of Meyer's work have repeated Farrer's statement that Meyer had difficulty with his employees and remained "aloof" from his men.[1] Unlike Wilson and Forrest, Meyer never settled down in a limited geographic area with a large group of men to assist him in his work. Because he had to climb mountains, peer into ravines, and cross deserts in order to find economically useful plants, he traveled thousands of miles accompanied simply by an interpreter, a guide, and sometimes an assistant. He did

have difficulty finding competent helpers who were willing to face hardships, but he retained the loyalty of dedicated employees. In 1906 and 1907
his Chinese guide journeyed with him across Korea, eastern Siberia, and
Manchuria, and then went on with him to Shanghai. Chow-hai Ting served
as his interpreter on all four of his expeditions. The same Russian interpreter who had traveled with him in eastern Siberia offered his services when
Meyer was ready to enter Russia again in 1909. His German-born interpreter of Russian and Turki accompanied him on the long trek from
Tashkent across the Mussart Pass into Mongolia, through the Altai Mountains, and then to Omsk in Siberia. Johannis de Leuw assisted him throughout the entire third expedition, which included two challenging trips into the
interior. Yao-feng Ting journeyed with him for ten months near Kingmen
and Ichang and remained at his side until his death. Two postcards mailed
months thereafter by Svend Lange, Meyer's interpreter in Siberia during the
alfalfa project, offer final evidence of the faithfulness of his employees.

Meyer inspired loyalty and affection throughout his life. In his youth in
Holland he earned the regard of the Janssens and de Vries. While he was
working as a gardener during his first year in America, P. H. Dorsett, A. J.
Pieters, and Erwin Smith became his lifelong friends. Fairchild believed in
him from the first time they met. In Asia consular officials of various
nationalities and missionaries of every denomination valued his friendship.
In America the staffs of the Plant Introduction Section in Washington and
of agricultural experiment stations and plant introduction gardens across
the country eagerly awaited his visits. Only a man who combined integrity
and intelligence with personal magnetism could have attracted the people
who became devoted to him, often after only a brief acquaintance.

During ten years in the field Frank Meyer carried out his promise to
"skim the earth for things good for man." Despite physical hardships and an
increasing sense of isolation, he continued to pursue his goal courageously.
For him life was never simple but his love of nature, his many friends, and
his belief that he was serving the needs of mankind made it fulfilling. He
could have no more fitting epitaph than the words that Fairchild wrote soon
after his death: "Meyer's field work is done. Whether his body rests beside
the great river of China or under some of the trees that he loved and
brought to this country, matters little to him. He will know that throughout
his adopted land there will always be his plants, hundreds of them—on
mountainsides, in valleys, in fields, in the backyards and orchards of little
cottages, on street corners, and in the arboreta of wealthy lovers of plants.
And wherever they are, they will all be his."[2]

Frank Meyer's pioneering work as an agricultural explorer in Asia
constituted a beginning; his death did not mark an ending, for the results of
his work still live and serve as a foundation for future accomplishments.

Meyer's Plant Introductions

THIS sampling includes only a fraction of Meyer's 2,500 introductions with the PI (Plant Introduction) numbers that the Department of Agriculture assigned each one. When Meyer made multiple collections, usually just the first is cited. Meyer's comments are quoted or paraphrased. For a complete list, see the USDA publication, *Inventory of Seeds and Plants Imported by the Office of Foreign Seed and Plant Introduction,* volumes 12–57.

Acer buergerianum Miquel — Trident maple
> PI 19411. Seed collected near Hankow on March 6, 1906. A very tall-growing maple, well adapted for use as an avenue tree.

Actinidia chinensis Planchon — Chinese gooseberry
> PI 45946. Seed collected in Hupeh Province on November 23, 1917. "A variety of Yang-tao bearing smooth fruits of various sizes. . . . Of high promise for mild-wintered sections of the United States. Combines the flavor of gooseberry, strawberry, guava, and rhubarb." (Dr. A. R. Ferguson of Auckland, New Zealand, is making a detailed study of this plant.)

Aesculus chinensis Bunge — Chinese chestnut
> PI 17736. Bud-sticks from the Western Mountains near Peking. Received by the USDA on March 1, 1906. "An ornamental shade tree with somewhat smaller leaves than the ordinary horse chestnut; when old gets to be very spreading. A very rare tree in north China and entirely new to America."

Agropyron cristatum (L.) Gaertner — Crested wheat grass
> PI 32406. Seed collected near Sarepta, Saratov District, Russia on November 28, 1911. A promising fodder grass occurring on very dry, sandy hill slopes. Of value for sandy lands in the semiarid belt of the United States.

Albizia kalkora (Roxb.) Prain — Silk tree
> PI 21969. Seed collected near Poshan, Shantung, September, 1907. Small ornamental tree. Flowers with pink stamens. Not very common in China. (Under PI 22618 Meyer added, "Bunge calls this *Acacia macrophylla,* which is, however, a totally different plant."

Astragalus sp. — Milk vetch
> PI 32186. Seed collected near Sminogorsk in southwest Siberia on September 24, 1911. Occurs on sandy pastureland. Browsed by cattle. Possibly of value as a forage plant in cool semiarid regions.

Brassica pekinensis (Lour.) Ruprecht — Chinese cabbage

PI 21625, 21626. Seed collected in Shantung on September 14 and October 2, 1907. A very large variety of white cabbage, said to grow up to forty pounds in weight and to be very solid. "One excellent feature of these cabbages is that they are far easier to digest than our varieties and never emit unpleasant odors while being boiled."

Carya cathayensis Sargent — Chinese hickory

PI 43952. Collected near Hankow at the request of Frank N. Meyer by Dr. Duncan Main, a missionary. Received by the USDA on December 18, 1916. The only hickory found in China. Thrives in narrow, moist valleys at the foot of mountains.

Castanea mollissima Blume — Chinese chestnut

PI 40508. Seed collected January 25, 1915, south of Sian (Xi'an) in Shansi Province. A large variety of Chinese chestnut propagated by grafting. "Seems on the whole more resistant to the bark disease than the ordinary strain of Chinese chestnut."

Catalpa bungei C. A. Meyer — Bunge's Catalpa

PI 16914. Cuttings received by the USDA on December 26, 1905. "A fine tree, said to be covered in spring with pink-white flowers; a favorite tree in old temple yards. This one comes from the Yellow Temple a short distance north of Peking."

Citrus ichangensis Swingle — Ichang lemon

PI 45931. Scions collected December 10, 1917, in Hupeh Province. "Chinese use only as room perfumers. Foreign residents use to make lemonade. May prove hardier than any other citrus fruit of economic importance."

PI 45937. An especially fine variety collected on December 30, 1917, at Ichang. Exudes a delightful fragrance and makes superior lemonade.

Citrus × *meyeri* Y. Tanaka (*Citrus limon* × *C. sinensis*?, according to Swingle; also called *C. limonia* Osbeck) — Meyer lemon

PI 23028. Plant collected at Fentai near Peking on March 31, 1908. Ornamental lemon, grown as a pot plant when dwarfed. Decorative in winter.

Coronilla varia L. — Crownvetch

PI 32305 (roots), 32414 (seeds). Both collected on dry slopes and in ravines near Saratov, Russia, on November 23, 1911. "Perennial legume, apparently very drought-resistant; of possible use as a forage and pasture plant."

Crataegus pinnatifida Bunge — Hawthorn

PI 17882. Seed collected near Changli. Received by the USDA on February 23, 1906. "A fine fruit for preserves and a very ornamental tree; is simply loaded in the fall with red berries and keeps its glossy-green leaves until late in autumn."

Daphne tangutica Maxim. — Daphne

PI 39914. Cuttings collected near Siku, Kansu Province, on November 17, 1914. A very beautiful evergreen bush of low, compact growth; foliage dark green and leathery; occurs in stony ravines and open woodlands at an altitude of 5,000 to 10,000 feet. Flowers white with a slight violet tinge, faintly scented. Berries bright red. This shrub is of high decorative value.

Diospyros kaki L. f. — Chinese persimmon

PI 16912. Cuttings from the Ming Tombs Valley. Received by the USDA on December 26, 1905. "A most valuable fruit. These bright orange-colored persimmons attain a diameter of 4½ inches and are perfectly seedless. Bears shipping extremely well. . . . Their taste is delicious and they would be highly esteemed in America as a table fruit." (This is the Tamopan persimmon, Meyer's first important discovery.)

PI 37525–37540, 37648–37658, 37661–37665, 37672–37678. Fine varieties of persimmons collected by Meyer south of Sian on his third expedition. Some were round, some had four vertical furrows, and others were flat with a horizontal incision.

Diospyros sinensis Hemsley
PI 23013. Acquired as a potted plant at Hankow on June 28, 1907. An evergreen shrub or small tree. Bears greenish-white, bell-shaped flowers; grown dwarfed in pots; rarely seen as a garden shrub.

Elaeagnus angustifolia L. — Russian olive
PI 27775. Cuttings collected near Tiflis in the Caucasus on March 22, 1910. Trees planted around fields as windbreaks. "Fruits large. Eaten fresh or dried or stewed in milk or boiled with sugar."

Euonymus japonica Thunb. — Japanese euonymus
PI 18566. Cuttings collected at Hankow. Received at Chico Plant Introduction Garden on May 18, 1906.

Fraxinus potamophila Herder — Khotan ash
PI 30143. Cuttings collected at Yarkand, Chinese Turkestan, on December 18, 1910, in an old graveyard. To be tested as an ornamental tree where rainfall is slight and summer temperatures high.
PI 30414. Collected as seed at Khotan on November 26, 1910. Able to stand considerable drought and alkali.

Ginkgo biloba L. — Ginkgo
PI 19390. Seed collected November, 1905, in the Western Hills near Peking. "A fine, spreading tree with leaves less strongly lobed than generally met with. Collected in an old temple garden."

Gleditsia heterophylla Bunge — Honey locust
PI 21968. Seed collected in Shantung, September, 1907. "A very spiny shrub or small tree growing in dry, rocky localities. May serve as a hedge plant in the Southwest."

Gleditsia sinensis Lam. — Soap-pod tree
PI 38800. Seed collected at Sian on January 7, 1914. Large-podded variety of soap bean. Drought-resistant. Recommended as ornamental and shade tree for mild-wintered and semiarid parts of the United States.

Glycine max (L.) Merrill (*Glycine hispida*) — Soybean
PI 19184. Seed collected near Newchwang, Manchuria. Received by the USDA on August 20, 1906. "A large variety of black soybean, a rare variety used for food and also for making a superior oil."
PI 19186. (The variety named 'Virginia'.) Also collected as seed near Newchwang. Received by the USDA on August 28, 1906. A medium-sized greenish soybean used to produce bean oil. The remaining material, pressed into large cakes, was exported as a fertilizer to Japan and southern China.

Hedysarum alpinum L.
PI 32187. Seed collected at Tomsk, Siberia, on August 22, 1911. "May possess value as a forage plant for the northern sections of the United States and may also serve as a factor in hybridization experiments to be made with the famous sulla (*Hedysarum coronarium*) in making it hardier."

Hordeum vulgare L. — Barley
PI 31796. Seed collected at Pustan Terek, Chinese Turkestan, on December 29, 1910. "An excellent large variety of hull-less summer barley grown by Kirghiz in mountain valleys at altitudes from 6,000 to 7,000 feet. Test in rocky and intermountain regions of the United States."

Juglans mandshurica Maxim. — Manchurian walnut
PI 44233. Seed collected at Shinglungshan on December 3, 1916. A wild walnut that grows into a stately tree. "Of value as a hardy shade tree; possibly also as a stock for Persian walnuts in cold localities."

Juglans regia L. — Chinese walnut
PI 35610. Seed collected at Tsinan (Jinan), Shantung Province, on April 4, 1913. A large variety of Chinese walnut; may thrive in valleys of southern Rocky Mountains. (PI 35612 was the rare "flat walnut.")

Juniperus chinensis L. 'Columnaris' — Columnar Juniper
PI 18577. Seed collected at Shan-haikwan. Received at Chico Plant Introduction Garden on May 18, 1906.

Juniperus squamata D. Don 'Meyeri'
PI 23023. Bought as plants at Peking on April 3, 1908, and taken by Meyer to Chico in June, 1908. "A specimen of remarkable beauty, said to come from southwestern Shantung."

Kolkwitzia amabilis Graebner — Beauty bush
PI 37480. Cuttings collected in the Ta hua Shan, Shensi Province, on December 29, 1913. A shrub growing four to six feet tall in rocky places at an altitude higher than 5,000 feet.

Larix sibirica Ledeb. — Siberian larch
PI 33317. Collected as seed at Saint Petersburg (Leningrad) on February 17, 1912. Of great value as a lumber tree and as an ornamental in the coolest sections of the United States.

Lathyrus pisiformis L.
PI 32192, 32193. Collected as seed near Tomsk, Siberia, from August 18 to 24, 1911. "A wild pea from two to five feet tall. Eagerly eaten by horses and cattle. The Siberian form deserves to be tested for forage purposes in the cooler sections of the United States. May prove extremely hardy."

Ligustrum quihoui Carr. — Privet
PI 38807. Seed collected near Nantotchu, Shensi Province, on January 21, 1914. "A privet found on rocky banks. Bears masses of small black berries. Evergreen foliage. Of value as hedge or border shrub, especially for mild-wintered, semiarid parts of the United States."

Ligustrum vulgare L. — Common privet
PI 26767. Cuttings from plants found on a dry, rocky mountainside near Sevastopol, Crimea, on January 11, 1910. "A low, bushy, semievergreen privet. May prove of value as an ornamental shrub."

Lilium sp. — Lily
PI 20355. Seed collected near Vladivostok on October, 1906. A wild lily, probably has scarlet blossoms. (This appears to be the scarlet lily Van Fleet used in hybridization. Fairchild referred to it as Korean; possibly he was confused because Meyer mailed his Korean collection from Vladivostok.)

Malus pumila var. *paradisiaca* (Medic.) C. K. Schneid. — Paradise apple
PI 27968. Cuttings collected at Geok-Tepe, Caucasus, on April 11, 1910. The true Paradise apple from its native habitat. Extensively used as dwarfing stock for apples. Very drought-resistant. May be useful in hybridizing a strain of bush apples.

Medicago falcata L. — Alfalfa
PI 32389. Seed collected in western Siberia, July 18 and October 4, 1911. Called 'Sholteek' by natives. "Great amount of selection and breeding may have to be done before ideal types evolve. Domestic animals devour it eagerly.

Remarkably resistant to drought. Great nutritive capacity. Test for semiarid belt of northwestern United States."

Myrica rubra Sieb. and Zucc. — Chinese strawberry

PI 22904, 22905. Seed collected at Tangsi (Dongsi), Chekiang Province, on June 25, 1907. Bears large, wine-red fruits, very pleasing to the taste. Can be eaten fresh, stewed, or preserved in spirits. The tree also is decidedly ornamental, especially when loaded with carmine fruits.

Olea europaea L. (*O. ferruginea*) — Common olive

PI 26801–26811. Collected at the Imperial Botanical Garden at Nikita, Crimea, on January 22, 1910. Cuttings from a very large olive tree, several centuries old. "Withstood temperatures of −2°F; unhurt, when other olives were frozen to the ground. Recommended for southern Texas and California."

Phyllostachys heterocycla (Carr.) Mitf. — Bamboo

PI 23233. Plants collected near Tangsi (Dongsi), Chekiang Province, autumn, 1907. Largest and most common kind of timber bamboo, 100 feet in height. Used in manufacture of ladders, water pipes, rain gutters, and as construction material for large sheds.

Meyer also collected other kinds of bamboo including *Phyllostachys* sp., PI 23235–23236, used in manufacture of furniture, tool handles, and baskets; *P. angusta* McClure, PI 23237, a very hard bamboo used for fine furniture; and *P. nigra* (Ladd ex Lindl.) Munro, PI 23240, a shining bamboo used for walking canes and pipe stems.

Picea meyeri Rehder and Wilson — Meyer spruce

PI 44149. Seed collected at Shinglungshan, China, on December 3, 1916. "A tall-growing spruce, often having bluish needles."

Pinus bungeana Zucc. ex Endlicher — White-barked pine

PI 17912. Seed collected in the Western Mountains near Peking. Received by the USDA on February 23, 1906. "A very beautiful pine tree with silvery-white bark; a slow grower but extremely striking when old. The bark peels off in flakes...and the foliage is not as dense as in most other pines."

Pistacia chinensis Bunge — Chinese pistachio

PI 17734, 17735. Collected as bud-sticks in the Western Mountains near Peking. Received by the USDA on March 1, 1906. The staminate form, PI 17734, "grows to very large dimensions. A very ornamental tree with graceful, pinnate foliage." The carpellate form, PI 17735, "bears heavy bunches of small scarlet and purplish-colored berries, a rather ornamental small tree."

Platycladus orientalis (L.) Franco (*Thuja orientalis*) — Oriental arborvitae

PI 22374. Collected near Peking on February 6, 1908, as cuttings. "A wonderful branch variation of *Thuja orientalis*. The Chinese call it 'the rising phoenix tree.' "

Populus × *berolinensis* Dippel — Berlin poplar

PI 26614. Cuttings collected on December 17, 1909, near Saint Petersburg (Leningrad). "A form of the so-called Berlin poplar, but much hardier than the type. Widely planted around St. Petersburg as a shade tree. Recommended for cold and uncongenial climates."

Populus tomentosa Carr. — White poplar

PI 22355. Cuttings collected west of Peking on January 21, 1908. The large-leaved Chinese poplar, remarkably straight and tall. May prove to be a very good street tree.

Prunus armeniaca L. — Apricot

PI 28953. Seed collected in Askabad, Turkestan, on June 9, 1910. Small freestone apricot with hard flesh and large, sweet kernel. (Meyer collected other apricots with sweet kernels: PI 28958 in Old Bokhara, PI 28960 in the Zaraf-shan Valley, and PI 28961 and 28962 in Samarkand.)

Prunus davidiana (Carr.) Franch. — Wild peach

PI 22009. Seed collected on October 5 and 7, 1907, near Tientsin. "Very resist-ant to drought and alkaline soil. The Chinese use this tree as a grafting stock for flowering peaches and plums; also for small bush cherries; even apricots are grafted on it."

Prunus davidiana var. *potaninii* (Batal.) Rehder (*Prunus persica* var. *po-taninii*) — Potanin's peach

PI 39899, 40007, 40008, 40009. All collected near Siku in Kansu Province from October 29 through November 9, 1914, PI 39899 as cuttings and the others as seeds. Found from an altitude of 4,000 to 7,000 feet.

Prunus × meyeri Rehder — Korean cherry

PI 20084. Seed collected on August 21, 1906, in the mountains of northern Korea. "A small wild cherry . . . quite handsome in appearance. Only two or three seen during the whole trip through northern Korea." (Thought to be of hybrid origin.)

Prunus persica (L.) Batsch — Feicheng peach

PI 21989. Collected near Feicheng on September 1, 1907. "Stones of the most famous peach of north China. The fruits grow as heavy as one pound apiece and are pale yellowish with a slight blush; meat white, except near the stone; taste excellent, sweet, aromatic, and juicy. Is a clingstone. Has extraordinary keeping and shipping qualities. The branches need propping up on account of the weight of the fruits."

On two later expeditions Meyer returned to Feicheng and collected PI 38178 in 1914 and PI 45320 in 1917.

Prunus prostrata Labill. — Siberian bush cherry

PI 28945. Collected July 9 to 11, 1910, in the mountains near Samarkand. A bush cherry found on stony and sterile mountain slopes and cliffs. "Bears multitudes of small red cherries of a sour taste.... It may possibly be hybrid-ized with the large-fruited sweet and sour cherries and therewith give rise to a race of bush cherries for drier sections of the United States."

Prunus pseudocerasus Lindl. — Tangsi cherry (See Appendix B)

PI 18587. Cuttings collected along the canal near Tangsi (Dongsi), Chekiang Province, with the aid of Alexander Kennedy, a missionary. Received at Chico Plant Introduction Garden on May 18, 1906. (This cherry is a different species from any grown in European or American orchards. It bloomed ten days earlier than any other cherry at Chico.)

Prunus tangutica (Batal.) Koehne (*Amygdalus tangutica*) — Bush almond

PI 39898. Collected as cuttings at Lantsai near Siku in Kansu Province on October 28, 1914. Found on cliffs and among rocks near the Siku River at 4,200 feet. Foliage small; fruits variable. Withstands drought, cold, and dry heat. Recommended as a factor for hybridization experiments to create hardy bush almonds. Could be used to develop an ornamental shrub for cool, semi-arid areas.

Pyrus betulaefolia Bunge — Wild pear

PI 21982. Collected as seed on October, 1907, in Shantung Province. Fruit not larger than green peas. Used all over China as a stock on which to graft pears. Stands alkali remarkably well. May be of value in alkaline regions as a stock.

Pyrus calleryana Decaisne — Callery pear

PI 45592. Over 100 pounds of wild pear seed collected near Kingmen (Jingmen) in October, 1917. Found in a variety of habitats. Highly resistant to fire blight. Used by the Chinese as a stock for improved pears.

PI 47261. "Purchased through Mr. John H. Reisner, University of Nanking, at the request of Mr. W. T. Swingle, for experiments being carried on to develop varieties of pears free from blight and also to be used as stock." Received by the USDA on March 11, 1919. (These seeds purchased through Meyer's good friend, John Reisner, almost certainly from the native sources that Meyer had developed at Kingmen, represent the fall harvest a year after his death and can be regarded as continuing and completing his pear project. Reisner did not function as a collector but as a link between the USDA and Meyer's sources of *Pyrus calleryana*. The Bradford, Whitehouse, and Capital ornamental pears are progeny of PI 47261.

Pyrus ussuriensis Maxim. — Wild pear of north China

PI 21918. Cuttings collected at Tungling on November 29, 1907. "A very thrifty form of the wild pear used everywhere in the north of China as a grafting stock for cultivated varieties of pears." (Under PI 44150, collected in 1916, Meyer notes that this pear may be immune to fire blight.)

Quercus variabilis Blume — Chinese cork oak

PI 21876. Acorns collected north of Peking on November 18, 1907. A handsome tree with long, serrated leaves. Stands drought well. May be of use in semiarid regions. (The only specimen known in cultivation in America is growing in Chevy Chase, Maryland, at David Fairchild's former home, In the Woods.)

Rosa odorata (Andrews) Sweet — Tea rose

PI 22449 originally; renumbered PI 44426. Collected as cuttings at the American Presbyterian Mission on January 30, 1908. Pale pink pillar rose. Blooms freely.

Rosa xanthina Lindl. — Rose

PI 17469. Collected as plants and cuttings near Peking. Received by the USDA on February 6, 1906. "A semi-double yellow rose. Is a very thrifty grower and able to withstand long droughts." (Meyer later collected this valuable rose in the wild in quantity in Shansi and Shantung provinces.)

Rosa xanthina f. *spontanea* Rehd. — Single rose

PI 21620. Collected as seed on August 23, 1907, in Shantung Province. "This beautiful single yellow rose grows in dry, rocky localities. . . . Produces masses of delicate yellow flowers in early summer."

Rubus nigrum L. — Black currant

PI 29142. Cuttings collected near Terek-Dawan, Russian Turkestan, on October 13, 1910. "Found growing in a cold, stony canyon at an elevation of over 9,000 feet above sea level. May be of value as a garden fruit in the most northern sections of the United States."

Salix matsudana G. Koidzumi 'Umbraculifera' — Willow

PI 17737. Collected as bud-sticks in the Western Mountains near Peking. Received by the USDA on March 1, 1906. "A remarkable willow that naturally forms a dense, flat, globular head."

PI 22450. Collected as cuttings on January 30, 1908. Needs no water supply beyond a scanty summer rainfall. (This interesting ornamental has been sadly neglected.)

Sorghum bicolor (L.) Moench (*S. vulgare*) — Dwarf sorghum

PI 22010. Seed collected in Shantung Province on August 12, 1907. "A very rare and dwarf variety of sorghum, not growing higher than three feet and making dense heads. Grows on shallow, sterile soils and matures much earlier than the taller-growing varieties. May do well in semiarid regions."

Meyer obtained the better-known 'Chusan Brown Kaoling' in 1908 from Dr. S. P. Barchet. A "dwarfy form of sorghum," PI 23231 came from the Chusan Islands, China.

Spinacia oleracea L. — Spinach

PI 20026, 20027. Collected as seed at Liaoyang, Manchuria, on June 20, 1906, and then at Antung, Manchuria, on July 12, 1906. "A good, large-leafed spinach grown in sheltered places all through the winter, producing greens until early summer."

Syringa meyeri Schneider — Dwarf lilac

PI 23032. Plants bought at Fengtai near Peking on March 31, 1908. "A small-leaved lilac bearing many panicles of purple flowers. . . . Used much in forcing; quite rare and expensive." Under PI 23033 Meyer added, "Has a future for Western people as a very graceful spring-flowering shrub of dwarf habit." (*S. meyeri* 'Palibin', popular in the nursery trade in England and America, is not Meyer's PI 23032 but another clone of *S. meyeri*. See P. S. Green, "*Syringa meyeri* cv. 'Palibin'," *Curtis's Botanical Magazine* 182, no.3(1979):117–20; Tab. 778.)

Triticum aestivum L. — Winter wheat

PI 31781. Seed collected at the oasis of Khotan, Chinese Turkestan, on November 24, 1910. "A good, hard, winter wheat called '*Al mecca boogdai*'. Said to have been introduced from Mecca."

Triticum durum Desf. 'Sela Turka' — Spring wheat

PI 32388. Seed collected at Chistunka, Siberia, on September 9, 1911. Hard-kerneled summer wheat. Resists drought. Early ripening.

Triticum turgidum L. (*T. aestivum*) — Poulard wheat

PI 32039. Collected on March 6, 1911, in the Tekes Valley, Tien Shan Mountains, Chinese Turkestan, at 3,900 feet. "A rare local variety of fine wheat of great excellence. Grains large, of a pale yellow color, ears very long. Flour made from this wheat makes a fine quality of substantial bread."

Ulmus carpinifolia Gleditsch 'Umbraculifera' (*U. campestris* var. *umbraculifera* [Trautv.] Rehder) — Kashgar elm

PI 30060. Cuttings collected at Khanaka, Chinese Turkestan, on December 5, 1910. Found in an old graveyard. Graceful, slightly drooping branches. "Recommended as an ornamental garden and park tree in semiarid regions and with slight irrigation in desert places."

Ulmus parvifolia Jacquin — Chinese elm

PI 22375. Cuttings taken on February 6, 1908. "A tall, spreading elm with many small branches bearing small leaves and flowering in the fall. I have seen only two specimens and these grow on the grounds of the Temple of Heaven at Peking, from where these scions are taken."

PI 37810. Seed collected south of Sian on April 14, 1914. "Very drought-resistant. Of value for mild-wintered semiarid sections as a lumber tree and as an ornamental."

Ulmus pumila L. — Siberian elm

PI 22975. Collected at Fengtai near Peking on March 31, 1908. "The Chinese elm, used all over northern China and Manchuria as an avenue, shade, and timber tree. Resists drought, extremes of temperature, and neglect remarkably well; will be a good shade tree for the semiarid regions of the United States."

(Now called Siberian elm; Meyer collected it repeatedly and in great quantities.)

Viburnum farreri Stearn (*V. fragrans*) — Fragrant viburnum

PI 37005. Cuttings collected at Peking on December 1, 1913. "A viburnum flowering in the spring before the leaves have fully come out, bearing fragrant white flowers carried erect as round panicles. . . . Of value in drier regions."

Viburnum macrocephalum Fortune — Chinese snowball

PI 22978. Bought as a plant at Suchow on April 26, 1908. "A tall bush bearing enormous umbels of white flowers, sometimes over one foot in diameter."

Zizyphus jujuba Miller — Jujube

PI 21618. The honey jujube collected at Laoling, Shantung, as seed on September 30, 1907. A remarkably sweet variety.

PI 22686. 'Lang' cuttings taken March 10, 1908, at Tsintse, Shansi Province. "A jujube tree that grows very large and spreads out very much, bearing small fruits of oblong shape, red color, and of a melting sweet taste; cannot be kept long."

PI 35253–35254. The seedless jujube, collected at Laoling, Shantung, on March 30, 1913. Served as sweetmeats or stewed.

PI 36854. 'Yu' cuttings collected at Peking on November 9, 1913. Large fruits of elongated shape, tapering toward the ends. Reddish-brown color, sweet taste, meat firm, foliage large.

PI 37484. 'So' cuttings collected January 6, 1914, at Sian, Shensi Province. Trees very gnarled and zigzag. Fruits round, shining brown-red, sweet. Obtained from J. A. Ross, postmaster at Sian.

PI 38249. 'Li' scions collected February 14, 1914, in Shansi Province at Anyihsien. Supposed to be the largest of all jujubes. Oval and larger than hens' eggs.

Zoysia japonica Steud. — Zoysia grass

PI 19425, 19426. Seed collected on July 15, 1906, near Aidjou, northern Korea, and on July 27, 1906, from the banks of the Yalu River in northern Korea. "A perennial grass growing but a few inches high, well adapted for lawn purposes. Needs mowing, in all probability, but once or twice a year and requires very little water. . . . There were donkeys continually browsing upon this grass, but it was one green velvet turf and will be excellent for golf links, lawns, etc."

Meyer Germplasm Available Today

THIS list is an attempt to record the location of Meyer germplasm before that information is completely lost. If anyone can offer additional data, please communicate with the author through the publisher.

Not all of Meyer's surviving introductions are included in this survey. Some, such as *Ulmus pumila,* have been so widely propagated that they are generally available. Ornamentals like *Juniperus squamata* 'Meyeri' have entered the nursery trade; the Chinese persimmon and the Meyer lemon are cultivated commercially. Others, including the Chinese chestnut and *Rosa xanthina,* as well as orchard and field crops, have made their largely unrecorded contributions as breeding parents. Identifying most of the plants that the USDA distributed freely in this country and abroad is impossible; yet examples occasionally appear. At the botanical garden at Yalta, Sylvester March of the National Arboretum recently saw fruits of jujube cultivars that the USDA had sent to Yalta long ago.

The USDA holds most of the germplasm listed below. The former USDA Plant Introduction Station at Chico, California, is now the U.S. Forest Service Plant Improvement Center, abbreviated hereafter as Forest Service Center, Chico. The following acronyms are used: AES (Agricultural Experiment Station); PI (Plant Introduction); SCS (Soil Conservation Service).

Acer buergerianum Miquel: PI 19411
  National Plant Materials Center, SCS, Beltsville, Md.
  Forest Service Center, Chico, Calif.
Acer truncatum Bunge: PI 18578
  Regional PI Station (S-9), Experiment, Ga.
  Forest Service Center, Chico, Calif.
Albizia kalkora (Roxb.) Prain: PI 21969
  National Plant Materials Center, SCS, Beltsville, Md.
Carya cathayensis Sargent
  The Arnold Arboretum of Harvard University, Jamaica Plain, Mass. (This is
    not Meyer's PI 43952 but germplasm reacquired from the Arboretum of
    the Chinese Academy of Forestry in 1982.)
Citrus × *meyeri* Y. Tanaka: PI 23028
  Nicholls State University, Thibodaux, La.
  Louisiana State University AES, Plaquemines Parish, La.
  Texas A & M AES and Texas A & I Citrus Center, Weslaco, and in the lower Rio

Grande Valley near Wesleco and Harlingen.

Glen Saint Mary Nurseries, Glen Saint Mary, Fla.

The Florida Crop Reporting Service listed 1,194 acres of the Meyer lemon (201,400 trees) in January, 1982.

Coronilla varia L.: PI 32305

National Plant Materials Center, SCS, Beltsville, Md.

Elsberry Plant Materials Center, SCS, Elsberry, Mo.

Crataegus meyeri Pojark.

The Arnold Arboretum, Jamaica Plain, Mass. (This is not Meyer's PI 27339 but germplasm reacquired from the Academy of Sciences, Moscow, in 1965.)

Diospyros kaki L. f. 'Tamopan': PI 16921

Fruit Crops Department, University of Florida, Gainesville.

Diospyros sinensis Hemsley: PI 23013

U.S. National Arboretum, Washington, D.C.

National Plant Materials Center, SCS, Beltsville, Md.

Glycine max L. Merrill 'Virginia': PI 17852

Glycine max L. Merrill 'Peking': PI 19186

National Seed Storage Laboratory, Colorado State University, Fort Collins.

Indigofera kirilowii Maxim.: PI 20127

Glenn Dale PI Station, Glenn Dale, Md.

Juglans regia L.: PI 18256

Regional PI Station (NE-9), New York AES, Geneva.

Juniperus chinensis L. 'Columnaris': PI 18577

U.S. National Arboretum, Washington, D.C. (Hedge)

Glenn Dale PI Station, Glenn Dale, Md. (Hedge)

The Huntington Botanical Gardens, San Marino, Calif.

Juniperus squamata D. Don 'Meyeri': PI 23023

The Arnold Arboretum, Jamaica Plain, Mass.

Larix sibirica Ledeb.: PI 36163

Arboretum, Northern Great Plains Research Laboratory, Mandan, N.D. Meyer traveled across the USSR in the winter of 1912 with a special appropriation for plants that would survive at Mandan. He repeatedly used this account to order seeds of hardy trees, including the Siberian larch. When PI 36163 reached Washington in September 1913, it was promptly sent to Mandan, arriving October 6, 1913. Though it came to the USDA "through Count von Sivers," it seems likely that it is a product of Meyer's special assignment to find hardy trees for Mandan.

Ligustrum quihoui Carr.: PI 38807

Glenn Dale PI Station, Glenn Dale, Md. (Hedge)

Ligustrum vulgare L.: PI 26767

Regional PI Station (NC-7), Iowa State University, Ames.

Lonicera fragrantissima Lindl. and Paxton: PI 40689

Glenn Dale PI Station, Glenn Dale, Md.

Maackia amurensis Ruprecht and Maximowicz: PI 20322 or 23 (originally grown as 19935)

Arboretum, Northern Great Plains Research Laboratory, Mandan, N.D.

Malus halliana Koehne: PI 38231

Mississippi Plant Materials Center, SCS, Coffeeville, Miss.

Myrica rubra Sieb. and Zucc.: PI 22905

Regional PI Station (S-9), Experiment, Ga.

Phyllostachys angusta McClure: PI 23237
Phyllostachys aureosulcata McClure: Renumbered PI 55713
Phyllostachys congesta Rendle: PI 23242 or 43, renumbered PI 80149
Phyllostachys nuda McClure: Renumbered PI 103938
    USDA Bamboo Collection, PI Station, Savannah, Ga.
    USDA Bamboo Repository, Fruit and Nut Tree Research Laboratory, Byron, Ga.
    American Bamboo Society Collection, Quail Botanical Gardens, Encinitas, Calif.
    David Andrews Collection, 14450 Homecrest Road, Silver Spring, Md.
Phyllostachys meyeri McClure: PI 23234, renumbered PI 116768
    The four bamboo collections listed above.
    The Arnold Arboretum, Jamaica Plain, Mass.
Phyllostachys vivax McClure: PI 23242 or 43, renumbered PI 82047
    Quail Botanical Gardens, Encinitas, Calif.
    Andrews Collection, 14450 Homecrest Road, Silver Spring, Md.
    The origin of several bamboos growing in Maryland and California is uncertain. The unidentified bamboos in the McIlhenny Jungle Garden, Avery Island, La., probably include some of Meyer's introductions.
Picea meyeri Rehder and Wilson:
    The Arnold Arboretum, Jamaica Plain, Mass. (This is not Meyer's PI 44149 but germplasm William Purdom collected in China in 1910 and 1912.)
Pinus bungeana Zucc. ex Endlicher: PI 17912
    Forest Service Center, Chico, Calif.
    Grave of William Woodville Rockhill, American Minister to China, East Cemetery, Litchfield, Conn. Rockhill told Fairchild and Meyer that he would like to be buried beneath a Chinese white-barked pine. His widow accepted Fairchild's offer of one of Meyer's specimens.
Pistacia chinensis Bunge: PI 21970
    National Plant Materials Center, SCS, Beltsville, Md.
    The Huntington Botanical Gardens, San Marino, Calif.
    Forest Service Center, Chico, Calif., along Station Road and Durham Highway south of Chico for about one mile. Fairchild wrote Meyer, "This avenue of *Pistacia chinensis* will be a monument to your exploration after we all are gone."
    Glenn Dale PI Station, Glenn Dale, Md. These trees are progeny of Meyer's introduction; Dr. William L. Ackerman brought them from Chico to Glenn Dale in 1959.
Populus × *berolinensis* Dippel: PI 26614
    Regional PI Station (S-9), Experiment, Ga.
Prunus pseudocerasus Lindl. (tentative identification): PI 18587 (The USDA has used this name to identify Meyer's Tangsi cherry for decades; however, it represents a complex that is not yet fully understood.)
    AES, University of California, Davis.
Prunus tangutica (Batal.) Koehne (*Amygdalus tangutica*): PI 39898
    AES, University of California, Davis.
Pyrus calleryana Decaisne: PI 45586, 45592, 47261
    Southern Oregon Experiment Station, Medford.
    Northwest Plant Germplasm Repository, Corvallis, Oreg.
    Glenn Dale PI Station, Glenn Dale, Md., maintains seedling progeny of PI 47261. (See note, *P. calleryana,* App. A.)

Quercus variabilis Blume: PI 21876
In the Woods, 8922 Spring Valley Road, Chevy Chase, Md.
Rosa xanthina Lindl.: PI 21620
The Arnold Arboretum, Jamaica Plain, Mass.
Sorghum bicolor (L.) Moench (*S. vulgare*) 'Chusan Brown Kaoling': PI 23231
Regional PI Station (S-9), Experiment, Ga.
National Seed Storage Laboratory, Colorado State University, Fort Collins.
Spinacia oleracea L.: PI 20026
Regional PI Station (NE-9), New York AES, Geneva
Spiraea cantonensis Lour.: PI 22993
Glenn Dale PI Station, Glenn Dale, Md.
Syringa meyeri Schneider: PI 23032
Regional PI Station (NE-9), New York AES, Geneva
Agricultural Research Station, Morden, Manitoba, Can.
The Arnold Arboretum, Jamaica Plain, Mass.
Syringa oblata Lindl. 'Alba' (*S. affinis*): PI 23031
Glenn Dale PI Station, Glenn Dale, Md.
Regional PI Station (NE-9), New York AES, Geneva. This lilac is maintained
at the University of New Hampshire at Durham.
Syringa persica L.: PI 40709
Regional PI Station (NE-9), New York AES, Geneva. This lilac is maintained
at the University of New Hampshire at Durham.
Triticum aestivum L. 'Changli': PI 17947
Triticum aestivum L. 'Ak-Mecca Boogdai': PI 31781
Triticum aestivum L. 'Kizil Boogdai': PI 31784, 31788
Triticum aestivum L. 'Ak Boogdai': PI 31789
Triticum aestivum L. 'Kara Boogdai': PI 32038
Triticum durum Desf. 'Afrikanski': PI 32175
Triticum durum Desf. 'Sela Turka': PI 32388
Triticum durum Desf.: PI 35314
Triticum durum Desf. 'Chernouska': PI 36003
Triticum turgidum L.: PI 32039
Small Grains Collection, Agricultural Research Center, Beltsville, Md.
Ulmus pumila L.: PI 22975, 40898
Northern Great Plains Research Laboratory, Mandan, N.D. Seedling progeny
of these elms has been widely distributed in cooperative tree plantings
throughout the northern Great Plains.
Viburnum farreri Stearn (*V. fragrans*): PI 37005
The Arnold Arboretum, Jamaica Plain, Mass.
Viburnum macrocephalum Fortune: PI 22978
Glenn Dale PI Station, Glenn Dale, Md.
Viburnum mongolicum (Pall.) Rehder: PI 36855
Glenn Dale PI Station, Glenn Dale, Md.
Zizyphus jujuba Miller
'Li', 'So', 'Sui Men', 'Yu': PI 38249, 37484, 38245, 36854
U.S. Forest Service Center, Chico, Calif.
'Li', 'So', 'Sui Men', 'Yu', 'Lang': PI 38249, 37484, 38245, 36854, 22686
Fruit Crops Department, University of Florida, Gainesville.
International Tree Crops Institute, U.S.A., Gravel Switch, Ky.
'Li', 'Lang', 'Sui Men': PI 38249, 22686, 38245

TVA reforestation project behind Norris Dam, Norris, Tenn.

'Li', 'Lang': PI 38349, 22686

Armstrong Nursery, Ontario, Calif.

John Hershey farm, Downington, Pa.

'So': PI 37484

Regional PI Station (NE-9), New York AES, Geneva.

'Silverhill', Edhegard', 'Swaboda'

These are probable Meyer introductions, but the original names and PI numbers have been lost. The USDA distributed these cultivars for testing at Silverhill, Ala., about 1920. Dr. Paul Lyrene of the University of Florida at Gainesville has collected and maintained them.

'Chico' or GI 7-62, GI 11-83, GA 8-86, 'Thornless': Progeny of PI 38249, 37484, 38245, 36854

U.S. Forest Service Center, Chico, Calif.

Fruit Crops Department, University of Florida, Gainesville.

International Tree Crops Institute, Gravel Switch, Ky.

In the 1950s Dr. William L. Ackerman used Meyer's introductions as breeding parents and grew 3,500 jujube seedlings at Chico, developing improved cultivars identified as GA 8-86, GI 11-83, and GI 7-62. Paul Thomson of California Rare Fruit Growers at Fullerton named GI 7-62 'Chico'. 'Thornless' is an Ackerman-Smith selection; Robert Smith continued Dr. Ackerman's work. In the late 1970s, Dan Barth of Gridley, Calif., identified these abandoned cultivars, as well as Meyer's 'Li', 'So', 'Sui Men', and 'Yu', and collected seeds and scions for Gregory Williams, Director of the International Tree Crop Institute, Appalachian Region. Though most of the old jujube planting at Chico was bulldozed in July 1983, rooted cuttings of these cultivars survive there.

Recipients of the Meyer Medal

Barbour Lathrop, *California*	1920	Robert Montgomery, *Florida*	1950
Louis Trabut, *Algeria*	1922	Walter N. Koelz, *Michigan*	1956
E. D. Fenzi, *Tripoli*	1923	Carl O. Erlanson, *Maryland*	1965
Charles T. Simpson, *Florida*	1923	Howard S. Gentry, *Maryland*	1966
Charles S. Sargent, *Massachusetts*	1923	Russell J. Seibert, *Pennsylvania*	1966
A. Robertson Proschowsky, *France*	1923	William Hartley, *Australia*	1967
Robert M. Grey, *Cuba*	1925	William Whitehouse, *Maryland*	1968
Charles P. Taft, *California*	1927	Knowles Ryerson, *California*	1968
Henry N. Ridley, *England*	1928	John L. Creech, *Maryland*	1969
Henry Nehrling, *Florida*	1929	Charles R. Enlow, *Indiana*	1970
G. P. Rixford, *California*	1930	Erna Bennett, FAO, *Rome, Italy*	1971
Vicary Gibbs, *England*	1931	Donovan S. Correll, *Washington, D.C.*	1972
Allison V. Armour, *New York*	1931	John G. Hawkes, *England*	1973
P. H. Dorsett, *Maryland*	1936	Howard L. Hyland, *Maryland*	1974
Kate Sessions, *California*	1939	Jack R. Harlan, *Maryland*	1976
David Fairchild, *Florida*	1939	Quentin Jones, *Maryland*	1978
Edmundo Navarro de Andradi, *Brazil*	1941	Frederick G. Meyer, *Washington, D.C.*	1981
Walter T. Swingle, *Washington, D.C.*	1947	Desmond D. Dolan, *New York*	1982
Harry T. Edwards, *Washington, D.C.*	1947	Charles M. Rick, *California*	1982
F. Wilson Popenoe, *Honduras*	1950		

NOTES

MEYER'S unpublished letters are the source of much of this account of his life and work. Many of these letters constituted his official reports to David Fairchild, head of the Foreign Seed and Plant Introduction Section of the USDA: others are addressed to his colleagues on the plant introduction staff. Unless an exception is noted, all are included in "Letters of Frank N. Meyer," Volumes 105–109, Project Studies, Division of Plant Exploration and Introduction, Record Group 54: Records of the Bureau of Plant Industry, The National Archives, hereafter cited as PI Letters, F. N. Meyer, RG 54, NA.

Letters written by his colleagues to Frank Meyer are in document boxes 3 through 18, Reports, Notes, and Other Records of Frank N. Meyer, Division of Plant Exploration and Introduction, Record Group 54: Records of the Bureau of Plant Industry, The National Archives. These boxes hereafter are cited as PI Records, F. N. Meyer, RG 54, NA.

The source of Meyer's letters to his family and friends in Holland is Frederike J. van Uildriks, "De Reiziger-Plant Kundige Frans N. Meijer en Zijn Werk," *De Aarde en haar Volken* (January/February, March/April, and July/August, 1919), hereafter cited as van Uildriks, "De Reiziger-Plant Kundige."

CHAPTER 1

1. Quotations from letters written November, 1906, October, 1907. All quotations not otherwise identified are from PI Letters, F. N. Meyer, RG 54, NA.
2. For further information about Western plant hunters who worked in China, see Alice M. Coats, *The Plant Hunters* (New York, 1969); B. J. Healy, *The Plant Hunters* (New York, 1975); M. Tyler Whittle, *The Plant Hunters* (Philadelphia, 1970).
3. For Fairchild's account of his early life and the establishment of the Foreign Seed and Plant Introduction Section, see his autobiography, *The World Was My Garden* (New York, 1938), pp. 14–36, 80–84, 106–17.
4. Nelson Klose, *America's Crop Heritage* (Ames, Iowa, 1950), pp. 115–18; Knowles Ryerson, "History and Significance of the Foreign Plant Introduction Work of the United States Department of Agriculture," *Agricultural History* 7(1933):121.
5. Fairchild described his search for a plant hunter in *The World Was My Garden*, pp. 284–85, 297, 309, 315.
6. Erwin F. Smith, "Frank N. Meyer," *Science* 48(1918):336.

CHAPTER 2

The chief source for this chapter is van Uildriks, "De Reiziger-Plant Kundige," pp. 2–3, 9–15, 22–23, 42, 50, 54. Additional information is from Leo Derksen, "De Onrust van Frank Meijer," *Panorama* 44, no. 20(1957):4–6; Meyer's two autobiographical letters, November 1, 1909, March 15, 1916 (PI Letters, F. N. Meyer, RG 54, NA); and personal letters written to A. J. Pieters and to P. H. Dorsett in 1902, 1903, and 1904 (PI Letters, F. N. Meyer, RG 54, NA).

1. The names of Meyer's father and siblings are from his will, filed July 18, 1918, Office of the Register of Wills, Probate Division, Superior Court of the District of Columbia, Washington, D.C.
2. Meyer's petition for naturalization, July 21, 1908, Immigration and Naturalization Service, U.S. Department of Justice, Washington, D.C.
3. Donald C. Peattie, "Erwin F. Smith, A Young Man's Impression," *Scientific Monthly* 25(1927):85–86; Harry R. Rosen, "Erwin F. Smith, Friend of Youth," *Mycologia* 19(1927):292–93.

CHAPTER 3

For Meyer's experiences in Mexico, Cuba, and Saint Louis, see van Uildriks, "De Reiziger-Plant Kundige," pp. 41–46, and personal letters to P. H. Dorsett and A. J. Pieters (PI Letters, F. N. Meyer, RG 54, NA).

1. Fairchild, *The World Was My Garden,* p. 315; for the description of Meyer's physical appearance, see Erwin F. Smith, "Frank N. Meyer," *Science* 48(1918):336.
2. Fairchild, *The World Was My Garden,* pp. 289, 312, 313, 316.

CHAPTER 4

This chapter is based on van Uildriks, "De Reiziger-Plant Kundige," pp. 49–56, and Meyer's correspondence with his colleagues at the USDA (PI Letters, F. N. Meyer, RG 54, NA).

1. A letter dated February 18, 1981, from the Library and Records Department, Foreign and Commonwealth Office, London, states that MacGregor worked for the Shanghai Municipal Council from 1904 until 1929; yet the council and the Shanghai *Municipal Gazette* knew him only as D. MacGregor (the signature that he used on his letter to Fairchild). Correspondence with the General Register Office, Edinburgh, Scotland, failed to disclose his first name.
2. Letter to Mansfield, September 16, 1905 (Box 5, PI Records, F. N. Meyer, RG 54, NA).
3. Knowles Ryerson, "Culture of the Oriental Persimmon," *University of California Agricultural Experiment Station Bulletin* 416(1927):36.

CHAPTER 5

See van Uildriks, "De Reiziger-Plant Kundige," pp. 57–59; letters to Dorsett and Fairchild (PI Letters, F. N. Meyer, RG 54, NA); and personal correspondence with Pieters (Box 7, PI Records, F. N. Meyer, RG 54, NA).

1. William L. Ackerman, "After-Ripening Requirements for Germination of Seeds of *Acer truncatum* Bunge," *Proceedings of the American Society for Horticultural Science* 69(1957):570.

2. Claire S. Haughton, *Green Immigrants* (New York, 1978), p. 332. Haughton describes the crisis that occurred when the 80,000 acres in South Carolina devoted in 1900 to the cultivation of rice dwindled within six years to 19,000 acres as a result of heavy lumbering above the coastal plain.
3. Fairchild, *The World Was My Garden,* pp. 316–18. Only one of the original cherry trees remains at In the Woods. The Outdoor Nursery School now occupies the premises. Children attending the school climb other trees, but they learn to treat "the Granddaddy tree" with affectionate respect. The dove tree (*Davidia involucrata*) that Meyer suggested planting there also survives.

CHAPTER 6

Meyer's letters to Fairchild, Dorsett, and Pieters form the framework of this chapter (PI Letters, F. N. Meyer, RG 54, NA). One personal letter to Pieters is in Box 7, PI Records, F. N. Meyer, RG 54, NA.

1. According to W. F. Donald, "China as a Most Promising Field for Plant Exploration," *Far Eastern Review* 12, no. 2(1915):48, the American consul general at Seoul said that Meyer had to slide down a mountainside to escape an attack by a tiger and then wired, "Attacked by a tiger. Send me some trousers." Meyer denied this story, explaining it as an attempt to relieve the tedium of a consulship at Seoul.
2. Ryerson, "History and Significance of Foreign Plant Introduction Work," p. 126; Sam Burgess, ed., *The National Program for Conservation of Crop Germ Plasm, A Progress Report on Federal/State Cooperation* (Athens, University of Georgia, 1971) p. 56. (This publication is largely the work of Dr. John L. Creech, then director of the New Crops Program.)
3. Alfred Rehder, "New Species, Varieties, and Combinations from the Herbarium and the Collections of the Arnold Arboretum," *Journal of the Arnold Arboretum* 2, no. 2(1920):123.

CHAPTER 7

See van Uildriks, "De Reiziger-Plant Kundige," pp. 64, 66–68, 79, and Meyer's letters to his associates in Washington (PI Letters, F. N. Meyer, RG 54, NA). A personal letter to Pieters is in Box 7, PI Records, F. N. Meyer, RG 54, NA.

1. Fairchild to Meyer, May 17, 1906 (Box 7, PI Records, F. N. Meyer, RG 54, NA).
2. Though Fairchild placed this incident at Harbin in his articles in *Asia* and in the *National Geographic,* as well as in his autobiography, Meyer's original letter describing the attack was written at Khabarovsk on November 22, 1906, before he traveled to Harbin.

CHAPTER 8

Meyer's letters to Fairchild and to Dorsett (PI Letters, F. N. Meyer, RG 54, NA) and Fairchild's letters to Meyer (Box 7, PI Records, F. N. Meyer, RG 54, NA) tell this story.

1. Stephanne B. Sutton, *Charles S. Sargent and the Arnold Arboretum* (Cambridge, Mass., 1970), p. 233.
2. van Uildriks, "De Reiziger-Plant Kundige," pp. 68–69.
3. Sutton, *Charles S. Sargent,* p. 237.
4. Fairchild, *The World Was My Garden,* p. 381.
5. Peter Bisset, "Frank Meyer's Rose Contribution," *American Rose Annual,* 1919, p. 39. See

also Charles S. Sargent, ed., *Plantae Wilsonianae,* Publication of the Arnold Arboretum no. 4, 2, part 2: 342. Sargent wrote, "The species was based by Lindley on a Chinese drawing of a double-flowered yellow Rose. This double Rose seems to have remained practically unknown until it was sent to Washington from Peking by Frank N. Meyer in 1907."

CHAPTER 9

Meyer's correspondence with Fairchild (PI Letters, F. N. Meyer, RG 54, NA) and with his parents (van Uildriks, "De Reiziger-Plant Kundige," pp. 83–85) form the basis for this chapter.

1. Elsewhere Meyer referred to this handgun as a revolver; however, this passage indicates that he carried a pistol, probably the Mauser model 1896 semiautomatic pistol nicknamed the "Broomhandle" because of the shape of the removable butt stock. Before the late 1890s, all handguns were single shot or revolvers. The semantic distinction between pistols and revolvers developed later. (Information from Woodward Arms, Annapolis, Md.)
2. From a letter written in China by Ambassador Nelson T. Johnson to his family in 1937. Neither Meyer nor Fairchild ever mentioned this incident, but an unsigned article ("The People Who Stand for Plus," *Outing* 53[1908]:69) relates that Meyer woke one night in Mongolia to find the knives of two would-be assassins within inches of his throat.
3. From a letter written from China to his family by Ambassador Nelson T. Johnson in 1937. Time dimmed his recollection in one respect. Ants herd aphids rather than aphids herding ants.

CHAPTER 10

This chapter depends primarily on Meyer's correspondence with Fairchild (PI Letters, F. N. Meyer, RG 54, NA).

1. Bisset, "Frank N. Meyer's Rose Contribution," p. 40.
2. For the lemon, see Roland McKee, "Chinese Dwarf Meyer Lemon Introduced," *Yearbook of Agriculture, 1926,* USDA, Washington, D.C., pp. 218–21. For the juniper, see Alfred Rehder, "New Species, Varieties, and Combinations from the Herbarium and Collections of the Arnold Arboretum," *Journal of the Arnold Arboretum* 3, no. 4(1922):207. For the lilac, see Donald G. Hoag, "Meyer Lilac: An Attractive Dwarf Shrub," *North Dakota Farm Bureau Research Bimonthly Bulletin* (a publication of the North Dakota State University Agricultural Experiment Station) 23, no. 9(1965):22–23.
3. Fairchild to Meyer, April 27, 1908 (Box 7, PI Records, F. N. Meyer, RG 54, NA); Frank Baker to Fairchild (Box 8, PI Records, F. N. Meyer, RG 54, NA).

CHAPTER 11

In addition to Meyer's letters to Fairchild (PI Letters, F. N. Meyer, RG 54, NA), sources include Fairchild, *The World Was My Garden,* pp. 345–47, and van Uildriks, "De Reiziger-Plant Kundige," pp. 89–91.

1. Fairchild's essay at the end of the volume entitled "The Published Descriptions of Seeds and Plants Collected in North and Central China, Manchuria, North Korea, and Eastern Siberia by Mr. Frank N. Meyer from September, 1905, to June 12, 1908," vol. 110, Project Studies, RG 54, NA.

2. J. W. Morrison, "Marquis Wheat – A Triumph of Scientific Endeavor," *Agricultural History* 34, no. 4(1960):182–88. Fairchild tells the story in *The World Was My Garden,* p. 438.
3. Meyer's note is attached to a clipping from the Coleman, South Dakota, newspaper dated August 27, 1908 (Box 7, PI Records, F. N. Meyer, RG 54, NA).
4. Klose, *America's Crop Heritage,* p. 124.
5. Fairchild to Meyer, September 28, 1908 (Box 9, PI Records, F. N. Meyer, RG 54, NA); Fairchild, *The World Was My Garden,* p. 381.
6. A flier announcing Meyer's lecture and clippings from the Brownsville *Daily Herald,* January 4, 6, 1909, supplement Meyer's account (Box 9, PI Records, F. N. Meyer, RG 54, NA).
7. Meyer's manuscript and the photographs that he chose as illustrations are in Box 6, PI Records, F. N. Meyer, RG 54, NA.

CHAPTER 12

See Meyer's letters to Fairchild, Robert A. Young, and Dorsett (PI Letters, F. N. Meyer, RG 54, NA) and also Fairchild's letters to Meyer (Box 8, PI Records, F. N. Meyer, RG 54, NA).

1. Sylvester March, supervisory horticulturist, U.S. National Arboretum.
2. Albert F. Dodge, William L. Ackerman, and Harold F. Winters, "Performance of Three Privet Introductions in the Upper Midwest," *American Horticultural Magazine* 44, no. 2(1965):92–93, 97–98.

CHAPTER 13

Meyer's letters to Fairchild, Dorsett, and Pieters provide the basis for this chapter (PI Letters, F. N. Meyer, RG 54, NA).

1. van Uildriks, "De Reiziger-Plant Kundige," p. 94.
2. Fairchild to Meyer, April 25, 1910 (Box 10, PI Records, F. N. Meyer, RG 54, NA).

CHAPTER 14

Except for three letters to Dorsett and Bisset, Meyer's letters to Fairchild form the framework of this chapter (PI Letters, F. N. Meyer, RG 54, NA).

1. Letters from the Smithsonian Institution dated November 25, 1910, December 12, 1910 (Box 9, PI Records, F. N. Meyer, RG 54, NA).
2. Donald C. Peattie, "Plant Hunters," *Yale Review* 34(1944):59.

CHAPTER 15

See Meyer's correspondence with Fairchild, Dorsett, and Bisset (PI Letters, F. N. Meyer, RG 54, NA). Meyer's itinerary report adds details of the journey south of Yarkand (Box 10, PI Records, F. N. Meyer, RG 54, NA).

1. Chinese Turkestan Exploration, Supplementary Report, November 1, 1911, p. 1, in "Foreign Exploration: Closed Projects," vol. 76, Project Studies, RG 54, NA.

2. Fairchild to Meyer, March, 1911 (Box 9, PI Records, F. N. Meyer, RG 54, NA).
3. Meyer to A. J. Pieters, January 27, 1911 (Box 9, PI Records, F. N. Meyer, RG 54, NA).

CHAPTER 16

Meyer's correspondence with Fairchild (PI Letters, F. N. Meyer, RG 54, NA) and his itinerary report for 1911 (Box 10, PI Records, F. N. Meyer, RG 54, NA) tell this story.

1. van Uildriks, "De Reiziger-Plant Kundige," pp. 148–50.

CHAPTER 17

This chapter is based on Meyer's letters to Fairchild (PI Letters, F. N. Meyer, RG 54, NA) and on van Uildriks, "De Reiziger-Plant Kundige," pp. 149–51.

1. Frank N. Meyer, *Agricultural Explorations in the Fruit and Nut Orchards of China,* Bulletin 204, Bureau of Plant Industry, USDA, Washington, D.C., 1911.

CHAPTER 18

Meyer's letters to Fairchild and one letter to Dorsett are the chief sources of this chapter (PI Letters, F. N. Meyer, RG 54, NA).

1. This letter (and others) from Meyer to Hugo de Vries are the property of the de Vries Plant Laboratory, University of Amsterdam.
2. Fairchild to Meyer, June 22 and July 19, 1911, Box 10; March 19, 1913, Box 12 (PI Records, F. N. Meyer, RG 54, NA).
3. Fairchild to W. W. Rockhill, July 17, 1914 (Box 16, PI Records, F. N. Meyer, RG 54, NA).

CHAPTER 19

Meyer's correspondence with Fairchild (PI Letters, F. N. Meyer, RG 54, NA) and his itinerary report (Box 10, PI Records, F. N. Meyer, RG 54, NA) form the framework of this chapter.

1. Burgess, ed., *The National Program for Conservation of Crop Germ Plasm,* p. 43.
2. Fairchild to Meyer, January 12, 1912 (Box 10, PI Records, F. N. Meyer, RG 54, NA).
3. van Uildriks, "De Reiziger-Plant Kundige," pp. 152–54.

CHAPTER 20

See letters and memoranda from Meyer to Fairchild and Dorsett (PI Letters, F. N. Meyer, RG 54, NA) and letters to Meyer (Box 11, PI Records, F. N. Meyer, RG 54, NA).

1. Frank N. Meyer, *Chinese Plant Names* (New York, 1911).
2. A copy of this bulletin is in Box 5, PI Records, F. N. Meyer, RG 54, NA.
3. Fairchild, "An Agricultural Explorer in China," *Asia* 21(1920):7, and *The World Was My Garden,* pp. 398–99.

4. Meyer's itinerary reports (Box 10, PI Records, F. N. Meyer, RG 54, NA).
5. E. I. Farrington, *Ernest H. Wilson: Plant Hunter* (Boston, 1931), p. 96.

CHAPTER 21

Sources include Meyer's letters to Fairchild, Dorsett, Grace Cramer, and Beagles (PI Letters, F. N. Meyer, RG 54, NA); correspondence from Fairchild, Dorsett, and Cramer (Box 12, PI Records, F. N. Meyer, RG 54, NA); van Uildriks, "De Reiziger-Plant Kundige," pp. 156–58.

1. Coats, *The Plant Hunters,* p. 132.
2. In addition to Fairchild's letters to Meyer, see his accounts of these events in *The World Was My Garden,* pp. 405–6, and in "The Discovery of the Chestnut Bark Disease in China," *Science,* n.s., 38, no. 974(1913):197–99.
3. Fairchild, *The World Was My Garden,* p. 107.

CHAPTER 22

Meyer's correspondence with Fairchild, Dorsett, Cramer, Bisset, and Beagles (PI Letters, F. N. Meyer, RG 54, NA) forms the framework of this chapter.

1. USDA form, "Data to be Furnished in Recommending Promotion of Scientific Employees" (Box 12, PI Records, F. N. Meyer, RG 54, NA).
2. H. N. Fisher, "Ligustrum Quihoui: A Plant Worth Using," *American Nurseryman* 101, no. 2(1955):10. (Dr. William L. Ackerman, research horticulturist, located and measured the hedge at Glenn Dale, Md.)
3. Mailing the two trees separately proved fortunate, for the other six did not arrive safely. The one tree received at Chico was "only fair" and twenty of the cuttings "alive but poor." A year later Beagles nevertheless had grown seven "first-class trees of this lot." (Supplementary Report, December 31, 1914, pp. 14–15, in "Northwestern China Exploration, 1912–1915," vol. 77, Project Studies, RG 54, NA).

CHAPTER 23

See Meyer's letters to Fairchild, Cramer, Bisset, and Beagles (PI Letters, F. N. Meyer, RG 54, NA) and his itinerary report (Box 10, PI Records, F. N. Meyer, RG 54, NA). Letters to Meyer from Fairchild, Cramer, and Bisset, and to Fairchild from Beagles and Sargent are in Box 13, PI Records, F. N. Meyer, RG 54, NA.

1. Vivian Wiser, *Protecting American Agriculture: Inspection and Quarantine of Imported Plants and Animals,* USDA Agricultural Economic Report 206 (Washington, 1974), p. 19. See also Roland M. Jefferson and Alan E. Fusonie, *The Japanese Flowering Cherry Trees of Washington, D.C.,* National Arboretum Contribution 4, Agricultural Research Service, USDA (Washington, 1977), pp. 7–15. This bulletin relates the part that Fairchild played in bringing the flowering cherry trees to Washington.
2. Fairchild, *The World Was My Garden,* p. 443.
3. Coats, *The Plant Hunters,* p. 133.
4. Fairchild, *The World Was My Garden,* pp. 338–39.
5. van Uildriks, "De Reiziger-Plant Kundige," p. 162.
6. Frank N. Meyer, "China, a Fruitful Field for Plant Exploration," *Yearbook of Agriculture, 1915,* USDA, Washington, D.C., p. 218. See also U. P. Hedrick et al., *The Peaches of New York,* Annual Report of the New York Department of Agriculture, 1916 (Albany, 1917), pp. 5, 6, 79.

CHAPTER 24

Meyer's four letters to Fairchild (PI Letters, F. N. Meyer, RG 54, NA) and his itinerary reports (PI Records, F. N. Meyer, RG 54, NA) are important sources for this chapter.

1. Meyer, "China, a Fruitful Field for Plant Exploration," *Yearbook of Agriculture, 1915,* USDA, Washington, D.C., p. 220.
2. Coats, *The Plant Hunters,* p. 132.
3. Reginald Farrer, "Mr. Reginald Farrer's Explorations in China," *Gardeners' Chronicle,* Series 3, 56:347; Farrer, *On the Eaves of the World,* vol. 2(London, 1917), p. 276.
4. Farrer, *On the Eaves of the World,* vol. 2, p. 276, and Farrer, *Gardeners' Chronicle,* Series 3, 58:1.
5. Farrer, *On the Eaves of the World,* p. 280; Farrer, *Gardeners' Chronicle,* Series 3, 58:1.
6. Coats, *The Plant Hunters,* p. 137; Healy, *The Plant Hunters,* p. 177. Both authors also follow Farrer in adding that Meyer had "similar trouble with his servants on other occasions." See p. 271–72 of the text for refutation of this charge.
7. Farrer, *On the Eaves of the World,* pp. 279–80; *Gardeners' Chronicle,* Series 3, 58:1.
8. Donald, "China as a Most Promising Field for Exploration," pp. 43–44; U. P. Hedrick et al., *The Peaches of New York,* pp. 3–5; Walter T. Swingle's memorandum concerning the wild peach and the bush almond (Box 12, PI Records, F. N. Meyer, RG 54, NA).

CHAPTER 25

See letters to Fairchild, Dorsett, and Grace Cramer (PI Letters, F. N. Meyer, RG 54, NA). Meyer's itinerary report is the only source for his journey back to Peking (Box 10, PI Records, RG 54, NA).

1. Meyer's will, filed July 18, 1918, Washington, D.C.
2. Meyer's letter to Paul S. Reinsch, American minister at Peking, April 3, 1914. (Because his original letter was lost in transit, he rewrote it in April.) Supplementary Report, December 1915, pp. 15-18 in "Northwestern China Explorations, 1912–1915," vol. 77, Project Studies, RG 54, NA. Meyer did not mention this incident in his letters to Washington, but he did ask Dr. Reinsch to send a copy of his letter to Fairchild.
3. E. I. Farrington, *Ernest H. Wilson: Plant Hunter,* p. 8. Wilson himself rarely rode in a sedan chair, but he explained that it must "go along with the party as an indication of the traveler's rank and authority." Farrer considered himself a "pathetic and heroic figure" when he made a journey accompanied only by a cook, a chamberlain, a groom, three soldiers, and four donkeymen (*Gardeners' Chronicle,* Series 3, 57:215).
4. Reinsch's reply follows Meyer's letter, note 2, above. Reinsch assured Meyer that the American Legation at Peking had made "vigorous representations" to the Chinese Foreign Office.
5. Cramer to Meyer, June 20, 1914 (Box 13, PI Records, F. N. Meyer, RG 54, NA). Winfield Scott Clime made the first motion pictures of men harvesting crops and was among the first to photograph airplanes in flight. After serving as a captain in World War I, he left the USDA and became an artist. He and Grace Cramer Clime lived in Chevy Chase, Maryland, and Old Lyme, Connecticut, before retiring to Florida. (Harold F. Winters, USDA, retired, who owns one of Clime's paintings, contributed this information.)
6. van Uildriks, "De Reiziger-Plant Kundige," p. 162.

CHAPTER 26

See Meyer's letters to Fairchild and to Grace Cramer Clime (PI Letters, F. N. Meyer, RG 54, NA); Meyer's itinerary (Box 10, PI Records, F. N. Meyer, RG 54, NA); van Uildriks, "De Reiziger-Plant Kundige," pp. 162–66.

1. Personal letter to Fairchild, June 21, 1915. This letter is now at the Fairchild Tropical Garden library, 10901 Old Cutter Road, Miami, Florida, Dr. John Popenoe, Director.
2. Donald, "China as a Most Promising Field for Plant Exploration," pp. 41–48. Donald wrote, "Although Mr. Meyer makes light of the dangers which he undergoes and the privations he must suffer, and mentions his difficulties only casually in connection with other things than his own personal comfort, a plant explorer must forego not only the ordinary luxuries of life, but almost its every comfort as well."
3. Sargent to Meyer, December 22, 1915, Supplemental Report, December 31, 1915, p. 63 in "Northwestern China Explorations, 1912–1915," vol. 77, RG 54, NA.
4. Jefferson and Fusonie, *The Japanese Flowering Cherry Trees of Washington,* pp. 7, 45; Fairchild, *The World Was My Garden,* p. 412.
5. Fairchild, *The World Was My Garden,* p. 443. USDA photographs 19433 and 19434 showing Fairchild greeting Meyer, who is carrying the cycad, are in the album picturing Meyer's travels from April 23 to September 14, 1915. This album is now in the library of the National Arboretum in Washington.

CHAPTER 27

Sources for this chapter include Meyer's letters to Dorsett, Fairchild, and Grace Clime (PI Letters, F. N. Meyer, RG 54, NA); Dorsett's letters to Meyer (Box 15, PI Records, F. N. Meyer, RG 54, NA); Fairchild, *The World Was My Garden,* pp. 381, 436, 443, 444, 454, 464.

1. McIlhenny also grew many acres of chili peppers for the manufacture of the Tabasco sauce that is still marketed by his family.
2. Frank N. Meyer, "Economic and Botanical Explorations in China," *Transactions of the Massachusetts Horticultural Society,* Part I (1916), pp. 125–30.
3. Frank N. Meyer, "China, a Fruitful Field for Plant Exploration," *Yearbook of Agriculture, 1915,* USDA, Washington, D.C., pp. 205–24.
4. The Washington Beltway bisected In the Woods, just missing the house itself. Several remaining acres of the property inside the Beltway and south of Connecticut Avenue are now owned by the Chevy Chase Recreational Association. Despite great losses of rare plant material, according to Dr. Frederick G. Meyer, supervisory botanist at the National Arboretum, a small but valuable collection of trees remains. This collection is protected by a group called Friends of In the Woods. The property is located at 8922 Spring Valley Road, Chevy Chase, Maryland 20015.
5. Fairchild, "An Agricultural Explorer in China," p. 13.
6. van Uildriks, "De Reiziger-Plant Kundige," p. 50.

CHAPTER 28

Meyer's letters to Bisset, Clime, Chandler, Dorsett, Fairchild, Howell, and Stuntz reflect his loneliness (PI Letters, F. N. Meyer, RG 54, NA). Letters and a cable from Fairchild and Dorsett to Meyer are in Box 15, PI Records, F. N. Meyer, RG 54, NA.

1. Letter from the auditor of Meyer's accounts, February 6, 1917 (Box 11, PI Records, F. N. Meyer, RG 54, NA).
2. Meyer's official accounts, November 18, 21, 1916 (Box 11, PI Records, F. N. Meyer, RG 54, NA).
3. Meyer discussed this problem in letters to Fairchild, Dorsett, Bisset, and Stuntz (PI Letters, F. N. Meyer, RG 54, NA). Fairchild commented on it in *The World Was My Garden,* pp. 424–25. For a balanced account of quarantine enforcement in this period, see Vivian Wiser, *Protecting American Agriculture,* pp. 17–22.

CHAPTER 29

The chief sources of this chapter are Meyer's letters to Fairchild, Bisset, Chandler, Dorsett, Galloway, Herbert Howell, Stuntz, and Young (PI Letters, F. N. Meyer, RG 54, NA); Meyer's itinerary (Box 11, PI Records, F. N. Meyer, RG 54, NA); letters to Meyer from Bisset, Dorsett, Fairchild, Murrill, and L. H. Bailey (Box 15, PI Records, F. N. Meyer, RG 54, NA); Meyer's letters to Reisner and Reimer (Box 16, PI Records, F. N. Meyer, RG 54, NA).

1. C. C. Thomas, "Chinese Elm in American Horticulture," *Yearbook of Agriculture, 1926,* USDA, Washington, D.C., p. 217.
2. Proposed resignation (Box 17, PI Records, F. N. Meyer, RG 54, NA).
3. van Uildriks, "De Reiziger-Plant Kundige," pp. 168–70.

CHAPTER 30

Meyer's letters to Bisset, Beagles, Chandler, Dorsett, Fairchild, Nathan Menderson, Stuntz, and Young (PI Letters, F. N. Meyer, RG 54, NA); his itinerary reports (Box 11, PI Records, F. N. Meyer, RG 54, NA); his correspondence with Reisner, Reimer, and Fairchild (Box 16, PI Records, F. N. Meyer, RG 54, NA) form the basis for this chapter.

1. For an account of the fiasco that occurred when the War Department tried to grow castor beans in America, see Fairchild, *The World Was My Garden,* pp. 463–64.
2. F. C. Reimer, "Report of a Trip to the Orient to Collect and Study Oriental Pears," pp. 4–6. This unpublished report was made available by Dr. Melvin N. Westwood, Department of Horticulture, Oregon State University, Corvallis.

CHAPTER 31

See Meyer's itinerary report (Box 11, PI Records, F. N. Meyer, RG 54, NA); Meyer's infrequent letters to Fairchild and Chandler (PI Letters, F. N. Meyer, RG 54, NA); his correspondence with Reisner and Liberty Hyde Bailey (Box 16, PI Records, F. N. Meyer, RG 54, NA).

1. Edward Gilchrist to Harlan P. Kelsey, USDA, July 15, 1930 (Box 16, PI Records, F. N. Meyer, RG 54, NA).
2. van Uildriks, "De Reiziger-Plant Kundige," p. 170.
3. Statement of Meyer's guide to Vice Consul Sokobin (Box 17, PI Records, F. N. Meyer, RG 54, NA).
4. Yao-feng Ting's statement to Sokobin and the report of R. P. Tenney (Box 17, PI Records, F. N. Meyer, RG 54, NA).
5. Statement of Ting to Sokobin and of the deck steward to R. P. Tenney (Box 17, PI Records, F. N. Meyer, RG 54, NA).

CHAPTER 32

The chief source of information about Meyer's death is the report that Sokobin filed on June 12, 1918 (Box 17, PI Records, F. N. Meyer, RG 54, NA). This report includes the statements by Meyer's guide and by the customs officer at Tikeng, as well as Form 192, Report on the Death of a U.S. citizen.

1. For the walking stick, see Leo Derksen, "De Onrust van Frank Meijer," *Panorama* 44, no.

20(1957):4, photograph, p. 6; for the dinner jacket, see Fairchild, "An Agricultural Explorer in China," *Asia*, p. 7.
2. Jan F. Meyer to Fairchild, August 22, 28, 1918 (Box 17, PI Records, F. N. Meyer, RG 54, NA).
3. *Horticulture* 28(1918):60; *American Nurseryman* 28, no. 1(1918):12, 14.
4. For Sargent's letter, see Sutton, *Charles S. Sargent*, p. 260. The comment about Sargent appears in S. B. Sutton, *In China's Border Provinces* (New York, 1974), p. 80.
5. Donald, "China as a Most Promising Field," p. 48.

CHAPTER 33

The letters of condolence, Fairchild's account of the memorial service, and Fairchild's correspondence with Jan F. Meyer are in Box 17, PI Records, F. N. Meyer, RG 54, NA.

1. Meyer's will, filed July 18, 1918, Washington, D.C.
2. Dr. Frederick G. Meyer rescued the photograph albums when the contents of a storeroom at the Agricultural Research Center were about to be discarded. Dr. John L. Creech salvaged Meyer's original negatives and prints. Though two albums later were taken to the USDA Photo Library and subsequently discarded, the remaining ten albums and many of the negatives and prints are at the National Arboretum in Washington, D.C.
3. Erwin F. Smith, "Frank N. Meyer," *Science* 48(1918):336.
4. Administration of Meyer's estate by the American Security and Trust Company, Washington, D.C., Administration 25027; Leo Derksen, "De Onrust van Frank Meijer," *Panorama* 44, no. 20(1957):5; Treasury Department to Dorsett, December 16, 1918, January 14, 1919 (Box 11, PI Records, F. N. Meyer, RG 54, NA).
5. Fairchild, "Foreign Plant Introduction Medal," *Journal of Heredity* 11, no. 4(1920):169–70.
6. Fairchild's and Galloway's proposals and L. H. Bailey's letter are in Box 16; letters from Wilson and Hicks are in Box 17, PI Records, F. N. Meyer, RG 54, NA.
7. Morrison's letter, January 5, 1931 (Box 16, PI Records, F. N. Meyer, RG 54, NA).
8. On August 18, 1924, Dorsett visited Meyer's grave (plot B, 324-12.6.18). He judged it to be in the northwest corner of the cemetery and described the marker and the planting (Dorsett, "China Trip," vol. 2, pp. 1217–19, in vol. 41, Project Studies, RG 54, NA).
9. In 1974 when Dr. John L. Creech went to China as a representative of the USDA Agricultural Research Service and attempted to visit Meyer's grave, he discovered that the cemetery had become a public park. This park is east of the Children's Palace within the triangle formed by Yenan Zhong, Nanjing Hsi, and Shin Men Streets. (A letter from the Library and Records Department, Foreign and Commonwealth Office, London, dated February 18, 1981, explains that the Bubbling Well Cemetery occupied a square formed by Bubbling Well Road [now Nanjing Hsi] to the north, Hart Road to the east, Avenue Foch [now Yenan Zhong] to the south, and Jessfield Road to the west.)

CHAPTER 34

1. Donald, "China as a Most Promising Field," p. 43.
2. Fairchild, *The World Was My Garden*, p. 371.
3. In 1942 the USDA transferred this program to the Soil Conservation Service. For a detailed discussion of this project, see "Windbreaks and Shelterbelts," Joseph H. Stoecheler and Ross A. Williams, pp. 191–99, *Trees, the Yearbook of Agriculture, 1949*, USDA, Washington, D.C.
4. I am indebted to Dr. Frederick G. Meyer and to Dr. John L. Creech for information about the current uses of Meyer's shade trees and ornamentals.

5. F. F. Weinard and H. B. Dorner, "Rosa Odorata as a Grafting Stock for Indoor Roses," *University of Illinois Agricultural Experiment Station Bulletin* 290(1927):455–62; Bisset, "Frank N. Meyer's Rose Contribution," pp. 39–40.

6. H. N. Fisher, "Ligustrum Quihoui: A Plant Worth Using," *American Nurseryman* 101, no. 2(1955):10.

7. William E. Whitehouse, John L. Creech, and G. A. Seaton, "Bradford Ornamental Pear—A Promising Shade Tree," *American Nurseryman* 117, no. 8(1963):7–8, 56–60; John L. Creech, "Ornamental Plant Introduction: Building on the Past," *Arnoldia* 33, no. 1(1973):20; Dennis Farney, "Meet the Men Who Risked Their Lives to Find New Plants," *Smithsonian* 11, no. 3(1980):129, 140. (See appendix A, *Pyrus calleryana,* PI 47261, for the origin of the parent stock of Bradford, PI 209840.)

8. William L. Ackerman, "Whitehouse Ornamental Pear," *Horticultural Science* 12, no. 6(1977):591–92. Whitehouse (PI 420995) and Capital (PI 459102) are seedling progeny of Bradford (PI 209840), a selected seedling of PI 47261.

9. Dr. Harold W. Fogle, Fruit Laboratory, Agricultural Research Center, Beltsville, Md., furnished this information about the current value of Meyer's wild peach. Dr. Kay Ryugo, Department of Pomology, University of California at Davis, researched the origin of the Nemaguard peach.

10. Dr. Catherine H. Bailey, professor emeritus, who worked on this project with Dr. Frederick Hough at Cook College of Agriculture, Rutgers, the State University of New Jersey, New Brunswick. The Fei peach at Rutgers was collected in 1933 by Peter Liu of Peking in villages south of Feicheng. I am indebted to Howard Hyland, retired chief plant introduction officer, USDA Agricultural Research Center at Beltsville, Md., for guiding me to Rutgers.

11. Harold F. Winters, retired chief of the Germplasm Laboratory, and Dr. Harold W. Fogle, Fruit Laboratory, USDA Agricultural Research Center, Beltsville, Md.

12. F. C. Reimer et al., "The Southern Oregon Branch Experiment Station: Its Development, Program, and Accomplishments, 1911–1962," Special Report 156, Oregon State University, Agricultural Experiment Station, Corvallis (July 1963), pp. 4–5. (This report and related information were made available by Dr. Melvin N. Westwood, professor of horticulture, Oregon State University, Corvallis.)

13. Paul M. Lyrene, "The Jujube Tree (*Zizyphus jujuba*)," *Fruit Varieties Jounral* 33, no. 3(1979):101–4; letters to the author dated March 31, 1981, July 22, 1982, August 24, 1982.

14. Roland McKee, "Chinese Dwarf Meyer Lemon Introduced," pp. 218–21.

15. Sam Burgess, ed., *The National Program for Conservation of Crop Germ Plasm,* p. 43.

16. Walter T. Swingle, "Trees and Plants We Owe to China," *Asia* 43(1943):295–96; Knowles Ryerson, "Plant Explorers Bring Valuable New Species," *Yearbook of Agriculture, 1932,* USDA, Washington, D.C., p. 298.

17. Deborah G. Strauss, managing ed., "Northwest Plant Germplasm Repository Director Reports on Successful East Asian Exploration," *Diversity* 1, no. 1(1982):13-14.

18. See Sutton's biography of Rock, *In China's Border Provinces,* and a series of articles that Rock wrote for the *National Geographic* from March, 1922, through October, 1935. After 1934 he devoted his time to ethnological studies.

19. Interview with Dr. Theodore R. Dudley of the National Arboretum.

20. Letter to the author, January 1, 1983.

21. Euan H. M. Cox, *Plant Hunting in China,* p. 192; B. J. Healy, *The Plant Hunters,* pp. 3, 177; Tyler Whittle, *The Plant Hunters,* p. 225.

CHAPTER 35

Letters from E. H. Wilson, C. G. Pfeiffer, and George Mitchell are in Box 17, PI Records, F. N. Meyer, RG 54, NA.

1. Coats, *The Plant Hunters,* p. 137; Healy, *The Plant Hunters,* p. 177.

2. Fairchild, Meyer's obituary in *Plant Immigrants,* Bulletin 142, Office of Foreign Seed and Plant Introduction, USDA, p. 1284 (dated February, 1918, which was before Meyer's death, but published January, 1919).

BIBLIOGRAPHY

MANUSCRIPT AND RECORDS COLLECTIONS

1. National Archives and Records Service—Record Group 54: Records of the Bureau of Plant Industry, Division of Plant Exploration.

   Project Studies:
   Vol. 41: "China Trip," Records of P. H. Dorsett.
   Vol. 76: "Foreign Exploration: Closed Projects, 1905–1915."
   Vol. 77: "Northwestern China Exploration, 1912–1915."
   Vols. 105–109: "Letters of Frank N. Meyer."
   Vol. 110: "Published Descriptions of Seeds and Plants Collected in North and Central China, Manchuria, North Korea, and East Siberia by Mr. Frank N. Meyer from September 1, 1905, to June 12, 1908."
   Vol. 149: "Explorations and Itineraries, 1897–1932."

   Reports, Notes, and Other Records of Frank N. Meyer, Boxes 3–18.
   Explorers, Maps and Routes, Box 32.

2. U.S. National Arboretum, Washington, D.C.

   Photographs taken by Frank N. Meyer on his journeys, June 1, 1907–March 24, 1917, Office of Foreign Seed and Plant Introduction, Bureau of Plant Industry, USDA. (Ten albums remain at the National Arboretum after the USDA Photo Library discarded two. Meyer's descriptive captions accompany the photographs and the negatives in the arboretum files.)

3. U.S. Immigration and Naturalization Service, Department of Justice, Washington, D.C.

   Petition for Naturalization, Frank N. Meyer, July 21, 1908.

4. Superior Court of the District of Columbia, Office of the Register of Wills, Clerk of the Probate Division.

   Administration of the estate of Frank N. Meyer by the American Security and Trust Company, Administration #25027.

   Will of Frank N. Meyer, filed July 18, 1918.

5. Other unpublished papers:

   Johnson, Nelson T. Letter to his family, 1937. This letter from the first American ambassador to China is quoted with the permission of his daughter, Betty Jane Johnson Gerber (Mrs. George C. Gerber), of McLean, Virginia.

   Meyer, Frank N. Letters to Hugo de Vries. These letters were provided by the Hugo de Vries Plant Laboratory, University of Amsterdam, Holland.

   Reimer, F. C. "Report of a Trip to the Orient to Collect and Study Oriental Pears," circa 1918. This report, which is filed at the Oregon Agricultural Experiment Station, Oregon State University, Corvallis, was made available by Dr. Melvin N. Westwood of the Department of Horticulture.

PUBLISHED MATERIAL

Ackerman, William L. "After-Ripening Requirements for Germination of Seeds of *Acer truncatum* Bunge." *Proceedings of the American Society for Horticultural Science* 69(1957):570–73.

―――. "Flowering, Pollination, Self-Sterility and Seed Development of the Chinese Jujube." *Proceedings of the American Society for Horticultural Science* 77(1961):265–69.

―――. " 'Whitehouse' Ornamental Pear." *Horticultural Science* 12, no. 6 (1977): 591–92.

Bisset, Peter. "Frank N. Meyer's Rose Contribution." *American Rose Annual* 1919, pp. 38–41.

Burgess, Sam, ed. *The National Program for Conservation of Crop Germ Plasm: A Progress Report on Federal/State Cooperation.* Athens: University of Georgia, 1971.
  This publication was prepared by a committee representing the agencies cooperating in the New Crops Program and is largely the work of the chairman, Dr. John L. Creech.

Coats, Alice M. *The Plant Hunters.* New York: McGraw-Hill, 1969.

Cox, Euan H. M. *Plant Hunting in China.* London: Collins, 1946.

Creech, John L. "Ornamental Plant Introduction: Building on the Past." *Arnoldia* (a publication of the Arnold Arboretum) 33, no. 1(1973):13–25.

Derksen, Leo. "De Onrust van Frank Meijer" ("The Restless Frank Meyer"). *Panorama* 44, no. 20(1957):4–6.

Dodge, Albert F., William L. Ackerman, and Harold F. Winters. "Performance of Three Privet Introductions in the Upper Midwest." *American Horticultural Magazine* 44, no. 2(1965):92–98.

Donald, W. H. "China as a Most Promising Field for Plant Exploration." *Far Eastern Review* 12, no. 2 (1915):41–48.

Fairchild, David. "The Discovery of the Chestnut Blight Disease in China." *Science,* n.s. 38, no. 974 (1913):297–99.

―――. "The Dramatic Careers of Two Plantsmen." *Journal of Heredity* 10, no. 6(1919):276–80.

―――. "A Hunter of Plants." *National Geographic Magazine* 36(1919):57–77.

―――. Obituary, Frank N. Meyer. *Plant Immigrants,* Bulletin 142, Office of Foreign Seed and Plant Introduction, Bureau of Plant Industry, USDA, Washington, D.C., 1919, pp. 1282–87 (dated February 1918, but published January 1919).

―――. "An Agricultural Explorer in China." *Asia* 21(1920):7–13.

―――. "Foreign Plant Introduction Medal." *Journal of Heredity* 11, no. 4(1920): 168–70.

―――. *The World Was My Garden.* New York: Charles Scribner's Sons, 1938.

Farney, Dennis. "Meet the Men Who Risked Their Lives to Find New Plants." *Smithsonian* 11, no. 3(1980):128–40.

Farrer, Reginald. "Mr. Reginald Farrer's Explorations in China." *Gardeners' Chronicle,* Series 3, 56 (1914): 347–48; 57(1915):109, 193, 337, 338; 58(1915):1.

―――. *On the Eaves of the World.* 2 vols. London: E. Arnold, 1917.

Farrington, Edward I. *Ernest H. Wilson: Plant Hunter.* Boston: Stratford, 1931.

Fisher, H. N. "Ligustrum Quihoui: A Plant Worth Using." *American Nurseryman* 101, no. 2(1955):10.

Haughton, Claire S. *Green Immigrants.* New York: Harcourt Brace Jovanovich, 1978.

Healy, B. J. *The Plant Hunters.* New York: Charles Scribner's Sons, 1975.

Hedrick, U. P., G. H. Howe, O. M. Taylor, C. B. Tubergen. *The Peaches of New York.* Annual Report of the New York Department of Agriculture for 1916. Albany: J. B. Lyon, 1917.

Hoag, Donald G. "Meyer Lilac: An Attractive Dwarf Shrub." *North Dakota Farm Research Bimonthly Bulletin* 23, no. 9, North Dakota State University Agricultural Experiment Station, Fargo, 1965, pp. 22–23.

Inventory of Seeds and Plants Imported by the Office of Foreign Seed and Plant Introduction. Vols. 12–57. U.S. Bureau of Plant Industry, USDA, Washington, D.C., 1906–1918.
These quarterly bulletins constitute a vital working tool that is available at land-grant colleges and state universities with agricultural experiment stations, at plant introduction gardens, and elsewhere.

Jefferson, Roland M., and Alan E. Fusonie. *The Japanese Flowering Cherry Trees of Washington, D.C.: A Living Symbol of Friendship.* National Arboretum Contribution no. 4, Agricultural Research Service, USDA, Washington, D.C., 1977.

Klose, Nelson. *America's Crop Heritage.* Ames: Iowa State College Press, 1950.

Lemmon, Kenneth. *The Golden Age of Plant Hunters: 1768–1836.* London: Phoenix House, 1968.

Lyrene, Paul M. "The Jujube Tree (*Zizyphus jujuba*)." *Fruit Varieties Journal* 33, no. 3(1979):100–104.

McKee, Roland. "Chinese Dwarf Meyer Lemon Introduced." *Yearbook of Agriculture, 1926.* USDA, Washington, D.C. 1927, pp. 218–21.

Meyer, Frank N. *Agricultural Exploration in the Fruit and Nut Orchards of China.* Bulletin 204, Bureau of Plant Industry, USDA, Washington, D.C., 1911.

———. *Chinese Place Names.* New York: Chinese and Japanese Publishing Co.; electrotyped for the Office of Foreign Seed and Plant Introduction, Bureau of Plant Industry, USDA, Washington, D.C., 1911.

———. "Seeking Plant Immigrants." *Journal of Heredity* 5, no.3(1914):111–21.

———. "Collecting in Turkestan." *Journal of Heredity* 5, no.4(1914):159–69.

———. "China, a Fruitful Field for Plant Exploration." *Yearbook of Agriculture, 1915,* USDA, Washington, D.C., 1916, pp. 205–24.

———. "Economic and Botanical Explorations in China." *Transactions of the Massachusetts Horticultural Society,* Pt. 1(1916):125–30.

Morrison, J. W. "Marquis Wheat—A Triumph of Scientific Endeavor." *Agricultural History* 34, no.4(1960):182–88.

Obituary, Frank N. Meyer. *American Nurseryman* 28 (1918):12, 14.

Obituary, Frank N. Meyer. *Horticulture* 28(1918):60.

"The People Who Stand for Plus: Frank N. Meyer, Scientific Explorer for the United States Government in China and Russia." *Outing* 53(1908):69–76.

Peattie, Donald Culross. "Erwin F. Smith, a Young Man's Impression." *Scientific Monthly* 25(1917):84–86.

———. "Plant Hunters." *Yale Review* 34 (1944):58–63.

Rehder, Alfred. "New Species, Varieties, and Combinations from the Herbarium and the Collections of the Arnold Arboretum." *Journal of the Arnold Arboretum* 2, no.2(1920):121–28; 3, no.4(1922):207–27.

Reimer, F. C., H. H. White, F. G. Gestner, H. H. Hartman, R. S. Besse. *The Southern Oregon Branch Experiment Station: Its Development, Program, and Accomplishments, 1911–1962.* Special Report 156(1963), Agricultural Experiment Station, Oregon State University, Corvallis.

Rosen, Harry R. "Erwin F. Smith, Friend of Youth." *Mycologia* 19(1927):292–93.

Ryerson, Knowles. "Culture of the Oriental Persimmon." *University of California Agricultural Experiment Station Bulletin* 416, Berkeley, 1927, p. 36.

_____. "Plant Explorers Bring Valuable New Species." *Yearbook of Agriculture, 1932,* USDA, Washington, D.C., 1932, pp. 297–302.

_____. "History and Significance of the Foreign Plant Introduction Work of the USDA." *Agricultural History* 7(1933):110–28.

Sargent, Charles Sprague, ed. *Plantae Wilsonianae.* 3 vols. in 6 books. Publication of the Arnold Arboretum, book 4, Cambridge, Mass.: Harvard University Press, 1915.

Smith, Erwin, F. "Frank N. Meyer." *Science* 48(1918):335–36.

Stoecheler, Joseph H., and Ross A. Williams. "Windbreaks and Shelterbelts." *Trees, the Yearbook of Agriculture, 1949,* USDA, Washington, D.C., 1949, 191–99.

Strauss, Deborah G., managing ed. "Northwest Plant Germplasm Repository Research Director Reports on Successful East Asian Exploration." *Diversity* 1, no.1(1982):13–14.

Sutton, Stephanne Barry. *Charles S. Sargent and the Arnold Arboretum.* Cambridge, Mass.: Harvard University Press, 1970.

_____. *In China's Border Provinces: The Turbulent Career of Joseph Rock, Botanist-Explorer.* New York: Hastings, 1974.

Swingle, Walter T. "Trees and Plants We Owe to China." *Asia* 43(1943):295–99.

Thomas, C. C. "Chinese Elm in American Horticulture." *Yearbook of Agriculture, 1926,* USDA, Washington, D.C., 1926, pp. 215–18.

van Uildriks, Frederike J. "De Reiziger-Plant Kundige Frans N. Meijer en Zijn Werk" (The Traveler-Botanist Frank N. Meyer and His Work). *De Aarde en haar Volken,* 1919 (January/February):1–24; (March/April):41–96; (July/August):145–71.

Weinard, F. F., and H. B. Dorner. "Rosa Odorata as a Grafting Stock for Indoor Roses." *University of Illinois Agricultural Experiment Station Bulletin* 290, 1927, pp. 455–62.

Whitehouse, William E., J. L. Creech, and G. A. Seaton. "Bradford Ornamental Pear: A Promising Shade Tree." *American Nurseryman* 117, no.8(1963):7–8, 56–60.

Whittle, Michael Tyler. *The Plant Hunters.* Philadelphia: Chilton, 1970.

Wilson, Owen. "The Travels of a Plant Hunter." *World's Work* 18(1909):11670–84.

Wiser, Vivian. *Protecting American Agriculture: Inspection and Quarantine of Imported Plants and Animals.* Agricultural Economic Report 266, Economic Research Service, USDA, Washington, D.C., 1974.

GENERAL INDEX

TAXONOMIC INDEX

315